THE
AMERICAN WEST
IN FILM

THE
AMERICAN WEST
IN FILM

Critical Approaches
to the Western

Jon Tuska

University of Nebraska Press
Lincoln and London

The American West in Film: Critical Approaches to the West-ern, by Jon Tuska. Originally published in the Greenwood Press series Contributions to the Study of Popular Culture, No. 11, Westport, CT, 1985. Copyright © 1985 by Jon Tus-ka. Reprinted with permission of the author and publisher.

Manufactured in the United States of America

First Bison Book printing: 1988
Most recent printing indicated by the first digit below:
1   2   3   4   5   6   7   8   9   10

Library of Congress Cataloging-in-Publication Data
Tuska, Jon.
    The American West in film: critical approaches to the Western / Jon Tuska.
    "Bison."
    Reprint. Originally published: Westport, Conn.: Green-wood Press, 1985. Originally published in series: Contribu-tions to the study of popular culture.
    Bibliography: p.
    Includes index.
    ISBN 0-8032-9411-5 (pbk.)
    1. Western films — History and criticism.   I. Title.
PN1995.9.W4T78 1988   CIP 87-30112
791.43'09'093278—dc19

For Vicki

O si non potuisti placere puella bona
Quam speras Musam posse placeri tuam?

The whites told only one side.
Told it to please themselves.
Told much that is not true.
Only his own best deeds, only
the worst deeds of the Indians,
has the white man told.

—Yellow Wolf of the Nez Perce

Errata

P. 7, line 2: politique *should read* parler politique.

P. 20, line 18: *He arrives because, ideologically he must, on Christmas Eve* should read *He arrives, because ideologically he must, on Christmas Eve.*

P. 76, line 7: *George Tecumseh Sherman* should read *William Tecumseh Sherman.*

P. 112, line 12: *the next day* should read *after this.*

P. 130: Add *Notwithstanding, Peckinpah was, until his death on 28 December 1984, the last truly notable director of Western films and, so far, no one else has emerged to equal his stature.*

P. 266, n. 18: *Woods, Michael* should read *Wood, Michael.*

P. 281, bib.: *Woods, Michael* should read *Wood, Michael.*

Contents

Illustrations

Introduction

I

THE AMERICAN WEST IN FILM is a book wholly devoted to the criticism of Western films from a number of different vantage points and employing a number of different critical methods. It is not a history of Western film production. That subject was addressed in THE FILMING OF THE WEST (Doubleday, 1976), a book which for a number of reasons I have withdrawn and intend to re-issue eventually in a revised and updated version. In film studies of somewhat more circumscribed scope, such as THE VANISHING LEGION: A HISTORY OF MASCOT PICTURES 1927–1935 (McFarland, 1982), I was able to combine film criticism with film history. This simply was not possible to do when it comes to a subject as exceedingly broad as the Western film. To combine the two would only produce a book so unwieldy that no publisher would be able to bring it out at a reasonable price.

A critic writing for the THE NEW YORK TIMES BOOK REVIEW complained that in THE FILMING OF THE WEST I did not deal at all with such issues as the way in which Native Americans or women have been treated in Western films. I did not do so because I did not feel I had sufficient space in that book to do them justice. The present undertaking, however, is concerned primarily with *what* was filmed, a critical survey of the fantasies, and very rarely the truths, about the American West recorded on film. These fantasies, I believe, are best contrasted with the historical realities of the American West and so I address the Western film in terms of structure, of *auteurisme*, of frontier legends, and of stereotypical contents, keeping historical reality at all times as the basic standard against which to measure the degrees of deviation and by this means to begin to understand the motivations behind the calculated distortions. Hence, in this book Native Americans and women have each been accorded a chapter.

Occasionally in these pages, I am concerned with Western fiction, but only in its relationship to what was filmed on the basis of it. THE AMERICAN WEST IN FILM is principally preoccupied with the social and psychological aspects of the systematic distortion and misrepresentation of our past and the possible influence this common practice in Western films exerted, and continues to exert, on the national character of Americans, on their international image as perceived by non-Americans, and, frankly, on the many potential dangers that may arise from what can only be termed an habituation to falsehood. I realize that this perspective is likely to spark controversy, because no one as yet has undertaken to evaluate Western films in terms of their ideological contents. Yet this is the best time to do it, when Western films are enjoying an unprecedented resurgence via cable television and are even highly praised by religious groups for their supposedly salutary morality. It is now even possible in many communities in the United States to watch Western films twenty-four hours a day, a situation which has not prevailed since the early days of television.

From the thousands of Western films which I have seen and on which I have compiled notes, I have chosen in this book to discuss at any length what may seem only a handful—although, in actuality, the number approaches several hundred. I have tried in every case to select films which are representative, or innovative, or adjudged by critics to be classics. Yet my ultimate purpose has not been the critique of any specific Western film. Rather, as in my course, "Images of the American West," which I have offered at a number of colleges and universities particularly for primary and secondary teachers, my intention is to provide the reader with the means to analyze and come to terms with the structure, formula, and ideology of *any* Western film. This is not the usual intention behind a book concerned with cinematic art and, insofar as it is not, it constitutes what I regard as the true uniqueness of my approach. The same holds true for my selection of photo illustrations. I have been guided by my aim to demonstrate the ideological contents of certain select Western films, rather than by any other consideration.

Quotations from foreign languages, unless they be extremely brief, appear in translation only, with the title of the book alone given in both the original and in translation. Unless otherwise noted, all such translations are by myself. I have found, while writing this book, that much valuable criticism of Western films has been published in French but so far has not been made available in English. The reader conversant in French is advised to seek out these references as contained in the footnotes and the bibliography.

I am a firm believer in dating. Accordingly, the first time a book or periodical is cited, it is followed in the text with the year of publication, with the exception of works originating in Classical Antiquity. Because the dating of films is, in my view, even more important, each film is followed by the name of the releasing company and the year of release. Once a book or periodical is dated in the text, it is not dated again even when cited again. With films, however, although they are dated only once in any given chapter, if cited in a subsequent chapter they are dated again because the year of release may be relevant in a number of different contexts and a reader cannot reasonably be expected to remember the date for every film cited.

II

Since it is my intention to employ the concept of historical reality as my basic standard for evaluation, I had best explain at the beginning what I mean by this concept and how I use it. Historical events cannot be recreated empirically. They can only be recreated by an elaborate process of inference according to logical principles, ideally taking all available evidence into account. Sallust confessed "in primis arduum videtur res gestas scribere" [to write an historical chronicle is to be regarded as especially difficult][1] and it has not changed since his day, save perhaps in the number and complexity of relevant factors which must be taken into account by an historian.

Morris R. Cohen in his book, THE MEANING OF HUMAN HISTORY (1947), conceived of the art of the historian as "something that involves literary skill but, even more, an imaginative capacity for seeing threads of connection between historic facts and significant issues."[2] He developed a model for the historian. This model was "the ideal of an imaginative reconstruction of the past which is scientific in its determinations and artistic in its formulations" and "is the ideal to which the greatest historians have ever aspired."[3] I would call such a model an historical construction. It is the recreation, as closely as possible, of a former reality in terms of what that reality was for those who were then living and perceiving it. The questions to be asked at this stage of historical inquiry are of this order: is all the available and pertinent evidence fully taken into account? are the determinations such that they can be verified by the known historical data? are the data themselves reliable? is the interpretation of the evidence logically consistent with the evidence and, internally, as an interpretation? how valid are the inferences and can they withstand logical scrutiny? Finally, the historian must be willing to admit that this historical construction is at best only probable and provisional.

"Pesez ce mot, l'ensemble," Taine wrote; "selon qu'on y songe ou non, on entre dans la maturité, ou l'on reste dans l'enfance" [Ponder carefully this word, totality; depending on how one does or does not consider it, one approaches maturity, or one languishes in infantilism].[4] The historian ideally ought to view an historical construction as both a totality and a series of totalities, each approximating more and more closely the historical reality being represented. What W.H. Watson wrote about methods of representation in his book, ON UNDERSTANDING PHYSICS (1938), could well be modified for the notion of historical constructions as a means of representing historical reality. "In the foregoing pages," he reflected, "it has been explained that in physics we choose the method of representation appropriate to our needs; that does not mean, however, that we are content to treat all methods of representation as on the same level of importance. A method which gives correctly the possibility of representing Nature with greater detail than another is thought of as the better method—and it is so when it is a question of showing detail. We think of the second method as an approximation of the first. We tend, therefore, to arrange methods in a series according to the degree of fineness of the pictures of phenomena that can be made by means of them, and of course from this point of view the last member of a series is the best.''[5] However, Watson hastened to warn that precisely because a form of representation ''has been in successful use for some years it is in danger of being looked upon as the best possible,''[6] and that in these matters, as in all others, scientists must as carefully look at the laws of the method of representation as they have for centuries looked at the laws of Nature.

With the discovery of new evidence, with the development of new techniques of representation, it should become possible to arrive at closer and closer approximations to a former historical reality. I would only add a consideration raised by Ludwig Boltzmann in that part of his GRUNDPRINZIPIEN UND GRUNDGLEICHUNGEN DER MECHANIK [BASIC PRINCIPLES AND EQUATIONS OF MECHANICS] translated by Rudolph Weingartner under the title ''Theories as Representations'': ''Insofar as we possess laws of thought which we have recognized as undoubtedly correct, on the basis of constant confirmation in experience, we can initially test the correctness of our pictures on them. However, the final and sole decision about the usefulness of the picture lies in the condition that it represents experience as simply and accurately as possible. And precisely in this we again have the test for the correctness of the laws of thought.''[7]

From this I would devise the following general principle: to the extent that an historical construction can be contradicted by verified evidence, to the extent that the method employed to determine an historical construction has led to such an unsuccessful termination of inquiry, to this extent both the historical construction and the method can be judged as unsatisfactory and can be discarded in favor of an alternative.

Once this has been done, and only then, ought ethics enter upon the scene as a rational examination of past human behavior evaluated according to a stated standard. I am, of course, making a distinction here, in accord with one Morris R. Cohen suggested in THE MEANING OF HUMAN HISTORY, a distinction between ''moral'' which can be said to refer to conduct and its conformity to certain rules and standards, and ''ethics'' which I would define as the rational and theoretic formulation of such rules. It was only after he had made this distinction that Cohen postulated that ''we cannot formulate an intelligible account of human history without the use of ethical categories and viewpoints.''[8] Now by this he did not mean that practice of Augustus Caesar of reading primarily to find examples which effectively illustrated his personal views on public or private life. In fact, modern logic would not support proving ethical theorems by means of historical examples, such as drawing an analogy between the last days of the Roman Republic and the present-day United States or as witnessed by the lunacy of a film such as THE FALL OF THE ROMAN EMPIRE (Paramount, 1964) which is set in the time of Commodus! Nor does modern logic justify the on-going American custom of teaching American history as a primary means of instilling patriotism and celebrating the blessings of uncontrolled capitalism, ignoring in Harvey Wasserman's words "the basic structural weakness of the system—it couldn't distribute purchasing power to the people because, by its very nature, it was geared to do exactly the opposite" and so "the 'high standard of living' of the new middle class took its payment in the cancerous gray of '100 percent Americanism,' in the immeasurable psychic deadweight of keeping other people down all over the world."[9] In fact, modern logic does not justify ever *proving* anything by means of history.

Rather, the philosophical use of ethical inquiry into human interaction in history, as in film criticism, has to do with a rational examination of the actual consequences of this interaction, whether real or imaginary. It is a philosophical, and never an historical, preoccupation. Contrasting Anglo-American culture with Sioux culture, Black Elk in BLACK ELK SPEAKS (1932) could not help but observe that in killing the buffalo "the Wasichus [white men] did not kill them to eat; they killed them for the metal that makes them crazy, and they took only the hides, only the tongues; and I have heard that fire-boats came down the Missouri River loaded with dried bison tongues . . . . Sometimes they did not even take the tongues; they just killed and killed because they like to do that . . . . I could see that the Wasichus did not care for each other the way our people did before the nation's hoop was broken. They would take everything from each other if they could, while crowds of people had nothing at all and maybe were starving. They had forgotten that the earth was their mother."[10] Harvey Wasserman diagnosed this kind of thinking as intrinsic to the profit system since, "as a linear rather than a cyclical device, the profit system found it better to waste and destroy than to conserve and reuse."[11] The situation had not changed appreciably in 1981 when then Secretary of the Interior James Watt, asked if his policies would not destroy what remained of the national treasure of natural resources for future generations of Americans, replied that as a born-again Christian he did not feel there would be many more generations.

What I am proposing as an additional perspective to historiography, as well as film criticism, is a re-invocation of the classical ideal of *humanitas*, to echo again in this context Max C. Otto's words from THINGS AND IDEALS (1924) and "let it be taken to heart that *soul* is not the name of a thing, but of a life; that the soul's salvation is not a commodity or a gift to be bought or begged, but a development to be attained; that to save one's soul is not an instantaneous deed, but a life-long adventure; not the rescue of an indefinable entity in preparation for a life to come, but the creation of a type of personality through loyalty to concrete values as these are at issue in everyday experience. It is an inner richness and ripeness, a sensitiveness to truth, to beauty, to the dignity of life." [12]

Only from such a perspective can we fully evaluate the whole meaning of the historical past, no less motion pictures which purport to represent or somehow comment on life in the past or at any time, human life as part *de rerum natura*. Because he had such a clear conception of *humanitas*, Mody Boatright could write in his essay, "On the Nature of Myth" (1954), that "ritualistic behavior is both repetitive and non-rational. It prescribes the pattern of behavior and relieves the individual of the responsibility of thought; the behavior springs from attitudes fixed by myth. Thus if I believe that America was made great by a collection of discrete individuals each pursuing his own selfish ends and if I believe that this process is still operative, I will not have to think to define my attitude toward welfare legislation." [13]

It is my opinion that reflections of an ethical kind are inappropriate to the kind of production history of the Western film which is narrated in THE FILMING OF THE WEST, but they are vital for dealing with the contents of Western films and, therefore, will preoccupy much of the critical commentary to be found in these pages, serving as an accompanying standard of value to that embodied in the concept of historical reality.

Many of the critics who have in the past addressed the subject of the Western film knew little or nothing about Western American history—except perhaps what they learned from watching the films—and, in their defense, insisted that any knowledge beyond this would have been irrelevant to appreciating a Western film. I would be more inclined to accept such a position if, correspondingly, in their critical remarks these same writers had made no comment about the historical accuracy of a particular film or had laid no claim on behalf of one filmmaker being more "realistic" than another in depicting the American West. Unfortunately, this has not been the case. In addition, most of these same writers have so ignored cinema history itself that whatever has happened is seen as having happened ostensibly because of some aesthetic consideration, rather than, as was and as continues to be most often the case, because of some behind-the-scenes event in film production, corporate machinations, or marketing strategy. To make matters still worse, many of these same writers who remarked on the historical accuracy of a film without knowing anything of history and who spoke authoritatively about production details without knowing anything about them also critically praised films they had never seen!

Since so much Western fiction and so many Western films are set in the past, it would seem a literary or media critic should, if only to avoid all manner of absurdities, know something about the historical reality of the period in which a particular fiction is set. William T. Pilkington and Don Graham co-edited and also contributed to a volume titled WESTERN MOVIES (1979) which illustrates nearly all of the shortcomings which occur when there is no concept of historical reality, either in terms of the contents of Western films or the history of Western film production, and their effort is also notable for its singular lack of an ethical perspective.

The reader is told in "Introduction: A Fistful of Westerns," which they co-authored, that "the collapse of the big-studio system spelled the end of the 'B' Western." [14] Anyone familiar with film production history will have a problem with this assertion. How is "the collapse of the big-studio system" to be interpreted since the big studios are still with us, although ownership may have changed? In 1981 Metro-Goldwyn-Mayer acquired United Artists for $400,000,000—and M-G-M had not made a "B" Western since 1929 and United Artists released its last one in 1950. Universal closed down its "B" unit in 1946, five years after Paramount had ceased financing its "B" Western series. Columbia Pictures discontinued its Gene Autry "B" series in 1953, but Columbia did not collapse. Companies such as RKO-Radio Pictures, which did cease production, did so for reasons unrelated to the studio system or "B" Westerns.

The same cavalier attitude toward the history of film production typically was carried over into the wider area of the history of the American West as portrayed in Western films. THE SEARCHERS (Warner's, 1956), while one of the most viciously anti-Indian films ever made, was defended by Professor Pilkington in an essay he wrote for WESTERN MOVIES by means of a citation of André Bazin's comment that John Ford in his later Westerns, including this one, strove for a "rehabilitation of the Indian." [15] All of which demonstrates that Professor Pilkington, albeit familiar with what Bazin had written, perhaps did not know that Ford's Comanches in THE SEARCHERS were played by Navajos who speak Navajo, that Ford deliberately although erroneously portrayed Indian captivity as generally driving into insanity most whites unfortunate enough to have undergone the experience, and that the entire film is in effect an argument in favor of killing Indians as the only solution to the "Indian problem." I even went so far as to communicate these objections to Professor Pilkington in a letter—only for him, in his reply to me, to wave them aside. In his view Ford's film was a myth about the past and, as such, has no relationship whatsoever to historical reality and cannot be approached in this fashion. I must disagree and one of my most fundamental reasons for disagreeing is that Native Americans were not, and are not, *mythical*. A film about the righteousness of killing Indians is making an ethical statement and the significance of such a statement must play an integral part in any critical approach to the film. It ought not merely be waved aside as an irrelevance.

PART I
VARIETIES OF MONTAGE

It is important for you to comprehend the need for
making the composition strictly depend on the content
and the aim of the work.

—Sergei Eisenstein[1]

1

Critical Theories about
Western Films

Later on in the course of their Introduction to WESTERN MOVIES, Pilkington and Graham included a list of "some of the more common critical approaches to Western movies."[2] Their list consisted of: (1) the "*auteur*" approach; (2) the "Western as history" approach; (3) the "Western as myth" approach; (4) the "literature into film" approach; (5) the "Western as allegory" approach; (6) the "decades" approach; (7) the "structuralist" approach; (8) the "genre" approach. Some of these approaches I feel are fruitless and some of them, or a combination of them, I have used in the writing of this book. By dividing the text into four parts—"Varieties of Montage," "Six Studies in Authorship," "Frontier Legends," and "Types and Stereotypes"—I have attempted to approach the Western film from four distinct perspectives. I believe, however, that it would clarify for the reader just why I selected these particular perspectives were I first to address the essential thinking behind each of the eight approaches outlined in the Introduction to WESTERN MOVIES, along with a few others the co-editors missed, and submit all of them to logical examination.

The co-editors defined *auteur* criticism as "founded on the belief that a film's director (or, less often, the screenwriter, occasionally a combination of the two) is the *auteur*, author, the shaping intelligence that stamps a motion picture with a distinctive style and vision of life."[3] There will be those, thoroughly conversant with the principles of the *auteur* theory, who will find a number of inadequacies in this definition. My concern is rather with a modification of the definition as given. Alan Lovell provided what I hold to be a more workable definition of the *auteur* approach. "By the '*auteur*' principle," he wrote in his essay, "Robin Wood—A Dissenting View" (1969), "I understand a descriptive method which seeks to establish not whether a director is a great director, but what the basic structure of a director's work is. The assumption behind this principle is that any director creates his films on the basis of a central structure and that all his films can be seen as variations or developments of it."[4] Andrew

Tudor in THEORIES OF FILM (1973) paraphrased Lovell's perspective to be a "working hypothesis through which we can make detailed analyses of a director's work. The real assumption of the process is that we can learn more about a director's films by considering them in relation to one another."[5] To this Tudor appended the observation that "to look at films as the work of an *auteur* involves close textual analysis rather than brief critical comment."[6] It is in Lovell's and Tudor's sense that I have applied the *auteur* principle in studying the six directors I have singled out in the next part of this book, men particularly well known for their Western films; albeit this same perspective could be applied to the Western films directed by any given director, indeed to a given director's films in general.

In criticizing the "Western as history" approach, Pilkington and Graham concluded that "carried too far . . . [this approach] seems a rather elementary and misguided method for evaluating Westerns, which have ordinarily been about a bygone era . . . . In the Western the way it really was in the old West is not nearly so important as the way Twentieth-century audiences *think* it was."[7] The first reservation I would have to this is that in order to know the differences between the way it was and the way modern audiences might think it was in the old West one is going to have to know indeed how it *really* was: one is going to have to become familiar with the closest approximation to the historical reality at issue. My second reservation is even more serious. I doubt if anyone is about to investigate what modern audiences do think it was like in the old West. What modern audiences? concerning what aspect of life or activity? where? when? and a dozen or more other questions would have to be researched; and even then with results less than reliable. About all we can actually learn from a Twentieth-century Western film is what filmmakers *wanted* modern audiences to think about what life was like in the old West. If we modify our perspective in this way, we are also in a position, not only to know the difference between the historical reality and the film's fantasy about that historical reality, but also something about those critics who, for whatever reason, insist on ignoring the historical reality when approaching a Western film. In short, knowing about the historical reality allows us to watch, close up, the workings of the phenomenon which has been going on for a long time but which George Orwell in NINETEEN EIGHTY-FOUR (1949) projected into the future when he described how "day by day and almost minute by minute the past was brought up to date. In this way every prediction made by the Party could be shown by documentary evidence to have been correct; nor was any item of news, or any expression of opinion which conflicted with the needs of the moment, ever allowed to remain on record. All history was a palimpsest, scraped clean and reinscribed exactly as often as was necessary."[8] It draws attention to the common bond between what in Communist countries is called propaganda and what in the United States is called entertainment.

The "Western as myth" approach is, in my opinion, a dead end. Pilkington and Graham did not see it this way. "Some kind of definition of the myth . . . ," they wrote, "is usually stated or implied in the critical analysis. Once a definition is established (or assumed), a particular Western may be seen as resting somewhere on the spectrum that stretches from total acceptance to total negation of the myth. STAGECOACH [United Artists, 1939], for example, is generally viewed as the archetypal Western because of its wholehearted endorsement of the myth, while a number of recent films . . . come pretty close to being wholesale denials of the myth." [9] Perhaps the reader has noticed how, either by oversight or sleight-of-hand, Pilkington and Graham moved from the idea of more than one myth—hence the need to define or assume such a myth— to writing within the very next sentence about "the" myth as if there were only one, as if myth itself, as concerns the Western, was univocal rather than multivocal. The truth is most critics of Western films who use this approach can come to no agreement as to what is meant by such words as "myth" or "mythical." Accordingly, I have found it a prudent policy to subsume what usually are referred to as "myths" in Western films under the heading of narrative structures and to deal structurally with them as varieties of montage. After all, there are far more differences than similarities between the epic myths that Homer and Vergil used and the commercial legendry manufactured by Hollywood for mass consumption; and what is referred to as a myth by most reputable mythologists is not, and was not, a fantasy designed to have box-office appeal the success of which is optimally measured by the positive difference between negative cost and world-wide gross receipts.

Although much has been written on the subject, I find that George Bluestone's NOVELS INTO FILM: THE METAMORPHOSIS OF FICTION INTO CINEMA (1957) is still the best book so far to have appeared. While I am a bit uncomfortable with just what is intended by the word "mythic," Bluestone's description of the adaptation process seems particularly apt. "What happens . . . ," he wrote, "when the filmist undertakes the adaptation of a novel, given the inevitable mutation, is that he does not convert the novel at all. What he adapts is a kind of paraphrase of the novel—the novel viewed as raw material. He looks not to the organic novel, whose language is inseparable from its theme, but to characters and incidents which have somehow detached themselves from the language and, like the heroes of folk legends, have achieved a mythic life of their own. Because this is possible, we often find that the film adapter has not even read the book, that he has depended instead on a paraphrase by his secretary or his screenwriter. That is why there is no necessary correspondence between the excellence of a novel and the quality of the film in which the novel is recorded." [10] Of course, not every film director would be capable of Robert Altman's honesty when Altman told me that he had lost interest in and so therefore never finished reading Raymond Chandler's THE LONG GOODBYE (1953) when he was at work on the screen version, THE LONG GOODBYE (United Artists, 1969). Howard Hawks admitted to me that he confined himself deliberately to only the second part of A.B. Guthrie, Jr.'s THE BIG SKY (1947) when he came to film the picture by the same title, THE BIG

SKY (RKO, 1952). But in this case reading the novel can have an almost electrifying effect when the conclusion of the second part, as Guthrie wrote it, is contrasted with the conclusion of Hawks' film. It is in fact singularly revealing of the *customary* interpretation Hawks was inclined to bring to a situation such as that presented by the novel, an interpretation completely at odds with Guthrie's effort to depict historical reality as opposed to a romantic fantasy about the past. Similarly, reading a novel or a novelized version of a film based on an original screen story, such as James Warner Bellah's SERGEANT RUTLEDGE (1960), can be instructive concerning what John Ford found attractive in Bellah's romantic vision of the West and what he felt had to be altered—altered, incidentally, not so much for cinematic reasons, that is, because certain characters or situations proved unfilmable, as for ideological reasons. Indeed, it is precisely in connection with ideological variances between author and film director that often the most profound contrasts can occur when comparing a written fiction with the filmed version.

Pilkington and Graham, perhaps because they were insensitive to the ideological dimension of interpretations in Western fiction no less than in Western films, in their remarks concerning the "literature into film" approach found that "the best studies of this sort are not content merely to point out differences in literary and movie treatments of the same storyline (such differences ought to be expected and therefore assumed). Instead, they speculate on what those differences tell us about the essential qualities and conditions of the two media."[11] This is a valid observation, as far as it goes; but speculations about the differences between the written medium and the film medium are not, as stated in this definition, really relevant to either Western fiction or Western films in terms of their "Western" content. Such speculations belong, rather, in the realm of general film theory.

Although it is technically non-fiction, Mari Sandoz' CHEYENNE AUTUMN (1953) provides a powerful and immensely illuminating contrast with John Ford's film, CHEYENNE AUTUMN (Warner's, 1964). That contrast is able to show us a great deal about the way Ford chose to distort history and even reveals some of his ideological motives. To give just one example. In her text, Sandoz related how President Lincoln "paid off some election favors by turning Indian agencies over to petty politicians, one man at least accumulating a fortune from his $1,200-a-year job. The Emancipation Proclamation was almost two years behind Lincoln, the Gettysburg Address a year and a week old when the Cheyenne men, women, and children were killed at Sand Creek."[12] In the Ford film, Edward G. Robinson as Secretary of the Interior Carl Schurz is seen standing before a portrait of Lincoln, his face reflected in the glass, asking the portrait, "Old friend, old friend, what would you do?" The scene implies that Lincoln, because of his compassion and his wisdom, would have known how to deal ably with the Cheyenne exodus, whereas, based on his actions with regard to Sand Creek, he would most probably have been indifferent unless absolutely forced to do something and, if forced, ineffectual, engaging in what the French call *politique*.

Whatever the weakness of their conception of the value of literary and cinematic comparisons, Pilkington and Graham outdid themselves when they came to the "Western as allegory" approach. In fact, they went so far as to regard the interpretation of an imaginative work as having an ontological reality equivalent to that of the work itself! This is something I have long suspected all too many professors of literature do covertly, but it is rare for them to come out and say it in so many words. "The propensity of directors and screenwriters to use the Western as a vehicle for allegory can scarcely be doubted," they wrote. "For instance, in the late 1960s and early 1970s many Westerns—THE WILD BUNCH [Warner's, 1969] and ULZANA'S RAID [Universal, 1972] have been interpreted this way—were not about the old West at all; they were really about the American involvement in Vietnam." [13] It does not matter to those critics who choose to interpret this as the "real meaning" of these films that, respectively, this was not what Sam Peckinpah and Robert Aldrich intended; indeed, in the end, the interpretations of such critics are ontologically *more* real to them than the films themselves and they expect a viewer after reading what they have written to think so, too.

" 'I often get credit for deep insights that are not even in my mind,' " Vicki Piekarski quoted Sydney Pollack in her career study of him for CLOSE-UP: THE CONTEMPORARY DIRECTOR (1981). " 'The French critics are great on this. They see a ray of sun in the corner of a frame and think I am talking about the evolution of a new civilization. At times, I am accused of maliciously destroying some concept or person, when I certainly did not intend that effect. Each person carries his own ideological framework, hangups, cultural conditions, and momentary concerns into a darkened theatre and interprets the motion picture in accordance with his frame of mind at the moment. That is a factor over which we have no control. If individuals feel boxed in by society, they may view Jeremiah [in JEREMIAH JOHNSON (Warner's, 1972)] as a hero. But that is not what I intended him to be. In fact, the audience is not getting what I hoped for out of the film. I wanted people to see and understand the bizarreness of Jeremiah's motivation. But the audience remembers things like the slapstick bear sequence and a good many other wrong things. The responsibility, however, is mine. If I failed in my intentions, perhaps I did not make a very good film.' " [14]

I recall that, when Ernest Hemingway read a critic who interpreted the sharks in THE OLD MAN AND THE SEA (1952) to symbolize literary critics and the giant marlin a great work of art, his response was that "simbolismo es un truco nuevo de los intellectuales" [symbolism is the new trick of the intellectuals]. It is the same with allegorical interpretations. My basic reasons for being wary of them are these. First, they cannot ever really be verified: not by asking the director, the screenwriter, other critics, or whom have you? Second, they are the most narrowly subjective of all subjective projections. Third, they are ultimately useless. When encountering them, you either agree or disagree; beyond that, they have no function and offer no real insight.

Even when it is known that a film was meant to have an allegorical interpretation, as for example HIGH NOON (United Artists, 1952), I do not see that this information makes HIGH NOON a better film nor can it heighten our appreciation of it as an example of cinematic art. HIGH NOON must succeed first and last as a dramatic *praxis*, a progress of the spirit (a concept explored at further length below), or not at all. Any allegorical meaning it may have had in 1952, subsequent to that time becomes largely an historical curiosity. Moreover, I do not perceive that I am making a significant statement about THE WILD BUNCH if I claim it is an allegory about the Vietnam War. What has that to do with the film I am watching, have watched, or am about to watch? If THE WILD BUNCH is a meaningful film, it must be so on the basis of internal and intrinsic qualities. What Northrup Frye said in THE CRITICAL PATH (1971) contra those literary critics who seem determined "to find the ultimate meaning of literature in something that is not literature"[15] might equally well be said against film critics who seek the ultimate meaning of a film in something that is not film. It is far more significant that a viewer can still watch THE WILD BUNCH and its concluding massacre of non-white people by four white men and not be disgusted by the experience than that this constitutes some kind of allegory. What is more, this was Peckinpah's point in making the film: our minds and words reflect a concern about humanity, but our hearts and our instincts prefer savagery. This is a proposition about the human condition and THE WILD BUNCH turns this proposition into a prescription. We get the English word prescription from the Latin: *prae scribere* [before writing]. This prescription was put into the film before it was made; and I, for one, prefer to deal with such prescribed meanings in THE WILD BUNCH, or in any film, than with some supposed allegorical meaning. Many times, it would almost seem, the projection of allegorical meanings is an attempt to escape coming to terms with the evident and deliberate meaning of a work of art.

The "decades" approach I find totally spurious. The idea, according to Pilkington and Graham, is "that many Westerns reflect the attitudes, beliefs, concerns, and deepest desires of the era (for convenience, read *decade*) in which they were made."[16] The authors provided two basic examples of this approach, "comparing different versions of the same story produced in different decades" and "contrasting the various screen 'biographies' of the life of some legendary figure" such as Billy the Kid or Wyatt Earp.[17] The same objections I raised with regard to the "Western as allegory" would apply equally here, but there is even a further, unverifiable supposition, namely that films, and in this case Western films, were somehow responsive to such things as "attitudes, beliefs, concerns, and deepest desires" of audiences. As an historian and as one who has seen at least once every surviving Western film, I must amend this idea somewhat. Westerns have, for the most part, *avoided* confrontations with audience attitudes, beliefs, and concerns. I believe this is what Michael Wood meant in AMERICA IN THE MOVIES (1975) when he observed that "entertainment is not, as we often think, a full-scale flight from our problems, not a means of forgetting them completely, but rather a rearrangement of our problems into shapes which tame them, which disperse them to the margins of our attention."[18] Further, I think we need only substitute the words "American West" for what Wood wrote about America and it will have a similar validity, that "the movies did not describe or explore America, they invented it, dreamed up an America all their own, and persuaded us to share the dream."[19]

I have arranged the parts of this book as I have so that—to take an example of an historical personality—by reading first about John Ford's world-view and then, in the section on frontier legends, about Wyatt Earp, it will be seen just how Ford's MY DARLING CLEMENTINE (20th-Fox, 1946) in its ideology and its interpretation of Wyatt Earp's historical significance is much more a reflection of John Ford and a twice-worked-over screenplay than of what the American public might have been thinking. I found in studying the Billy the Kid legend in my book, BILLY THE KID: A BIO-BIBLIOGRAPHY (1983), that the "decades" approach did not hold water; the same will be found in this book in the part devoted to frontier legends. Moreover, in a chapter such as that concerned with the images of women in Westerns, it will be seen that the roles assigned to women have changed very little, if at all, over eight decades.

The very idea that there could be such a thing as a "decades" approach seems to have been derived from Henry Nash Smith's VIRGIN LAND: THE AMERICAN WEST AS SYMBOL AND MYTH (1950); at least this is the book most frequently cited by students of popular culture as a primary demonstration of how to deduce the sentiments supposedly felt by a wide number of people by analyzing a sampling of their popular fiction. Yet, this is precisely what Smith's book does *not* do. In his "Preface to Twentieth Anniversary Printing," Smith confessed that "on rereading the book now I am forced to the chastening realization that I was guilty of the same kind of oversimplification I ascribed to others. Although I had gained some theoretical perspective on the nature of fictions from Bergson, Lévy-Bruhl, and Vaihinger, my attitude toward popular beliefs about the West was in practice often reductionistic . . . . The vestiges of dualism in my assumptions [between what he meant by symbol and myth] made it difficult for me to recognize that there was a continuous dialectic interplay between the mind and its environment, and that our perceptions of objects and events are no less a part of consciousness than are our fantasies."[20]

Smith did spend two chapters analyzing the formulae of dime novels and he also tried to examine attitudes toward the American West to be found in fictional works by such authors as Timothy Flint, Emerson Bennett, and James Fenimore Cooper. His book is an experiment in perspective, an attempt to view the Westward movement through the propaganda and fictions inspired by it, or related to it. However, Smith's premise in approaching the dime novel, that "the individual writer abandons his own personality and identifies himself with the reveries of his readers,"[21] is far-fetched if not the sheerest wool-gathering. The reading public may pick an author who comes closest to its collective reveries, or an author who, in C.G. Jung's sense, may try to compensate in his fiction for what he feels is lacking in the spiritual climate of his age; but, ultimately, the mood of the reading public is formed by such a confluence of factors as to be unknowable and incapable of measurement. Smith's methodology, while entertaining, cannot, as he himself later admitted, demonstrate by intuition any correlation between popular fiction and popular sentiment that is meaningful, that can somehow be measured or even verified negatively, that is, by some result that would prove to be inconsistent with such an hypothesis.

This might also be the place to deal with the notion of dichotomies which appears to be associated with both the allegory and "decades" approaches. Pilkington and Graham found dichotomization praiseworthy, but upon closer investigation any application of pseudo-Kantian categories of absolute antinomies to films leads up a blind alley. Typical is Jim Kitses' list, compiled for his book, HORIZONS WEST (1969), where he dichotomized dialectical antinomies between "The Wilderness" and "Civilization," so that, to take one instance, in contrasting "The West" with "The East," Kitses postulated that "The West" embodied America, "The East" Europe, "The West" equality, "The East" class, and so on. I suspect that much of this kind of dialectical thinking is an outgrowth of a misreading of the highly fanciful frontier theories of Frederick Jackson Turner. In any event, it overlooks the fact, as Morris R. Cohen pointed out in A PREFACE TO LOGIC (1956), that "the law of contradiction does not bar the presence of contrary determinations in the same entity, but only requires as a postulate the existence of a distinction of aspects or relations in which the contraries hold."[22]

Andrew Tudor in THEORIES OF FILM submitted this tendency of "reducing analysis to a formula simplification of a few themes" to a critical and logical examination and concluded, rightly I believe, that "dichotomization can be at best only an epistemological weapon. Its claim to ontological universality is deeply problematic."[23] Instead of dichotomies, I find Cohen's "principle of polarity" a more useful concept. "In physical science," Cohen wrote in A PREFACE TO LOGIC, "the principle of polarity would thus be represented by the principle of action and reaction, and the principle that wherever there are forces there must be resistance. Philosophically it may be generalized as the principle, not of the identity, but of the necessary copresence and mutual dependence of opposite determinations . . . [and] progress might be made . . . if we recognized the indeterminateness of certain issues as to whether certain things exist or not, by asking how and in what sense."[24] Applied to Kitses' elaborate dichotomies, or to those of Peter Wollen in SIGNS AND MEANING IN THE CINEMA (1969) which he applied to John Ford's films in particular, this would mean that, depending on how or in what sense the descriptive notion was being used, "The West" in Kitses' list could embody the class system, as historically it did in time, rather than just "The East"; and that in Wollen's system, where, according to him, Ford's films equate the Irish, Indians, and Polynesians "as traditional communities, set in the past, counterposed to the march forward to the American future,"[25] these groups upon closer analysis may not warrant being clumped together any more than any other three groups in Ford's films.

Pilkington and Graham defined the "structuralist" approach as an effort "to discern the underlying and governing structural configuration of a given discrete entity," and they concluded that the results of its use "are interesting, if hardly definitive."[26] Since I feel that a structural method is the most productive means through which to approach the varieties and patterns of narrative in Western fiction and in Western films, naturally I am not in accord with their view. In the next chapter I explain in some detail what I mean by narrative structures and I define and make distinctions between the three general narrative structures found in Westerns—the formulary Western, the romantic historical reconstruction (or historical romance), and the historical reconstruction. These are followed by further refinements. I take as my point of departure Aristotle's PO-ETICS; but, for my purpose here, I should like to present only two basic concepts which it will do well to keep in mind throughout this book. These are the concept of *praxis* and the concept of transformation through narrative rhythm.

In his introductory essay to S.H. Butcher's translation of Aristotle's POET-ICS (1961), Francis Fergusson questioned what Aristotle meant by the word "*action (praxis)*" which I would translate as "progress," being nearer to the meaning of the original Greek word, and which is consistent, I believe, with the meaning T.S. Eliot attached to the word "progress" when in "The Love Song of J. Alfred Prufrock" (1917) he referred to "one that will do to swell a progress, start a scene or two . . . ."[27] "One thing must be clear, first of all," Fergusson wrote, "that *action (praxis)* [progress] does not mean deeds, events, or physical activity: it means, rather, the motivation from which deeds spring . . . . It may be described metaphorically as the focus or movement of the psyche toward what seems good to it at the moment—a 'movement-of-spirit,' Dante [called] it . . . . When Aristotle [said] 'action' (*praxis*) [progress] in the POETICS, he usually [meant] the working out of a motive to its end in success or failure."[28] This is the spirit in which I interpret what I call the "progress" of a Western film, the motivation from which deeds spring and the focus or movement of the narrative toward what seems good at the moment to one or another, some or all, of the characters.

In his review of Kenneth Burke's book, A GRAMMAR OF MOTIVES (1945), Fergusson discussed the role of transformation in Classical tragedy. In commenting on "the transformation represented in OEDIPUS REX," Fergusson noted that "Oedipus' ideas are certainly different at the end of the play from what they were at the beginning, but the change in his ideas appears to result, not from thinking, but from suffering and direct experience—a development of the man himself. This transformation is shown in the whole tragic rhythm of 'Purpose to Passion to Perception,' or, as Mr. Burke [called] it in this book, Poiema-Pathema-Mathema.''[29]

I have found, in dealing with the Western film, that it is only rarely that the hero changes so that he or his ideas are different at the end than at the beginning, albeit quite frequently the heroine will change her ideas, usually about the hero (including her emotional commitment to the hero) and, almost as often, about the hero's ideas, such as, that violence and blood-letting are truly prerequisites for life, liberty, and the pursuit of property. This will become exceedingly evident in the chapter devoted to women. Accordingly, I have modified this concept which, after all, is derived from tragedy (and Westerns are almost never tragic in the Classical sense). I perceive transformation—how things are different at the end from what they were at the beginning—to be transformation through narrative rhythm: the result of a number of incidents in the plot so arranged as to bring about and, at times, even make seem inevitable the state of affairs at the end of the film.

The last approach Pilkington and Graham listed is that of genre, but they had a quirky and peculiar definition for it, claiming that ''in genre analysis all films are of equal interest. Thus BILLY THE KID VS. DRACULA [Embassy, 1966] is potentially as significant to the genre critic as, say, Arthur Penn's THE LEFT-HANDED GUN [Warner's, 1958]'' and that ''it encourages the critic to explore an individual motion picture in the broadest possible generic context and to show how the film enlarges and alters the form or type to which it properly belongs.''[30] From the way they referred to it, one might almost assume that they were writing about structural criticism and not genre criticism. Actually, genre criticism as they defined it cannot be said to exist. The major questions which genre critics have addressed are what is a Western and what is not, what makes the films in the Western genre different from other films, and how does one best arrive at a definition of a Western? The answer to this last question is usually supplied somewhat tautologically by deriving from a group of supposedly Western films a definition of what a Western is and then to declare this group to be examples of Westerns because they meet the criteria. In this, I again find myself in agreement with Andrew Tudor and accept as a definition of the Western genre that it is that genre containing films classed as being Westerns by my particular society. Only sometimes do I deviate from this consensus approach, for example, with ONE FLEW OVER THE CUCKOO'S NEST (United Artists, 1975); but, when I do, I am aware of it, make special note of it, and am willing to have my arguments dismissed as invalid. However, virtually all discussion concerned with genre is in the area of film theory and has no real place in a critical appraisal of specific Western films.

There have been other attempts to approach the structure of the Western film besides those mentioned by Pilkington and Graham. Jean-Louis Leutrat's effort in LE WESTERN (1973) is quite possibly the most intelligent, but, before I come to it, there are a few others that ought to be cited if only because they vie in degrees of silliness. An outstanding example of the latter, to be sure, is that system concocted by Philip French for his book, WESTERNS (1974). French presumed Westerns to reflect the political policies of various American presidents, or merely presidential candidates. "The overall style of the typical Goldwater Western," French asserted, "would be slack and expansive; its rhetoric would be sententious, broadly humorous, woolly; its visual surface would involve a casual acceptance of the landscape; the moral tone would be generous but ultimately unforgiving . . . . "[31] Conversely, "the content of the Kennedy Western would tend to feature the following ingredients: a slightly diffident hero capable of change and development, with a rather unostentatious professionalism, though prone to a sense of anguished failure; there would be an accent on the need for community activity . . . . "[32] Even right-wing commentator William F. Buckley got a type of Western identified with him. Hence, for French, "all of Anthony Mann's films of the 'Fifties are Kennedy Westerns (except for his final masterpiece MAN OF THE WEST [United Artists, 1958], written by the liberal television playwright Reginald Rose: a real Buckley movie, whereas Mann's Kennedy films were scripted by the ultra-right-wing Borden Chase) . . . . But Budd Boetticher's films, with their close stylistic affinities, are Buckley movies . . . . On another level, one would note that John Wayne's THE ALAMO [United Artists, 1960] was a Goldwater Western which, under the guise of saying 'better Tex than Mex' in its account of the first tragic stage in the winning of Texas from the Mexicans, was actually affirming 'better dead than Red,' with rhetorical material about the Republic of Texas (as opposed to American democracy) seemingly drawn from the Blue Book of the John Birch Society."[33] Here is another variety of the allegorical approach combined with the Henry Nash Smith thesis. The pity of it, I suppose, is that French was convinced that he was writing something cogent, if not profound, about Western films.

The components of the structure of a genre such as that of the Western are perhaps best derived from exemplary works rather than any appeal to something extraneous, something not only not film but not even fiction or history—notwithstanding the argument that many political notions, because they correspond to no known reality, are therefore fictional. French's confusion seems to have come about as a consequence of identifying a convention of the genre with the genre itself. Once this had been done, it became possible to project anything into a particular Western.

A somewhat more complicated attempt was propounded by Will Wright in his book, SIXGUNS & SOCIETY: A STRUCTURAL STUDY OF THE WESTERN (1975). Wright's thesis was that the *types* of people in Western films have not changed over the years, only the ways in which they interact. Choosing for his illustrations those Westerns which, since 1930, have grossed more than four million dollars in film rental and then analyzing their respective structures, he came up with four basic plot types. These he termed the classical plot, the vengeance variation, the transition theme, and the professional plot. Unfortunately the actual plots of the films he selected to illustrate these basic plot types do not fit into his categories at all without all manner of exceptions and unconventional interpretations. The classical plot, according to Wright, "is the story of the lone stranger who rides into a troubled town and cleans it up, winning the respect of the townsfolk and the love of the schoolmarm."[34] As a definition, this may be fine; but where Wright encountered an insurmountable problem was in trying to force all the Western films he labeled "classical" into this definition as a category. Further, he broke down the classical plot into what he called sixteen separate functions. I shall not go through all of them, but the first function is: "The hero enters a social group."[35] Since DUEL IN THE SUN (Selznick, 1948) is among the films Wright classed as classical and since it is the heroine who, at the beginning, enters a social group, he had to engage in a little sleight-of-hand. "More interesting," he wrote, "is the fact that, instead of a gunfighting hero coming to the ranch, we have Pearl, a scared, confused, half-Indian girl. In fact, Pearl is the hero; for, if we substitute her for the standard male hero and make one more transformation, we will find that DUEL IN THE SUN corresponds exactly to the basic meanings of the typical plot."[36] The "one more transformation" we have to make is to accept for the function—"the hero is revealed to have an exceptional ability"—that Pearl's "remarkable ability is not demonstrated in fighting but in sex. Where the other heroes have physical or shooting strength, she has sexual strength."[37] Wright's last two functions—that "the society accepts the hero" and that "the hero loses or gives up his social status"—are even more difficult, if not altogether impossible, to reconcile since Pearl is never accepted socially and the only way she gives up her special status at the end is when she and Lewt McCanless shoot each other to death.

Another problem was presented by other Westerns he tried to cram into this group. CANYON PASSAGE (Universal, 1946) and DODGE CITY (Warner's, 1939) do not really qualify for the first function—"the hero enters a social group"—because the hero in CANYON PASSAGE is the owner of a freighting business in Jacksonville, Oregon, where the action is set while the hero of DODGE CITY is cited at the beginning of the picture as being one of the founders of Dodge City; and Wright had an even stickier problem reconciling these heroes with his second function: "the hero is unknown to the society." Wright also had to stretch a point for his sixth function—"there is a conflict of interest between the villains and society"—in the case of CANYON PASSAGE because he decided to make Bragg, a Jacksonville tough, the villain in the film, whereas the villains are actually the Rogue Indians who stage an attack during the final reels. If Wright had designated the Rogue Indians as the villains, however, and thus wrought agreement with his sixth function, he would still have been stumped by his eighth function: "there is a strong friendship or respect between the hero and a villain." But then, this does not apply to the hero's relationship with Bragg, either. For DUEL IN THE SUN, Wright felt it particularly worked since Lewt and Pearl become lovers, in Wright's words "a passionate friendship."[38]

For Leutrat in LE WESTERN, the structure of the Western film is best broken down into three components: the situations, the personages (including heroes, companions of the heroes, the villain, the woman, and the Indian), and a world. This last is further sub-divided into space and what Leutrat termed "*des décors*," which I would translate as scenery. To these, he added yet a fourth component, social groups, which are also sub-divided into groups which are itinerant and groups which are sedentary. I feel Leutrat was definitely on the right track and I should not wish to undertake my own structural analysis without first acknowledging the importance of his contribution.

2

The Structure of the Western Film

I believe the Western story can ideally be broken down into three categories, determined strictly on the basis of function. I have already identified these categories as the formulary Western, the romantic historical reconstruction (historical romance), and the historical reconstruction. However, before defining these categories further, I should like first to point out that the formulary Western and the romantic historical reconstruction share a common link: the romance. Now, the romance has changed very little since we inherited the form from Classical Antiquity. The ancient Greeks divided romance into three stages. The first, the *agon*, means a conflict of some sort. The second stage is the *pathos*, the life-and-death struggle. The third and final stage is the *anagnorisis*, the recognition. There is an optional middle term which, when present, proves pivotal in determining whether the story is merely formulary or a romantic historical reconstruction and this is the *sparagmos*, the mangling.

The Perseus myth, in simple form, without the later embellishments of Ovid and Apollodorus, well illustrates the stages of the romance. There is a helpless old king whose kingdom is menaced by a devouring sea monster. Each year an innocent victim is offered to the sea monster in propitiation until, finally, the choice has fallen on the king's beautiful daughter. At this juncture the hero, Perseus, comes on the scene, kills the sea monster, and thus rescues the princess. In due course he marries her and inherits the kingdom. The *agon* is the conflict between the people of the kingdom and the sea monster. As in most Classical romances, the princess is motherless and her father impotent to save her life. The *pathos* is Perseus' struggle with the sea monster in which the monster dies. If the stage of the *sparagmos* is added to the telling, Perseus is badly mangled during the death-struggle. The *anagnorisis* is the recognition that the sea monster *had to be killed*, not propitiated, in order for the kingdom to enjoy true happiness, peace, and prosperity.

This structure of the romance is basic to the plot structure of the formulary

Western. There is a conflict within the community. The hero eventually decides to take part in the conflict and his involvement precipitates the death-struggle between himself and one or more villains. The recognition is that an orderly society is not possible until the conflict with the villain or villains has been resolved through the hero's intervention.

The hero need not come from outside the community. Rather, it is true of him, as Vergil said it was true of Jupiter, "deus dabit his quoque finem"—a god will put up with just so much of such things. Perceiving the conflict, the hero determines to take a hand. In RIDER OF DEATH VALLEY (Universal, 1932) directed by Albert Rogell, Tom Mix, cast as Tom Rigby, is a successful rancher in the district. Bill Joyce, played by Willard Robertson, has made a rich gold strike and Fred Kohler, as Lew Grant, kills him without learning the location of the mine. As a consequence, Joyce's little girl Betty, played by Edith Fellows, is orphaned. Dr. Laribee, played by Forrest Stanley, and Lew Grant are just about to seize the map to the mine from Betty's hands when Tom Rigby enters on the scene. He has Betty tear the map into three parts, giving a part to each of the men. Helen Joyce, Bill's sister, played by Lois Wilson, arrives from the East intent on taking possession of Betty and the map. Rigby, knowing that Doc and Lew intend to steal the map from Helen, refuses to give up his piece. He tells Helen that she will get his help whether she wants it or not. He proposes that the four of them leave Betty at his ranch and venture out to examine the mine. It turns out that he has the last third of the map. After a series of mishaps, the four find themselves at the mine in the middle of the desert. The only horse remaining is Rigby's mount, Tony. Rigby sends Tony back to his ranch to bring help. There is no water at the mine and the little that is left in the canteens must be shared by all. Lew dies from thirst and exposure. Now comes the *sparagmos*. Rigby decides to head himself into the desert to see if he can locate the search party. Doc secretly takes the water out of Rigby's canteen and substitutes sand. Leaving the other canteen in Helen's care, Rigby sets out. The ordeal is very great and he eventually collapses due to the heat and the lack of water. He is found by his men who have been led to the spot by Tony. Recovering, he mounts Tony and the others follow him to the mine where Doc, in an attempt to get at water, has lit a charge of dynamite. Tom saves Helen only seconds before the explosion which kills Laribee.

In RIDER OF DEATH VALLEY, the hero ends up with the heroine, but this need not be the case. In SHANE (Paramount, 1953) directed by George Stevens, the hero comes from outside the community, becomes involved in the conflict within the community between the nesters and a cattle baron who believes in free range, and, after the final death-struggle with the villains, he rides off alone. There are three different instances of mangling in the film: Shane's fight with Chris, a tough working for the cattle baron; Shane's fight with Joe Starrett, the nester for whom he works, when Shane decides that he, and not Starrett, must face the cattle baron and his hired gun in a showdown and Starrett stubbornly thinks it is his responsibility; and, lastly, Shane is wounded in the showdown.

The reason that I regard the *sparagmos* episode, when it is included, to be pivotal between the formulary Western and the romantic historical reconstruction (historical romance) is that in the formulary Western the hero always lives through the mangling, no matter how horrible it might be. In the romantic historical reconstruction there is another option: the hero may die from the mangling. An illustrative example is provided by what C.G. Jung termed the "child archetype" in the book on which he collaborated with Karl Kerényi, ESSAYS ON A SCIENCE OF MYTHOLOGY (1963). In Western fiction this "child archetype" made its appearance relatively early in Bret Harte's story, "The Luck of Roaring Camp" (1868). In Harte's story, when a mining camp prostitute dies in childbirth, the males in the camp adopt the orphan as a community endeavor and their care and concern for the infant completely transform their lives. Peter B. Kyne wrote a variation of this story in his "Broncho Billy and the Baby" which ran in THE SATURDAY EVENING POST in 1909. G.M. Anderson read the story, liked it, and, for fifty dollars, bought screen rights to Kyne's central character. The first Broncho Billy film in which Anderson starred, BRONCHO BILLY'S REDEMPTION (Essanay, 1910), made use of the character's name, but not of Kyne's plot. This had to wait for THE OUTLAW AND THE CHILD (Essanay, 1911). In this short film, a little girl, scarcely more than a baby, daughter of the sheriff, is found in the middle of the Mojave desert by Broncho Billy, a desperate outlaw being pursued by her father. Billy undergoes terrible sufferings in the desert in order to save the child's life and to return her safely to the sheriff's home. The mangling, however, proves to have been too much and Billy expires at the end of the picture.

Kyne so liked the story that he decided in 1911 to expand it into a short novel he titled THE THREE GODFATHERS which was also serialized in THE SATURDAY EVENING POST before it was issued in book form. It was filmed the first time as THE THREE GODFATHERS (Universal, 1916) directed by Edward LeSaint. Harry Carey was the star, the leader of an outlaw trio that comes upon an infant in the desert while trying to escape from a pursuing posse. It was filmed again as MARKED MEN (Universal, 1919) directed by John Ford, again with Carey in the lead; again as HELL'S HEROES (Universal, 1929) directed by William Wyler; as THE THREE GODFATHERS (M-G-M, 1936) directed by Richard Boleslawski; as THE THREE GODFATHERS (M-G-M, 1948) directed by John Ford; and as a made-for-television movie, THE GOD CHILD (ABC, 1974) directed by John Badham.

What happens in a formulary Western happens because the formulary structure demands it. The hero triumphs because the formula requires that the hero triumph. What happens in a romantic historical reconstruction happens for an *ideological* reason. This is how the circumstances surrounding the American Revolutionary War are usually taught in primary school: the British prey upon the innocent Colonials; the British have to be killed; the Colonials suffer at Valley Forge, but in the end they triumph. They triumph because, *ideologically*, they have the right on their side and right always triumphs eventually. It is quite the same in a film such as John Ford's second make of THE THREE GODFATHERS story. Three outlaws, played by John Wayne, Pedro Armendariz, and Harry Carey, Jr., rob a bank and are pursued into the desert by Sheriff "Buck" Sweet, played by Ward Bond, and his posse. The outlaws come upon a wagon at Tarapin Tanks. A tenderfoot in an effort to get water (reasoning much the same as Dr. Laribee in RIDER OF DEATH VALLEY) has blown up the tanks and left his pregnant wife alone in the wagon. The three outlaws become the newly born baby's godfathers, promising the dying mother they will save her baby. A passage in a Bible instructs them to take the baby to New Jerusalem and that they must follow a star at night in order to get there. Both Pedro Armendariz and Harry Carey, Jr., die during the *sparagmos* of crossing the desert. When Wayne collapses, they return in shadow and song to urge him onward. It seems as if he can go no farther when he discovers a donkey. Again as prophesied in the Bible, the donkey helps him transport the child to New Jerusalem. He arrives because, ideologically he must, on Christmas eve. Sheriff Sweet is waiting for him there and arrests him. It does not matter. Wayne has been redeemed through the *sparagmos*. He is alive, not merely because the formula requires him to survive because he is the hero, but because he is a villain redeemed through divine intervention. His redemption, and not a convention of the formulary fictional mode, transforms him into a hero. After a year in prison, he will be released and able to assume the responsibilities of parenthood through raising to maturity the child whose life he saved.

Of course, when the ideology is different, as it is in THE OUTLAW AND THE CHILD, the villain, although he may behave as a hero, dies as a result of the *sparagmos*; in this case the ideology prohibits redemption through suffering. In HOMBRE (20th-Fox, 1967) directed by Martin Ritt, Paul Newman was cast as the hero, John Russell, a man whose white parents were lost to him in an Indian raid and who was then raised by the Apaches. Known generally only as Hombre, Russell inherits a boarding house and decides to try living more as a white man. He trades the boarding house for a passel of horses and then leaves town aboard a stagecoach. The other passengers include an Indian agent who has embezzled $12,000 in funds intended for the Indians, his young wife, a young married couple, a sensuous woman named Jessie Brown, and the leader of an outlaw gang who plans to hold up the stagecoach in order to rob the Indian agent. "Put yourself on the winning side for a change," Hombre is told in town by a Mexican friend named Mendez. "Is that where you are?" Hombre asks Mendez. "Being a Mexican is closer to being white than being an Apache," Mendez tells him. This is the ideology which motivates all the events in the film.

A good way to approach any Western to determine if it is formulary, romantic, or historical is to separate it into the three distinct parts already mentioned:

Purpose, Passion, and Perception. The Purpose of HOMBRE is to explore the question of the winning side. The Passion of the film is characterized by Hombre's attempts to live more as a white man and this conflict leads to a death-struggle which occurs once he boards the stagecoach. His is the burden of saving the money and the passengers. Now, in a formulary Western, Hombre would be the unambiguous hero; he would save the passengers after a death-struggle with the villains; and the Perception at the end would be that he behaved as he did because he was a hero. A trivial Perception, perhaps, but *the* Perception to be found in virtually every "B" Western ever made and there have been thousands of them. Since this is not the Perception at the end of HOMBRE and since there is an ideology at work, rather than a formula, it is apparent that it is a romantic historical reconstruction. In his effort to save the money and the lives of the passengers, Hombre has to revert to his Apache savagery. Yes, he does win out. But there is another ideological precondition involved in this particular plot, one rather common in Western films: when an Indian and a white man confront one another, one must vanish, that is, die. Hombre, in fighting the white villains, becomes again as an Indian; and so, as an Indian, he must die at the end so that white society can prosper without having to concern itself with inferior races notwithstanding that they might magnanimously sacrifice their lives to make that prosperity possible. According to this ideology, we can regard the dead with gratitude and grant them a posthumous dignity they were denied in life precisely because they are dead.

Many more instances of historical reconstructions can be found in Western fiction than in Western films. While I engage in a more detailed discussion of this mode of Western plot structure in the part on frontier legends, for now let it suffice that an historical reconstruction is to be regarded as an attempt to re-create a situation or an individual from the history of the American West without any ulterior ideological motive. It is not formulary because there are no formulae in human history, with all due respect to such historians as Oswald Spengler and Arnold Toynbee who thought otherwise. It is not romantic because, while ideology might motivate some people some or all of the time, all persons do not at all times behave according to a specific, prescribed ideology. A good example of an historical reconstruction would be TOM HORN (Warner's, 1980) directed by William Wiard.

In 1900, after Horn came back from working as a mule handler during the Spanish-American War, he was again hired by Wyoming cattlemen to act as a range detective. He was supposed to fight rustling which meant, in practice, that he was a hired killer. On 18 July 1901, dressed in his father's hat and yellow slicker, fourteen-year-old Willie Nickell was shot from ambush. Deputy U.S. Marshal Joe La Fors set up a meeting with Horn at his office in Cheyenne and had Undersheriff Leslie Snow and Charlie Ohnhaus, a court reporter, hidden so they could witness and Ohnhaus record what was said. Horn was drunk and Ohnhaus stated at Horn's trial that, when asked casually by La Fors how far away he had been when Willie Nickell was killed, Horn boasted "about 300 yards. It was the best shot I ever made, and the dirtiest trick I ever done. I thought at one time that he would get away."[39] The next day, 13 January 1902, Horn was arrested. At his trial, Horn insisted that he and La Fors were just "joshing." The evidence was extremely flimsy but, nonetheless, Horn was convicted and on 9 January 1903 he was sentenced to hang. While in jail waiting first for his trial and then for his appeal and his petition to the governor, Horn wrote his autobiography. The last letter he wrote was to his close friend, John C. Coble, a Wyoming cattleman. It was dated at Cheyenne, 20 November 1903. "All that supposed confession in the United States marshal's office was prearranged," Horn wrote Coble, "and everything that was sworn to by those fellows was a lie, made up before I came to Cheyenne. Of course, there was talk of the killing of the boy, but La Fors did all of it. I did not even make an admission, but allowed La Fors to make some insinuations . . . . This is the truth, as I am going to die in ten minutes."[40]

Steve McQueen was cast as Horn in TOM HORN; he was also the executive producer of the film. The time frame by omission of events extraneous to the basic storyline is acceptably condensed. In history, Horn escaped jail with another range detective, Jim McLeod, also accused of killing a sheepherder from ambush. Both were easily recaptured. In the film, Horn is alone when he escapes; but the omission of McLeod does not distort the accuracy of the event as it concerned Horn. McQueen's understated performance is exactly right to convey the combination of self-assurance, fundamental kindliness, irony, occasional perplexity, and cold-blooded competence of the historical Horn. Richard Farnsworth, cast as John C. Coble, Linda Evans as Glendolene Kimmell, the schoolteacher of part-German, part-Polynesian extraction who was profoundly in love with Horn, and Slim Pickens as a sympathetic sheriff provide fine support. The hanging is appropriately grim, albeit it is not shown that Horn's neck was not broken and that he died slowly; seventeen minutes after the trap was sprung, two physicians pronounced him dead. What *is* shown is that Horn kept his nerve to the very end. "The unflinching stare of his keen eyes which one sometimes encountered," Glendolene Kimmell recalled, "was the signal-light of a sublime nerve—a nerve which enabled him to look a horrible death in the face and smile. This was one reason why his enemies so hated him. They could imprison him, they could kill him—they might even torture him—but they could never make his soul cringe, his nerve falter."[41] It is due to McQueen's subdued performance that Horn is seen to exhibit these qualities without the obvious romanticism with which Kimmell portrayed them. The film has Horn's last words spoken correctly: "That's the sickest-looking bunch of damned sheriffs I ever saw."

There are dozens of parallels from American history which this film might suggest, the returning Vietnam veteran being only the most recent, where the same community that hires killers to kill for it turns on them after the need or desire for them has disappeared. But TOM HORN makes no such appeal. It is concerned with its historical subject and any such parallel is clearly to be drawn gratuitously by the viewer.

I must emphasize that my method for making structural distinctions between the modes of the Western has to do primarily with the manner in which situations and persons *are treated*. However, having distinguished between the formulary, romantic, and historical modes, the formulary and romantic, while united on the basis of dependence on romance, are also further distinguished by the fact that the romantic mode, in addition to its dependence on ideology, has a patina of historicity usually lacking in the formulary Western. This patina is invoked so that the ideology motivating the sequence of events will appear to have somehow an *historical* validity. Beyond this, there is the matter of heroes.

"The ancients have left us examples of epic poems in which the heroes provide the entire interest of the story," Leo Tolstoy wrote in WAR AND PEACE (1862–1869), *ne plus ultra* among historical reconstructions, "and we are still unable to accustom ourselves to the fact that for our epoch history of that sort is meaningless."[42] The formulary Western and the romantic historical reconstruction, because of their debt to romance, embody and promote readily identifiable heroes. There are no heroes in an historical reconstruction because there are no heroes in history; albeit, in history, there have been myriad human beings who have been capable of heroic behavior in given circumstances. I suppose the difference comes to this: a hero in a formulary Western or an historical romance is a hero by definition; in the historical reconstruction he is a character capable of heroic behavior not by definition but as the result of character and boundless other factors. Tom Horn, as Steve McQueen portrayed him, while at times sensitive and at others accomplished, is not a hero, nor a villain, but rather a somewhat remarkable and unique individual suddenly caught up in a process of historical change which he cannot fathom in time to save himself.

It was Frank Gruber in his book, THE PULP JUNGLE (1967), who first set forth what he considered to be the seven basic plots to be found in Western fiction. While in what follows I am indebted to this original notion of his, there are several distinct differences between his views and mine. First, I do not regard what he called a plot anything of the kind, but rather a matter of setting or situation. Second, all such notions may be true of formulary Westerns or romantic historical reconstructions, but they are not true of historical reconstructions since history, and especially the stunning diversity of people and events in the American West in the nineteenth century, can never be limited to seven, or seventy, basic situations. Third, in amending Gruber's list, I have not only altered it with my own refinements, but I have also accommodated a wholly separate group of seven basic plots devised by Mody Boatright in his essay, "The Formula in Cowboy Fiction and Drama," which appeared in WESTERN FOLKLORE (April, 1969). Although I might also have chosen far more than two paradigms to illustrate each of these seven basic plot situations, I felt that two were indeed adequate for each.

1. *The Pioneer Achievement Story.* Under this heading would be included all stories dealing with the construction of a railroad, a telegraph, a stage-coach line, or a wagon cartage company as well as stories centering on wagon train journeys, construction of toll roads, of long and/or large cattle drives. Also under this heading would be those stories where the hero attempts to expand his own business enterprise or one for the community, such as fencing in his land or a dam-building project. The villain or villains will oppose the proposed achievement because of rivalry in love, hope of profit or advantage from the failure, or because of a grudge, motivated in the case of a white villain, less motivated or not motivated at all in the case of Indians. Also allied are stories telling of the efforts of a hero, a villain, or a villain who becomes a hero to build up an empire. If the story has the hero doing this, he succeeds; if he is a villain who becomes a hero or who has a change of heart, defeat is accepted with grace, while success is crowned by recognition of social values, such as, the good of the community is perceived as being more important than an empire. If the villain undergoes no change of heart, defeat signifies the triumph of Populist, or democratic, values over incipient fascism or monopolistic capitalism.

NORTH OF 36 (Paramount, 1924) directed by Irvin Willat was based on a novel of the same title by Emerson Hough. It was remade a second time as THE CONQUERING HORDE (Paramount, 1931) directed by Edward Sloman and a third time as THE TEXANS (Paramount, 1938). The contents of the screen story were changed in each adaptation, but not the essential ingredient: driving a large trail herd to a railhead for shipment. THE TEXANS was directed by James Hogan. In history, the first cattle were dispatched from Abilene to Chicago on 5 September 1867, but not according to this picture. It was presumably some time earlier, in 1865, when Randolph Scott, cast as a former Confederate soldier, arrives at Indianola, Texas, and helps out heroine Joan Bennett who is also a gun-runner. Scott, however, bows out when Bennett begins recruiting for Maximilian in Mexico. Bennett is in love with rebel leader Robert Cummings. Scott switches to wearing buckskins and Raymond Hatton—who often played Scott's sidekick in early sound Westerns in Paramount's Zane Grey series—joins him as his pard. Robert Barrat is the chief carpetbagger in the area. He wants to tax Bennett's cattle and thus drive her into ruin. This Scott will not permit to happen. Together with Bennett's cowhands, he drives her cattle across the border into Mexico. In a matter of twelve hours or so, an incredible 10,000 cattle are herded to the Rio Grande and make a spectacular crossing, a high-point in all three versions of the story (although the motivation is always different, much of the footage is the same, an obvious inducement to remake the film). Presently Bennett decides to drive the cattle back across the river and head them to Abilene for shipment East. Barrat is empowered to bring the cattle forcibly back to Texas for tax evasion. Having run amok in Mexico with

Maximilian, Cummings now joins the drive. The Comanches, whose land the herd must cross, ask for a single steer in payment, but this price is too high for the whites. The Comanches attack. The whites are rescued by Barrat and the militia/Cavalry. Once the Indians are driven off, Bennett's crew is arrested for tax evasion and the herd is started back to Austin. The Comanches attack a second time and, during the fray, Hatton kills Barrat. The militia/Cavalry then decides to escort Bennett and her group to the Kansas border. When, after the herd reaches its destination, Cummings joins the Ku Klux Klan, Bennett throws him and her Confederate sympathies over and realizes she loves Scott.

It is typical in the Pioneer Achievement Story that there be some extraordinary undertaking which leads to a break-through wherein the future will be brighter than the past. In THE TEXANS the Comanches are irrelevant to the storyline except for dramatic purposes. No recognition is accorded to their claim to their tribal land and the demand that the trail crew surrender a steer to them is treated as an irrational demand for unjust enrichment by indolent savages. Instead of viewing Reconstruction for what it was—the economic exploitation of the defeated South by Northern investors—the situation is reduced to the formulary figure of a greedy villain played by Robert Barrat; once he is killed, the community easily heals itself. The ideology is quite clear: this single murder is all that is required, and not the extremism demonstrated by Bennett early in the film and by Cummings throughout. Hatton commits the murder in such a way that the Comanches will be blamed and this is considered morally acceptable for a sidekick, although it possibly would not have been so much so had the hero done it. The heroine is a fool who does not know her own mind until nearly the end when she sees how mistaken she was to love Cummings and that Scott, who will work hard in her behalf, is readily the better man. With the money realized from sale of the herd, her future and Scott's will be affluent and happy.

The achievement in a Pioneer Achievement Story need not come about only as the result of hard work, human endurance, or community effort. It can happen as a consequence of technology. The U.S. Cavalry in the West generally rode by fours. In SPRINGFIELD RIFLE (Warner's, 1952) directed by Andre de Toth, a technological Pioneer Achievement Story, as in most Cavalry Westerns, the men ride by twos. A horse herd is stolen from the Cavalry. Gary Cooper, cast as a major, is accused of retreating from action because he made no attempt to retrieve the horses. He is drummed out of the service with a yellow stripe painted down his back. Phil Carey, a fellow officer, is in on the secret plan to get to the bottom of a gang running horses South for use by the Confederacy. Cooper tells his wife, played by Phyllis Thaxter, that he cannot go back East with her; there is something he has to do first. He and Carey fight and Cooper is arrested and charged with trespassing on military property. Cooper is put in a cell with two men suspected of being in with the horserunners and Cooper joins up with them. It turns out that two ranchers, played by David Brian and Lon Chaney, Jr., are leading the gang, but the real mastermind is

Paul Kelly, cast as the commanding Union officer. The gang rustles a Union horse herd and Carey is killed during the raid, gunning David Brian before he falls. A good part of the film was shot at Lone Pine, California, with the snow-covered mountains for background. "This is a man's world out here," Kelly tells Thaxter, "and you just don't belong." Once Thaxter is out of the way, Kelly sees to it that everyone who knows Cooper is a spy is killed. Then Kelly has Cooper charged with being the head of the horse rustlers. "Big Boy" Williams, cast as a sergeant, helps Cooper escape and with Springfield rifles and some troopers they go out to capture the gang. There is a blood bath of bad men being shot down and a chase on horseback of Kelly by Cooper. At the end of the picture, Cooper is told that the new technology of the Springfield rifle, so decisive in defeating the horse rustlers, will also have a salutary effect on the war effort and then on the winning of the West.

This is the commonest attitude toward technology in Westerns before 1970. After that date, this ideology would occasionally be reversed, so instead the theme becomes that of preserving the wilderness in the face of the onslaught of technology. Such a film—MAN IN THE WILDERNESS (Warner's, 1971) would be an example—is a negative Pioneer Achievement Story. It reverses the conclusion according to what, in logic, is known as *tolendo tolens*, that is, by denying the minor premise, what is asserted in the major premise is denied in the conclusion. Reserving comment on its content, in MAN IN THE WILDERNESS directed by Richard C. Sarafian, the pioneer achievement being sought is to transport a boat overland for the purpose of expediting the fur trade. The plot is so set up that it occurs to those attempting this achievement that what they are trying to do is wrong: therefore, they abandon the boat so the wilderness can be preserved. In terms of actual history, this kind of negative Pioneer Achievement Story is as much a fantasy as THE TEXANS.

2. *Picaresque Wanderers and Searchers.* This plot setting is found more frequently in Western fiction than in Western films. The hero can be a roving cowhand, gunfighter, or mountain man. The narrative follows him from place to place where he becomes involved in various adventures, usually to the betterment of those with whom he comes in contact, or, more rarely, for purposes of personal spiritual growth. Also included in this group are those stories where a hero, or a hero and a companion, set out to find some thing or some person: a gold mine, or hidden loot, or a shrine, or a ruins of some kind. Where the search is for a person, quite often this setting is combined with the Justice/Revenge Theme below and deals with revenge, or, less frequently, with proving the innocence of the hero, the hero's companion, or some other person close to the hero.

An excellent example of this plot setting is COWBOY (Columbia, 1958) directed by Delmer Daves, based on Frank Harris' autobiography. Jack Lemmon, cast as Harris, works as a clerk in a Chicago hotel and falls in love with a Spanish-American woman who is going back to Mexico. Harris pays cattleman Glenn Ford $3,800 to join up with Ford's cattle company on the trail. Harris learns how to be a cowboy during a series of picaresque adventures. Ford is a particularly demanding task master. Brian Donlevy, cast as a disillusioned law man who has quit his profession because he is sick of killing, is one of the more interesting characters Harris meets. When Harris finally does get to Mexico, he finds the señorita married. He decides to continue his nomadic life.

Frequently in stories employing this plot setting part of the ideological message is that women are fickle and that a man is therefore better off wandering. Sometimes, as in WILL PENNY (Paramount, 1968) directed by Tom Gries, this decision to keep wandering can be shown as extremely painful; at other times, as in MONTE WALSH (National General, 1970) directed by William Fraker, the decision, while sad, is made to seem inevitable. In COWBOY, it is light-hearted and high-spirited, perhaps because the Harris character is still a young man and there will be other chances for him to settle down.

In J.W. COOP (Columbia, 1972) directed by and starring Cliff Robertson, this plot setting is combined with the contemporary West for background. The film opens to Coop rodeoing in prison. When he is released, he follows the rodeo circuit. As Coop wanders around in Texas, the state is shown to be dominated almost exclusively by harassing law men, fascist and racist promoters, and people with empty lives. Coop picks up a hippie girl, played by Christina Ferrare, and they go on the circuit together. Once Coop gets to the championship finals, he proposes to the girl and she leaves him. Coop breaks his leg and comes in second. Next he tries riding a bull with his leg in a cast and gets mauled. Ferrare, who is reading C.G. Jung's MAN AND HIS SYMBOLS (1964), explains to Coop at this point that the reason she rejected him is that he wanted to settle down on a horse ranch. The somewhat complicated ideology of this plot indicates that a man must be circumspect: he must know when to quit and, in the modern West, when he wants to settle down, the woman may not. Because Coop does not know when to quit, he persists at trying to win at rodeoing when it is no longer possible for him to do so. Because the woman rejected settled life, he remains a loner. Very often, if not always, the reason a wanderer or a searcher goes on being a wanderer and a searcher is because he is obsessed, either about a woman or by some goal he hopes to achieve. Obsession leads inevitably to his being alone.

3. *The Ranch Story/Town Western.* This plot setting focuses on a background consisting of cattle or horse ranching. The emphasis may be on ranch life or town life, depending on whether the action takes place principally on the range or within the confines of a Western town. The conflict usually concerns some sub-group within the ranching community, rustlers, nesters, sheepmen, mustangers, capitalist exploiters (local or from

the East), or dishonest bankers. The hero may be either a member of the existing community or an outsider who rides into a community and takes sides in an existing or emerging conflict.

SHOWDOWN AT ABILENE (Universal, 1956) directed by Charles Haas is a Ranch Story/Town Western in which Jock Mahoney was cast as a Confederate veteran returning after the war. While he was away, Lyle Bettger has managed to build up a land and cattle empire. He also runs the town and is engaged to marry Martha Hyer. There is an interesting—and *very* telling—shot of Mahoney and Hyer talking with Bettger's reflection in a mirror standing between them. This is a signal to the viewer of what is to come: Bettger must be removed. There is friction between the farmers and the cattlemen. Mahoney is being forced to pick a side by the farmers who want him to resume his old job as sheriff. Mahoney, however, is not up to it. He keeps his gun in a drawer and feels himself impotent to use it again, no matter what the provocation. Even when Mahoney agrees to assume the sheriff's job, he refuses to wear a gun. Bettger, who lost his right hand as a child because of Mahoney, asks Mahoney now to act as his right hand. When a friend of Mahoney's is beaten up in a ruckus, he confesses to Mahoney the underlying ideological prescription of the film: "It's funny that a man has to fight to live at peace." Mahoney then tells Bettger and Hyer the bad news: he accidentally shot Bettger's only brother during the war. Bettger goes berserk. Hyer does not help matters when she rejects Bettger's suit because she has finally discovered that it is Mahoney whom she really loves. The viewer is supposed to feel no sympathy for Bettger: he still has his cattle empire and the town. However, he *did* lose his right hand, his brother, and Hyer all because of Mahoney. Mahoney goes one even better. He clandestinely unloads Bettger's gun. As a consequence, when Bettger confronts his arrogant trail driver in a show-down and is killed it is really Mahoney's doing that Bettger gets plugged. Bettger's death does have a positive affect on Mahoney. His impotence suddenly gone, he picks up Bettger's gun and shoots down the trail driver. This not only wins Mahoney happiness and wealth, but it reinforces a number of the secondary prescriptions in the film: crippled men become ambitious to compensate for their infirmities and the only way to deal with them is for them to die; greedy and ambitious men will do each other in; and, finally, a good man *must* resort to violence if he is going to bring about peace and personal prosperity.

COUNT THREE AND PRAY (Columbia, 1955) directed by George Sherman is in the vein of the fiction of Harold Bell Wright, a rural preacher who wrote such sentimental and inspirational novels as THE SHEPHERD OF THE HILLS (1907) and THE WINNING OF BARBARA WORTH (1911). The film opens with three veterans returning to a town made up entirely of ex-Confederates or Confederate sympathizers, two of them in gray, Van Heflin in blue. Naturally enough, Heflin is hated. Notwithstanding, he is determined to pursue a career as a preacher. He discovers Joanne Woodward—the bright moment in this picture—squatting at what is to become the parsonage. She falls in love with Heflin and he sets about to make her duly devout. When the wife of one of Heflin's parishioners does not want to attend his service, her husband gives her a black eye and the incident is treated as quite a joke. Because the flesh is weak, Heflin keeps getting into fistfights; but the community increasingly comes to believe in him and to help him build a church. Raymond Burr, cast as the chief heavy and leader of a gang of ex-Confederates, does not want the church. His being an ex-Confederate is just another manifestation of his generally anti-Christian nature. He is dispatched, Heflin gets the church built, Heflin and Woodward marry.

Both of these films embody a strong endorsement of community spirit, a celebration of American middle-class life, and a reassurance of the promise of the future now that the war is over. Andrew Bergman in his book, WE'RE IN THE MONEY (1971), made the assertion that Westerns, because of their fundamental commitment to hopefulness, were therefore unpopular in the years of the Great Depression. The truth of the matter is that more Westerns were made during this period than at any other time, especially after 1932 when the possibility of making sound pictures outdoors had been proven to be economically profitable. The only economic factors which have any real relevance to a film's plot are usually those presented within the context of the film, rather than those outside of it. The Ranch Story/Town Western emphasizes that all hard-working middle-class individuals and families will fare well once the trouble-makers are removed from the community, generally by killing them off, if events themselves do not manage it.

4. *The Justice/Revenge Theme.* Buck Jones best summed up the guiding philosophy behind this plot setting when in THE SUNDOWN RIDER (Columbia, 1932) he remarks: "I pay my debts, both kinds." In many of the Westerns employing this plot setting, justice is equated with revenge; but in an appreciable number a distinction is made between the two, revenge being morally dubious and even dangerous when it takes the place of due process. The hero, depending on how revenge and justice are treated, may seek vengeance and be persuaded instead to seek justice; or the hero may seek justice through due process, be foiled, and have to turn to revenge, becoming either a villain or arriving at a dialectical synthesis in which the resolution of the plot finds justice and revenge somehow aspects of a higher principle. If a sense of historical "progress" is a theme in this plot setting, revenge is usually seen as having been superseded by honest due process; however, if due process has become corrupt, it is generally corrected by reverting again to revenge as a balancing measure. In view of the vast number of formulary Westerns and romantic historical reconstructions which have employed this plot setting either as a part or as the whole motivation of the story, it has obviously been an attractive dramatic situation for filmmakers. Two ma-

jor varieties of stories utilizing this plot setting are the vengeance plot/hero variety and the vengeance plot/villain variety. Complementary to this bifurcation, in the vengeance plot/hero variety a crime is committed against the hero and he sets things right—the *active* ending—by killing the villain or villains responsible, or—the *passive* ending—by seeing the villain or villains killed (or by himself turning the villain or villains over to the law to be dealt with accordingly). When Cable Hogue in THE BALLAD OF CABLE HOGUE (Warner's, 1970) is told, "Vengeance is mine, saith the Lord," Hogue responds that that is all right, as long as the Lord does not take too long and Hogue can watch. No less a divine than St. Thomas Aquinas once suggested that the heavenly blessed would spend eternity watching the damned suffer in Hell and—although his theology differed—John Calvin wrote in his INSTITUTES OF THE CHRISTIAN RELIGION (1536–1559) that the righteous are able to observe "the wicked bringing upon themselves the just destruction to which they are destined."[43] Walter Van Tilburg Clark's THE OX-BOW INCIDENT (1940) and the film based on it directed by William Wellman both draw their significance through presenting an antithesis to justice which is disguised and mistaken revenge. Such an alternative termination usually shows the accused and punished to have been innocent.

THE MAN FROM COLORADO (Columbia, 1948) directed by Henry Levin opens with the Civil War. Glenn Ford, cast as a Union colonel, orders his troops to fire upon a Confederate band despite the fact that these men are holding a white flag. Ford tells William Holden, his second in command, that the two of them make a good team. Returning home after the war, they discover that Ray Collins, cast as a grasping capitalist mine owner, has disenfranchised all the men who joined the Union army and has jumped their claims. Ford is appointed a federal judge and Holden becomes his marshal. Both Ford and Holden are in love with Ellen Drew, but Drew agrees to marry Ford. Holden begins to have reservations about Ford, suspecting that the war turned him into a killer. In retaliation over Collins' swindle, some of the veterans become outlaws. Holden stands up for them, whereas Ford has become "blood simple," hanging veterans with enthusiasm. In a *dénouement* reminiscent of William S. Hart's HELL'S HINGES (Triangle, 1916), Ford dies in a fiery inferno after the town has been set ablaze. Holden, who survives, believes in a higher justice than any Ford practiced and goes to Washington to appeal on behalf of the veterans.

The ideology of this film would have the viewer believe that the federal government is needed to protect small businessmen and workers from cruel exploitation by greedy industrialists. This kind of faith in just government is frequently invoked when abstract justice is the issue, rather in the spirit of Honoré de Balzac's physician, Benassis, who remarks in THE COUNTRY DOCTOR (1833) "a statesman ought always to imagine Justice with the poor at her feet, for justice was only invented for the poor."[44]

There is no such belief in a just federal government in GOOD DAY FOR A HANGING (Columbia, 1959) directed by Nathan Juran. Here the community is shown as being able to solve its own problems, including the administration of justice. There is a bank robbery. Two of the bandits are killed as is the town marshal leading the pursuing posse. Another of the bandits, played by Robert Vaughn, is wounded. He is captured by Fred MacMurray whose daughter was once in love with him. MacMurray is made temporary marshal. Vaughn insists that he was not the one whose bullet killed the marshal. Not only does MacMurray not believe Vaughn, he is so intent on seeing him hang that he goes to the extreme of beating up his defense attorney. MacMurray claims that he saw Vaughn do the shooting and his testimony convicts Vaughn at his trial. The town inexorably turns against MacMurray once it is learned that he will function as the executioner: he so obviously relishes the job. An effort is undertaken to get Vaughn's death sentence commuted. Even MacMurray's daughter, played by Maggie Hayes, sides with Vaughn. MacMurray is asked to surrender his badge. Vaughn then breaks out of jail, slaps down Maggie Hayes, and laughs at the stupidity of the townspeople for believing him to be innocent. MacMurray is asked to pin on the badge again. "Who's going to look after us fools, if you don't?" a townsman asks.

The ideology informs the viewer that, while vengeful feelings might seem inappropriate, mercy is often wasted on the undeserving. A strong posture of rigid law and order is the only true antidote to the inclination toward moral laxness which both encourages criminals to think they can defeat justice and blinds the ordinary, well-meaning citizen into thinking that capital punishment is too severe a penalty.

5. *The Indian Story.* In this plot setting, an Indian, an Indian tribe, or several Indian nations are either the principal focus of the story or the principal motivation of the actions of the other characters in the story. Generally the law of miscegenation has applied, so while a white man might marry an Indian woman, she comes to die in the course of the story. Rarely, as will be seen in the chapter on "Images of Indians," an Indian woman might live and ride off with the hero; and even more rarely a white woman might choose to live with an Indian male and survive the end of the picture.

The Indian story, as the Pioneer Achievement Story, is particularly notable for having a negative as well as a positive dimension. In GUNS OF THE TIMBERLAND (Warner's, 1960) directed by Robert D. Webb, if loggers Alan Ladd and Gilbert Roland successfully execute their timber contract, they will destroy the watershed protecting a fertile valley of a ranching community: to succeed would be a negative achievement even though the timber is needed for railroad ties and, therefore, for technological progress. The negative dimension of the Indian Story can be found in all those films in which the U.S. Cavalry is confronted by anti-progress and anti-civilization "renegade" Indians who have broken away from Anglo-American custody or in which some other segment of the white community, intent on progress, is hampered by Indians. In fact, the negative dimension is more common in the Indian Story than it is in the Pioneer Achievement Story perhaps because "renegade" Indians are the antithesis of pioneer achievement. The Indian Story also need not focus on an Indian as the central or point-of-view character, or even a group of Indians; the white characters can always remain in the forefront. This is certainly the case in DUEL IN DIABLO (United Artists, 1966) directed by Ralph Nelson.

This film was based on Marvin H. Albert's APACHE RISING (1957). In the novel when Ellen Graf is rescued from Indian captivity, she is told, " 'You were even a wife to one of them.' " " 'Not because I wanted to be,' " she protests. " 'Then why were you? Any decent white woman would kill herself before . . . . ' "[45] When the novel was adapted for the screen, this interchange did not make it into the screenplay. This was not because of any squeamishness since similar episodes are commonplace in Western films in any given decade; no, rather the shift in the film's ideological emphasis necessitated the change. James Garner is married to an Indian woman who is killed and scalped, presumably by a white man. Garner sets out to find the murderer. He signs on as a scout with the Cavalry. Sidney Poitier, cast as a gambler, goes along with the Cavalry in order to break horses. There is a ridiculous Indian fight in which the Indians get lopped off in great numbers, albeit, finally, the troop is pinned down. It turns out that Dennis Weaver, cast as Bibi Andersson's husband, did in Garner's wife. Weaver is captured by the Apaches, tied upside down on a wagon wheel, his head over a raging fire so that his brains boil, his screams heard by the besieged whites all through the night. Bibi Andersson resorts to prayer and is rewarded the next morning when Cavalry reinforcements arrive, dispersing the Indians. There is even a brief moment of sympathy for the Apaches. "I wonder if they will stay on the reservation this time?" Andersson asks Garner. "Why should they?" he responds.

The ideology of the film instructs us that savagery must be punished. The Indians cannot really help that they are savages and so they are simply killed. The Dennis Weaver character, however, is a white man who should have known better; because he still behaved as a savage, his death is incredibly savage. After Constantine the Great had his vision in which he was informed by the God of the Christians, "In hoc signo vinces" [In this sign you will conquer], Christianity became the official state religion of the Roman Empire. Ever since that time, the Christian God ostensibly has been on the side of those who believe in Him as opposed to those who do not. In DUEL IN DIABLO Bibi Andersson again proves the truth of this belief, as have many other whites in Westerns who have successfully prayed for intercession on their behalf against heathen Indians. Finally, while there may be no good reason for the Indians to remain on the reservation, there is also no place for them in the new society that is emerging. The most charitable solution that can be devised is simply to kill them.

Sidney Poitier's presence is purely gratuitous in this film. The Western, on the whole, has never dealt any more realistically with the issue of blacks on the frontier than with any other historical reality. Arthur Gordon's novel, RE-PRISAL (1950), which focuses on the fight for civil liberties in then contemporary Georgia, when it was filmed as REPRISAL! (Columbia, 1956) directed by George Sherman, had its locale shifted to Oklahoma, its time-frame set back seventy-five years, its point-of-view character altered from a black to an Indian, played by Guy Madison, who wants to pass for white so he can own land and pursue a career as a rancher. True, Madison is a mixed-blood; he feels, therefore, that he ought to be able to choose with which racial group he will identify. When he first rides in, there is a trial in progress in which Michael Pate and other bigoted heavies are being tried for supposed abuses of the Indians who live in a segregated village outside of town. Kathryn Grant was cast as an Indian maiden toward whom, despite her race, Pate is attracted, whereas white heroine Felicia Farr is attracted to Madison. Ralph Moody, cast as Madison's Cherokee grandfather, wants Madison to return to his own people. Madison calls him a "stupid old Indian" and retains him as a servant on the ranch which he buys. When one of the heavies is shot down by an Indian, the townspeople, learning of Madison's racial identity, want to lynch him for the crime. After the heavies murder Madison's grandfather, Madison shoots them down. This so impresses the townspeople that they are now seemingly prepared to overlook Madison's racial impurity. However, he decides to head out, Felicia Farr following after him.

REPRISAL! might be superficially termed "pro-Indian," but to do that would be to ignore the one-settlement cultural values which dominate its ideology. I shall have more to say about this phenomenon later on in these pages. Madison's identification with the whites involves him in repudiating his Indian heritage and the conclusion of the film does not find him any more willing to accept this heritage than he was at the beginning. Instead, he is isolated, neither wanting to be an Indian nor able, really, to pass for a white. If the reasoning behind the change from blacks to Indians in the film was to address seriously the problem of racism in the United States, it did not happen. Rather the ideology states: here is a man of mixed racial background. His dilemma is that he cannot really be white and he does not want to be either a savage, renegade Indian or a drunken, defeated Indian. What is he to do? What he does is he rides off; he vanishes, and with him his problem.

6. *The Outlaw Story.* Under this heading can be subsumed all those stories dealing with a hero forced into outlawry for whatever reason, or the outlaw who is somehow reformed—the plot dilemma of the good bad man. Sometimes outlaws are portrayed as being undeserving of viewer sym-

pathy, but in "psychological" Westerns this is altered to an explanation that outlaws are psychologically disturbed, even psychotic, and are best understood in this light.

THE LIFE OF JOHN WESLEY HARDIN (1895) was found among Hardin's papers after his death on 19 August 1895. It narrated his version of the events of his life from the time he shot and killed a black slave at fifteen through his imprisonment and studying law at the penitentiary at Huntsville, Texas. He was released in February, 1894. His wife, Jane, mother of his son and two daughters, had died in 1892. Callie Lewis, whom Hardin married on 8 January 1895, left him shortly after the wedding and refused to see him again. He was practicing law after a fashion, drinking heavily, gambling, and sharing rooms at the Herndon Lodging House with Mrs. Helen Bulah M'Rose. He was standing at the bar in the Acme Saloon when old John Selman stepped through the swinging doors behind Hardin and shot him in the back of the head.

THE LAWLESS BREED (Universal, 1953) directed by Raoul Walsh is a good example of the Outlaw Story. Much is made at the beginning of the film about Hardin writing his own memoirs. Rock Hudson, cast as Hardin, gets out of prison at the beginning of the picture. He gives his autobiography to a newspaper editor. The film then reverts to backtelling via Hudson's spoken narration. Hardin shoots a crooked card sharp in a fair fight. The card sharp's brothers, played by Glenn Strange, Hugh O'Brian, and Lee Van Cleef, take after him. Hardin is forced into a gun fight with Van Cleef and kills him. When Hardin goes to his father's ranch to get his girl friend, she blows out a kerosene lamp by lifting its glass without burning her fingers. She perversely agrees with Hardin's father, played by John McIntyre, that Hardin must stand trial before she can marry him. Hardin tries to raise money for his defense by racing horses. McIntyre, in a dual role, also plays Hardin's uncle in this sequence. Hardin's girl finally rejects him as a killer just before she herself is accidentally killed by a posse chasing Hardin. The Texas Rangers now set out after him. Rosie, a dance hall girl played by Julia Adams, tells Hardin that they are exactly alike. The two of them settle down on a horse ranch. Rosie does not like this life and wants Hardin to return to gambling until Hardin proposes marriage, whereupon she is overwhelmed, becomes a "new" woman, and, after the ceremony, announces she is pregnant. Hardin is arrested by the Rangers and because of popular opinion is sentenced to twenty-five years in prison. After sixteen years, he is granted a full pardon. His homecoming to Rosie and their son is highly sentimental. When Hardin soon after is shot in the back while unarmed in a saloon in town, the youngster becomes convinced that if you do not take up guns you will not have to use them.

THE LAWLESS BREED is the embodiment of the theme of the good bad man *par excellence* when it comes to the Outlaw Story. Throughout the film Hardin murders no one; he is forced into every fight. Yet there is no attempt made to explain *why* Hardin is singled out for persecution. Even his conviction at the trial is due to social prejudice and not the consequence of anything he did. One might say that the film illustrates a criminal as victim, except that Hardin is not shown to be a criminal, merely a victim. The ideology is subtly covert: relish your comfortable middle-class life because look here at a man who yearned for nothing else, but to whom it was denied!

In A MAN CALLED SLEDGE (United Artists, 1971) directed by Vic Morrow, a film produced after the end of the Hays Office code which insisted that crime must not only not pay but be punished, James Garner and his pard are stage robbers. The pard is shot in the back after winning at poker. Garner, in a spectacular display of the gunfighter's art, finishes off the killers. He then organizes a gang, including Dennis Hopper and Claude Akins, and decides to steal a gigantic gold shipment. Everyone in the towns in this picture is so trigger-happy he is ready to slap leather over anything. Garner tells his men about the gold shipment guards, that they are not professionals, whereas the members of the gang are. Garner has no interest in getting old; he just wants a good life before the bullet or the rope. To get at the gold, Garner has to be taken inside a prison as a prisoner. The robbery sequence itself is appropriately suspenseful. Garner proceeds in a poker game to win the shares of the other gang members. They are naturally resentful and take after him. Garner then kills them, one by one, his girl friend getting plugged in the process. Garner then leaves both the dead girl and the gold behind, and rides off.

The plot has definite similarities with that of SAM WHISKEY (United Artists, 1969) directed by Arnold Laven and THE TREASURE OF SIERRA MADRE (Warner's, 1948) directed by John Huston. In an odd *volte-face*, the viewer, after enjoying the planning, the theft, and the subsequent killing, is supposed to believe that Garner suddenly realizes that the lust for gold cost him something infinitely more precious, the life of his girl friend. In BUTCH CASSIDY AND THE SUNDANCE KID (20th-Fox, 1969) directed by George Roy Hill, the viewer feels a definite, sympathetic affinity with the two robbers, although, contrary to what happened in history, they are presumed to have been shot down in Bolivia. Garner pays no such price. His chicanery is punished only to the extent that he gets neither girl nor gold.

7. *The Law Man Story*. This plot setting includes not only town marshal and sheriff stories, but all manner of rangers, U.S. and deputy U.S. marshals, agents of the Department of Justice, range and stock detectives, insurance company investigators, and even occasionally a vigilante or a bank examiner. It is an excellent vehicle, when combined with the Justice/Revenge Theme, to raise all manner of legal and moral issues, or when combined with the Outlaw Story; whereas, when combined with the Ranch Story/Town Western or with the Indian Story (as in TELL

THEM WILLIE BOY IS HERE) [Universal, 1970], it can address social and psychological issues.

HIGH NOON (United Artists, 1952) directed by Fred Zinnemann stands as a sort of line of demarcation between law man stories prior to it and law man stories after it. In DEATH OF A GUNFIGHTER (Universal, 1969) directed by Allen Smithee, based on a novel by Lewis B. Patten, Richard Widmark was cast as a town marshal. Before HIGH NOON, town marshals were generally honest and capable, or dishonest, or just inept. When they were honest and capable, their heroics more often than not took on a quality of the superhuman. HIGH NOON attacked this premise, showing a law man to be human and deeply troubled. In DEATH OF A GUNFIGHTER, Widmark's job is killing trouble-makers and it is this fact which slowly turns the townspeople against him, the local banker leading the opposition. As the elderly law man played by Joel McCrea in Sam Peckinpah's RIDE THE HIGH COUNTRY (M-G-M, 1962) or the elderly major played by John Wayne in John Ford's SHE WORE A YEL-LOW RIBBON (RKO, 1949), Widmark has to put on spectacles to read fine print, in this case his notice of dismissal. As in HIGH NOON and so many post-HIGH NOON instances of the Law Man Story, the film ends with a terrific shoot-out. The ideology wishes to impress upon the viewer that a community, perfectly willing to hire a killer when the need exists, is also willing to go to any lengths to get rid of him once his job seems to be done. The law man's position in the community has no intrinsic value attached to it; rather it can become a source of community embarrassment.

However, no such hypocrisy can be found in FIRECREEK (Warner's, 1968) directed by Vincent McEveety, a veteran from television Western series, es-pecially GUNSMOKE. The film opens to Henry Fonda and his gang riding. Jack Elam and Gary Lockwood, gang members, would rape a young woman named Leah, played by Brooke Bundy, but Fonda puts a stop to it. Leah is given a five dollar gold piece and forgets all about the episode. The gang then rides into Firecreek and sets about terrifying the whole town. James Stewart is the part-time sheriff. Inger Stevens is attracted to Fonda. She tells him that he is living in the past; he accuses her of being even a worse example of someone living in the past since she has buried herself in Firecreek because the man she loved has been dead for ten years. Lockwood, Elam, and the other gang mem-bers feel that Barbara Luna has "a way to make a man ache." When the sim-ple-minded stable boy, who is Stewart's assistant, catches one of the gang trying to rape Luna, he accidentally shoots him. The gang holds a public wake that night in the center of the town street. Dean Jagger, a storekeeper, tells Stewart to stay out of it; the town, made up of losers, is dying. Fonda confesses to Stevens during their sexual encounter: "I can't gamble with bein' a nobody. I've been that." He derives his sense of identity from his gang. Stewart's wife, who is expecting, asks him: "Why did we settle for less?" The gang hangs the simple-minded stable boy while the townspeople remain mute; Stewart is shot in the leg. "Arthur is dead because I didn't do something about them in the beginning," Stewart tells Jagger. "The day a man decides not to face the world, he'd better step out of it." Stewart goes out into the street and through a hide and seek game finishes off the members of Fonda's gang. When Fonda would plug the wounded Stewart, Stevens shoots Fonda, much as the Quaker wife played by Grace Kelly in HIGH NOON shoots Robert Wilkie in the back when he is about to kill her law man husband. It is an integral part of the general ideology of Westerns to show women ready and willing to resort to killing, if necessary. This was hardly an innovation in HIGH NOON; heroines even in the Broncho Billy Westerns are quite wont to wield firearms when called upon to do so. I recall Gloria Steinem remarking on the ironic shift in political name-calling as applied to women: when they opposed war in 1917 they were called conservative; when they oppose war today they are called radical. In the Western, women, if they are heroines, must endorse violence and even be willing to become violent themselves.

These plot settings, as should be obvious, only rarely exist as pure types, but instead usually appear in a number of different combinations. But having made these distinctions, I am only partly in accord with Jean-Louis Leutrat who wrote in LE WESTERN that "the Western is bathed in ideology. Product of a capitalistic system, fashioned to be sold and helping to make sales (as cigarettes among television viewers) [N.B. this book was written in 1973], transmitted throughout the world, the American cinema *par excellence*, an expression so to speak of the ideology of the United States, it is at the same time a fantasy process born of that country, as well as a means of looking at it."[46] Such a charge cannot be made against the historical reconstruction, but where it does apply, in connection with the romantic historical reconstruction, perhaps Leutrat did suggest what is indeed a fruitful method to determine what *is* the ideology being transmitted. A viewer might well ask: if I knew nothing about the United States but what I have seen in this film, what would I say was the philosophy the filmmaker saw as motivating human behavior and human events and how has he gone about selling it to me? Moreover, not even the formulary Western entirely escapes this charge of possessing an ideology, albeit one of a most rudimentary kind. The villain must be killed or otherwise somehow removed from the community before the "good life"—as defined by the formula—becomes possible. What truly distinguishes the romantic historical reconstruction from the formulary Western is the wide variety of ideologies which can be transmitted by means of it.

"It is because most of us get our philosophies of the course of human events and their value from our school textbooks in history," Morris R. Cohen wrote in THE MEANING OF HUMAN HISTORY, "that those who wish to control popular opinion seek to dominate or determine the kinds of history textbooks in our schools."[47] It is too simplistic to assume, when it comes to Western films, that the ideology in a particular film is merely accidental or intended to reflect the values of the society which produced it. There is always that aspect which Leutrat mentioned, selling an ideology throughout the world; and "selling," as Daniel Bell observed in THE CULTURAL CONTRADICTIONS OF CAPITALISM (1976), is "the most striking activity of contemporary America."[48] The ideology controls how events are structured while, again in Bell's words, "in the technical nature of cinema, the event—the distance (close-up or long shot), the duration of the 'clip,' the concentration on one character rather than another, the pace and rhythm of the images—is 'imposed' on the spectator as he sits enveloped . . . in the darkness of the movie house."[49] I know from personal experience how difficult it is to get an individual to view a film critically, keeping foremost the rational, discerning mental faculties. The seduction is hardly less strong than has been the conditioning. Indeed, since the average American sixteen-year-old, exclusive of theatrical movies, has watched 16,000 hours of television, the seduction can seem more real than any life experience, the collective fantasy reinforced subliminally so often that plot formulae and plot expectations (resulting from the formulae) might almost be regarded as indelibly shaping a viewer's perspectives on life just through the power of sheer repetition.

PART II
SIX STUDIES IN AUTHORSHIP (*AUTEURISME*)

Ces sortes de spéculations ne donnent point de génie à ceux qui en manquent; elles n'aident pas beaucoup à ceux qui en ont, et le plus souvent les gens de génie sont incapables d'être aidés par les spéculations. A quoi donc sont-elles bonnes? A faire remonter jusqu'aux premières idées du beau quelques gens qui aiment le raisonnement, et qui se plaisent à réduire sous l'empire de la philosophie les choses qui en paroissent les plus indépendantes, et que l'on croit communément abandonnées à la bizarrerie des goûts.

[These kinds of speculations do not confer genius on those who are devoid of it; they are not of much help to those who are possessed of it and for the most part persons of genius are incapable of being helped by means of such speculations. Of what good, then, are they? They enable those people who love reasoning to refer back to the first principles of beauty, to find pleasure in reducing to the domain of philosophy those things not associated with it, most independent of it, and which commonly one is persuaded have been abandoned to the bizarre whimsies of taste.]

—Bernard de Fontenelle[1]

3

John Ford

In the course of a long and distinguished career, John Ford directed more than fifty Western films for theatrical release. MARKED MEN (Universal, 1919), MY DARLING CLEMENTINE (20th-Fox, 1946), and THE THREE GOD-FATHERS (M-G-M, 1948) are dealt with elsewhere in this book. Of the remaining Ford Westerns, I intend to confine myself here to THE OUTCASTS OF POKER FLAT (Universal, 1919), THE IRON HORSE (Fox, 1924), STAGE-COACH (United Artists, 1939), FORT APACHE (RKO, 1948), SHE WORE A YELLOW RIBBON (RKO, 1949), RIO GRANDE (Republic, 1950), THE SEARCHERS (Warner's, 1956), SERGEANT RUTLEDGE (Warner's, 1960), TWO RODE TOGETHER (Columbia, 1961), THE MAN WHO SHOT LIB-ERTY VALANCE (Paramount, 1962), and CHEYENNE AUTUMN (Warner's, 1964).

THE SUN SHINES BRIGHT (Republic, 1953) was a remake of Ford's earlier JUDGE PRIEST (Fox, 1934) and was, according to Ford himself, his favorite among his films. While neither the original nor the remake can be called a Western, I am convinced that a contrast between their respective structures can cast a decisive light on Ford's Western films. JUDGE PRIEST was the second in a trilogy with Will Rogers that Ford directed in the early 'Thirties. Breaking down its structure into components of Purpose, Passion, and Perception, the Purpose of the film is anticipated even before the credit crawl when the viewer sees Will Rogers on the bench as Judge Priest. Following the credits, the film opens in the judge's courtroom where Jeff, played by Stepin Fetchit, is being prosecuted by ex-Senator Maydew, played by Berton Churchill. It is established nearly at once that the judge is running for re-election and that the former senator is opposing him for the office. Three major sub-plots are introduced and developed during the Passion portion of the film. The first major sub-plot is the discovery that Bob Gillis, a mysterious figure in this small rural

Kentucky community in 1890, is in fact a distinguished war hero, having demonstrated extraordinary bravery on the side of the Confederacy during the last year or so of the struggle, and this despite his having been previously convicted of murder and sentenced to life imprisonment; moreover, Gillis is actually the father of Ellie May Gillespie, the heroine played by Anita Louise, and he has been keeping his relationship to her a secret because he does not want his prison background to compromise her socially within the community. Obviously, this is wrong thinking and when Gillis is placed on trial on a trumped up charge of assault with a deadly weapon, Henry B. Walthall, cast as the local minister, sets the record straight and sees that the truth comes to light. A court trial is used to acquit a social outcast.

A second major sub-plot is the love affair between Jerome Priest, the judge's nephew played by Tom Brown, and Ellie May. Jerome is a newly graduated lawyer and the judge promotes the love affair in the face of his sister-in-law's opposition; she would rather have her son marry Virginia Maydew, the ex-senator's daughter, and she regards Ellie May as a no-account because of her obscure parentage. The judge tells his sister-in-law that she fortunately has enough personal dignity for the whole family and so he need not be concerned with it.

The third major sub-plot is what might be regarded as the judge's relationship to the ante-bellum South, his continuing friendship with fellow Confederate veterans (at one point they are seen playing croquet and drinking mint juleps) and his attitude toward the principal black characters: his housekeeper played by Hattie McDaniel and Stepin Fetchit who becomes the judge's "man"—blacks belong properly to the servant class, the role assigned to the "loyal souls" in D.W. Griffith's THE BIRTH OF A NATION (Epoch, 1915); and, although the viewer does not know *when* the judge's wife and two children died, the relationship the judge still maintains with them. This last is revealed in one scene where the judge's image is reflected in the glass covering the portrait of his wife and children hanging in his bedroom; and, after talking to it for a while, the judge with a folding chair adjourns to the cemetery so he can speak even more intimately to his deceased wife sitting beside her grave. It is, in fact, when the judge is thus occupied that he observes Bob Gillis putting flowers on Ellie May's mother's grave and comes to the same conclusion the viewer does: Gillis must be Ellie May's father.

The Perception at the end of the film is that, given time and a little right-minded connivance, everything will surely work out for the best. The judge is re-elected; Jerome and Ellie May are to be married; and in the final scene of a parade Bob Gillis is grabbed from the sidelines and induced to march right alongside the other Confederate veterans. The emotion accompanying the Perception is that the "forgotten man"—to recall the production number with which THE GOLDDIGGERS OF 1933 (Warner's, 1933) directed by Mervyn LeRoy concludes—will be recognized, that the sacrifices the common man made in the Great War, as the sacrifices Bob Gillis made in the Civil War, will not go unsung by the community and that men of such evident virtue as Judge Priest will be exalted.

Structurally, THE SUN SHINES BRIGHT is a flawed work, not so much because of shortcomings in the screenplay or in Ford's direction as because the director's cut was re-edited by Republic prior to its release. Two essential Fordian sequences were deleted: that in the opening courtroom scene where the charges against Mallie Cramp, the local madam, brought weekly by Prosecuting Attorney Maydew and dismissed weekly by the judge, are again set aside by the judge; and that in which the judge goes into his bedroom and addresses the portrait of his deceased wife. The first scene in its present abbreviated form, while it might confuse a modern viewer as to why Mallie Cramp is in court and what it is she does for a living which so outrages Maydew, was acceptable to movie-góing audiences of the 'Fifties somewhat accustomed to this kind of screen "short-hand" through deletion. The second cut, however, is definitely more serious from both an aesthetic and structural point of view. At the very end of the film, Judge Priest, played by Charles Winninger, is seen to enter his house. He passes through a dark shadow and walks into his bedroom. Had the deleted scene not been removed, the viewer would realize that he was going to report his re-election to his deceased wife's portrait. But, since the scene is absent, one can understand why J.A. Place in her book, THE NON-WESTERN FILMS OF JOHN FORD (1979), was able to romanticize the conclusion and felt that the judge is "alone at the end of this film, alienated visually from both the audience and from the community he nurtured: he moves into the past as it moves into the future he made possible."[2] Further, had the earlier scene been left in, a viewer would see in the final scene a repetition of the conclusion of SHE WORE A YELLOW RIBBON where Captain Nathan Brittles, after his return to Fort Starke and his appointment as chief of scouts, must venture out into the fort cemetery to share this news with *his* deceased wife.

Viewing the film as it exists, the Purpose of THE SUN SHINES BRIGHT is established at once. Ashby Corwin, played by John Russell, returns to the small rural Kentucky community of his youth and introduces himself to Lucy Lee Lake, played by Arleen Whelan, the adopted daughter of Dr. Lewt Lake. Corwin tells Doc Lake right off that of all the children the doctor has delivered into "this vale of tears"—as Doc Lake refers to it—he is the blackest of the black sheep. Cut to the judge's courtroom where the viewer quickly learns that the judge is up for re-election and that the prosecuting attorney is running against him. Two cases are brought before the bench. The first is that of a black youth, U.S. Grant Woodford played by Elzie Emanuel, who is being tried because he refuses to go to work to support his Uncle Pleasant. From the outset Jeff, again played by Stepin Fetchit, is the judge's "man." Jeff joins U.S. in performing "Dixie," causing a commotion that finds the judge participating with his trumpet and that summons the judge's political cronies including Doc Lake, who is the county physician, joined by the local dog catcher and a merchant. U.S. is assigned by the judge the job of distributing his calling cards among workers curing tobacco and to do nothing that would interfere with his ability to play the banjo. Mallie Cramp's case is next. The Purpose of the film, therefore, is that the judge, who represents the spirit and definitely not the letter of the law, is running for re-election in a community fraught with moral intolerance.

There are also three major sub-plots in the Passion, but they differ from those in JUDGE PRIEST. The first is for General Fairchild to admit that Lucy Lee is his granddaughter and thus release the community from the moral tension his intense denial of this family relationship has imposed on it. Intimately connected with this major theme of the sub-plot is the minor theme of Ashby's courtship of Lucy Lee which, once General Fairchild acknowledges her as his granddaughter, culminates in their betrothal. The second major sub-plot is the return of Lucy Lee's mother. She comes back for one last look at her daughter before she dies. As a social outcast, she stays at Mrs. Cramp's brothel. Her final request is for a public funeral with a hearse, a funeral procession, and a service to be read over her. The judge leads the procession and reads the service. For his text he takes John 8:5–11 in which Jesus tells the accusers of a woman taken in sin: "He that is without sin among you, let him cast the first stone." In St. John's Gospel, Jesus also absolves the woman, telling her to "go, and sin no more." The judge makes no reference to this, but the idea is manifest since shortly after the service, Mrs. Cramp, who pays for the hearse and the burial, and the other prostitutes, all of whom are in the funeral procession and in church for the service, book passage on the riverboat. The third major sub-plot has to do with U.S. who is accused of raping a hill-country man's daughter. An unruly mob comes to town led by Buck Ramsey, played by Grant Withers, a nasty heavy who earlier in the film got into a fight with Ashby over Lucy Lee's good name. The judge prevents the mob from lynching U.S., for which he is exalted by the mob itself when the hill-country man's daughter regains consciousness and identifies Buck Ramsey as her assailant.

John Ford's brother, Francis Ford, is employed as comic relief in JUDGE PRIEST where he continually disrupts Maydew's orations by trying to hit with tobacco spittle a spittoon that is constantly being moved further out of reach. He is also on hand in THE SUN SHINES BRIGHT, this time as a mountain man who is such a crack shot that he can fell Buck Ramsey when the latter attempts a getaway in Lucy Lee's buggy, the bullet literally zigzagging as his spittle did in JUDGE PRIEST when it hit the spittoon even after it was placed behind a leg of the prosecutor's table. What is important here is the judge's observation: "Good shootin', comrade. Saves a trial." This comes from the same man who saved U.S. from execution without a trial. It is somehow supposed to be evident that the *truly* guilty can do without a trial.

In JUDGE PRIEST, Hattie McDaniel leads a black chorus singing "My Old Kentucky Home." This song is sung again by blacks in THE SUN SHINES BRIGHT, with the exception of only a word—from " 'tis summer, and the darkies are gay" to " 'tis summer, and the children are gay." Beyond this concession, the blacks still know their place in white society and keep it, although they can carry subservience too far as when Uncle Pleasant tries to kiss the judge's hand after he saves U.S. from the lynch mob. Young men and young women pair off at the town hall dance; but this is something reserved for youth. The older women in the community are believers in abstention and have formed an alliance while the older men believe in drinking and male companionship, each sex having become isolated from the other. Brief reference is made in JUDGE PRIEST to the fact that the judge belongs to a political machine. In THE SUN SHINES BRIGHT, the judge is frequently joined in tableau with his fellow political cronies. When he is re-elected, it means his cronies are also re-elected; just as, in life, when John Ford was hired to direct a film, his stock company went with him.

The Perception of the film comes with the narrow tally of votes: 1,700 to 1,701. The judge casts the deciding vote himself. A sign carried by the hill-country people in the parade with which the film concludes reads: "He Saved Us From Ourselves." He did it by a very, very slim margin. The values of American society, as Ford regarded them, masculine camaraderie and habitual drinking, young romantic love, the separation of the sexes in the later years, recognition that prostitutes, albeit victims of society, have hearts of gold, and the conviction that blacks will keep their place if they are left free of needless persecution: these values are threatened in this film and are saved *by just one vote*. It is a vote for Judge Priest who makes quite a point of not judging his fellow man, except in such a case as that of Buck Ramsey, and then he is saved the effort by a well-placed bullet. It is not certain any longer that everything will work out for the best; in fact, things may not work out at all unless,like the judge in defending U.S. from the lynch mob, or in leading the funeral procession, or in bringing Lucy Lee and her grandfather together, one is willing to take a stand and maintain it no matter what the opposition.

By the time Ford came to direct THE LAST HURRAH (Columbia, 1958), the aging politician and his cronies are *not* re-elected; the community is abandoned to the money-changers, city-slickers, and moral hypocrites. All three of these films conclude with a victory parade, symptomatic of Ford's romance with martial displays. In JUDGE PRIEST, recalling the parade in THE BIRTH OF A NATION where the "Little Colonel" leads the Confederate troops off to war, it is an occasion for the community to pull together. In THE SUN SHINES BRIGHT the victory parade passes the judge's house, the judge and Jeff on the front porch, the judge with tears in his eyes: military regimen and discipline, unquestioning faith in heroes and leaders, might yet save us, as it saved the judge's community, if only at the last minute. In THE LAST HURRAH it is not the protagonist's victory parade; he has been forgotten by his community and all that is left for him is to die. The protagonist, played by Spencer Tracy, moves through the frame in retrograde motion to the direction of the parade.

As many another, I once asked John Ford if he did not feel that as he grew older his pictures became darker in tone, a mood of reassuring confidence giving way slowly to anxious hope and finally to a sigh of futility. He made chewing motions with his mouth, as he often did when he was less than completely at ease, and then said, succinctly and positively, "No." The structures of his films, however, contradict this negative. And there is one thing more. John Ford was a chronic alcoholic.

Andrew Sinclair's biography, JOHN FORD (1979), is mostly an exercise in apologetics for Ford and so it was only to be expected that when the subject of drinking came up he wrote that Ford "hardly ever drank during the making of a movie. Liquor was banned on the set; but when the shooting was over, he would call for his bottles and his friends."[3] This overlooks incidents such as MISTER ROBERTS (Warner's, 1955) where the principal reason Ford and Henry Fonda did not get along and Ford was replaced by Mervyn LeRoy was that Ford was drinking more than a case of beer a day and was quite often drunk on the set. Dan Ford, Ford's grandson, was somewhat more candid about the matter in PAPPY: THE LIFE OF JOHN FORD (1979) and he described typical moments such as how Ford, when Ward Bond died, "spent almost twenty days in an alcoholic fog. He refused to eat or to see anyone, and he drank until his eyes grew cloudy and distant, until his cheeks looked shrunken and hollow."[4] Or how, after he finished filming 7 WOMEN (M-G-M, 1966), Ford "went on a binge that lasted for weeks. He drank as though he were trying to do more than blur the edges; he drank as though he were trying to find real oblivion."[5]

It would be foolish to ignore this, the alcoholism that was the reverse side of Ford's sentimentality.

II

In her book, MARK TWAIN & BRET HARTE (1964), Margaret Duckett wrote of Harte that "he once assured Ralph Waldo Emerson that the gambler and the prostitute had contributed more than churches to the cultural aspects of civilization in the West, a position he supported in fiction describing the bare wooden ugliness of some of the Protestant churches on the frontier."[6] Walter Blair in MARK TWAIN & HUCK FINN (1960) defined what he called the "Harte formula": there is "good in the heart of an outcast."[7] In an earlier chapter I traced the influence of the central idea in Harte's story "The Luck of Roaring Camp" through a number of films, Ford's MARKED MEN and THE THREE GODFATHERS among them. But a Harte story that well illustrates both the point that Harte made to Emerson and which utilizes what Professor Blair meant by the "Harte formula" is "The Outcasts of Poker Flat" (1868).

In "a spasm of virtuous reaction, quite as lawless and ungovernable as any of the acts that had provoked it,"[8] Poker Flat ejects a group of undesirables: gambler John Oakhurst, prostitutes known familiarly as "The Duchess" and "Mother Shipton," and a confirmed drunkard called "Uncle Billy." Escorted out of town and warned not to return, this quartet decides to ride across a steep mountain range to the town of Sandy Bar. Coming to a wooded amphitheatre, less than half way there, the group, primarily because of the Duchess, comes to a halt. Oakhurst remarks on "the folly of 'throwing up their hand before the game was played out,' "[9] but he, too, halts with them. Tom Simson, a young man known as "The Innocent" of Sandy Bar, and his fiancée, Piney Woods, happen to ride into their camp. The two are on their way to Poker Flat to be married. Uncle Billy, as Harte described him, is the prototype of the drunken buffoon Francis Ford almost invariably portrayed in his brother's films. "Suddenly," Harte told the reader about Uncle Billy, "an idea mingled with the alcoholic fumes that disturbed his brain. It was apparently of a jocular nature, for he felt impelled to slap his leg again and cram his fist into his mouth."[10]

They decide to make camp for the night, the three women sleeping in a wooden cabin, the men outside. During the night Uncle Billy steals away with their mounts, leaving them stranded. Fortunately a little over a week's provisions, which Simson had with him, have been stored in the cabin. Then a snow storm comes. " 'Luck,' " Oakhurst tells Simson, " 'is a mighty queer thing. All you know about it for certain is that it's bound to change. And it's finding out when it's going to change that makes you. We've had a streak of bad luck since we left Poker Flat—you come along, and slap you get into it, too. If you can hold your cards right along you're all right.' "[11]

The Purpose of this story is clearly to show the quixotic character of luck and the importance of not throwing up your hand too soon. The group is snowed in for a week. This is the Passion and during this time Mother Shipton starves herself to death, saving her rations for Piney Woods. Finally it is determined that Simson must make his way as best he can to Poker Flat to get help. Oakhurst sets in an extra supply of wood for the Duchess and Piney and, after kissing the Duchess tenderly, he says that he will accompany Tom as far as the canyon. The fire goes out that night; Oakhurst does not return. The Duchess in the cold puts her head upon Piney's shoulder. When the rescuers from Poker Flat arrive, they find the two dead, huddled and frozen together, so that "you could scarcely have told, from the equal peace that dwelt upon them, which was she that had sinned."[12] At the head of the gulch, "pulseless and cold, with a Derringer by his side and a bullet in his heart," they find Oakhurst, "still calm as in life, beneath the snow . . . he who was at once the strongest and yet the weakest of the outcasts of Poker Flat."[13] The Perception is not only that the "outcasts" are not at all what they may have seemed, but in Oakhurst's case he was the "strongest and yet the weakest" because he had run into a streak of bad luck and had thrown up his cards before the game was played out.

When Ford directed his film version of the story, H. Tipton Steck did the screenplay and the sources given were Harte's stories "The Outcasts of Poker Flat" and "The Luck of Roaring Camp." To this should have been added "A Protégée of Jack Hamlin's," since the Passion portion of the film was derived mostly from this source. There is a framing story. Harry Carey was cast in a dual role, as Square Shootin' Lanyon in the framing story and John Oakhurst.

As the film opens, Lanyon is the proprietor of a gambling house in Arizona. He is in love with Gloria Hope, cast as his ward, Ruth Watson, in the framing story, and as Sophy; but he believes she loves Cullen Landis, cast as his adopted son Billy in the framing story and Tommy Oakhurst. When Billy announces that he intends to leave town to seek gold, Lanyon asks Ruth if she is tired of town life and she responds that she likes it now because she is in love. Lanyon takes this to mean that she is in love with Billy, but from her expression the viewer knows it is Lanyon whom she loves. Lanyon decides that he will suppress his own love for Ruth so she can be happy with Billy. At this point he picks up Bret Harte's story "The Outcasts of Poker Flat" and imagines himself in the role of gambler John Oakhurst.

Cut to a scene of Cherokee Sal dying after giving birth to a son. There is a comic interlude as all of the rough miners pass the hat and select Oakhurst to be the boy's guardian. The action then jumps twenty years into the future. Oakhurst is gambling on a riverboat and on board is the roué Ned Stratton who dupes young women, promising them marriage if they will run away with him and then deserting them. Sophy, Stratton's latest conquest, in "A Protégée of Jack Hamlin's" succumbs to Stratton's wiles *before* he abandons her; not so in the film: Sophy refuses him and, angry, he deserts her. In a dramatic scene Oakhurst prevents Sophy from committing suicide. Too disgraced to return home, Sophy becomes Oakhurst's ward and he takes her to live at his gambling hall in Poker Flat where she joins the Duchess and another dance hall girl, both of whom are now under Oakhurst's chaste and generous care. Tommy, Oakhurst's adopted son, is grown into manhood and he deals faro for Oakhurst. He falls in love with Sophy. Oakhurst feels a pang at this turn of events because he himself has fallen in love with Sophy. Stratton shows up. He begins to berate Sophy and Tommy enters upon the scene. The two struggle and Stratton shoots Tommy. Oakhurst then overpowers Stratton and tells him he had best start praying that Tommy does not die. There is a tense scene, waiting on Tommy's fate, until the news comes that he will live. Oakhurst decides that his gambling hall is no place for a young woman and tells Sophy as much. She responds that she likes it because she has fallen in love. Oakhurst assumes that she is in love with Tommy. Watching the way she nurses the recovering Tommy, Oakhurst makes her promise that she will marry him once he recovers.

A few moments before Sophy's marriage to Tommy, she sends Oakhurst a note, informing Oakhurst that it is he whom she really loves. To preserve their happiness, Oakhurst convinces the head of the local vigilantes to burn down his gambling hall and drive him out of town. When Tommy and Sophy return from their honeymoon, they are shocked to find the gambling hall in smoking ruins. Tommy confronts the vigilante leader and forces the truth out of him. Then, determined to join his foster father, Tommy takes Sophy and they go in pursuit of Oakhurst. They overtake him only to be caught in a terrible snow storm without provisions. Oakhurst makes the ultimate sacrifice, dissembling that he intends to go for help while he actually goes outside and shoots himself.

Reading this story has an electric effect on Lanyon. He goes to Ruth and discusses her relationship with Billy. She reveals her love for him and they embrace. Lanyon observes, just before the fade, ''That fellow in the book was a durn fool.''

THE IRON HORSE was the second so-called ''epic'' Western of the silent era, THE COVERED WAGON (Paramount, 1923) directed by James Cruze having preceded it. Both films consist of the sheerest fantasy. Ford's subject in THE IRON HORSE is the construction of the first transcontinental railroad, but most of the film is devoted to Indian-hating and Indian-killing. The attitude of the Anglo-American Colonists toward Indians was embodied in the Declaration of Independence. In Thomas Jefferson's words: ''He [King George III] has excited domestic insurrections amongst us, and has endeavoured to bring on the inhabitants of our frontiers, the merciless Indian Savages, whose known rule of warfare, is an undistinguished destruction of all ages, sexes, and conditions.'' The Colonists did not believe that Native Americans were capable of independent action. ''Eternal children,'' Jefferson, who was considered something of an authority, wrote to John Adams on 20 April 1812, ''they were too immature themselves to launch a campaign of resistance; hence they had to have been manipulated or tampered with by crafty adults, most likely renegade whites or foreign agents.''[14] James Madison also expressed a similar concern. ''Next to the case of the black race within our bosom,'' he wrote in a letter to Thomas L. McKenney on 10 February 1826, ''that of the red on our borders is the problem most baffling to the policy of our country.''[15] Only to the extent that Ford's films, and his Westerns in particular, embody these attitudes would I agree with Peter Bogdanovich in his book, JOHN FORD (1978), that ''it would be instructive (in fact schools might do well making it a regular course) to run Ford's films about the United States in historical chronology—because he has told the American saga in human terms and made it come alive.''[16]

Ford dedicated THE IRON HORSE to Abraham Lincoln. Lincoln is a character in the first sequence and he can feel the inevitability of American history. Cut to those who also feel it and would defy it—the Indians. They are led by a white man, played by Fred Kohler. Kohler and the Indians sneak up on a man and his son at their campfire. The son hides. The father is captured. When the man recognizes Kohler as a white, Kohler splits his skull with an axe. In building the railroad, a title informs the viewer: ''There is no white labor. It is necessary to bring in Chinese people.'' George O'Brien, cast as the son of the murdered man who is now an adult, bosses the railroad crew. Other ''foreigners'' are hired to work with the Chinese. O'Brien says to his loyal Irish co-workers: ''With these foreign laborers making trouble, we Americans must stick together.'' A lone Indian is shown riding a horse, his arms folded, smoking a cigar, while his squaw stumbles alongside carrying several packs. When Kohler leads his Indians in an all-out attack on the railroad, the foreigners tend to be shirkers and have to be forced to fight. They definitely ought to be ashamed since the white women do not stint to join in the fight to kill Indians. A group of Pawnee scouts who are "good Indians" because they support the white man's notion of one-settlement culture leads the rescue as O'Brien strangles Kohler.

All the attitudes displayed in THE OUTCASTS OF POKER FLAT and THE IRON HORSE come together in Ford's first sound Western, STAGECOACH. As the film opens, Geronimo, "that old Apache butcher," as Doc Boone calls him, is again on the rampage. Boone, played by Thomas Mitchell, and Dallas, the town prostitute, played by Claire Trevor, are compelled to leave Tonto by the Ladies' Law and Order League. Lucy Mallory, played by Louise Platt, is a Southern woman, delicate, pregnant, on her way to meet her husband who is in the Cavalry. Hatfield, a gambler, played by John Carradine, joins these three, along with a whiskey drummer and the sheriff, on a stage driven by Andy Devine through hostile Indian country. Hatfield hopes to protect Miss Mallory, having served in her father's Confederate regiment. Jean-Louis Rieupeyrout in LA GRANDE AVENTURE DU WESTERN [THE GREAT ADVENTURE OF THE WESTERN] (1964) expressed his belief that John Ford in his Western films "created a world apart, which demands in order to be appreciated a profound sympathy with its personalities and their epoch, viewed through the inevitably distorting lens of legend, quite after the manner of a Bret Harte and all those storytellers of that noble line." [17]

STAGECOACH was based on a short story titled "Stage to Lordsburg" by Ernest Haycox and Haycox, in turn, may have been influenced by Guy de Maupassant's short story about a prostitute aboard a coach during the Franco-Prussian War, "Boule-de-suif" ["Pot of Fat"]. But Rieupeyrout was the first to my knowledge to see the parallel between the characters in Ford's film and Bret Harte's fiction. Haycox' name for his prostitute character was Henriette. "Thus," Rieupeyrout wrote, "Hatfield comes right out of Poker Flat and Roaring Camp where he was acquainted with Dallas (ex-The Duchess, ex-Henriette) and Boone (ex-Uncle Billy). It is not just the initial view of the situation in the film's exposition that owes something to Bret Harte: the doctor and Dallas are the 'outcasts' of Tonto and, if Hatfield is not so explicitly, he is very nearly." [18] At the outskirts of Tonto the local banker, played by Berton Churchill, who has absconded with a mine payroll gets on board and *en route* to Lordsburg the Ringo Kid joins the group. Ringo has just broken out of prison to revenge himself on the Plummer gang for having killed his brother and the sheriff intends to see Ringo back in jail rather than lose his life in a gunfight with the Plummers. Characteristic of the nonsense which some critics are able to project into Ford's Westerns, Joseph McBride and Michael Wilmington wrote in their book, JOHN FORD (1974): "The coach is America, a nation of exiles, riven with warring and contradictory factions; the Indians are the wild forces of Nature; the pregnant woman is Liberty; the banker is the corrupt Republican Establishment, the spokesman for selfish individualism; the benevolent sheriff is Roosevelt; the Plummer gang are the Axis powers; Buck, the driver, and his Mexican wife 'Hoolietta' are the ethnic mixtures which give the country its democratic character." [19] Did they mean *Julietta*? At any rate, she is never seen and Andy

Devine as Buck is on hand strictly for comic purposes. Personally, I do not see how reading this kind of socio-political fantasy into the characters makes STAGECOACH a better film.

The stage is beset by raging Indians and they give chase across the salt flats. When Ford was readying the script for production, he viewed a print of RIDERS OF THE DAWN (Monogram, 1937) directed by Robert N. Bradbury, a "B" Western starring Jack Randall in which there is a terrific race across the same salt flats—outside Victorville, California—and stunt man Yakima Canutt, doubling for Randall, did his famous stagecoach trick for the film, dropping down between the horses, hanging onto the tongue of the stage, letting go, with the coach pounding over him, and then grabbing onto a rope at the rear of the stage, pulling himself up, and regaining the top of the coach. Ford decided to use a variation of this stunt and contracted Canutt to perform it. When Ford was set to shoot the sequence, he told Canutt that he was an expert at how fast horses could run and that he wanted the camera car to move at forty-five miles an hour. Canutt insisted that the horses would not run that fast, thirty-seven miles per hour, absolute tops. Ford would hear nothing of it, but in the end Canutt proved himself right. Once the film was completed, the cast and crew assembled for the "wrap" party. Bert Glennon was the cinematographer. Ford overheard someone remark that it was an excellent Western. "Thanks to Yakima Canutt," Glennon responded. "It was the first time I worked for John Ford," Canutt told me subsequently, "and it was the last."[20] Yet, this notwithstanding, Andrew Sinclair in JOHN FORD claimed that "through his series of films . . . Ford regulars included the stunt man Yakima Canutt" and that "Canutt was one of Ford's beloved stunt men."[21]

In THE BATTLE AT ELDERBUSH GULCH (Biograph, 1914) directed by D.W. Griffith, when the whites are besieged in a blockhouse by Indians and the battle looks lost, the heroine, Lillian Gish, is shown and creeping downward into the frame is a cocked revolver, illustrating the sentiment that a woman is better off dead than a captive of the Indians. The same thing happens in STAGECOACH. As Lucy Mallory is praying, her face lit with an angelic light, Hatfield's gun comes into the frame. He is killed suddenly by an Indian, the gun dropping; while, tears running down her face, Lucy whispers, "Do you hear it?" It is a bugle announcing the arrival of the Cavalry which hacks its way through the Indians. All that is left is for Ringo to go to Lordsburg and with three bullets in his rifle shoot down the Plummers and then get into a buckboard with Dallas. Since they are both social outcasts, they obviously belong with each other, free, according to Doc Boone, from the blessings of civilization.

The Perception of the film is that the price one pays for the prospect of a happy life is violence. The Indians have to be killed and the Plummers have to be killed before such a prospect can be realized. Most of all, in the exciting chase sequence, killing Indians is shown to be exciting. I am not about to say that Ford was an ineffectual filmmaker. In my opinion STAGECOACH is his best Western film. But that opinion does not compel me to remain blind to the film's ideological content.

In the late 'Forties Ford began directing a remarkable series of Westerns which combined his love for Roman Catholic imagery, military pomp, heavy drinking, buffoonery, with an almost mystical treatment of Western fantasies, showing the West as John Ford would have wanted it to have been. Foremost among this group was what has since been called Ford's Cavalry trilogy, FORT APACHE, SHE WORE A YELLOW RIBBON, and RIO GRANDE. André Bazin, among the French critics, cited this trilogy as supposedly marking Ford's political rehabilitation of the Native American when, in fact, nothing could be further from the truth. Ford knew nothing about Native Americans and was basically contemptuous of them. Beginning with the filming of STAGECOACH, Ford chose, when he could, to locate his Westerns in Monument Valley, on the Navajo reservation, and he had whatever tribe the script called for—Apaches, Kiowas, Comanches, Cheyennes—played by Navajos. What the Cavalry trilogy did mark was the advent of Ford's collaboration with James Warner Bellah.

Bellah was born at New York City in 1899 and was graduated from Columbia University in 1923 with a Bachelor's degree. He was a second lieutenant during World War I in the 117th squadron of the Royal Air Force and, after the Armistice, he served with the rank of captain in General Haller's Expedition for the Relief of Poland. Bellah worked in advertising in New York City from 1923 to 1925 while simultaneously teaching English at Columbia. He served as special correspondent in China in 1927–1928 and in Europe in 1928 for AERO DIGEST; in 1929 he went as a correspondent for THE SATURDAY EVENING POST to the West Indies and Central America. During World War II, Bellah served in the 1st and 80th Infantry Divisions and as an American officer on the staff of Admiral Lord Louis Mountbatten at the headquarters of the Southeast Asia command. He saw combat service under General Stilwell, General Wingate, and Colonel Philip Cochran in Burma, emerging from the conflict with the rank of colonel and honored with the Legion of Merit, the Bronze Star, the Air Medal, and the Commendation Medal. Bellah's first novel was SKETCH BOOK OF A CADET FROM GASCONY (1923) and it indicated the preoccupation with military subjects which would inform most of his subsequent fiction. However, it was not until after World War II that he began writing his memorable stories set at Fort Starke during the Indian campaigns. Several of these stories, some of which Ford used as the basis of his Cavalry trilogy, were collected later in the anthology volume REVEILLE (1962).

Dan Ford in PAPPY: THE LIFE OF JOHN FORD recorded that "from the first time John read 'Massacre' "—the short story on which FORT APACHE was based—"he was drawn to it. Beyond its vigorous prose and its spirit of aristocratic militarism, it seemed to articulate all his wartime emotions, his fascination with the American military tradition, and the special nobility he felt was born of combat."[22] Notwithstanding, Dan Ford was also sufficiently circumspect to admit that Bellah's Fort Starke stories "are heavy on rape and racism, and their message about the Indians is clear: the only good one is a dead one." [23] The Indians in "Massacre" are given no tribal designation and they function only to dramatize a conflict between white men. Ford, however, in the screen adaptation made them Apaches under the leadership of Cochise. In his novel THE APACHE (1951) Bellah wrote thus about the Apaches: "It can be the phase of the moon that maddens Apaches, or a word from the memory of a medicine chief, or a strange flower by the trailside, or an omen of blood in a stone; because Apaches hate life and they are the enemies of all mankind, even unto each other. That is what Apache means: enemy." [24]

In "Massacre," Bellah based his character of Brevet Major General Thursday loosely on the Custer legend. When the Indians leave their reservation, Thursday meets with the chiefs and shows his contempt for them, telling them he thinks they are "recalcitrant swine" and "without honor or manhood." He leads his company into battle with them and, when his force is overwhelmed, he commits suicide by shooting himself. Bellah's point-of-view character in most of his Fort Starke stories is Lieutenant Flintridge Cohill. Cohill comes upon Thursday's body. "Glory," Bellah wrote, "is a jade of the streets who can be bought for a price by anyone who wants her. Thursday wanted her but his pockets were empty, so . . . Cohill took his . . . gun from Thursday's dead hand. He threw out the cylinder and jerked the five ball cartridges and the one empty case into his left hand. He spun the gun far out into Crazy Man Creek." Cohill conceals Thursday's suicide because, for him as for Bellah, "there are ways of living that are finer than the men who try to live them, and a regiment has honor that no man may usurp as his personal property." [25]

In FORT APACHE Thursday, demoted to a lieutenant colonel in the screenplay, comes from the East to take command of Fort Apache. Played by Henry Fonda, Thursday has with him his daughter, Philadelphia, played by Shirley Temple, who falls in love with a young lieutenant newly graduated from West Point, played by John Agar. The Irish composition of the Cavalry is emphasized with Ford repertory players such as Ward Bond as Sergeant O'Rourke, Victor McLaglen as Sergeant Mulcahy, and Dick Foran as Sergeant Quincannon. A group of new recruits is being trained amid rough-housing and drinking and a post dance. Cochise, played by Miguel Inclan, leads his Apaches off the reservation and John Wayne, cast as Captain Kirby York, rides out to convince Cochise to come back. Thursday will have no such pandering to the Indians. He meets with Cochise, demands that he come in because he signed a treaty that he and his people would stay on the reservation, and, if Cochise refuses to obey, he intends to force him into obedience. Thursday, however, knows nothing about fighting Indians and he and his command are wiped out, while York and a detail on the sidelines and under orders to remain there witness the "massacre." At the end of the film, in a powerful endorsement of Ford's belief in the glory of defeat, York tells newspaper reporters that Thursday's example was such as to "make them better men."

What most critics subsequently have tried to ignore when dealing with this film is that as far as Ford was concerned Thursday *was* a hero. "The end of FORT APACHE anticipates the newspaper editor's line in LIBERTY VAL-ANCE, 'When the legend becomes a fact, print the legend.' Do you agree with that?" Peter Bogdanovich asked Ford in the interview included in his book, JOHN FORD. Ford, in answering the question, revealed more than how very little *he* knew about American history. "Yes," he said, "—because I think it's good for the country. We've had a lot of people who were supposed to be great heroes, and you know damn well they weren't. But it's good for the country to have heroes to look up to. Like Custer—a great hero. Well, he wasn't. Not that he was a stupid man—but he did a stupid job that day. Or Pat Garrett, who's a great Western hero. He wasn't anything of the sort—supposed to have shot Billy the Kid—but actually one of his posse did. On the other hand, of course, the legend has always had some foundation."[26] In the film, Thursday does not commit suicide. His death, while clearly unnecessary and the result of stupid-ity, is still heroic; his memory is sanctified because of *how*, not why, he died.

In the short story, "The Devil at Crazy Man," Bellah articulated what I term the John Ford/James Warner Bellah racial nightmare. " 'They used to fight each other,' " Major Allshard remarks to the post doctor of the Indians. " 'But now it's a race war against the white man—ultimately to the death.' "[27] Although the copyright information for SHE WORE A YELLOW RIBBON credits a Bel-lah story titled "War Party," the film was actually based on a composition of elements from "The Devil at Crazy Man," "Big Hunt," and "Command." They, as all of Bellah's Fort Starke stories, appeared first in THE SATURDAY EVENING POST. "Command," indeed, was later translated by the State De-partment into Thai for the THIS IS AMERICA program just shortly before Bel-lah wrote the dialogue for Ford's U.S. Navy documentary, THIS IS KOREA (Republic, 1951). SHE WORE A YELLOW RIBBON opens to narration de-claring that the Kiowas (mispronounced "Keeowas") are supposedly uniting with the Comanches, the Apaches with the Cheyennes—in short, the John Ford/James Warner Bellah racial nightmare. They are forming an alliance against the white men. "One more defeat as Custer's," the narrator tells the viewer, "and it will be a hundred years before another wagon train dares cross the United States." It may be interesting to note in this context that the population of the United States was 38,500,000 in 1870 and that it rose to 50,100,000 in 1880. The Native American population during the same decade was less than two mil-lion and by the turn of the century this would be reduced to less than a half million. Ford had seen Howard Hawks' RED RIVER (United Artists, 1948) and he followed Hawks' lead in casting John Wayne as the aging Captain Brit-tles. Brittles in a reverent tone reads aloud the casualty list after the battle at the Little Big Horn.

In DRUMS ALONG THE MOHAWK (20th-Fox, 1939), Ford cast John Big Tree as his solitary Christianized Indian whose dialogue is confined for the most part to yelling "Hallelujah" in a coarse, guttural voice. He was cast again in SHE WORE A YELLOW RIBBON as Pony That Walks, a friend of Brittles, who wants peace and who, at their meeting, continually bellows "Hallelujah." FORT APACHE has a different version of a stagecoach race across the salt flats, much family sentiment, and several songs. In SHE WORE A YELLOW RIBBON, the songs are on the sound track, more emphasis is placed on the courtship romance of Joanne Dru by Flint Cohill, played by John Agar, and Ross Pennell, played by Harry Carey, Jr., both young lieutenants. Unlike either FORT APACHE or RIO GRANDE, the film was shot in color and several early scenes, especially the one where Captain Brittles sits at his deceased wife's grave, are aglow in the hues of late sunset. Victor McLaglen, cast here as Sergeant Quincannon, brawls his way through several minutes in the post bar where Francis Ford, in his Uncle Billy characterization, is the bartender. The Indian problem is solved deftly by running off all the Indians' horses and they are thus forced through the humiliation of having to walk back to the reservation. U.S. Grant, Sheridan, and Sherman all sign Brittles' order to become chief of scouts and Ben Johnson, cast as Sergeant Tyree, formerly of the Confederate Army, regrets only that there was not "a fourth ace," Robert E. Lee, as a signatory.

RIO GRANDE was based on Bellah's story, "Mission with No Record." Just as Sam Peckinpah rewrote FORT APACHE for his screenplay, THE GLORY GUYS (United Artists, 1965) directed by Arnold Laven, he used many of the plot ingredients from RIO GRANDE in his own MAJOR DUNDEE (Columbia, 1965); nor was he alone in such indebtedness. The Apaches in Ford's film raid a wagon train and kidnap a group of children, taking them across the border into Mexico. John Wayne, cast as Lieutenant Kirby Yorke, middle-aged and with an "e" added to his name since FORT APACHE, is ordered by J. Carrol Naish, ineptly cast and giving a poor performance as General Phil Sheridan, to try and get them back. Yorke's son, whom he has not seen for fifteen years, is a recruit, along with Ben Johnson as Trooper Tyree and Harry Carey, Jr., as Trooper Daniel "Sandy" Boone. Yorke's ex-wife, played by Maureen O'Hara, shows up and, upon first seeing her, Sergeant Quincannon, played by Victor McLaglen, makes the sign of the cross. O'Hara wants their son to quit the Cavalry. The young man refuses and Yorke lectures her about honor. Wayne and O'Hara are serenaded by the Regimental Singers, played by the Sons of the Pioneers, while they dine. This is only one of several songs: Phil Sheridan is serenaded, there is singing around the campfire. It all ends happily, of course. The mission is successful. The children are saved and the Apaches killed. Wayne and O'Hara find their love restored and are both equally proud of their son's prospects in the Cavalry.

It is a basic tenet in most of Ford's Westerns that there is a certain element of society, be it Indians, or the Plummer gang, or the Cleggs in WAGON-MASTER (RKO, 1950), that simply must be killed off before a truly stable community can be established. It is quite the same with the Clantons in MY

DARLING CLEMENTINE. THE SEARCHERS is, therefore, somewhat unique in that it shifts the stress from the community to the individual. The theme of Indian captivity, however, is played up more than it was in RIO GRANDE.

There was a trend in the 'Fifties to introduce anti-hero elements into formulary Western fiction, but this trend became even more evident in romantic historical reconstructions. It was usually accomplished as in Alan LeMay's THE SEARCHERS (1954) and Will Cook's COMANCHE CAPTIVES (1960)—to take as examples two novels filmed by John Ford—by splitting the traditional hero into two distinct characters. Alan LeMay split his hero into Amos Edwards, a dark figure, and Mart Pauley, a young man (but in the novel *not* a mixed-blood) adopted as a boy by the Edwards family; Will Cook split his hero into Jim Gary, a lieutenant in the Cavalry, and Guthrie McCabe, sheriff of Oldham County, Texas. The idea of splitting, of course, did not originate in the 'Fifties' as far as Indians were concerned and in the chapter devoted to images of Native Americans in Western films I trace it all the way back to James Fenimore Cooper. The real novelty in the 'Fifties was the splitting of the leading *white* characters.

In LeMay's novel Amos Edwards' two nieces are taken captive by the Comanches. One of them is raped and killed. The other, Debbie, is apparently still alive and for nearly six years Amos and Mart search for her. LeMay's Comanches are irredeemably savage whatever the talk about their sacred lands. Conversely, Amos and Mart become nearly superhuman during their ordeal. Amos is patently intent on killing Debbie because of the humiliation she has experienced by being made the wife of a Comanche war chief. In this he is frustrated and, providentially, he dies at the hands of a Comanche squaw. Mart finds Debbie and, together, they rediscover their once innocent love—or, the reader is led to believe they do.

Ernest Wallace and E. Adamson Hoebel in their book, THE COMANCHES: LORDS OF THE SOUTH PLAINS (1952), made the point that while "captive white children were generally initiated into the tribe by a series of terrifying experiences in which the Indians tried their courage by brutal treatment and threats of destruction," it was equally true that "some of the most hardened warriors are known to have wept because a captive of whom they had become fond returned to his own people."[28] Such a perspective tends to humanize the Comanches, but LeMay, and Ford after him, would have no part of it. "Most of the village had emptied," LeMay described the final battle when the Texas Rangers joined by a band of Tonkawas swoop down to massacre war chief Scar's village, "but at the far end a great number of Comanche people—squaws, children, and old folks mostly—ran like wind-driven leaves in a bobbing scatter. The Rangers were riding through to join the Tonkawas in the running fight that could be heard far up the Wild Dog; but they made it their business to stamp out the resistance as they went. The dreadful thing was that the fleeing people were armed, and fought as they ran, as dangerous as a torrent of rattlesnakes. Here and there lay the body of an old man, a squaw, or a half-grown boy, who had died rather than let an enemy pass unmolested; and sometimes there was a fallen Ranger.''[29] The reader is supposed to be reassured that only "sometimes" was there a fallen Ranger, amid all those bodies of "molesting" Comanche old men, squaws, and half-grown boys; and reassured also that the killing of old men, women, and half-grown boys, because they are "as dangerous as a torrent of rattlesnakes," is justified.

While the movie version of THE SEARCHERS is regarded as a cult film among many critics and even filmmakers who like its staginess and remarkable photography, in terms of its ideology it was Ford's most vicious anti-Indian film yet. His idea of comedy had Jeffrey Hunter, cast as Mart Pawley, kick a rotund squaw out of bed so she rolled down an incline. White captives of the Comanches are depicted as having become hopelessly insane as a result of their captivity. John Wayne was cast as Ethan Edwards, a name modification (as was Mart Pawley) from the spelling given in the novel which is indicative of the way in which the character was modified in order to remain consistent with John Wayne's screen persona. As in Wayne's portrayal of Tom Dunson in RED RIVER, Ford wanted the Ethan Edwards character to embody some anti-hero elements, but never to the extent that he would be in danger of completely losing the viewer's sympathy. Also, Ethan does not die at the end of the film.

"Ethan Edwards is perhaps Ford's most ambiguous character," J.A. Place wrote in THE WESTERN FILMS OF JOHN FORD (1974). "In him are all the qualities that make a Western hero—strength, individualism, self-sufficiency, leadership, authority."[30] When stated in this fashion, these are more or less admirable qualities. It is only when a viewer has become sensitive to the way in which the Comanches are misrepresented and exploited in this film that another series of words occur to describe Ethan: fanaticism not strength, monomania not individualism, alienation not self-sufficiency, obsessionalism not leadership, dogmatism not authority. Debbie, played by Natalie Wood, is rescued. It is Mart, not Ethan, who kills Scar. Joseph McBride and Michael Wilmington in JOHN FORD, apparently unaware of the fact that Ford turned the Mart Pawley character into a mixed-blood and what his reason was for doing so, wrote that "like Martin, she [Debbie] has accepted her dual heritage; resigned to her role as Scar's wife ('These are my people'), she nevertheless remembers her childhood ('I remember . . . from always') and is fluent in both English and Comanche. Miscegenation has not destroyed her identity, but deepened it."[31] To the contrary, because of miscegenation Mart had to be changed to a mixed-blood. Debbie has co-habited with an Indian; at the end she could only be linked with a man who is, if not morally, at least racially dubious.

Because of its similarity in plot, TWO RODE TOGETHER should be considered next, out of chronological sequence. In Will Cook's novel, COMANCHE CAPTIVES, Guthrie McCabe is hired by the U.S. Cavalry to bring back white captives from among the Comanches. He is accompanied on this mission by Jim Gary. All the white captives these two discover have been transformed into brutish animals as a result of their captivity and the one adolescent boy

McCabe does bring back commits a vicious murder and is hanged by the morally outraged whites. Jim Gary rescues Janice Tremain, the niece of a U.S. senator, who for five years has been the captive wife of Stone Calf. Gary kills Stone Calf, but he finds he must reject Janice because "he was a prudish man who wanted all women pure, until they were married at least."[32] This was not so much a consideration for Mart Pauley in Alan LeMay's novel as for men generally on the real American frontier where there were very few single women to be had, virgins or otherwise. McCabe for his part is saved from Amos Edwards' fate by being enslaved by the Comanches and only rescued by Jim Gary once he has learned the value of friendship and the virtue of community spirit.

The enslavement is not to be found in the film version. McCabe, played by James Stewart, describes Indian life-style as brutish and their speech as "grunts Comanche." Ford outdid the novel in showing white captives as having been reduced to groveling animals while many of the Comanches, including Woody Strode as Stone Calf, prefer simulated Mohawk hairpieces to traditional tribal hair styles. Apologists for Ford's racism declare that his films are more myths than actual historical renderings, in the manner of the character who both in the novel and the film comments, concerning his wife, "If I can give her comfort in a lie, God won't kick me out of heaven." What these apologists forget—and an observation which cannot be stressed enough in this book—is that Native Americans are *not* mythical and that the lies told about them in Ford's Western films could scarcely be expected to engender any greater social and cultural understanding. The Jim Gary character, played by Richard Widmark, is given from among the settlers a virginal heroine, played by Shirley Jones, whereas the Janice Tremain character was changed into a Mexican woman played by Linda Cristal. McCabe, not Gary, kills Cristal's Indian husband. When at a dance at the fort the white women are shocked because Cristal did not kill herself after she was taken captive rather than co-habit with an Indian, McCabe righteously defends her by saying: "She didn't kill herself because it was against her religion." McCabe, who has consorted with whores, is thenceforth paired with Cristal. Ford's formula was reinforced: moral outcasts belong together.

In a brief foreword to his fictionalization of SERGEANT RUTLEDGE, James Warner Bellah told how he and Willis Goldbeck had come up with the story idea and managed to interest Ford in filming a picture about a black soldier—in Bellah's words: " . . . the thought that no one yet had bothered in any way to present the story of the colored soldier and his contribution to the Western march of American empire."[33] Bellah also recorded how "toward the end of shooting when Mr. Ford was shaping his terminal dramatic scenes, one projectionist had tears in his eyes after running one of them in daily rushes . . . " and how one of the script clerks "turned around to me with goose pimples on her arms and her mouth stuck half open—after Mr. Ford shot another one."[34] And here is how Bellah described the Apaches who had escaped from the reservation: "Crossed in blood some, mad dog all—with the insensate goad of youth. Red-eyed with tiswin, tulupai from the night before—and justified to their ancient, senseless savagery by Old Man's talk. Of the ancient days. Of freedom in the mountains. Of Cochise and Mangas—and Geronimo now dead or taken."[35] The renegades rape a white girl. "All nine did it to her. On the beaten path. There before the house she had been born in. With her family dead about her. Then, because they couldn't stand her gibbering, they killed her as they would a broken animal, and rode off."[36] When Rutledge is first introduced, the reader is told that he would not couple "with Indian blood, because he'd come a long way from savagery himself and couldn't go back";[37] and when the black Buffalo soldiers object to the attitude of their white officer, their collective growl rises "like hot bile in their throats. It came free in jungle protest with fury bubbling in it."[38]

It is clear in the novel that Rutledge killed Major Dabney, something not clear in the film. Using a trial, as in JUDGE PRIEST, to dramatize innocence—Rutledge is charged with rape and murder of a white girl and murder of her father—Ford's film is only a reversal of a principal theme in THE BIRTH OF A NATION, still the only time in which a black is shown on screen actually attempting to rape a white woman. Ford borrowed Orson Welles' technique from CITIZEN KANE (RKO, 1941) where a character begins to narrate the past and is plunged into shadow as he or she is speaking; but the film is badly structured insofar as the witnesses at Rutledge's trial narrate episodes (or epidodes are shown) where they were not present and of which they could not know of their own experience. One of the ways in which audience sympathy is gained for Rutledge is by showing how, while he is under close military arrest, he helps kill Indians rather than attempt to escape. "It ain't the white man's war," Rutledge tells a dying black bugler. "We're fighting to make us proud." Woody Strode was cast as Rutledge. It did not matter, however, whether Strode was playing a black or an Indian as in TWO RODE TOGETHER. When on location for a John Ford picture, the outhouses were segregated without distinction: whites and non-whites.

SERGEANT RUTLEDGE is even more stage-bound than THE SEARCHERS; most of the exteriors were shot on indoor sets. Nor did this aspect lessen when Ford came to direct THE MAN WHO SHOT LIBERTY VALANCE. It became more prevalent. The short story on which the film was based was by Dorothy M. Johnson, but James Warner Bellah worked on the screenplay, in collaboration with Willis Goldbeck.[39] This is not too surprising in view of Ford's conviction, as he once expressed it to me, that no one knew more about the history of the West than James Warner Bellah. The names and characters were again changed in significant ways from the original story. James Stewart was cast as Ransom Stoddard, a U.S. senator at the beginning of the film who narrates the story in flashback, John Wayne as Tom Doniphon, the man who really shot Liberty Valance and let Stewart take the credit. Stewart and Wayne were older men when they made this film, and they looked their ages. Doubtless, though, they were actors with whom Ford felt comfortable. But Ford's apologists will not even permit this much of a concession. "Perhaps the oddest thing about the film is that most of the actors in Stoddard's recreation were older, by decades, than the characters they are playing," Joseph McBride and Michael Wilmington wrote in JOHN FORD. "Ford's detractors found this the limit of absurdity, as if the old man had slipped into dotage. But we are not seeing the characters as they were in the past. Nor are we seeing them altered by the memory of an old man (Stoddard or Ford). They are the people of the film's present projected back into the past, acting out its fateful moments but incapable of altering them."[40] I guess it is possible to rationalize anything.

Woody Strode was cast as Tom Doniphon's man, "my boy," as he is referred to in the script. Wayne wears a peaked Stetson, as did Harry Carey. Andy Devine, as in STAGECOACH, is given a large Mexican family. "Out here," Doniphon tells Stoddard, a dude lawyer from the East, "a man settles his own battles," and again the point is reinforced that harmony is only really possible by removing recalcitrant elements through death. As Luke Plummer in STAGE-COACH, Liberty Valance is dealt aces and eights in his last poker hand, only in his case, as played by Lee Marvin, he is pleased about it. At the end, after the remark about printing the legend, Vera Miles, as Mrs. Stoddard, remarks of the West: "It was once a wilderness. Now it's a garden."

Perhaps Richard Drinnon, while addressing the Westward movement as a whole in FACING WEST: THE METAPHYSICS OF INDIAN-HATING AND EM-PIRE-BUILDING (1980), summed up best the final vision of Ford's Westerns. "For Homer's Greeks and North American tribal peoples alike, the West was the land beyond, Spiritland, the land of mystery, of death and life eternal. It was not a Dark and Bloody Ground to be 'won.' But for Anglo-Americans it was exactly that, the latest conquest. Yet how could they conclusively 'win' it? If the West was at bottom a form of society, as [historian Frederick Jackson] Turner contended, then on our round earth, Winning the West amounted to no less than winning the world. It could be finally and decisively 'won' only by rationalizing (Americanizing, Westernizing, modernizing) the world, and that meant conquering the land beyond, banishing mystery, and negating or extir-pating other peoples, so the whole would be subject to the regimented reason of one-settlement culture with its professedly self-evident middle-class val-ues."[41]

I never asked Ford if he had read Mari Sandoz' CHEYENNE AUTUMN with its vision—"In the great expanse of earth and sky and all the things between there was nothing without a reason."[42]—so different from his, both in his early Westerns and in those which came later. He seemingly did become ambivalent and disillusioned about his fantasy West, which is to say that he could perhaps no longer believe in it himself. He confided to Peter Bogdanovich: "I've killed more Indians than Custer, Beecher, Chivington put together, and people in Europe always want to know about the Indians. There are two sides to every story, but I wanted to show their point of view for a change. Let's face it, we've treated them very badly—it's a blot on our shield; we've cheated and robbed, killed, murdered, massacred, and everything else, but they kill one white man and God, out come the troops.''[43] He told me that he included in CHEYENNE AUTUMN the episodes with James Stewart as Wyatt Earp and Arthur Kennedy as Doc Holliday as comic relief in what he honestly believed to be a tragic story.

Yet, his film is not a tragedy. Ford apparently felt compelled to have the Cheyennes prove immediately successful in their 1,500-mile trek to their homeland rather than tell the truth which was certainly to be had in Mari Sandoz' history. The biggest absurdity in the picture is to have Edward G. Robinson as Secretary of the Interior Schurz, after talking to Lincoln's portrait, decide to come out to the Black Hills, meet with the Cheyennes, and magnanimously give them their reservation on the spot. What he did in history—in U.S. CONGRESS 46th. 2nd session. Senate Report 708—was to say, ''the Indians should be taken back to their reservation,'' by which he meant they should be taken back to Indian Territory from whence they had fled.

Ford's weaknesses as a director of Western films were of two kinds. Ideologically he couched his racism behind a facade of apparent paternalism, something John Wayne began to imitate. Dramatically, his penchant for excessive sentimentality, low comedy, and stereotypical, brawling male characters tended to create films which now seem slow and at times rather dull. These defects are partially offset, however, by his masterful use of outdoor locations, pictorial splendor, and images of memorable composition and striking beauty. '' 'Pappy' was a painter with a camera—a rock of strength to his friends and acquaintances,'' John Wayne wrote to me shortly after Ford's death. ''Many will miss him; I most of all.''[44] Perhaps this points up the most rewarding aspect of many of Ford's Westerns, their portrayal of human friendship, certainly of itself one of the most important social factors in the Westward expansion.

4

Howard Hawks

In an interview with Joseph McBride and Gerald Peary in FILM COMMENT (May-June, 1974) Howard Hawks said, "I learned right in the beginning from Jack Ford, and I learned what not to do by watching Cecil DeMille."[45] When I took a crew to where Hawks lived in Palm Springs to videotape what proved to be my last conversation with him—he died shortly thereafter—he told me how Peter Bogdanovich had got it wrong in his article, "Taps for Mr. Ford," in NEW YORK MAGAZINE (October, 1973). Ford had not said, "Goodbye, Howard" once followed by a "I mean *really* goodbye"; he had said goodbye to Hawks seven or eight times.[46] There is no question that the men had a high regard for each other. But this is not to say that, however much they might borrow bits of business from each other, their films had many common or shared themes. Even if Ford had not said that he admired Hawks for the austerity and stoicism in his films, albeit certainly not in these words, referring instead to his own films as "corn," it could be deduced by comparing the films themselves. "Where Ford's long shot/close-up editing idealizes his characters," John Belton wrote in "Howard Hawks" in Volume Three of THE HOLLYWOOD PROFESSIONALS (1974), "the same sort of cutting in Hawks' films humanizes his."[47]

Hawks himself was not a sentimental man and probably for this reason his characters lack sentimentality. They face the world squarely and refuse to be controlled by external forces or influences. He would have agreed with Marcus Aurelius, in the book known as THE MEDITATIONS, that "the god within you should preside over a being who is virile and mature, a statesman, a Roman, and a ruler; one who has held his ground, as a soldier waiting for the signal to retire from life's battlefield and ready to welcome his relief; a man whose credit need neither be sworn to by himself nor avouched by others. Therein is the secret of cheerfulness, of depending on no help from without and needing

to crave from no man the boon of tranquillity. We have to stand upright ourselves, not be set up.''[48] Sometimes, as in the Tom Dunson character played
by John Wayne in RED RIVER (United Artists, 1948), this aggressive stoicism
can be taken too far; but sometimes, as in the John T. Chance character in RIO
BRAVO (Warner's, 1959), all the humors, as it were, are in balance and we
are intended openly to admire it.

In his Westerns, above all, Hawks charted the course of his stoic hero, from
a man who found fulfillment in male camaraderie and female companionship to
a man who was increasingly isolated and stood alone, detached but never in-
different. Jacques Rivette, writing about Hawks' film, MONKEY BUSINESS
(20th-Fox, 1952), in an essay titled "Genie de Howard Hawks" ["Genius of
Howard Hawks"] for CAHIERS DU CINÉMA (May, 1953), remarked on how
"one recognizes in this a classic conception of man; one cannot become great
save through experience and maturity; at the end of his journey, a man's old
age is his judge."[49] In his later years, Hawks mastered what only a very few
ever have: he learned to be cheerfully alone. Had he not lived by himself, the
accident which caused his death might not have proved fatal; but had he known,
and had he had to make a conscious choice, I wonder if he still would not have
preferred living alone.

"I decide to make a film whenever the subject interests me," Hawks told
Jacques Rivette and Francois Truffaut in an interview published in CAHIERS
DU CINÉMA (February, 1956). "It may be on auto racing or on aviation; it
may be a Western or a comedy; but the major drama for me is the one which
has as its subject a man in danger . . . . When I made RED RIVER, I thought
that it might be possible to make an adult Western, for and about mature people, and not one of those about mediocre cowboys. And at that time, everyone
was looking to make intelligent Westerns . . . . ''[50]

RED RIVER is regarded by critics as Hawks' first Western, although, technically, BARBARY COAST (United Artists, 1935) preceded it as did THE
OUTLAW (RKO, 1943). Both of these projects were less than successful, and,
while THE OUTLAW will be discussed in the chapter on Billy the Kid, Howard Hughes took over the picture from Hawks very early in the game and it
would perhaps be specious to impute Hawks with either credit or blame. BAR-
BARY COAST is another story. Set in San Francisco around 1850, the plot
concerns Miriam Hopkins, who arrives on a boat from the East, finds that her
betrothed is dead, and decides matter-of-factly that she will become a gold-dig-
ger. Edward G. Robinson runs the largest gambling establishment in town and,
upon meeting Hopkins, remarks, "I hope you like San Francisco. I own it."
In the motion picture shorthand of the day, they evidently sleep together, but
Hopkins is less than enthusiastic, regarding their association as purely a business arrangement, and Robinson becomes obsessed, first with Hopkins' fidel-
ity, and second with making her love him. Joel McCrea was cast as a prospector who likes poetry and, when he encounters Hopkins on the trail one day while
she is out riding, he gives her a volume of Shelley's poems which causes Rob-

inson to fly into a paroxysm of jealousy and suspicion. McCrea has divided women into those who are innocent and those who are tainted. He regards Hopkins as one of the former until he sees her in Robinson's casino. He proceeds to lose all his hard-earned gold to her at her roulette table.

Walter Brennan, cast for the first time in a Hawks film as a grizzled old-timer, assures McCrea that "things'll be simpler in the East." "Sure will . . . for poets and failures," McCrea responds. In the name of law and order, the vigilantes waylay Robinson's right-hand man, played by Brian Donlevy, and string him up. This may be democracy in action, but from the looks of the vigilantes democracy seems almost mob rule. Some critics have said that, based solely on the characters played by Hopkins, McCrea, and Robinson, one might not be certain how it will come out; but the formulary plot structure—a sensitive miner, a basically innocent, family-oriented heroine whatever her pretensions, and a greedy villain—makes the outcome inevitable.

I would underscore this point because in making RED RIVER Hawks was far more concerned with consistency of character than he was with plot conventions. Indeed, he turned around Borden Chase's ending of BLAZING GUNS ON THE CHISHOLM TRAIL (1948), the novel on which the film was based. Chase had the Dunson character die at the end. For Hawks, such an ending was unacceptable. Matt, played by Montgomery Clift, originally at fourteen years of age threw in his lot with Dunson and has too much regard for him to kill him, just as Dunson, in his own way, has too much regard for Matt to carry through his threat to kill him. The way Chase drew Dunson, he was the stereotype of the tyrannical big rancher who must die in order to give the next generation, in Chase's words, "the promise of a new day."[51] Donald C. Willis probably put it best in his book, THE FILMS OF HOWARD HAWKS (1975), when he wrote that "the extent of Matt's feeling and respect for Dunson is measured by the difference between the tentative acts of defiance he does commit and the absolute acts he could and probably should commit. His action here is little more than the equivalent of Groot's [Walter Brennan] 'You was wrong, Mr. Dunson.' Matt and Groot disagree with Dunson but, unlike him, aren't so sure of themselves that they want to interpose their own will."[52]

John Ford contended that STAGECOACH (United Artists, 1939) made John Wayne a star, but RED RIVER proved him to be an actor. "I didn't know that big sonofabitch could act," was how Ford put it. He himself began casting Wayne as an older man and Wayne, as he grew older, found that the public preferred him this way. "He read the script for RED RIVER," Hawks once told me, "and said, 'I don't know whether I want to play an old man.' I said, 'you're going to be an old man pretty soon, and you ought to get used to it. And you also better start playing characters instead of that junk you've been playing.' So he said, 'How do I show that I'm old?' and I said, 'Did you ever see me get up? Just do it that way.' So he did it and he saw the film and he said, 'Lord, I'm old.' He didn't have to do a lot of damn silly things to get that impression across."[53]

In the same conversation, Hawks recalled how when he was casting BAR-
BARY COAST, "they brought in Walter Brennan. I looked at him and laughed.
I said, 'Mr. Brennan, did they give you some lines?' And he said, 'Yeah.' I
said, 'Do you know them?' And he said, 'With or without?' I said, 'With or
without what?' He said, 'Teeth.' I laughed again and said, 'Without.' He turned
around and read the lines. I said, 'You're hired.' When we were going to do
RED RIVER, there was a line in the scenario; it said, 'The cook's name was
Groot.' He said, 'What are we going to do?' I wasn't worried. I said, 'Remember how we met, that "with or without teeth?" Well, I got an idea that you're
going to lose your teeth in a poker game with an Indian. And every night he
makes you give them back.' 'Oh,' he said, 'we can't do that.' I said, 'Yes, we
can.' "[54]

The Indian who won Brennan's teeth was Chief Yowlachie, a Yakima who
had appeared in the first two-color Western, WANDERER OF THE WASTE-
LAND (Paramount, 1924) directed by Irvin Willat. It was based on the Zane
Grey novel by the same title. Hawks worked at Paramount in those days and
he urged them strongly to film at least two or three Grey stories a year. His
interest in Westerns was apparent already this early in his career. Noah Beery,
Sr., was the chief heavy in WANDERER OF THE WASTELAND. For RED
RIVER, Hawks cast Beery's son, Noah, Jr., Harry Carey, and Carey's son,
thereby making the film, among other things, a generational tribute to decades
of Western filmmaking.

For Montgomery Clift it was the first of a five-picture contract he had signed
with Hawks. He was enthusiastic about his part and waited with anticipation
for what he felt would be his big scene, when he takes the herd away from
Wayne and leaves Wayne behind, wounded, on the trail. After the scene was
shot, Clift went to Hawks and complained that it had not turned out to be so
big, after all. Wayne never even looked at him. While Clift spoke his lines,
Wayne continued to stare over the saddle of his horse into the distance, with
his back more or less to Clift. Finally, Wayne said simply, "I'm gonna kill
you." Hawks laughed and chided Clift for thinking he could best Wayne in any
scene.

It was Wayne's opinion that Borden Chase had rewritten MUTINY ON THE
BOUNTY (1932) as a Western with the Tom Dunson character a surrogate for
Captain Bligh. "When Hawks bought the story," Wayne told me, "I felt I
could play an old man. He wanted to have Cooper. What he was aiming at was
Cooper and Cary Grant to play Cherry. That was what he wanted. Now, his
idea of the old man was that he was becoming senile and he was afraid. In the
last scene, there was a great chance for me to play a coward. This was how he
conceived of it. He had Walter Brennan in and I sat there and listened to them.
Hawks is a very easy man to talk to, but Brennan evidently had been giving
him the thing, 'I'll teach this guy to play an old man,' because Brennan was
playing that part when I first met him and he was about thirty years old. He
really always was an old codger. He said, 'I'll fix it, Mr. Hawks. We'll get

some springs and his legs will do this.' I listened. 'Oh, Christ,' I thought, 'what have I got myself into?' Hawks said, 'Yep, that's good, sounds very good.' He sent for a prop man. I didn't want to say anything with everybody together. I waited until the following morning and then I went to see Howard. 'Mr. Hawks,' I said, 'you been down to Texas lately?' 'Yes, Duke,' he said, 'I've been down there a little.' I said, 'Have you ever noticed how the older these strong men are, the top ranchers, how much straighter they get and how much more personality and power they have as they reach maturity?' He said, 'I get it, Duke.' I never had any more trouble. There was another scene. Two fellas stand up to me. Howard said, 'This is Academy Award stuff, Duke. Show you're afraid.' I told Howard that it might be Academy Award stuff to show that I was afraid, but I wasn't gonna be no goddamn coward. I'd been strong all through the picture. The kid, Clift, loved me because I was a man he *could* love. But, sure, I told Howard I could be afraid, but not a coward. That's the way we played it.''[55]

Some time later when I repeated this conversation to Hawks, he told me that that was how he got "that big sonofabitch" to act, that he performed better when he was angry or stubborn and determined—which, after all, was the essence of the Dunson character.

"Dunson travels a rough course in which human obstacles, removed by him with a rare violence, count for more than physical obstacles," Jean-Louis Rieupeyrout wrote in LA GRANDE AVENTURE DU WESTERN. "From murder to brawling, he arouses a singular antipathy, as opposed to the traditional characterization of the hero one is fond of following in this film genre, and yet appearances are misleading. Dunson winds up convincing and pleasing us because even his rudeness is brought about through his intent to force a superhuman task to its rightful conclusion."[56] Hawks changed the Dunson character because he regarded his determination as a virtue taken to an almost insane extreme and the structure of the film was also changed so that Dunson could retain his integrity and the viewer's esteem for his determination, if not for his methods. This reduces to absurdity Borden Chase's complaint in FILM COMMENT (Winter, 1970–1971) that the ending to Hawks' film is inconsistent with everything leading up to it. The structural change in the ending was made necessary because of the way the Dunson character itself was conceived.

The cattle drive in RED RIVER *is* brought to its rightful conclusion even though it is in Kansas and not, as Dunson intended, in Missouri. Surely one of the reasons Dunson would not kill Matt, even had he been able to bring himself to try it, is because Matt was successful: he achieved what he set out to do. This is a value for the Dunson character which supersedes all other values and it was this same value which, at the very beginning of the picture, prompted Dunson to leave the wagon train he was with and the woman he loved. Dunson could scarcely be anything but pleased to see the same value holding true for Matt.

In John Ford's films about superhuman tasks, all the way from THE IRON

HORSE (Fox, 1924) to CHEYENNE AUTUMN (Warner's, 1964), although they might be successful in their terminations, the feeling at the end is one of ambivalence, concern over whether it was worth it; certainly there is an acute awareness of what it has cost and what was lost irretrievably. Ford's answer to T.S. Eliot's question in "The Love Song of J. Alfred Prufrock," "And would it have been worth it, after all , . . . "[57] was less optimistic and assuring than was Hawks'. A.B. Guthrie, Jr., termed stories of this kind "an adventure of the spirit" and the difference between Hawks' view of such adventures and Ford's is made still more clear in THE BIG SKY (RKO, 1952). In THE BIG SKY, the way Guthrie wrote and structured it, Jourdonnais' daring trek up the Missouri ends with him and most of his men being killed by the Blackfeet. The novel is divided into five parts, spanning the years 1830–1843, but Hawks confined the screenplay to only Part Two, that concerned with Jourdonnais. It was, Hawks told me, the most dramatic moment in the novel and, therefore, of still more significance is the fact that in Hawks' film Jourdonnais, undergoing even more hardships than in the novel, is successful and the journey is brought to what, for Hawks, was its rightful conclusion. His sympathies were more Roman than Greek; he preferred comedies—satisfying terminations—to tragedies culminating in frustration or resignation. However much Hawks' stories and characters might demonstrate a stoical attitude, he was not a Stoic.

The narration at the beginning of the film version tells of the first white men to venture through 2,000 miles of hostile Indians to open up the Great Northwest, or what historians now call the Old Northwest. When Kirk Douglas, cast as Jim Deakins, and Dewey Martin, cast as Boone Caudill, join in the singing and dancing in a saloon, their emotional buoyancy is far more integrated into the film story than are similar moments in a Ford film. As with Tom Dunson, the Boone Caudill character in the film is altered from its literary prototype. "I wanted to show the mountain man . . . for what he was," A.B. Guthrie, Jr., wrote of Boone in his essay "The Historical Novel" which appeared in MONTANA: THE MAGAZINE OF WESTERN HISTORY (Fall, 1954), "or what he seemed honestly to me to have been—not the romantic character, the virtuous if unlettered Leatherstocking, but the engaging, uncouth, admirable, odious, thoughtless, resourceful, loyal, sinful, smart, stupid, courageous character that he was and had to be."[58] Such a character was of no interest to Hawks. Boone Caudill, for Hawks, was a man much as the Matthew Garth character played by Montgomery Clift in RED RIVER: his initiation into manhood comes about as a result of his participation in a superhuman task.

As in RED RIVER, the men are given a choice by Jourdonnais, played by Steven Geray, of either quitting or sticking it through to the end. Desertion is not so much of an issue as is the necessity of the men to control their lustful impulses toward the Indian maiden being taken on the journey, Teal Eye, played by Elizabeth Threatt, the daughter of the Blackfoot chief, who, Jourdonnais hopes, will make the Indians friendly and willing to trade. Arthur Hunnicutt was cast as Uncle Zeb—an uncle of Boone's—and in a moving soliloquy he characterizes the white man's sickness as "grab," first grabbing everything they can grab, and then grabbing from each other. "Poor Devil," a demented Blackfoot from a different part of the novel, was interpolated; in the film, as played by Hank Worden, he becomes integrated and vital to the group. Hawks included a scene where the Indians follow along the shore before they attack the men on the boat which Ford varied for a similar sequence in THE SEARCHERS (Warner's, 1956) and which Budd Boetticher copied in RIDE LONESOME (Columbia, 1959).

"The undercurrent of homosexuality in Hawks' films is never crystallized," Peter Wollen wrote in SIGNS AND MEANING IN THE CINEMA, "though in THE BIG SKY, for example, it runs very close to the surface. And he himself described A GIRL IN EVERY PORT [Fox, 1928] as 'really a love story between two men.' For Hawks men are equals, within the group at least, whereas there is a clear identification between women and the animal world . . . . Man must strive to maintain his mastery. It is also worth noting that, in Hawks' adventure dramas and even in many of his comedies, there is no married life. Often the heroes were married or at least intimately committed to a woman at some time in the distant past but have suffered an unspecified trauma, with the result that they have been suspicious of women ever since. Their attitude is 'Once bitten, twice shy.' This is in contrast to the films of Ford, which almost always include domestic scenes."[59] Wollen also extended his comparison to include Budd Boetticher's Westerns where, he felt, there was "no obvious place for women at all; they are phantoms, who provoke action, are pretexts for male modes of conduct, but have no authentic significance in themselves."[60]

I think Wollen has more of a case with regard to what he wrote about Boetticher, a point which merits discussion in the chapter devoted to him; but when it comes to Hawks, I believe he exaggerated. While Wollen was unquestionably correct that Ford conceived a woman's role in the West as primarily domestic, Hawks' view was not so much homosexual as asexual. "He was not a demonstrative, relaxed sort of man," Lauren Bacall, who became the embodiment of a "a Hawksian woman," wrote about him in her autobiography, BY MYSELF (Knopf, 1978). "He was inscrutable, speaking quietly in a fairly monotonous voice. He seemed very sure of himself."[61] Observing Hawks' relationship with his wife Slim, Bacall was puzzled. "I could never really connect with Slim and Howard's relationship. They seemed temperamentally different—Howard was clearly crazy about her, but, undemonstrative as he was, I never felt a sense of fun or sex between them."[62]

Leigh Brackett, who worked on and off as a screenwriter for Hawks, notably among his films on his subsequent Westerns, RIO BRAVO, EL DORADO (Paramount, 1967), and RIO LOBO (National General, 1970), and who, Hawks was fond of saying, he thought "wrote like a man" perhaps came closest to the mark. "He doesn't like losers, or antiheroes," she reported in "Working with Hawks" in TAKE ONE (October, 1972). "He values bravery, strength, expertise, loyalty, all the 'masculine' virtues (though Lord knows I've known women who had a damned sight more of them than some of the men I've known; it isn't sex, it's the individual). So why should he give his women a position of equality—often, indeed, dominance—in a genre that usually relegates them either to being decorative in the hero's relaxed moments, or to looking doleful as the hero goes off about his business? I suspect that it's because Hawks doesn't like women in their *negative* aspect, and until he can accept a female character, as the hero must, as another man, or an asexual *human being* with the attributes he respects, he can't like her. And if he didn't like her, he wouldn't know what to do with her. Hawks has to like all his people (the villains are kept down to a minimum) and this is why such a great deal of affectionate good humor comes through in films like RIO BRAVO and HATARI! [Paramount, 1962]."[63]

Hawks was displeased with Joanne Dru's performance in RED RIVER, but there was not much he was able to do about it, Margaret Sheridan, the actress he had cast initially, discovering she was pregnant two days before location shooting was to begin. Elizabeth Threatt, as an actress, was not much better portraying a Hawksian heroine. Physically, and in terms of her costume in the final scenes, she was clearly a Pocahontas stereotype. But the structure of the film, as well as the way her character was drawn, required that she be universally respected among the members of her tribe, not only because of her status as a chief's daughter, but even more because of her fortitude, her moral strength, and her downright ability to know her own mind and proceed accordingly. Such characteristics may be regarded as "masculine" in a certain cultural setting, but for Hawks they were virtues, and they had nothing to do with a person's gender.

II

It would be of value to contrast Hawks' approach to making Western films with that of Sam Peckinpah. "The Western," according to Peckinpah, "is a universal frame within which it is possible to comment on today."[64] For Hawks it was otherwise. "To me," I recall him saying, "a Western is gunplay and horses. It's about adventurous life and sudden death. It's the most dramatic thing you can do."[65]

HIGH NOON (United Artists, 1952) directed by Fred Zinnemann, released almost a decade before Peckinpah directed his first theatrical Western, might nonetheless be said to embody Peckinpah's viewpoint. Neither Hawks nor John Wayne particularly liked the film; they felt it lied about what they conceived of as the frontier spirit. Hawks felt that Gary Cooper's role in HIGH NOON showed him to be less than a professional, indeed very nearly a loser. He recalled what he had wanted Tom Dunson to represent in RED RIVER and in scripting RIO BRAVO he wanted a story about a sheriff threatened by a lawless element who is not afraid, who does not ask anyone for help, but who gets it anyway because of the kind of man he is and because he has the kind of character that inspires loyalty in others. The others are Dean Martin, cast as a man who was driven to drink by a relationship with a woman but who struggles to regain his self-esteem; Walter Brennan in his customary role as a feisty oldtimer; and instead of the younger man, played by Lloyd Bridges in HIGH NOON, who tries to move in on the sheriff's old girl friend, Ricky Nelson was cast as a youngster who has to prove himself in order to be accepted by men whom he admires. Ward Bond was cast as a character whose offer of assistance is rejected because he is too old and has other people who depend on him. Unlike the cowardly townspeople in HIGH NOON, Bond takes a hand anyway, and is killed. This incident is similar to the situation confronting the character played by Thomas Mitchell in ONLY ANGELS HAVE WINGS (Columbia, 1939) and I tend to agree with Donald C. Willis' conclusion in THE FILMS OF HOWARD HAWKS that "RIO BRAVO is almost the same movie as ONLY ANGELS HAVE WINGS, only longer, more loosely structured, and imperfectly cast." [66] Angie Dickinson played Feathers, the best portrayal in a Hawks Western of a Hawksian heroine; she and Wayne express their affection for each other mostly through aggressive banter.

Peter Bogdanovich in an interview with Hawks in THE CINEMA OF HOWARD HAWKS (1962) quoted him as saying: "In RIO BRAVO Dean Martin had a bit in which he was required to roll a cigarette. His fingers weren't equal to it and Wayne kept passing him cigarettes. All of a sudden you realize that they are awfully good friends or he wouldn't be doing it. That grew out of Martin's asking me one day, 'Well, if my fingers are shaky, how can I roll this thing?' So Wayne said, 'Here, I'll hand you one,' and suddenly we had something going . . . . " [67] How we know that the two are friends is that Wayne will not roll a cigarette himself for Dean Martin; he will only keep giving him the makings. It aptly symbolizes Hawks' personal code and, in fact, the point of the whole film.

Robin Wood in his book, HOWARD HAWKS (1968), spent most of his time speculating on Hawks' characters in his films as if they were real people, a technique he presumably adapted from the way academics like to analyze literary fiction. His findings have as much and as little validity as subjective projections ever have, but, curiously, when he approached the issue of Hawks' use of racial stereotypes—the French-Canadians (and I might add Poor Devil and Teal Eye) in THE BIG SKY or the Mexican played by Pedro González-González in RIO BRAVO—he was on even shakier ground. "One can say that the very existence of such stock figures is itself insulting, and this is fair enough; one can, I suppose, go on from that to complain that Hawks is unthinkingly helping to perpetuate the insult; but that is rather different from finding actual racial malice in his attitude. He is simply—and very characteristically—making use of the conventions (and the actors) that are at hand, and not questioning their initial validity. He takes the stock figure of the comic, cowardly, gesticulating, garrulous Mexican and, by eliminating the cowardliness while playing up the excitability, builds up a character whose dauntlessness and determination win our sympathy and respect even as we laugh at him." [68] To me, at best this is being mincing, at worst, an exercise in apologetics. The truth of the matter is that Hawks, as Ford, was a racial elitist and a viewer just has to accept this attitude in his films; and, albeit disapproving of its presence, move on to other considerations—but not so swiftly that one forgets that in the world of Hawks' films self-evidently the white man belongs to a master race and that, in quieting our objections, we are expressing our willingness to endorse tacitly this racial bias in order to participate in other, more pleasant aspects of Hawksian fantasy.

In an essay titled "El Dorado" contained in FOCUS ON HOWARD HAWKS (1972), Peter Bogdanovich claimed that "Hawks' vision of the world is tragic: his men are gallant, brave, reckless, but it is the facade for a fatalistic approach to a world in which they hold a most tenuous position." [69] This may apply to "marked men" in Hawks' films, but for his heroes it is utter nonsense. One is never in doubt during RIO BRAVO that the sheriff will come out of it alive; nor do doubts arise concerning the fate of the characters played by John Wayne in either EL DORADO or RIO LOBO. Hawks' alteration of the conclusion Borden Chase intended for RED RIVER was indicative of his basic attitude toward his heroes. In EL DORADO a gunfighter played by Christopher George is on the side of big rancher Bart Jason, played by Edward Asner, and calls it "professional courtesy" when he prohibits his men from shooting Wayne in the back. At the end of the film Wayne finishes off the George character with a rifle. "You didn't give me a chance," the character complains before he dies. "You're too good to give a chance to," Wayne tells him. What in this is tragic?

In Hawks' Westerns, the aging characters played by John Wayne take on an increasing significance as, for him too, "a man's old age is his judge"—to echo Jacques Rivette's words—and in the process the judgment of old age is brought to bear on the values of the Hawksian hero. "As Wayne declines in years and physically deteriorates," Gregg Ford wrote in "Mostly on RIO LOBO" for FILM HERITAGE (Fall, 1971), "director Hawks, in compensatory fashion, insistently endows him with greater apparent dignity and self-respect." [70] In the same essay Gregg Ford also recognized that while RIO BRAVO, EL DORADO, and RIO LOBO are thematically very closely related, structurally they represent a graduated return to the journey and search theme of Hawks' earlier Westerns. The focus in RIO BRAVO is on the jailhouse and the surrounding urban world is one of great danger, typical of the paranoia of the "town Western" variety of the Ranch Story/Town Western plot setting. EL DORADO is partially a "town Western" and is partly set outside of town. In RIO LOBO, the story embodies a revenge theme and is structured in the form of a quest. In Hawks' journey films, according to Gregg Ford, male adventurers are denied "the prefab shielding of any inviolate womb-like redoubt" and they are sent out "wandering, desultorily, exposed to the transcience and chaos and unknown of a genuine ordinary social milieu. In RIO LOBO, Hawks toys with topography to evolve a fleetingness, an elusiveness, an impermanence . . . . ." [71]

In EL DORADO Robert Mitchum, cast as the drunken sheriff whom Wayne decides to help out, serves as a good balance to Wayne's powerful screen presence. There is no such balance in RIO LOBO, mostly because it was a low-budget production and there was little money left over in the budget after paying Wayne's salary. Jennifer O'Neill proved she had a titillating body in SUMMER OF '42 (Warner's, 1971), but Hawks found her neurotic personality and awkwardness when asked to act before the camera insurmountable difficulties. The company was on location at the Old Tucson town set in Arizona when Wayne departed for Hollywood to receive his Academy Award for TRUE GRIT (Paramount, 1969). Upon his return to the set, Hawks and everyone else, and even Wayne's horse, wore a patch over one eye.

Andrew Sarris had commented that John Wayne was the preeminent incarnation of the Western hero and that not until he had been given his due as a player would the full stature of both Ford's and Hawks' Western films be appreciated. It was therefore all the more ironic that the one award Wayne received from the Academy should have been for a Western directed by Henry Hathaway.

5

Henry Hathaway

The same French critics who have usually had so many praises to sing in behalf of John Ford and Howard Hawks have been uncommonly reserved when it comes to Henry Hathaway. "Inevitably," Jean-Louis Rieupeyrout wrote in LA GRANDE AVENTURE DU WESTERN concerning HOW THE WEST WAS WON (M-G-M, 1963), "the juxtaposition of three styles as personal as those of Henry Hathaway—paradoxically the best here—of George Marshall and John Ford serves to bring about a distinct disequilibrium further amplified by the necessity where each one of them was in the position of creating a shared language for a three-headed camera to the destruction of the field of vision." [72] The essential words are "paradoxically the best here." Why should the high quality of Hathaway's work be paradoxical?

HOW THE WEST WAS WON is not a good film. Ideologically, it begins with the voice of Spencer Tracy on the sound track assuring the viewer that little more than a hundred years ago the Far West was a wilderness that had to be "won from Nature and primitive man." The whole motive behind this great effort toward winning is that "Americans have a way of acting out their dreams." The dialogue is filled with sparkling interchanges such as that between a mountain man, played by James Stewart, and a pioneer woman, played by Carroll Baker:

Baker: Are them Injun girls pretty?
Stewart: Well, ma'am, I guess that depends on how long it's been since you seen one.

This scene occurs in the opening section, "The Rivers," directed by Henry Hathaway. Carroll Baker's family is preyed upon by river pirates, headed up by Walter Brennan, and, although Stewart comes to their rescue, Baker's father, played by Karl Malden, is killed in the fracas. Beyond the distortion of history, the racism, and the supportive dialogue, there is also the matter of personal styles to which Rieupeyrout was referring. The styles are indeed quite different and, whatever individual havoc they produce when joined together sequentially, the transition from Hathaway's strong, self-possessed, realistic characters to John Ford's stylized treatment of some of the same characters in "The Civil War" section is an abrupt one, as abrupt in fact as a transition from crisp characterization to sentimentality can ever be. Suddenly, there are all the Ford trademarks: the love of the military, the admiration for Phil Sheridan and George Tecumseh Sherman, the necessity for commitment to a cause, even a cemetery shot of the stone marking the Stewart character's cenotaph (his body was lost in action).

Although we all like to think that some opinions are better informed than others, usually our own, for me there is no paradox at all in Hathaway's screen work being "the best here." His superior ability at treating Western themes in this case becomes obvious because he and Ford were working with some of the same characters and on the same picture; and for this same reason it may be more evident than when contrasting Hathaway's best Westerns with Ford's. I use the words "superior ability" because Hathaway, as Hawks, shared in the abstract many of Ford's values, but unlike him he did not sentimentalize their presentation.

Recalling his years of apprenticeship in an interview with Rui Nogueira for FOCUS ON FILM (Summer, 1971), Hathaway spoke of how he worked as Victor Fleming's assistant director on Fleming's version of THE VIRGINIAN (Paramount, 1929) and on "all those early Westerns—all of the Zane Greys, the ones I did over again. I mostly learned from them how to handle people. I would take a script home and think, Now what would I tell these people to do to make the scene, how would I start it, where would be the climax, how would I get out of it, how do I get rid of people, where would I play it—in front of the fire or on the couch, what would I do? And I'd make up my mind and I'd make a lot of notes and then I'd see what they did. Entirely different! But you learn." [73]

In LE WESTERN, quoting from the interview with Henry Hathaway which appeared in POSITIF (March, 1972), Jean-Louis Leutrat wrote about the early sound Zane Grey series with which Hathaway began his directing career that "Henry Hathaway informs us that 'there was a contract with Zane Grey stipulating that in order to retain the rights these films must be remade every seven years.' But, the director added, 'They were not absolute remakes: they had little differences. The heroes were less "heroic."' . . . New screenplays were written.' Precisely. It is not possible to remake a film 'absolutely,' unless we have two totally identical works: there are always, at the very least, variations. But 'little differences' can become 'big differences,' a modification so-to-speak." [74]

Frank Gruber in ZANE GREY: A BIOGRAPHY (1970) cited Hathaway as saying that Grey himself was a "quiet, easy-spoken man. 'He didn't talk much,' says Hathaway, 'but he listened a lot, and he was always working on a new story. His books were marvelous. There was always something fresh and different about them."[75] Gruber made the claim that it was at Grey's insistence that the remakes which Hathaway directed were filmed on location, but it was Hathaway who found the locations and made splendid use of them. In fact, this is what makes these early films so outstanding: the subdued heroics, noted by Hathaway himself, and the way in which he employed scenic locations as an integral part of each film. For John Ford Monument Valley *was* the American West. Just as for Howard Hawks, whose four Westerns with John Wayne were all filmed around Tucson, there is in Ford's films no real sense of the land or the variety of its effects, its wonders, and its changing influence, even when there is a change of seasons as in THE SEARCHERS (Warner's, 1956) or CHEYENNE AUTUMN (Warner's, 1964). Yet, what marvelous tonalities could and did Henry Hathaway manage to evoke in the multiple locations he used for the filming of TRUE GRIT (Paramount, 1969). Of the three, I would say that Hathaway alone made the land a character in his films, not just a backdrop with human activity in sharp focus in the foreground. Ford used the changing seasons as a way to mark the passage of time in THE SEARCHERS; in TRUE GRIT the magic of autumn comprises a theme parallel but ultimately unrelated to the human activity, the shifting colors, the majesty and beauty of Nature, a world unto itself until the final scene, shot during winter, at the grave site, but even here the viewer is more conscious of its spiritual significance than are the characters on the screen.

Wendell Mayes worked on the screenplay for FROM HELL TO TEXAS (20th-Fox, 1958) and, in an interview with Rui Nogueira in the same issue of FOCUS ON FILM as the interview with Hathaway, Mayes recalled that Hathaway was "very easy for a writer to work with. He's absolutely dreadful for actors to work with, he's probably the toughest sonofabitch in Hollywood. He is tough for a reason. Hathaway is not the most articulate man in the world and he maintains control of his set and of his crew and his actors by being cantankerous and rather cruel sometimes. He knows what he's doing, he isn't doing it out of hand. He's doing it deliberately because this is the way he's discovered he can work. It isn't true with a writer. He's a very gentle man when you sit down with him in a room to write. He doesn't feel he has to browbeat you."[76] In the novel TRUE GRIT (1968) by Charles Portis, the character LaBoeuf, played by Glenn Campbell in the film, does not die; Mattie Ross, played by Kim Darby in the film, loses an arm; and Rooster Cogburn, the role John Wayne felt perfectly suited for him, is dead at the end. Marguerite Roberts, who worked on FIVE CARD STUD (Paramount, 1968) for Hathaway, did the screenplay for TRUE GRIT and the scene between Wayne and Darby at the family plot where Darby offers Wayne a grave beside hers was totally Roberts' addition. These changes, too, may seem to be only little differences, but they are significant ones. The aging hero and the adolescent heroine survive the end of the film intact whereas the younger man, LaBoeuf, the Texas Ranger, the one for whom in a film by Ford or Hawks the adventure would be a learning experience, an initiation into manhood, does not. "Justification and vindication of integrity are prime motivating forces for many Hathaway heroes and heroines," Kingsley Canham wrote in "Henry Hathaway" in Volume One of THE HOLLYWOOD PROFESSIONALS (1973), "yet the attainment of these goals often turns into a Pyrrhic victory since the pursuit has completely occupied their existence and has worn them into a shell so that they find little to celebrate."[77] This perspective, so evident in TRUE GRIT, was already apparent in Hathaway's Zane Grey remakes.

THE HERITAGE OF THE DESERT (Paramount, 1932) was the first film Hathaway directed, made originally in a silent version in 1924 by Paramount and directed by Irvin Willat. Hathaway chose contract player Randolph Scott to star in the role of Jack Hare who, in the earlier film, had been played by Jack Holt. There is an elemental crudity about both this film and the next, WILD HORSE MESA (Paramount, 1932), but it has mostly to do with the ensemble playing; Scott and Sally Blane—they played hero and heroine in both—received most of the director's attention, their delicate romance acting as counterpoint to the camera's awareness of the outdoor locations. Some stock footage from the previous makes of these films was interpolated, but the matching was extremely well done, considering the hiatus of nearly ten years between productions.

Particularly notable among Hathaway's entries in this series the next year are MAN OF THE FOREST (Paramount, 1933), TO THE LAST MAN (Paramount, 1933), and THE THUNDERING HERD (Paramount, 1933). MAN OF THE FOREST (1920), one of Grey's better novels, was first filmed in 1921 by Zane Grey Productions directed by Benjamin B. Hampton. Al Auchincloss, played by Harry Lorraine, sends for his two nieces to take over his land empire; Claire Adams and Charlotte Pierce played the nieces. Carl Gantvoort was cast as Milt Dale, the man of the forest who hides the women from Lem Beasley's scheming. The 1926 remake by Paramount featured Jack Holt in the role of Milt Dale. The nieces were trimmed to a single heroine, played by Georgia Hale. When the niece is sent for by her dying uncle, Jack frustrates Beasley's devilish plan to murder her by abducting and hiding her in his forest retreat. Warner Oland played Beasley. Georgia Hale grows suspicious of her benefactor's intentions and so has him jailed. Milt escapes with the assistance of his pet cougar, confronts Beasley, and settles the score, the heroine coming to realize that Beasley was behind her uncle's death. In Hathaway's version, Randolph Scott was cast as Brett Dale. He hides heroine Verna Hillie, playing Harry Carey's daughter, from Noah Beery's schemings. Beery murders Carey and has Scott arrested for the crime. Scott's pet lion helps him escape. Interestingly, Beery is shot down by Blanche Frederici, cast as his housekeeper, who becomes jealous of the attentions he begins paying the heroine.

In TO THE LAST MAN Hathaway introduced Shirley Temple to the screen. Gail Patrick was cast as Temple's mother. According to Frank Gruber in ZANE GREY: A BIOGRAPHY, in one scene Temple's "pet pony was to enter, be slapped on the rump by the little girl, and then leave. That was the way the scene was rehearsed, but when the camera rolled for the take, things did not work out that way. The pony entered, was slapped by the little girl, and promptly raised up its hind legs and began kicking the tables and dishes to pieces. With the camera still rolling, the little girl dressed down the pony, and in clear, ad-libbed lines, told the animal how badly it was behaving and ordered it to leave the party. The scene rolled to its conclusion and the entire cast and crew applauded the little girl for her excellent ad-libbed dialogue and handling of the scene."[78] Hathaway wanted Paramount to sign her, but the studio did not; Fox Film Corporation did instead. Esther Ralston was cast as the heroine and, in addition to her fighting with the heavies to save hero Randolph Scott's life, Hathaway filmed a nude swimming scene—this was before the crack-down by the Hays Office—with Ralston appearing as a primeval woman in a Western paradise. The scene anticipated that in FROM HELL TO TEXAS where hero Don Murray decides to take a bath at midnight in clear moonlight only to find spunky heroine Diane Varsi doing the same, unashamed of her own nudity and fully determined to watch Murray take off his clothes! There is also a direct line between the determined Shirley Temple in this film and Kim Darby almost four decades later.

Indians were used strictly for dramatic purposes in THE THUNDERING HERD, with Noah Beery back as the principal heavy. But here, as elsewhere in Hathaway's remakes, not only were the heroics more subdued, but Randolph Scott, Harry Carey, and Raymond Hatton formed a male fighting unit, quite similar to later groups united in a common purpose in films such as THE SONS OF KATIE ELDER (Paramount, 1965) and TRUE GRIT.

The basic plot of TO THE LAST MAN is that of a mountain feud transferred to the West. Perhaps the most effective film Hathaway directed incorporating this plot was THE SHEPHERD OF THE HILLS (Paramount, 1941) which also features two other themes common to Hathaway Westerns, that of revenge and the restoration of family honor. THE SHEPHERD OF THE HILLS was also Hathaway's first picture with John Wayne. Based on the sentimental and allegorical novel by Harold Bell Wright, the film opens to revenuers hunting moonshiners in the mountains. Wayne is being raised by his family to kill his father who, many years before, deserted his mother, now dead. In a graveside sequence, reminiscent iconographically of similar scenes in numerous Ford films but quite different dramatically, Wayne swears that he will avenge his mother. Harry Carey comes to the hills, helps the sick and enfeebled, and buys Moaning Meadow, the homestead of Wayne's father and mother. "As long back as I can remember," Betty Field says of Wayne, "he's either fightin' agin yuh or for yuh." Carey's good works hurt the moonshine business, but Field and others regard him as "the good shepherd." Once Wayne learns that Carey is his father, he sets out to kill him. Carey shoots Wayne, but Wayne survives. Learning that Carey was away serving a prison term, he is reconciled with him. As with so many of Hathaway's Westerns—including THE TRAIL OF THE LONESOME PINE (Paramount, 1936), the first three-color outdoor Western and, as

THE SHEPHERD OF THE HILLS, a family feud story—the climax is ambiguous rather than, as in most Westerns, reassuring of values set forth by the principal characters. The same can be said for THE SONS OF KATIE ELDER where, at the end of the film, only two of the four brothers survive the feud with Hastings, played by James Gregory, and Hastings' son, played by Dennis Hopper. "In John Ford's films," Kingsley Canham wrote, "violence is seen as a threat to the peace of the community, which, unless it is stemmed by law and order or channeled by military service, leads to anarchy. Only one instance springs to mind of a Hathaway hero rejecting violence as a solution, and that is in THE TRAIL OF THE LONESOME PINE when Fred Stone persuades Fred MacMurray to let the death of his girl friend's brother go unavenged in the interests of peace in the community."[79]

However, while the argument in the majority of Hathaway's Westerns may be in favor of violence, the perspective is different. Richard Drinnon in FACING WEST: THE METAPHYSICS OF INDIAN-HATING AND EMPIRE-BUILDING observed that the fantasy image of Daniel Boone "became the prototype for a series of American folk heroes who were disinclined to fight but driven to HIGH NOON [United Artists, 1952] confrontations by dire circumstances."[80] In a footnote he added that "the barbarity of the villain(s), and the hero's sense of honor, overcame the promptings of conscience or surrogate conscience, as the schoolmarm functioned in Owen Wister's THE VIRGINIAN. In real life Alvin C. York, the World War I hero who grew up on the Wolf River in the Cumberland Mountains, was a more recent exemplar. When Sergeant York died in 1964, the Associated Press obituary noted that he had served in the 82nd 'All-American' Division, that 'Onward Christian Soldiers' would be sung at his funeral, and that his strong religious convictions were part of his legend: 'Once a conscientious objector, he went on to answer his country's call to World War I and killed 25 Germans and captured 132 more virtually single handed in the battle of Argonne forest.' From Boone's day to York's, men who heroically overcame principle to kill for their country frequently enjoyed all-American status."[81]

In the interview with Rui Nogueira, Hathaway, talking about the making of 13 RUE MADELEINE (20th-Fox, 1946), related getting a call from Darryl Zanuck who was in charge of production at Twentieth Century-Fox when Hathaway was a contract director there, "and he said, '[Louis] De Rochemont has been working on this story for over a year. He's had writers and writers and writers. Now, for Christ's sake, take this stuff and read it, and come down and tell me whether or not you think there is any possibility of a script. If not, I'm going to junk it. He's been working on it too long.' So I took all the stuff upstairs and I went through it for a couple of days and I told Darryl that there were an amazing number of technical things about it but it had no story. So he said, 'Well, how can we get a story into it?' So I said that I'd worked on the original VIRGINIAN (as a matter of fact, I'd worked on two VIRGINIANS), and I said that the story of THE VIRGINIAN would suit this perfectly because the leading man is responsible for the death of Steve but, although he had to kill Steve, he felt that Trampas was responsible for having had to kill him so he goes on a man-hunt after Trampas. Well, we had that same situation put into 13 RUE MADELEINE . . . . ''[82]

Howard Hawks brought Alvin C. York's story to the screen in the fanciful SERGEANT YORK (Warner's, 1941), but it was Hathaway, not Hawks, who, with some consistency, incorporated in his Westerns the theme from Wister's novel and much of Zane Grey's fiction about men forced by circumstances into violence. For example in RAWHIDE (20th-Fox, 1951) Tyrone Power, cast as a bumbling Easterner, and Susan Hayward with her young niece are traveling on a stagecoach. A gang waiting to steal a gold shipment takes them captive. Once Hayward and Power escape, the outlaws try to take revenge on the niece which pushes Power into a very effective display of violence. In FROM HELL TO TEXAS, hero Don Murray is falsely accused of having killed one of R.G. Armstrong's sons in cold blood. Murray flees from Armstrong and Armstrong's other sons, who are in pursuit, and meets a trader played by Jay C. Flippen who reminds him that "convictions must fit the time and place." When the inevitable showdown occurs, Murray, who has stopped running and has decided to fight, remarks: "Like the man said, there's a time and a place." Rooster Cogburn, being cross-examined in TRUE GRIT, when asked how many men he has killed in the last four years, needs a clarification whether "shot or killed" is meant before admitting to twenty-three, but justifying himself with the statement, "I never shot nobody I didn't have to."

In GARDEN OF EVIL (20th-Fox, 1954) Susan Hayward hires Gary Cooper, Richard Widmark, and Cameron Mitchell to help her save her husband who has been buried in a mine cave-in. They are stalked on the way to the mine by Apaches wearing Mohawk hairpieces. After they rescue her husband, played by Hugh Marlowe, he repudiates Hayward, insisting she was interested only in the gold. "You took him too far," Cooper tells Hayward. "You took him over his head. You made him into a coward and he hates you for it."

They are surrounded by Apaches and Hayward would remain behind while the others slip out after dark, but Cooper slugs her and takes her along with them. Mitchell is killed by an arrow. Hugh Marlowe is taken by the Apaches and they find his body, crucified upside down—something only Hollywood Apaches would do—[83] and filled with arrows, about which Cooper remarks: "We all have a cross. That was his." Finally, it is just Hayward, Cooper, and Widmark. Widmark stays behind to cover Hayward and Cooper while they slip away. Once they are safe, Cooper leaves Hayward to go back and help Widmark. "Somebody always stays," he tells Hayward. "Everywhere in the world someone always gets the job done." By the fade, although it was too late for Widmark, it is not too late for Cooper and Hayward to follow Widmark's dying advice and build a home.

Hathaway's heroines are not prime candidates for domestic life, as are Ford's, nor are they asexual, as are Hawks'. They are frequently involved in the action,

from Barbara Fritchie in THE LAST ROUND-UP (Paramount, 1934), based on
Zane Grey's THE BORDER LEGION (1916), through the roles played by Susan Hayward and Kim Darby. They rarely lack character, but they are more
likely to follow the lead of the hero than ever to initiate any action themselves
and, often, the action they do propose is rejected by the heroes as foolish.

Unquestionably, some of Hathaway's weakest films as a director have been
Westerns, NEVADA SMITH (Paramount, 1966), a flaccidly routine revenge
story, and FIVE CARD STUD with Robert Mitchum in the role of a maniacal
killer in preacher's garb which he played better in THE NIGHT OF THE
HUNTER (United Artists, 1955) directed by Charles Laughton. Perhaps the least
of Hathaway's Westerns, and one he himself disclaimed, is BRIGHAM
YOUNG—FRONTIERSMAN (20th-Fox, 1940). Mark Twain in ROUGHING
IT (1872), when he encountered the Mormons on his trip West, dealt with the
issue of polygamy in this fashion. ''With the gushing self-sufficiency of youth
I was feverish to plunge in headlong and achieve a great reform here—until I
saw the Mormon women. Then I was touched. My heart was wiser than my
head. It warmed toward these poor, ungainly, and pathetically 'homely' creatures, and as I turned to hide the generous moisture in my eyes, I said, 'No—
the man that marries one of them has done an act of Christian charity which
entitles him to the kindly applause of mankind, not their harsh censure—and
the man that marries sixty of them has done a deed of open-handed generosity
so sublime that the nations should stand uncovered in his presence and worship
in silence.'' [84] Hathaway's approach was no less frivolous. ''What's the difference between a white man and a Mormon? Don't know . . . 'bout fifty wives,
I guess''—is about as close as his film comes to dealing with the issue at all,
tending therefore to make the sententious comments about bigotry vague and
meaningless.

On the other hand, SHOOT OUT (Universal, 1971), based as was an earlier
film, THE LONE COWBOY (Paramount, 1934) directed by Paul Sloane, on
Will James' THE LONE COWBOY (1930), is one of Hathaway's very best
Westerns and a decidedly different treatment of many of the same story ingredients which can be found in WILL PENNY (Paramount, 1968) directed by
Tom Gries. SHOOT OUT opens to Gregory Peck getting out of prison. His
partner in a bank robbery shot him in the back and so he was caught. Peck
wants revenge. So far, one has a typical Hathaway plot-line. Peck is expecting
some money on a train, being brought to him by a prostitute who was once
apparently in love with him. What he gets instead is her little girl—the mother
died on the way—and Peck is unsuccessful in trying to get someone else to
adopt Decky, as she is called, played by Dawn Lyn. ''Reverend, you are mean,''
Peck tells a preacher who refuses him. ''Perhaps,'' the preacher replies, ''but
not mean enough to get rid of a child in her presence.'' From this point on the
story is concerned with the gradual humanization of the Peck character. The
interchanges between Decky and the Peck character are some of the most touching
and poignant Hathaway ever got onto film. Peck's former partner sends some

hired guns after Peck. Peck and Decky stop off during a rain storm to stay at a ranch owned by a widow, played by Susan Tyrrell, who lives with her small son and, in her loneliness, has turned to drink for companionship. Peck's former partner is killed by one of his own hired guns and Peck, in turn, kills the hired gun. The *dénouement* of the film is more ambiguous than even that of TRUE GRIT, an aftermath of sadness and indefinable loss that is nearly palpable. Rarely in any Hathaway film is the acting so underplayed as it is here, the characters so delicately and affectingly drawn. But, of course, Peck does have his revenge; the code is upheld; "somebody [does get] the job done."

6

Anthony Mann

I can think of no director of Western films—including Ford and Hawks—who has inspired such enthusiastic accolades among French critics as has Anthony Mann. André Bazin in his essay, "The Evolution of the Western," contained in the second volume of WHAT IS CINEMA? (1971) edited and translated by Hugh Gray, claimed "each of Mann's films reveals a touching frankness of attitude toward the Western, an effortless sincerity to get inside its themes and there bring to life appealing characters and to invent captivating situations."[85] Indeed, Bazin went so far as to insist that "anyone who wants to know what a real Western is, and the qualities it presupposes in a director, has to have seen DEVIL'S DOORWAY [M-G-M, 1950] with Robert Taylor, BEND OF THE RIVER [Universal, 1952] and THE FAR COUNTRY [Universal, 1954] with James Stewart. Even if he does not know these three films, he simply has to know the finest of all, THE NAKED SPUR [M-G-M, 1953]."[86] Finally, Bazin celebrated Mann's "natural gift for direct and discreet use of the lyrical and above all his infallible sureness of touch in bringing together man and Nature, that feeling of the open air, which in his films seems to be the soul of the Western."[87]

There are a number of unstated premises and assumptions in this praise. In his Introduction to an earlier version of Jean-Louis Rieupeyrout's LA GRANDE AVENTURE DU WESTERN, also included in WHAT IS CINEMA?, Bazin stated that "the Indian, who lived in this world [of the American West], was incapable of imposing on it man's order. He mastered it only by identifying himself with its pagan savagery. The white Christian on the contrary is truly the conqueror of a new world."[88] Seemingly in contradiction to such a view is Jim Kitses' formulation in HORIZONS WEST that "Mann's style creates a world that is hard and punishing towards moral disorder, unnatural, extreme behavior. Justice emerges not from within the individual soul or through a social dialectic: standing outside and above man there exists a cosmic equilibrium, a natural law which demands a paying of dues."[89]

If there is posited in Mann's Westerns—as, in agreement with Kitses, I believe there is—a world-view which implies the existence of a natural order that can be plunged into disequilibrium through human concupiscence, philosophically there is no *logical* reason to presume that Native Americans would be excluded from its compass. Further, it ought to follow that an attempt to establish "man's order" in place of the natural order would be a sin of the first magnitude against equilibrium. But these are the contradictions in Mann's films. Native Americans *are* excluded from the natural order which apparently pertains only to the activities of white men and the conflict, or *agon*, in many of Mann's Westerns is precisely the conquest of the natural order. "Yes," Anthony Mann said in his interview in POSITIF (September, 1968), "the struggle of the elements, amongst them or against them, brings good results. The actors and the technical crew need to struggle against something. The snow is a very useful element and yields a myriad of plastic effects. Besides there is the breath of the horses and the actors, the difficulties of the terrain, the contest to overcome these difficulties. In a studio one is able to achieve nothing such as this. Moreover, the actors love this way of shooting and the freedom is most welcome. The management is not there to annoy you and you can do what you want to do."[90]

However, to probe this issue more deeply, the natural order in Mann's Westerns has nothing to do with Nature; it is specifically a *moral* order. It is divorced from the classical and medieval tradition which conceived of Nature and human morality as manifestations of an underlying unity, *de rerum natura maxima*—of the nature of things in the highest degree. The elements of Nature are in Mann's world-view often antagonistic to the moral order, and Indians no less than moral reprobates among the whites are regarded as extensions of that antagonism. Might this not perhaps justify Rieupeyrout's lyrical and encompassing description of the West of Mann's films in LA GRANDE AVENTURE DU WESTERN?—:"From the North to the South, from Canada to the Rio Grande, from Colorado to the Dakotas, in this West prey to the unchecked influx of civilization, the Indian prowls, mute witness, sometimes cruel, who shares the privilege of desperate roaming with a motley bunch of whites, inhabitants of the troubled world on the fringes of that same civilization: declared bandits (WINCHESTER 73 [Universal, 1950]), gangs meanwhile on the horizon (MAN OF THE WEST [United Artists, 1958]), cowboys splintering away from the crew, etc. All of them, white or red, noble-minded or vile, obstinate builders or profiteers without scruples, haunt the world of Mann's Westerns in a heterogeneous cross-section of a human geography perfectly set in place and carefully portrayed in terms of the moral dimensions and of the dramatic colors of these locales and of the epoch."[91]

As if in support of such a view, the French release title for CIMARRON (M-G-M, 1960) is LA RUÉE VERS L'OUEST: THE RUSH WESTWARD; but I have a problem with Rieupeyrout's terming the Indians in Mann's Westerns mute witnesses. When in WINCHESTER 73 James Stewart and Millard

Mitchell, after leaving Riker's, are riding along the trail at night, the Indians are anything but mute; and the same thing is true in BEND OF THE RIVER when the wagon train led by Stewart makes camp for the night. Indians are rather a perpetual menace, even if they are nowhere in evidence—as when John McIntyre's body is discovered by Stephen McNally and his two thugs in WIN-CHESTER 73 and one of the thugs inquires: "Why do they always scalp them that way?" When Jed, played by Victor Mature, Gus, played by James Whitmore, and Mungo, played by Pat Hogan, at the beginning of THE LAST FRONTIER (Columbia, 1955) move across a clearing, they are suddenly surrounded by Indians who literally seem to come out of the earth itself. The Indians claim their furs and mounts and, when Jed would fight, Gus reminds him of the hopeless odds and that they are fortunate to escape with their lives. In THE NAKED SPUR a party of Blackfeet Indians is caught between a cross-fire by the whites and slaughtered to the last man. "The massacre," Kitses wrote, "shattering for us in its efficiency, in retrospect appears inevitable."[92] Desperate roaming, as it is portrayed in these films, is scarcely a privilege. Indians are perceived as an extension of the savagery of Nature which must be destroyed. The white man's moral order is indeed in direct opposition to the traditional notion of the natural order.

THE DEVIL'S DOORWAY was Mann's first Western film. Robert Taylor was cast as "Broken Lance" Poole, an educated Shoshoni who is decorated for bravery in the Civil War. Returning home, Poole begins to build up a large ranch for himself and some of his people. Louis Calhern, cast as Verne Coolan, attempts to cheat Poole out of his land, claiming that as an Indian Poole is a ward of the United States government and not entitled to land ownership under the Homestead Act. Poole retains Orrie Masters, played by Paula Raymond, to defend his rights. They fall in love, but the romance is doomed from the beginning, Poole sorrowfully concluding that "a hundred years from now it might have worked." The rule of miscegenation applies even more rigorously in a film of this vintage than it would have in the historical period being depicted: Poole cannot survive the fade. The Cavalry sweeps down on Poole's ranch and Poole dies in the massacre of the tribe, defending his land. The ideology of the film would indicate that even an Indian willing to take the white man's road will be destroyed by the white man's prejudice. The moral point being made is: if Indians, or any other non-white racial group, are willing to accept white man's values, they ought to be permitted to live as white men. What critics at the time who celebrated the racially enlightened viewpoint of this film seem to have missed is the strong propaganda in favor of one-settlement culture. This is a far more pernicious variety of racism since it permits viewer and critic to think that THE DEVIL'S DOORWAY is what is termed a "pro-Indian" picture. I cannot agree with Kitses that "the film ends on a strange note of dark exaltation—victory through death—and celebrates the uncompromising quality of the character."[93] To the contrary, Poole is a *compromised* character. What is his victory? That he dies at the end? That he dies in his uniform trying to be a white man, with a white man's property values? That the viewer admires him for his struggles to behave as a white man, even though he is no match for the racial intolerance of the white community? If there is a victory in this film, it is the more subtle (because overlooked by almost everyone) victory of the notion of one-settlement culture. The Indian was not allowed cultural integrity—the right to have his own culture independent of the white community—in 1865 and he was not allowed to have it in 1950 when Mann directed this film. In the words of a federal marshal whose voice was monitored on a radio transmission on the night of 26 April 1973 reprinted in VOICES FROM WOUNDED KNEE (1974): "If we see one of them long-haired hippie dudes jump out of that bunker in front of us with long black hair with pigtails, we got a search 4 [a search party] out there, and if we capture him, first off we're gonna cut off his hair."[94]

Charles Silver in THE WESTERN FILM (1976) felt "it can be argued that the basic thrust of Anthony Mann's work grew out of 'psychological' Westerns like [Raoul] Walsh's PURSUED [Warner's, 1947]. Mann's films are not psychological so much as they are neurotic. His hero is perfectly embodied in James Stewart. Their five films in five years literally created a new Western type, nearly as compelling as John Wayne, but possessed of obsessions, self-doubt, and emotional eccentricity. (John Ford was to later bring the two together with profound results in THE MAN WHO SHOT LIBERTY VALANCE [Paramount, 1962])."[95] I agree with the first part of this statement, with some reservations, but not at all with the reference to THE MAN WHO SHOT LIBERTY VALANCE. The intention of Ford's film, it appears to me, is to demonstrate that the character played by James Stewart could not have survived in the "wild" West without someone like the John Wayne character to look out for him; whereas the John Wayne character could not prosper once "law and order" were established, with the attendant political subtleties and indirections. The Stewart hero in Mann's Westerns is obsessed, as is the Randolph Scott hero in Budd Boetticher's Westerns, but unlike the Scott hero, he is not alone. Sometimes the hero's relationship with a male companion does not last—in BEND OF THE RIVER, THE NAKED SPUR, THE FAR COUNTRY—but sometimes it does—in WINCHESTER 73 and THE MAN FROM LARAMIE (Columbia, 1955)—though the Stewart hero is nowhere as close to the character played by Wallace Ford in the latter as he is to Millard Mitchell in the former. In fact, Stewart's relationship with Mitchell is one of the most interesting aspects of WINCHESTER 73. Throughout the film, Mitchell is constantly in support; on three occasions he brings Stewart a cup of coffee. At the end, when Stewart and Shelley Winters are embracing, he stands to the left of them in the frame with a perplexed and ironic expression, as if to say: What happens now? In most variations of the Picaresque Wanderers and Searchers plot setting, of which WINCHESTER 73 is an example, the hero's male companion, if he has one, dies at the end, so the heroine can take his place, the prototype *par excellence* of initiation into the world of adulthood. The curious Stewart/Mitchell relationship is underscored in the scene where Winters' fiancé, Steve, before Dan Duryea shoots him, is humiliated by Duryea by being forced to bring Duryea and Winters coffee. Duryea even tells Steve to wear an apron, and Duryea's gang joins in the ridicule.

The Winters character is herself no less interesting. When she is first seen, Wyatt Earp, played by Will Geer, is forcing her to leave town on the stagecoach. Stewart would interfere, before he learns Earp's identity, and Earp tells him—incredibly!—that the people of Dodge City might object to the presence of dance hall girls over the holidays. It is the Fourth of July. Winters is the only dance hall girl being asked to leave. It may be a variation on Bret Harte's "The Outcasts of Poker Flat," and, if it is, then Winters would clearly be a prostitute—she boasts to Steve when she meets him later in the film that she successfully earned money while waiting for him in Dodge. When Universal remade the film, WINCHESTER 73 (Universal, 1967) directed by Herschel Daugherty, perhaps since this was a movie made for television the problem was resolved by making the character, played by Barbara Luna, a card sharp. I suspect that the reason Millard Mitchell appears in the final scene is because the screenplay was unwilling to commit itself to the customary "they married and lived happily ever after" conclusion so typical of the Ranch Story/Town Western plot setting. Not only is Winters' profession ambiguous, but, whether voluntarily or not, the viewer does see her riding around the countryside with Duryea after Steve is killed and it is Winters who manipulates Duryea into the position that gets him killed when Stewart enters the saloon where the two of them have been amusing themselves.

Stuart N. Lake wrote the original story for WINCHESTER 73 and for reasons that will become evident in the chapter later devoted to the Wyatt Earp legend he probably could not resist the temptation to make Earp a character. Earp, as portrayed by Will Geer in Mann's film, is as highly idealized as he is in John Ford's MY DARLING CLEMENTINE (20th-Fox, 1946); nor, indeed, is this the only link between WINCHESTER 73 and Ford's sentimental view of American history. When Stewart and Mitchell join up with Jay C. Flippen, a Cavalry sergeant whose detail is surrounded by Indians, because the sergeant is from Pennsylvania Stewart gives him a little useful advice about Indians. They never fight at night because they are afraid that if they die the Great Spirit will lose track of their souls. He also tells him that the reason Custer lost the battle at the Little Big Horn is because the Sioux had repeating rifles and Custer's regiment did not. After shooting a great many Indians, Stewart directs everyone to concentrate their fire on the chief, played by Rock Hudson. If they kill him, the nameless tribe will retreat—which is exactly what happens. And then—a truly strong link with Ford—the battle over, Flippen tells Stewart he wishes Stewart and Mitchell could have been at the battle of Bull Run. They *were* there, Stewart tells Flippen, only on the other side. In a patriotic moment, they shake hands.

The most fundamental plot setting in WINCHESTER 73 is that of the Justice/Revenge Theme. Stewart is after his brother, played by Stephen McNally, because McNally killed their father. Obviously this, too, was found to be unacceptable when the film was remade since in the remake the equivalent character murders not his own father, played by Dan Duryea (the only actor retained, albeit recast, from the original), but the hero's father, and is therefore pursued by his cousin. The shoot-out between Stewart and McNally in Mann's film, with the scream of ricocheting rifle bullets colliding against rocks all around the antagonists, is perhaps one of the most effective gun duels staged in a Western film up until that time and not even this episode was attempted again for the remake which begins with the announcement that two hundred and twenty troopers died at the Little Big Horn because the Indians, with their Winchesters, had superior fire power.

For Mann, how the hero related to his gun was important. "Gary is magnificent when he walks down a street with a Winchester under his arm," he said of Gary Cooper. "Jimmy [Stewart] himself is also magnificent when he clutches a Winchester. He studied a long time learning how to use it. His fingers became completely at home with it. In addition we had an expert from the Winchester company . . . . Knowing how to use something is the only way in a Western to achieve realism."[96] It is this sense of expertise which combines with the atmosphere of violence in Mann's Westerns to make them so dramatically compelling, but it remains the potential for violence that is most important. Although individual acts of violence may erupt and pass quickly, it is their intimations which hover and their repercussions which reverberate and distantly echo. " . . . This is true of great drama," Kitses quoted Mann in HORIZONS WEST, "that it needs violence because the audience is sitting there and they are experiencing things, and then in order for it to take hold the dramatist really needs . . . to express an emotion, for the character to go through something that the audience *feel* for."[97] This quite definitely happens in BEND OF THE RIVER when the rabble Stewart hires to help him transport a shipment of supplies to a newly settled community turns on him, intent on stealing the supplies to sell them at a profit to a nearby mining camp, and beats Stewart almost senseless. The tension which has been delayed from the beginning of the film, and delayed, and delayed some more, suddenly breaks, and Stewart becomes a one-man demon, frantically determined to get the supplies back no matter what the cost. A similar episode occurs in THE MAN FROM LARAMIE; in fact, two such episodes occur. There is one at the very beginning, where the Barb riders come upon Stewart's men and wagons at the salt lakes and Stewart is roped and dragged through a fire, his wagons burned, and his mules shot; this leads to a terrific fistfight later in town. And there is the episode where Stewart is captured by Barb riders on Barb land, much later in the film, and Alex Nicol as Dave Waggoman shoots Stewart with deliberation through the palm of his left hand. This event precipitates the last round of violence.

The Stewart hero, in the Mann Westerns made after WINCHESTER 73, is almost always indirect in his behavior. At the beginning of BEND OF THE RIVER, when he saves Arthur Kennedy from a lynching, Kennedy asks Stewart, "Why did you step in?," and Stewart replies casually, "Well, I just don't like hanging." When five Indians surround the wagon train Stewart is leading, Stewart and Kennedy creep out of camp under the cover of darkness: Kennedy kills one, Stewart four. It is an incident such as this, visual action never underscored by dialogue, which establishes the violent nature inherent in the Stewart character and prepares the viewer for the coming outburst. Jay C. Flippen, cast as the *paterfamilias* of the wagon train and Julia Adams' father, informs Stewart that "when an apple is rotten, it'll spoil the whole barrel"—in a single sentence the condensed "wisdom" of a thousand "B" Westerns—to which Stewart replies, "There's a difference between apples and people." This statement would seem to remove BEND OF THE RIVER from the ideology of similar Pioneer Achievement plot setting Westerns—John Ford's WAGONMASTER (RKO, 1950) notably among them—but, because of the fashion in which the plot is resolved, it proves to be a red herring. Soon after the wagon train arrives in Portland, Oregon, gold is discovered, and Flippen remarks to Stewart, "Missouri and Kansas were like this when I first seen them. It was the men who came in to steal and kill who changed things." This reaffirms the delusion that moral evil comes from outside the community. Stewart, it turns out, was a border raider during the Civil War, but after he kills Kennedy and retrieves the stolen supplies, this is forgotten. Flippen magnanimously reflects, "There is a difference between apples and men"; but the plot does not demonstrate the proposition: while occasionally a rotten apple reforms, others are still hopeless reprobates and must be killed.

At first, when the wagon train pulls out of Portland, Julia Adams stays on to work in a saloon. She changes her mind by the end of the picture and is ready to settle down with Stewart. "In practice," Mann remarked in his interview for CAHIERS DU CINÉMA (May, 1956), "one always interpolates a woman into the ballad because without her a Western will not sell."[98] In THE NAKED SPUR, which I personally do not regard as Mann's best Western, the Stewart hero is pursuing Robert Ryan for having killed a marshal. Stewart is a bounty hunter. He gets Ralph Meeker, a dishonorably discharged Cavalry officer, and Millard Mitchell, a prospector, to join him in the hunt. Ryan is traveling with Janet Leigh when he is captured. "The longer we ride," Ryan tells Leigh, "the more things can happen." Surely, Ryan belongs among Mann's most philosophical villains. "Choosin' the way to die makes no difference," he says later on. "Choosin' how to live. That's the hard part." Every time violence erupts, Leigh does nothing except stand around and watch. Her presence is even more extraneous than that of Winters in WINCHESTER 73 or of Adams in BEND OF THE RIVER, although she is on hand, once Ryan is dead and Stewart decides to bury him rather than claim the bounty, to head to California with Stewart. Before censuring Mann too much, however, for regarding women as irrelevant, it should be observed in his behalf that he was in the forefront of his time in including in his Westerns heroines who were neither prim nor vestal. He went so far in preproduction of MAN OF THE WEST as to want

Gary Cooper to go off with the Julie London character despite his being married and her having just been raped. This the front office would not permit. A hero did not behave in that fashion and, even were he single, he could not be rewarded with such blatantly "soiled" merchandise. It is my suspicion that had fewer restraints been placed on Mann, he would have included heroines with far more depth and complexity. It was not merely that a woman had to be interpolated into the ballad, but a certain kind of woman, the traditional Western heroine.

In THE FAR COUNTRY, there are two heroines. Ronda Castle, a villainous saloon-owner played by Ruth Roman, made more interesting by both the storyline and by Mann's direction, and the virginal Renée Vallon played by Corinne Calvet. The film is supposedly set during the Klondike gold rush, and Ronda Castle is accused of having ruined Skagway and then Dawson. "I trusted a man . . . ," she tells Stewart, "*once*." At the end, she is shot by John McIntyre who is the leading villain. Calvet, dressed as a child, a tomboy with pig-tails, is the heroine with whom Stewart winds up. For much of the film, the Stewart hero is very similar to Ronda Castle insofar as he trusts no one and wishes to concern himself with no one. When, on the way to Dawson, Ronda and her men are caught in an avalanche and Stewart's partner, Ben Tatum played by Walter Brennan, would go back to rescue them, Stewart wants no part of it. Then, in a line right out of Howard Hawks' RED RIVER (United Artists, 1948), Brennan tells Stewart, "You're wrong, Jeff." It is not until the final reel, after outrage after outrage, including having seen Walter Brennan shot down and having been severely wounded himself, that Stewart finally relents and faces down the villains, killing Bob Wilkie, Jack Elam, and, after McIntyre plugs Ronda, McIntyre.

William R. Meyer in THE MAKING OF THE GREAT WESTERNS (1979) made the claim that Mann's "talent for bringing out incisive points about his fictional men and women is one of the reasons he's respected as one of the greatest makers of Westerns" and that this was "never so evident as in THE MAN FROM LARAMIE."[99] I would be more in accord with this assertion were it not for the numerous structural inconsistencies in the film which were a direct result of a surprisingly inept adaptation of the original story, THE MAN FROM LARAMIE (1954) by T.T. Flynn, which also appeared as a serial in THE SATURDAY EVENING POST. These inconsistencies might be illumined to the best advantage by comparing the plot of the original story with the screen version.

Will Lockhart is in the freighting business. As the novel opens, he is at the salt lakes loading four big freight wagons with salt. Nearby are the charred remains of a fleet of wagons burned out by marauding Apaches. Charley Yuill, "an odd mixture of Scot father and Indian mother,"[100] works for Will. Lieutenant Evans is commanding a patrol out of Fort Roxton. He stops where Lockhart is working and assumes that Will is employed by Barb, the ranch empire owned by Alec Waggoman, but Lockhart tells him that he is renting salt rights from the Half-Moon ranch. Barbara Kirby also stops. She informs Will that the salt lakes are now owned by Barb, that the lease changed hands about a week ago. In the distance Will can see that Barb riders are approaching. Dave Waggoman, Alec's only child (Barbara is his niece; her mother, Alec's sister, is dead and Barbara now lives in town with her father), and Vic Hansbro, Barb's foreman, are leading the men. Barbara is engaged to marry Frank L. Darrah, a young, ambitious merchant, who also lives in the nearby town of Coronado. It is Hansbro in the novel who orders Lockhart roped down, his wagons burned, and his mules shot, leaving only enough mules for Lockhart and his men to ride out of there. He probably would have gone further but Lieutenant Evans and his patrol return. "Young Dave Waggoman might have settled reasonably. But Hansbro had crowded Dave. Hansbro was the man, not Dave Waggoman."[101] Everyone leaves, except for Lockhart and Charley. Will, it turns out, is a captain in the Cavalry, on a leave of absence, searching for the man in the area who is selling rifles to the Apaches. His brother was killed in a recent attack. Will has traced the shipment of two hundred rifles and ten thousand rounds of ammunition from New York to New Orleans and he suspects it is now *en route* to Coronado, New Mexico, and to Frank Darrah.

Alec Waggoman is going blind due to cataracts. It is a well-kept secret, but Darrah learns of it. "The day word flashed out that Alec Waggoman—the great Alec Waggoman—was half-blind, that day three long, ruthless decades of old scores would stir and take life. They'd be after Alec Waggoman quickly. After Barb. They'd move in like pack wolves racing to hamstring a great lamed buck. In his day, building, expanding, holding Barb, Alec Waggoman had been completely ruthless. He'd get no better once he was considered helpless."[102] This obsession with property, acquiring it and holding it, was characteristic of formulary Western fiction in the period beginning in 1902 with THE VIRGINIAN and extending into the 'Seventies. It is Darrah's master plan to marry Barbara and thus be next in line to inherit, through her, the Barb empire, figuring that Dave is too hot-headed and foolish to hold it.

When Hansbro and Dave ride into town, Lockhart is there and he beats Hansbro in a fight, badly. "This was something Hansbro could understand. This sort of cruelty was Barb's own language, and the town could read it, too."[103] Alec, when he learns of what happened to Will's wagons, agrees to reimburse him for all losses. When Will goes to George Freall's bank to collect the money, Freall senses "depths of experience and understanding in this man, forged into the calm of self-awareness. In Lockhart, a warmth, a sincerity, and a spontaneous humor evidently took life without cynicism. Savoring what was good, Freall guessed. Weighing events calmly with that smiling, indolent self-assurance. A man, Freall decided now, who had mastered himself, whose smiling reserves would not be mastered."[104] On the very positive side, Stewart's achievement, and Mann's, in projecting a totally different kind of hero in their collaboration, a man who is unsure of himself, fearful of his vulnerability, drawing strength from obsession rather than from conviction, is a decided contrast with Flynn's typical formulary hero.

Alec unloads on Hansbro. " 'Better believe this, Vic! Starting now, I'm not keeping an oversize bully boy to help Dave get into trouble! . . . I'd fire you now if I thought it'd help Dave! I'm warning you now! If you're near Dave's next fool move and don't stop him, I'll bust you to a cowhand! If you help him, I'll fire you! Pull your pay and ride if you don't like it!' " [105]

Chris Boldt, a henchman working for Darrah, is told by Darrah to pick a fight with Lockhart and kill him. When the scheme backfires, Darrah kills Boldt. Lockhart, because of the abortive fight, is blamed and arrested. Kate Canaday, a spirited, middle-aged woman who owns Half-Moon, gets Lockhart released into her custody. She wants him to manage her ranch. Will avails himself of the opportunity to trace what happened to the shipment of guns which disappeared from Darrah's warehouse right after Boldt was killed. He rides onto Barb land, is spotted by Dave, and the two shoot it out. Dave's gun hand is hit by one of Lockhart's bullets. He has his men pinion Lockhart. " . . . Will stiffened against the blow Dave evidently meant to strike with Will's own gun. Then in pale rage, Dave shoved the gun muzzle at Will's left palm and pulled the trigger." [106]

Barbara, against the advice of her father and Kate, agrees to marry Darrah. On his way into town to get medical attention for his hand, Dave meets Darrah on the road. Darrah shoots him, thinking Lockhart will be blamed. Will, meanwhile, rides to the Half-Moon where Kate bandages his hand and urges him to go into town to the doctor. "He might lose the hand. His army career would end. The future would be bleak indeed for Will Lockhart." [107] Charley Yuill arrives and tells Will he has located the rifles in an old powderhouse. Will instructs him to watch the powderhouse while he goes into town. Hansbro has a meeting with Darrah and Darrah promises Hansbro that he will have a permanent job as foreman once Alec dies and Barbara comes into Barb. Hansbro and young Dave had rustled some cattle from Barb and sold them to Darrah when Dave needed money. Hansbro now plants evidence pointing to Kate Canaday. Alec, believing the evidence, burns out Half-Moon and then heads into the hills to meditate. Hansbro follows him and pushes him from his horse down an incline, believing him to be dead. However, with the help of Kate's dogs, Alec is found and brought to Kate's burned-out ranch. Will has a shoot-out with Hansbro on the trail and Hansbro confesses his association with Darrah before he dies. Darrah, pursued by a posse, tries to make a getaway. He is jumped by Indians and scalped. Dave's gun—the reader is to believe the Indians would take a scalp and not a gun!—is found on his body, exonerating Lockhart. Kate ends up with Alec. " 'Alec made me a kinda business proposition. Dave's dead, an' Alec won't see his own victuals before long. I ain't got a roof now. So Alec's got an idea I can run both ranches from Barb. Usin' my eyes an' his brain, like he had a brain.' " [108] Will and Barbara come together in a clinch.

THE MAN FROM LARAMIE is a complex formulary Western combining the Ranch Story/Town Western and Justice/Revenge Theme and, in view of the capitalistic accumulation by Alec Waggoman in the past and Frank Darrah in the present, the Pioneer Achievement plot settings, as well as the brief use of the Indian story plot setting, functioning as a subsidiary motive and nemesis in the plot resolution. In adapting such a story for the screen, the plot, of course, had to be simplified and stream-lined, unnecessary characters excluded, and scenes condensed. The art of adaptation, however, is all in the doing. In Mann's film, James Stewart as Will Lockhart is a freighter who camps for the night near where some freight wagons had been attacked some years before. In the next scene, he unloads his wagons at a store owned by Barbara Waggoman, played by Kathy O'Donnell. She has a suspicious Indian working for her and Will wonders if he is somehow connected with the gun-running he intends to investigate. The Indian does nothing; Will is made suspicious by the mere fact that he is an Indian. When Lockhart goes out to load up what Barbara tells him is free salt, he is set upon by Barb riders led by Dave Waggoman, played by Alex Nicol, his wagons burned, and his mules are being systematically shot, until Vic Hansbro, played by Arthur Kennedy, rides up and halts the proceedings. Will pays off his men. He stays behind because he wishes to learn who has been selling repeating rifles to the Apaches. Charley O'Leary, played by Wallace Ford, chooses to help him. ''I doubt if we spoke ten words coming down here,'' he tells Lockhart, ''but I feel I know you.'' He heads North in order to gather information. Lockhart goes into town where he beats up Dave and then starts beating up Hansbro before Alec Waggoman, played by Donald Crisp, comes on the scene, stops the fight, and offers to pay Lockhart for his losses. Hansbro and Barbara Waggoman are in love. She wants to leave the territory, but Hansbro wants to remain, convinced he will inherit half of Barb.

Lockhart, we now learn, is seeking the man who killed his brother. He is befriended by Kate Canaday, played by Aline MacMahon, the only one who has held out against Barb's land greed. Jack Elam, cast as the town drunk, is killed after he attacks Lockhart at night. The Indian from Barbara's store is seen in the background. Lockhart is blamed for Elam's death and jailed. Kate gets him released into her custody because she needs him at her ranch.

Alec Waggoman, the viewer finds out, is going blind, but no cause is given. Dave and some of his men, patroling Barb land, see Lockhart. A gun battle ensues and Dave is wounded in his hand. While Dave's men hold him, Dave shoots Lockhart through the left palm. He then rides off to the high country where he has cached two hundred rifles he wants to sell to the Apaches. Hansbro, having been told by Alec that there will be no inheritance if Dave is not kept out of trouble, trails Dave. When he discovers what Dave plans, the two shoot it out, and Dave is killed. Alec blames Lockhart and, after the funeral, goes gunning for Will. Because of his failing eyesight, he misses Lockhart, and rides off chagrined.

Next, Alec decides to find out what Dave was doing in the high country. He takes Hansbro with him. The two struggle on the trail and Alec falls off his horse, down a cliff. Lockhart finds Alec and takes him to Kate's ranch. Rather incredibly, Kate is able to patch up Lockhart's hand without need of a doctor or fear on Will's part that he might lose it. Alec tells Will that Hansbro was behind the whole thing. Lockhart discovers Hansbro signaling the Apaches. He destroys the rifles but he cannot bring himself to kill Hansbro. Hansbro tries to get away, but the Apaches surround and kill him. Alec is completely blind—the fall did it. Lockhart rides off alone in the end.

No motive is provided for Dave Waggoman to be selling rifles to the Apaches. In fact, such an action would be against his own best interests, since the rifles would undoubtedly be used against Barb. Hansbro as a villain in Mann's film blunders into killing Dave and Alec's fall is shown to be the consequence of desperation. In brief, the screenplay portrays wrong-doing as more accidental than deliberate, in contrast to the calculated viciousness of Flynn's characters in the novel. In WINCHESTER 73 when John McIntyre ventures alone to sell rifles to the Indians, he is surrounded and killed. The same thing happens to Hansbro in THE MAN FROM LARAMIE, albeit the rifles have been destroyed. Yet both Dave and Hansbro were willing to meet alone with supposedly savage Apaches and had expected to get away with it. This naiveté is rather hard to believe. Because of the way her role was cut, the Barbara Waggoman character has absolutely no function in the film, not even the stereotyped heroine role of Barbara Kirby in the novel.

Jim Kitses felt that "in THE MAN FROM LARAMIE Mann and his scriptwriter Philip Yordan [were] clearly attempting a loose reworking of OEDIPUS REX within the genre."[109] There is no such suggestion in the novel and in the film, if Hansbro has a motive, he is fearful Alec will discover the rifles and fire him, figuring he will suspect him, and not Lockhart, of having murdered Dave. What is there in this that could possibly smack of patricide?—to say nothing of Alec's being a widower! "Mann's tendency," Kitses continued, "was always to work towards the heightened drama of family relationships: he bemoaned the lack of courage in producers who would not allow him to make Lockhart still another son to Waggoman . . . . "[110] Could a viewer, already stretching credulity to accept Alec as a man capable of building up a cattle empire despite such evident lack of judgment as revealed in his obliviousness to Dave and Hansbro (and Kate, although more so in the novel than in the film) accept such a sudden alteration in his character? If indeed Mann was prevented from scripting in this alternative ending, I doubt if lack of courage aptly describes the producers' objections.

Mann was scheduled to direct NIGHT PASSAGE (Universal, 1957), based on a novel by Norman A. Fox and starring James Stewart, but he had a falling out with Stewart, and James Neilson directed the film instead. Thus Mann's last collaboration with Stewart remains THE MAN FROM LARAMIE. Regarding the five films in terms of their shared patterns, Indians, when present, are a savage menace but are never characterized; heroines have almost no function and contribute virtually nothing to the story. I disagree with Kitses that Mann's heroes join the community only after "being literally *beaten* into line. . . ."[111] The ending of WINCHESTER 73 is too ambiguous for a viewer to presume this. THE NAKED SPUR ends with Stewart riding off alone with Janet Leigh. In BEND OF THE RIVER, the hero does join the community; in THE FAR COUNTRY, he may stay in Dawson, but one cannot be sure and, historically, what happened once the gold rush was over is not addressed. In THE MAN FROM LARAMIE, the hero rides off alone, apparently to resume his army career. In none of the endings of these films, however, is there anything akin to what Kitses meant by "the hero not so much integrated as exhausted by his compulsion to pursue an unnatural course, not educated so much as beaten by a struggle against profound forces that operate as a kind of immutable law." What can be said in Mann's behalf is that he was uncommonly versatile in his choice of locations and settings.

Mann loved, he told CAHIERS DU CINÉMA (June, 1966), "la montagne et les torrents, les sous-bois et les cimes neigeuses" [the mountain and the torrents, the lower forest and the snow-covered summits . . .].[112] WINCHESTER 73 was set in Arizona and filmed, in part, at Old Tucson. BEND OF THE RIVER was set in Oregon, the THE NAKED SPUR in lower forests, near torrents and summits, THE FAR COUNTRY in Washington, Alaska, and Canada, and THE MAN FROM LARAMIE in New Mexico. Unlike either Ford's obsessive use of Monument Valley or Hawks' of Old Tucson, Mann's variety of locations is as challenging as his plot ingredients: Indian fighting and outlaws, wagon trains and riverboats, gold rushes and mining communities, bounty hunting and ranch life.

In THE TIN STAR (Paramount, 1957) Henry Fonda was cast as a worldly wise, somewhat sad, extremely capable bounty hunter, passing on his knowledge and his skill to a younger man, played by Anthony Perkins. If Kitses was right and Mann did want to develop a relationship between Alec Waggoman and Will Lockhart at the conclusion of THE MAN FROM LARAMIE, this film would appear to have evolved from that desire. But Kitses went further. "With Alec Waggoman and Lockhart it is a case of age, arrogance, and power being checked by moral doubt and a drive for the truth inspired by the younger man. But with THE TIN STAR, the pattern is more complex, the idealism of youth stiffened by the wisdom and power that is passed on by Hickman [Fonda], who in turn is forced to face himself through the example of Owens [Perkins]. In both cases the younger man fills out the psychological structure, functioning both as something of a son to the older and as an embodiment of his youth, and in this way triggering action and change."[113]

The two Westerns directed by Mann which, in my view, present his various themes with the greatest coherence are THE LAST FRONTIER and MAN OF THE WEST. The triad hero of THE LAST FRONTIER, perceived as a delicately balanced unity at the beginning of the film, separates in the course of the plot and—had Mann been able in this case to conclude it as he wanted—would be seen to fragment completely by the end. James Whitmore's Gus represents, if not wisdom and power, then at least common sense and reality. Victor Mature's Jed represents the middle ground between Gus and the wild, free life represented by Pat Hogan's Mungo. After they are robbed of their guns, horses, and furs by Red Cloud and his braves who do not want them ever to return because the blue coats have come, they arrive at the fort. Guy Madison, cast as Captain Riordan, hires them as scouts. Jed wishes to become a soldier so he can wear a uniform, but Riordan tells him that he just is not civilized and it is not possible. Jed wants to know what being civilized means. Riordan tells him that being civilized is the opposite of being savage, being civilized is being part of a family. Here, again, Mann's ignorance of Native Americans and the premium Native American culture placed on family relationships caused him to set up a false dichotomy.

The plot now expands to include the John Ford/James Warner Bellah racial nightmare in addition to the Custer legend, so much a part of Ford's FORT APACHE (RKO, 1948). Robert Preston, cast as Colonel Marston, assumes command at the post. He is ambitious and is fired by what he feels was the unfairness of the War Department in punishing him for losing 1,500 men in a reckless attempt during the Civil War to seize enemy artillery. Red Cloud's Sioux are in the process of making an alliance with the Assiniboines so as to form a united front against the whites. Jed is attracted to Colonel Marston's wife, played by Anne Bancroft. "I care for you," he tells her. "I need you." "How can I help you?" she asks. Perhaps the answer is to be found when they have sexual intercourse while everyone at the fort is distracted by the antics of a young Sioux brave.

In a later conversation, Riordan, referring to Marston, admits, "We have animals among us, too." "Why don't you kill him?" Jed asks. "Because then we'd be animals, too," Riordan responds. It is Marston's intention to lead a concerted attack against the allied Indians. Out on reconnaissance with Jed, Marston falls into a bear trap. Jed refuses to help him unless Marston agrees to give up his notion of attacking the Indians. When Marston rejects Jed's terms, Jed abandons him. He feels he must do it, for Riordan, for the white men at the fort, for Bancroft. When he sees their unanimous disapproval, he regrets himself, goes back and rescues Marston. "She wouldn't let you do it, would she?" Marston taunts him. Once back at the fort, Marston tries to frame Jed, only for Jed to escape over the stockade wall. Mungo tells Jed that he is heading back into the wilderness, going back to the mountains. He tells Jed that Jed cannot join him, that Jed no longer belongs there. Presumably this conversation is intended to be pivotal, to indicate that Jed has gone so far toward civilizing himself by saving Marston's life that he is no longer suited to a "savage" existence. The white men, as the Indians, kill; but the white men, as far as this film is concerned, kill so as to stop killing in the future. Such a crazy kind of logic is really no logic at all, but it has passed for logic in the Western world since the days when the Israelites found the Promised Land and also found it occupied by other people who did not "belong" there, or since the days when Julius Caesar began his COMMENTARII with the words "Gallia est omnes divisa en partes tres" [Gaul is divided into three parts . . .] without consulting the Gauls about the division;[114] and so Mann is scarcely alone at fault. Employing Gus as scout, Marston leads his command against Red Cloud and he and the Cavalry are wiped out. After Gus dies in Jed's arms, Jed, who was watching the battle prior to this from the sidelines, rushes into the fray and gets the Infantry to retreat.

"The story of this trapper who cannot see civilization but for the uniform, while obviously suited neither to one nor the other . . . ," Philip Yordan, who worked on the screenplay, told CAHIERS DU CINÉMA (February, 1962), "it is one of the most beautiful subjects for a Western . . . . He was supposed to die at the end, but Columbia imposed on the final treatments what constitutes a stupid *happy ending*. It was a very bitter subject because one was attacking the savage as well as the civilization that succeeded in producing hateful people such as the colonel . . . . "[115]

As false as I find Mann's dichotomy, I will concede Yordan's view, and the film would be better than it is were Jed to die. What happens instead is that he is not disillusioned with the Anne Bancroft character, nor she with him—it always annoys me when I see a female character falling for the male line: "I need you"; she will stay on at the fort, looks dreamily at Jed, and Jed is duly proud of having been promoted to the rank of sergeant.

Even more explicitly than THE LAST FRONTIER, MAN OF THE WEST confronts the problem of human evil. Here it is dynamically evoked by Dock Tobin, played by Lee J. Cobb, a malevolent *paterfamilias*—in contrast to the good one played by Jay C. Flippen in BEND OF THE RIVER. Gary Cooper, cast as Link Jones, was once an associate of Dock's, but he escaped from his influence and wants to forget all about that part of his past. This proves impossible. Julie London, cast as Billie Ellis, functions as a sexual component to the violence which Jones' *rencontre* with Dock and his gang unleashes. Jones, who would avoid violence, is forced to become more violent even than those he opposes. It is in the course of the Passion, in which the necessity if not also the efficacy of the hero's violence is being demonstrated, that Billie is brutally raped. I have already mentioned the reason which caused Mann to end this film with Link and Billie, although survivors, doomed to pursue their own separate ways. As a heroine, surely, she is even more questionable than Shelley Winters in WINCHESTER 73 or the Anne Bancroft character in THE LAST FRONTIER or the Ruth Roman character in THE FAR COUNTRY. That old and deep-seated prejudice ostracizing a woman who has been raped still wins the day in MAN OF THE WEST and making the Link Jones character a married man was only a shameless evasion.

Mann's weakest Westerns are those which were remakes. THE FURIES (Paramount, 1950), based on a novel by Niven Busch, is basically a rehash of the plot of Busch's DUEL IN THE SUN (1944). A passionately disturbed woman, played by Barbara Stanwyck, turns against the young step-mother her cattle baron father marries, throwing a scissors in her face. Banished from her father's ranch, she takes up with a worthless gambler who previously rejected her love and conceives an elaborate scheme of revenge. Mann's remake of CIMARRON stresses exciting action at the expense of character—just the opposite from Wesley Ruggles' superior CIMARRON (RKO, 1931)—and, while occasionally the use of studio exteriors unpleasantly destroys the illusion and distracts the viewer in films such as BEND OF THE RIVER, here studio exteriors are preponderant, totally incongruous with a plot which opens with a land rush and proposes to show the psychological and economic changes which the imposition of a complex social order wrought in the West. Where, the viewer wonders, are those torrents, those lower forests, those snow-covered summits?

It is a valid question, I feel, because of the emphasis Mann traditionally gave to his locations, an emphasis he shared with Henry Hathaway. Also, like Hathaway, Mann was never confined in his themes, or, if you will, his *idées fixes*, the way Ford was, or even Hawks and Boetticher. The effort he made in the plots of his films to depict violence in a realistic way and to probe both its moral and psychological character is far more searching, and therefore more satisfying, than anything attempted by Sam Peckinpah. Mann said it best himself, about the best parts of his Western films: "A Western is a wonderful thing to do because you take a group of actors who have acted on the stage or who have acted in rooms and now you take them out into the elements, and you throw them against the elements and the elements make them much greater as actors than if they were in a room. Because they have to shout above the winds, they have to suffer, they have to climb mountains . . . . '' That, in a very fundamental way, is a distillation of the very essence of the American frontier experience, and Mann tried, perhaps harder than most, to capture it in film.

7

Budd Boetticher

Although he began his career with ONE MYSTERIOUS NIGHT (Columbia, 1944), an entry in Columbia Pictures' Boston Blackie series starring Chester Morris, signing his name Oscar Boetticher, Jr., the first film he signed as Budd Boetticher was the BULLFIGHTER AND THE LADY (Republic, 1951). The latter was produced by John Wayne, and John Ford, then associated with Republic studios, assisted in cutting the film. That year also marked Boetticher's emergence as a director of Western films with THE CIMARRON KID (Universal, 1951). In it Audie Murphy was cast as Bill Doolin.

Pardoned from a prison term as the picture opens, Murphy is on a train held up by the Dalton gang and he becomes a suspect. A railroad detective who originally framed Murphy wants to frame him again. Murphy escapes, fighting his way out, and rides off to the Daltons' camp. Two simultaneous bank robberies, extremely well staged with good tension, are executed in Coffeyville, Kansas, during which the Daltons are shot down. Murphy as Doolin takes over what is left of the gang and leads them in a series of daring raids. Cimarron Rose, played by Yvette Dugay, is in love with Bitter Creek, played by James Best. "I always want to be with you," she tells Bitter Creek. When Bitter Creek is killed during a train robbery, Rose, one of the few Hawksian heroines in a Boetticher film, keeps her head. The idea is to substitute lead for gold at each check point on the way, but lawmen are always present in hiding, waiting to seize the Doolin gang. Rose tips off Doolin that his plan has been discovered by the law. Doolin makes it to Roy Roberts' ranch and there meets Beverly Tyler, cast as Carrie Roberts, with whom he is in love. Carrie takes away Doolin's gun while he is asleep and informs Marshal Sutton, played by Leif Erickson, of his presence. Doolin is arrested. Carrie tells Doolin that this is the best way for them. Roy Roberts promises Doolin that his ranch will be given to Carrie and to him as a wedding present once Doolin gets out of prison. "You're lucky, Carrie," Cimarron Rose says. "I wish Bitter Creek and I had had that same chance."

The structure of this film was to become commonplace in later Boetticher Westerns. It is circular. The hero begins where he ends up.

"I am not faithful to history when it risks making a mess of the film," Boetticher remarked in an interview published in CAHIERS DU CINÉMA (September, 1963). "For example, in THE CIMARRON KID I rewrote entirely the sequences of the attack of the James and Dalton brothers because it was impossible to film such things as they happened. When the film was shown to the inhabitants of a city where such a raid had taken place in the 1880s, seven old-timers came forward who had made it through the raid and escaped from the bullets. They declared that an attack such as I had shown was faithful to history. They would have been too young or would have hidden themselves during the fray. Right off the city awarded me a medal for having so faithfully respected the historical truth. At that point I wanted to say that the cinema must remain before all else a diversion and frequently it has a tendency to be no more than that. It tends rather to arrange historical reality and produce a good film, one that takes hold of the moment, rather than scrupulously to respect history and make a boring and tiresome film as so many one sees today." [116]

Boetticher was wrong about the James brothers; they are not in the film. But the statement is certainly accurate when it comes to the view of historical reality embodied in his Westerns: it is something to be "arranged" for the sake of drama. The war between the Anglo-Americans and the Seminoles is usually divided into the First Seminole War and the Second Seminole War. A viable argument might be made that it was just one continuous war, which, of course, it was; but for Boetticher, as for most filmmakers, it was "before all else a diversion." In SEMINOLE (Universal, 1953), Anthony Quinn was cast as Osceola, the Seminole leader, and, leading the Anglo-American forces, Richard Carlson as Major Degan and Rock Hudson as Lieutenant Caldwell. "Killing Indians in the swamps is no different than killing Indians in the forest," Carlson comments, "and I'm an expert at killing them." While campaigning in the swamps, a man and a cannon sink in quicksand. The major wants the cannon saved. The lieutenant saves the man instead. As far as the major is concerned, this is only another act of insubordination in a series of such acts. Under a flag of truce, the major tricks Osceola and he is taken prisoner. Concurrently Hudson is placed under military arrest and sentenced to be shot. The heroine, played by Barbara Hale, with the help of the Seminoles saves Hudson. Hugh O'Brian, as Kajeck, becomes the new chief of the Seminoles, after Quinn dies. "He loved all people," Barbara Hale sums up Osceola. "That's what made him great."

The ideology of the film is such that the viewer is led to believe that the cruelty and injustice of the war against the Seminoles was largely the result of a fanatical, Indian-hating officer rather than official American governmental policy. In the words of Thomas Jefferson in 1807, "in war, they will kill some of us; we shall destroy all of them." [117] Osceola's obvious nobility in loving everyone and his greatness, in the film, bring him only death in a wretched prison. Nothing is shown the viewer to explain how the Seminoles came to be occupying the Florida swamps to begin with, nor is it ever very clear why the war is being fought.

It was also in his CAHIERS DU CINÉMA interview that Boetticher remarked that "what is important is what the heroine provokes, or rather what she represents. She is the one, or rather the love or fear she inspires in the hero, or else the concern he feels for her, who makes him act the way he does. In herself the woman has not the slightest importance."[118] To an extent, I suppose, this was already true as early as THE CIMARRON KID, but it became a firmly fixed *modus vivendi* by the time Boetticher directed WINGS OF THE HAWK (Universal, 1953), the Western which directly preceded his most notable achievement, the series with Randolph Scott which began with SEVEN MEN FROM NOW (Warner's, 1956). The scene is 1911 in Mexico. Van Heflin, cast as "Irish" Gallagher, opens the film by narrating how he and his partner were mining during the Mexican revolution. The Mexican militia tries to seize the mine and Heflin fights it out with Colonel Ruiz, played by George Dolen. Heflin's partner is killed, but Heflin escapes, the militia giving pursuit. The militia is wiped out by a group of "insurrectiones" (sic) led by Julia Adams costumed in tight pants, sombrero, and bandoliers. The reason, she tells Heflin, that she has become an insurrectionist, rather than grabbing a sewing bag, is because there are not enough real men left. It is not too long, however, before Adams realizes that Heflin is indeed a real man; and, after they are captured and put in jail, the two of them kiss. In a particularly well-photographed sequence, a gun is lowered into Heflin's cell that casts a shadow against a wall which alarms a guard. The savagery of Colonel Ruiz, who has become the provincial governor, produces a considerable number of casualties. Heflin throws in his lot with the insurrectionists and using explosives helps decimate Ruiz' troops. Adams' sister, Elena, played by Abbe Lane, is in love with Ruiz, but she comes up empty handed when Ruiz is shot down trying to make a getaway with her.

In HORIZONS WEST, Jim Kitses, contrasting Boetticher's female characters with those of Hawks, observed that "if Boetticher's women do not have to become men to be taken seriously (as Hawks' must), they remain somewhat on the margins, their shifting *persona* reflecting the drives of hero and villain."[119] I cannot agree with this, either as it pertains to Boetticher's Westerns prior to the Scott series, or to the Scott series itself. Yvette Dugay is a far more attractive character in THE CIMARRON KID, playing Cimarron Rose, than is the Carrie Roberts character who is ostensibly the heroine. And this is still more the case in WINGS OF THE HAWK where Julia Adams quite definitely is in the role of a Hawksian woman—doing far better at it, incidentally, than most of the heroines in Hawks' Western films. What being in love with Carrie Roberts gets Bill Doolin is another jail stretch, albeit with the promise of a ranch once he gets out. This is anti-historical in terms of what actually happened to Doolin—he was shotgunned to death by a posse of Oklahomans in 1896—but it serves to reinforce traditional middle-class American values as they were then conceived. Whatever her last lines, the Cimarron Rose character, with her willingness to ride with the Doolin gang and share their outlaw life-style, is actually an anticipation of the Raquel character played by Julia Adams in WINGS OF THE HAWK. As Western heroines, these characters constitute nearly a total fulfillment of the Hawksian prescription.

Moreover, what Boetticher himself stated with regard to the heroine as *primum mobile*, a prime mover behind all the action and behavior of the hero, is an exact description of Adams' role and her effect on the Van Heflin character. She literally causes him to change from a cynical, avaricious miner intent on minding his own business to an astonishingly capable revolutionist. Abbe Lane, cast as Adams' sister, is more or less a trope for the Carrie Roberts character; only here the values are reversed: conventional marital life within the Establishment proves both unattainable and reprehensible.

It is in the Scott series that the Hawksian heroine vanishes completely. The heroines in this series still function as *prima mobilia*, but they have undergone a change in status: in themselves they are not of "the least importance." Kitses was far more accurate when he wrote that in the Scott series "marriages are pathetic, shattered by death, betrayed, or weak . . . . ." [120] To which might be added Charles Silver's observation in THE WESTERN FILM that frequently the Scott character "passes judgment on women for being satisfied with weak men whom he deems unworthy of them." [121]

André Bazin hailed SEVEN MEN FROM NOW as an "exemplary Western" when it first appeared and Jean-Louis Rieupeyrout seconded him when he wrote about the film in LA GRANDE AVENTURE DU WESTERN. He incorporated into his remarks a quotation from Boetticher's CAHIERS DU CINÉMA interview. "If one takes . . . the vigorous and engaging SEVEN MEN FROM NOW, a small masterpiece representative of the cream of a 'B' series without ambage, the know-how of Boetticher emerges in a clear light. Supported by a scenario by Burt Kennedy, prime testimony of the success of this film, this Western without pretensions, is how it constitutes in effect a composite ideal of the genre: characters sparing in effusions but master of their actions down to the most decisive ('Even if it isn't a question of revenge, my characters, men or women, are always decided about the way in which they are going to behave. They have chosen how they will proceed.'), an account of concentrated dynamicism that erupts brutally in successive explosions, a remarkably 'significant' utilization of the natural setting." [122]

I accept without equivocation Boetticher's statement but not Rieupeyrout's effort at extension. The characters in the Scott series are indeed masters of their behavior. What they are not masters of, what they have no control over at all, are external factors, and these external factors often cause them to respond in terms of certain kinds of actions. The whole time they are responding, they behave according to the characters they have assumed, the *personae* which are theirs, and this gives an element of ritual to their interaction. But they are masters only of their *personae*, not of their circumstances. I am reminded of Epictetus' Entry 17 in THE MANUAL: "Remember that you are an actor in a play of such a kind as the author may choose; if short, of a short one; if long, of a long one. If he wishes you to act the part of a poor man, see that you act the part naturally; if the part of a lame man, of a magistrate, of a private person, do the same. For this is your duty: to act well the part that is given to you; but to select the part, belongs to another." [123] Scott says it all in DECISION AT SUNDOWN (Columbia, 1957): "Where I come from a man doesn't celebrate when he acts the way a man is supposed to."

In their book, THE DIRECTOR'S EVENT (1970), Eric Sherman and Martin Rubin, drawing a parallel between Boetticher's view of the Western and his fascination with bullfighting, noted that "Boetticher's style establishes the same delicate balance between ritual, terror, and beauty. His heroes . . . are involved in an unending quest for honor, which once undertaken cannot be abandoned. The rituals of the *corrida* are a metaphor for the moral code in all of Boetticher's films." [124]

In SEVEN MEN FROM NOW, the Scott character tracks the men who held up a Wells, Fargo station and killed his wife. In the course of his search, the Scott character encounters an Eastern couple, the Greers played by Walter Reed and Gail Russell, and they are joined by two outlaws, played by Lee Marvin, the obvious leader, and Donald Barry. Greer is secretly transporting the stolen gold taken from the Wells, Fargo station. Confronted by the Scott character's moral fortitude, he regrets his participation, stands up to Marvin, and is killed. Indians are used merely for dramatic purposes, that is, to stage an attack, and the film concludes after the Scott character guns down Lee Marvin. Burt Kennedy worked on the screenplay for SEVEN MEN FROM NOW as he did for the next film in the series, THE TALL T (Columbia, 1957). In the latter, after losing his horse in a bet with his former employer that he can ride a seed bull, the Scott character hitches a ride on a stagecoach chartered by Willard Mims and his wealthy heiress wife, played respectively by John Hubbard and Maureen O'Sullivan. Richard Boone, Henry Silva, and Skip Homeier, cast as outlaws, hold up the stage and kill the driver, as they have the station master and his small son. Mims proposes a ransom and the Scott character and Maureen O'Sullivan are kept alive while the outlaws wait for the ransom money to arrive. Playing on their mutual suspicions, the Scott character undermines Boone's two cronies and finally, after killing them, confronts Boone. The Scott character would let Boone ride off, but Boone has done too much to get the ransom money and, as Lee Marvin before him, dies in a shoot-out.

"I felt that Boone really loved Randy in the picture, to the point of being terribly attracted to him physically," Boetticher told Sherman and Rubin in the interview for THE DIRECTOR'S EVENT. "He would have liked to have been Randy. There's no reason that a man can't love another man. It doesn't have to be a homosexual thing. I think only weak people are afraid of that. If you have a lot of balls, you can say whatever you want." The authors quoted a line given to the villain played by Claude Akins in COMANCHE STATION (Columbia, 1960), the last entry in the series: "I've come too far to turn back now." "That was more or less the same ending that we used with Marvin in SEVEN MEN FROM NOW, and with Boone in THE TALL T. It had to happen. You can't back away from a situation like that . . . . All of my villains have definite ideas about what they want to do. They may realize halfway through their association with Scott that they're wrong, but by then they're too far committed. They're past the point of no return. That's why, morally, Boone had to come back, maybe knowing that he was going to die." [125]

"In every one of the Scott pictures," Boetticher added, "I felt that I could have traded Randy's part with the villain's." [126] It might take some stretching for this to be applied to *all* of the Scott pictures equally, but it is certainly true for THE TALL T. The Scott character is living alone on a small spread where he cannot afford to hire help. "I'm alone," he tells Mrs. Mims when they have been taken prisoner. When the Scott character and Boone talk soon after this interchange, Boone tells Scott he should not be alone. He confides that he's sick of his two sidekicks; he wants his own place. "A man should have something that is his own, something that belongs to him." After her husband is shot by Henry Silva, Mrs. Mims confesses to Scott that she knew he had married her only for her money, but that it did not matter, because she was lonely. "You can't always wait for something to happen," Scott tells her. "Sometimes you have to up and take it." After which he kisses her, but the viewer has the distinct impression that, no less than Mims or Boone and his sidekicks, Scott sees Mrs. Mims' money and her loneliness as his main chance. "Some things a man can't ride around," Scott tells Mrs. Mims as he goes about cleaning up the villains. At the end, he puts his arm around the heroine and utters the banality, "Come on. It's going to be a nice day."

"Boetticher's West," Jim Kitses wrote, "is quite simply *the world*, a philosophical ground over which his pilgrims move to be confronted with existential choices wholly abstracted from social contexts." [127] This sounds good, but I am not sure how true it is. Unquestionably, in the Scott series Boetticher was using the Western as a genre to probe moral issues and to define his view of how a man is supposed to live; but the choices his characters make are not "wholly abstracted from social contexts." The context is quite definite in THE TALL T. Mrs. Mims is the total victim. Her father neglected her because he had wanted a son; her husband married her for her money; Boone and his henchmen take her captive for ransom; Scott sees her as a way out of poverty—he lost his best horse and his ranch is anything but prosperous. The social *and economic* context is always in the foreground.

All of the films in the Scott series begin *in medias res*. Boetticher dispensed with the beginnings of his stories in order to concentrate on the middles and the conclusions. As he told Sherman and Rubin, "because that's where the action is. I establish that something drastic has already happened at the beginning . . . ." [128] DECISION AT SUNDOWN, filmed next, also follows this same pattern, albeit with a difference: whereas the first two were largely "outdoor" pictures, Boetticher's camera capturing some striking cloud formations in THE TALL T, here he was concerned with what is termed a Town Western. All of the essential action is centered in town and the surrounding countryside is, in this case, irrelevant. The script was by Charles Lang, Jr., and, whether or not this was the reason, the characters are all verbose about life in general and their personal situations in particular.

The Scott character has been trailing Tate Kimbrough for three years because, while Scott was away during the Civil War, Kimbrough supposedly seduced Scott's wife and, after he deserted her, she committed suicide. Scott and his close friend, Sam, played by Noah Beery, Jr., arrive in town on Kimbrough's wedding day. Karen Steele, in the first of three heroine roles in Boetticher Westerns, is the bride. John Carroll, cast as Kimbrough, has been carrying on a long affair with a prostitute named Ruby, played by Valerie French, and French is helping him get dressed before he puts in his appearance at the church. Scott shows up just as the ceremony is about to begin and suggests the wedding be called off since by sundown Karen Steele will be a widow. Kimbrough "runs" the town and he sends his hired guns, led by the sheriff, played by Andrew Duggan, to kill the Scott character who, with Sam, holes up in the livery stable. "Why does this man want to kill you?" Steele asks Carroll. "Maybe because he doesn't understand about women as I do." When Steele goes to see Scott in the stable, she suggests: "So maybe you didn't lose anything that was really worthwhile." Scott slaps her mightily on the behind and ejects her forcibly out the door. When Sam tries to tell him the truth about Mary, his deceased wife—that she was promiscuous and that Kimbrough was not the only one—Scott will not let him finish, but throws him out, too. Sam is shot in the back by one of Kimbrough's hired guns and his last words to the town doctor, played by John Archer, are, "Mary was no good."

The men of the town are congregated at the hotel bar. "This is our town," Doc tells them. "We're responsible for everything good or bad that happens in it." Ray Teal, cast as a local rancher, says, "A man's got to draw the line somewhere if he wants to go on living with himself." He and his men disarm Andrew Duggan's gunmen, leaving Duggan alone to face Scott. Duggan is killed in a walk down, Scott cutting his hand badly. The bartender expresses the general sentiment that the Scott character "coming to town was all we needed." The town regains its sense of self-respect and Kimbrough is finished. He goes out to meet Scott in the street, only for Valerie French to shoot him, a casual wound but sufficient to call off the duel before one or the other of them is killed. Carroll and French leave town together. Doc and Karen Steele pair off. Scott is left alone, and rides out alone, having learned the truth about his wife and having lost a close friend.

In Boetticher's moral vision, as in John Ford's, a man of questionable character can be linked only with a prostitute, a virgin only with an embodiment of bourgeois values. Howard Hawks, impressed with the episode where Scott tries to fight a gun duel while wounded, reminiscent of James Stewart in similar circumstances in Anthony Mann's THE FAR COUNTRY (Universal, 1954), included a similar scene in EL DORADO (Paramount, 1967).

In Revelation 3: 16–17, St. John told the church of the Laodiceans: "I know thy works, that thou art neither cold nor hot: I would thou wert cold or hot. So then because thou art lukewarm, and neither cold nor hot, I will spue thee out of my mouth." "I hate insecurity," Boetticher told Sherman and Rubin in the interview with them. "Although I never thought of it before, I probably don't like those middle-of-the-road characters in my films, so I get rid of them. I get rid of all those friends around me, too. Boy, the minute I sense that—whap! Cut off their heads! And you can cut off a man's head, as I have done in Mexico, when you're cold and hungry and without a penny, if you still have some moral integrity." [129] Which explains, after its fashion, why Sam has to die in DECISION AT SUNDOWN: he argues for a middle-of-the-road position.

BUCHANAN RIDES ALONE (Columbia, 1958) is the weakest film in the Scott series, and WESTBOUND (Warner's, 1958), while it has some interesting ingredients, is almost equally disappointing. Lucien Ballard, Boetticher's cinematographer on BUCHANAN RIDES ALONE, in an interview with Leonard Maltin in BEHIND THE CAMERA (1971) commented that the story had originally been a Batjac property which Boetticher had "bought from John Wayne without his knowing it. And everyone thought it was great, Wayne said it was the best story he'd had in years and he was angry at having let it go. So one night I took a plane out to the location, and Budd handed me the script. I read it before I went to sleep, and the next morning I went to him and said, 'Have you read the script?' He said, 'No, I only read the original treatment and I assumed . . . ' I said, 'You'd better read it, it's the worst piece of crap I've seen in years.' He went away and read it, came back and said, 'You're right.' So he started rewriting it at night, during lunch breaks, all during shooting. He was still working on it during lunch hour on the last day we were shooting." [130]

The novel on which Charles Lang Jr.'s screenplay was based was THE NAME'S BUCHANAN (1956) by Jonas Ward, a house name under which William Ard wrote at the time. The first in a continuing series of novels currently being written by William O. Turner under the Jonas Ward name, Buchanan in THE NAME'S BUCHANAN is a hero typical of formulary Western fiction in the 'Fifties. "He was tall," we are told, " . . . with the look of a wild animal in his battered, unshaven face." [131] Buchanan's face was battered as a result of leaving the service of Mexican revolutionist, Luis Campos. Buchanan is carrying five thousand in gold for his service below the border. When he finds the raped body of Maria del Cuervo on the trail, he helps save her life. Boetticher, in the film, cut out any such scene, and the viewer only hears about the rape—which does not alter the fact that a woman causes all the trouble. Buchanan next rides across the border into Agrytown in Southern California. Ard drew a weak parallel between the Agrys who run Agrytown and Southern Californians, a parallel which Boetticher did not stress at all in his film. "By hell," Buchanan reflects about his money and the high price of everything in

Agrytown, "Campos couldn't steal it but these armed thieves in Agrytown will." [132] Juan del Cuervo, bent on revenge for his sister's rape, rides into town and guns down Roy Agry, the rapist. Buchanan interferes, is beaten up badly, and is thrown into jail with Juan. Simon Agry, Roy's father, is running for the U.S. Senate and is also the local judge. Don Pedro, Juan's father, intends to buy his son's freedom. " 'Senor Simon,' " he says, " 'we believe puts material things above all else.' " [133] The trial is so popular that Deputy Waldo Peek charges a dollar a head admission. Juan is sentenced to hang, but Buchanan is let off, Lew Agry, Simon's brother, and the sheriff taking all his gold and sending a couple of deputies along with Buchanan to murder him as soon as he is out of the county. " . . . What the hell was this to come home to," Buchanan reflects. "Were these who raped, bullied, and cheated, his fellow Americans, his brothers? It was hard to take, hard to have the dream shattered so completely." [134] This is the point where Boetticher cut away from the novel, in fact a little before this because such a sentiment would not fit his view of the Western milieu. Ard, on the other hand, softened the indictment by the end of the novel. " 'Yes,' " he had Don Pedro tell Buchanan, " 'I would certainly not want to judge all Americans by the acts of the Agrys,' " to which Buchanan replies, " 'Fair enough. And I won't measure out Mexicans by that—by Campos.' " [135] Insofar as Ard's novel could be taken as a parable, Agrytown falls into two camps, the greedy, power-driven Agrys and Simon Agry's right-hand man, Abe Carbo, and the faceless cowards who make up its citizens and permit the Agrys to flourish. For Boetticher, the parable was changed somewhat. In the novel, all the Agrys are killed and Abe Carbo with them; in the film, Abe Carbo inherits their town and, the viewer feels confident, will continue in their tradition. The Scott character rides off alone.

What ruins the film is the way the plot, usually so geometrically precise in a Boetticher film, becomes haphazard and then unravels completely. The Scott character, incredibly, leaves gang members so sloppily tied that they easily undo themselves, mount the horses he conveniently left behind, and overtake Juan and L.Q. Jones cast as the deputy who saved Scott's life when he was taken out of town to be murdered, killing Jones and recapturing Juan. Also, an impression which began with DECISION AT SUNDOWN is confirmed by this film: Boetticher was unable to handle crowd scenes. When many characters are present, as during the trial, he did not know what to do with them, in contrast to a director such as Anthony Mann who was a master at crowd scenes, and most of the time the streets of Agrytown are so devoid of people Simon Agry's concern about losing votes seems idiotic.

WESTBOUND is the most conventionally formulary of the Scott series. The Scott character, in the Union Army during the Civil War, is charged with setting up daily stage runs over 2,000 miles to bring gold East from California. On his way to Julesburg, Colorado Territory, Scott meets Red Miller, played by Michael Dante, who has lost an arm while in service. He keeps looking at a small portrait of Karen Steele, his wife, telling Scott at one point, "She's the prettiest girl in the whole Territory." to which Scott responds, " 'Cepting one, maybe," by which he means Virginia Mayo, the woman with whom he was in love before the war began and who, he learns upon his return, is now married to villain Clay Putnam, played by Andrew Duggan. Putnam and his gang, led by right-hand man Michael Pate, set out to frustrate Scott's efforts. Putnam is a Southern sympathizer, as is his wife, while Pate is merely out for himself. Scott sets up a swing station at the Millers' farm. The first time the viewer sees Karen Steele she is out in the field plowing, dressed in tight-fitting pants, her hair perfectly coiffed. In THE PROUD REBEL (Buena Vista, 1958) directed by Michael Curtiz, an Alan Ladd vehicle from the previous year, heroine Olivia de Havilland is shown out plowing the field in her long skirts. In Boetticher's film, the sexual fantasy concerning Karen Steele had to take precedence over verisimilitude.

Red Miller is called "half a man," and even comes to view himself that way—one of Boetticher's middle-of-the-road characters. When he is shot down, Scott remarks: "Nothing works for him. That shot was meant for me." His death, however, places Scott in the position of having to choose by the final reel one of the two heroines, a theme to which I return in the chapter on women. The idea of "America first" soon emerges when Scott is told by the townspeople that, while they, too, are sympathetic with the South, they are willing to back Scott against "Putnam and his kind." Mayo comes to the swing station to tell Scott that Michael Pate is a professional killer and that Scott should avoid him. Scott shows her the door. It is a dumb play all the way around, since this attempt only fires her husband's obsessive jealousy. When Pate and the gang kill a stage full of people, including a little girl, Putnam breaks with Pate, while Mayo, in turn, decides to leave Putnam over Pate and Putnam's jealousy. The town gathers around Scott and helps him shoot down Pate and the gang. Putnam rides in to help, but Pate fells him, Putnam's last words to Scott being a request that Scott take care of Mayo. Cut from this to Scott getting out of the stage in which Mayo is sitting, as they pull up at the swing station. Karen Steele is pleased to see Scott until she notices Mayo and then holds herself in suspense until it becomes evident that Mayo is going back East and Scott staying behind. Their romance will now have an opportunity to flower. It is, as I have said, a disappointing film, but at its worst it is competently directed, the characters are consistent, and the action, once the formulary conventions are accepted, is credible.

"Above all, avoid trickery, gimmicks," Boetticher said in an interview published in POSITIF (January, 1970). "In the Western you have to avoid these things up front. For a film director, it is an excellent education. After all, one must give precedence to character over action, not hesitating to improvise the function of the background scenery, to change the scenario, to love the landscapes and to understand them, getting rid of a cameraman afraid to take risks, knowing, with a few words or with some images, to stress a character or an action, not to be afraid of silence, not to abuse violence, not to hesitate to attack conventional myths, to have a serious sense of humor.''[136]

If Boetticher not only hesitated but failed to attack conventional myths in WESTBOUND, if his sense of humor in BUCHANAN RIDES ALONE was more inept than serious, in declaring RIDE LONESOME (Columbia, 1959) his best Western I am not saying that it is completely lacking in these faults, only that they are not quite so apparent and, in terms of the film's many excellences, irrelevant. "In general," Jim Kitses wrote, "the Boetticher hero as created by Scott can be said to possess (or be moving towards) a great serenity, the knowledge that we are fundamentally alone, that nothing lasts, that what matters in the face of all this is 'living the way a man should.' Especially in the late films the hero has had it all—love, position, security—and lost it all. This makes the figure oddly anachronistic, a man who continues to assert values out of an image of himself that has its roots in the past . . . . 'Some things a man can't ride around.' This stoicism arms the character with a grace that is an impenetrable armor against the temptations and threats of life. More typically, the hero survives through intelligent calculation and a capacity for self-control in facing danger.''[137]

The film opens to Scott riding through a defile of high rocks near Lone Pine. He captures Billy John, played by James Best, who shot a man in the back in Santa Cruz. Billy John has set a trap for him. He is surrounded by men armed with rifles who have their sights on Scott, but Scott values his life less than Billy values his: he will simply shoot Billy John. A similar situation develops later on in the picture when Billy John holds a Winchester pointed at Scott's abdomen and Scott does not flinch. It is, as Charles Silver wrote in THE WESTERN FILM, Scott's "inherent irony which makes his characters more complex" than is usually the case in Western films, and this becomes especially apparent in RIDE LONESOME.[138]

As the story develops, Boetticher's exteriors are lyrical, notable for the use of natural light. Yet, precisely when the spaces are the most expansive, as in riding across a flat desert, the atmosphere and tension compress the emotions to claustrophobia. Scott brings Billy John to a stage swing station where he encounters Pernell Roberts and James Coburn, two men with the reputation of being outlaws, and Karen Steele, wife of the station manager. Her character has no first name and she is referred to as Mrs. Lane throughout the film. A stage comes rolling in, the driver and passengers dead. Billy John's men have gone to get his brother, Frank. The Mescaleros are on the warpath. Death and danger appear to be encompassing.

In a dialogue interchange, Coburn asks Roberts why the Indians are on the warpath. "We're white," Roberts tells him. "That's enough." He then goes on to tell Coburn a story about a married couple who seemed happy until one day the wife up and shot her husband. The parallel is obvious: women and Indians are alike; they cannot be trusted. Roberts and Coburn want Billy John because the territory has offered amnesty to anyone who captures him. It will mean a new life for them. But all whites are drawn together, no matter what their cross-purposes, by the unity of racial loyalty, justified by attributing racism to the Mescaleros.

That night, commenting on Steele's absent husband, Scott tells her, "He left you alone." "I can take care of myself," she replies. "If you were mine," Scott says, "you wouldn't have to." This dialogue reinforces the role assigned to a Boetticher heroine.

The next day, the Indians offer to trade a horse for Karen Steele. It is the horse Steele's husband was riding. She breaks into tears, an act which according to Burt Kennedy's screenplay shames the Mescaleros. When the five whites pull out the next day, the Indians track them, their shame insufficient to cool their lust. In an effective tracking shot, Scott and Roberts are talking and ride past Indians in the distance, waiting until they come fully into the shot before charging at them. They race to a deserted building and hold them off; even Karen Steele shoots one. "Sure beats all, don't it?" Roberts remarks, surveying the dead Indians. "What a man'll put himself through to get a woman."

Karen Steele is costumed in a very close-fitting riding skirt and an uplift brassière, the camera invariably positioned so as to emphasize her profile. While she is standing before a mirror combing her hair, Roberts and Coburn watch her. "She's the kind that has a need, a deep lonely need only a man can get at," Roberts tells Coburn, explaining why, in his opinion, Steele will not long remain a widow. Roberts, who earlier remarked that Steele is just about the most perfect "all over woman" he has ever seen, now claims to Coburn that he knows what he knows about her from her eyes. Coburn looks again at her upraised breasts as she continues to comb her hair and Roberts has to remind him, "I said in her *eyes*," and the two break into an adolescent chuckle. However, the viewer is supposed to take all this seriously, since Roberts, as the Richard Boone character in THE TALL T, wants to settle down—"A man gets halfway, he ought to have something."—and he proposes marriage to Karen Steele; in fact, the film ends with the implication that she will marry him.

Roberts feels he has to kill Scott to get Billy John. "I've gone too far . . . ," he tells Coburn, "I can't turn back now. I just plain can't." When they arrive at a camp near a hanging tree, Roberts tells Steele, after proposing to her (i.e., he would be obliged to look after her), that he must kill Scott, "There are some things a man just can't ride around." Scott, later, confesses to Steele that Billy John's brother once hanged his wife, who looked much as Karen Steele, from the hanging tree. It becomes apparent that Scott is after the brother, Frank, played by Lee Van Cleef, and not Billy John at all. When Frank arrives, Scott shoots it out with him, Roberts and Coburn siding him against the rest of Frank's gang. After which, Scott turns over Billy John to Roberts, giving him his chance. But there is a warning. If Roberts does not go straight, Scott tells him, it will be Scott who will come after him. As the four ride off to Santa Cruz, Scott burns the hanging tree.

COMANCHE STATION (Columbia, 1960) is in many ways a remake of RIDE LONESOME and employs many of the same themes. The Scott character buys Mrs. Lowe, played by Nancy Gates, from Comanche Indians who wear their hair as Mohawks and who occupy the Lone Pine region in California where in actuality they never went—nor did the Mescaleros except in films such as RIDE LONESOME. Mrs. Lowe's husband has offered a reward for her return, substantial enough to attract Claude Akins and his two young, but equally crooked, sidekicks to help him kill Scott and, since the reward is the same whether alive or dead, to bring back her corpse. The sidekicks are played by Richard Rust and Skip Homeier. The idea about killing Mrs. Lowe is Akins' and, after Homeier dies in a skirmish with the Comanches, Rust balks at a double murder. Akins kills Rust and, in turn, is killed by the Scott character. Some ten years prior to this time Scott's wife was taken captive by the Comanches and, with every white woman whose freedom he secures, he keeps hoping someday to come upon his wife. In Boetticher's favor be it said, however unrealistic and stupid his images of Indians, unlike John Ford he did not show Indian captivity to reduce most whites to brutish insanity. Scott informs Mrs. Lowe that had she been his wife, he would have gone after her himself, rather than merely offering a reward. Hence, he is chagrined at the end when he learns that her husband is blind. He rides off alone into the distance.

In 1959 Boetticher divorced his wife of thirteen years and wed Debra Paget in a marriage that lasted all of three weeks; Paget's previous marriage in 1958 to a singer lasted ten weeks. Boetticher disappeared into Mexico where he spent seven years filming a documentary about a bullfighter, spent some time in prison, nearly starved to death, had frequent bouts of heavy drinking, had a lung removed surgically, and finally surfaced in 1968 with the film, titled ARRUZA, which remains in obscurity. He sold a screenplay he had written while in Mexico. It was filmed as TWO MULES FOR SISTER SARA (Universal, 1970) directed by Don Siegel and starring Clint Eastwood and Shirley MacLaine, the latter a prostitute disguised as a nun—thus the title for the film and a magnificent composite image of Boetticher's ideal of woman. He also directed and scripted A TIME FOR DYING (Etoile, 1971) filmed in Europe, produced by and starring Audie Murphy. He wrote an autobiography, WHEN, IN DISGRACE . . . , which seems not to have found a publisher, married Margo Jensen in 1969, and began to be acclaimed as a director of Westerns, particularly by the French. Yet I have the suspicion that Boetticher's autobiography would prove more interesting than any of his films.

The metaphor of life as a bullfight was an interesting innovation in Boetticher's Westerns; and, although the hero does eventually triumph and is always a hero, the victory is anticlimactic to the ritual of the struggle. Boetticher once remarked about his characters that ''if they get killed on the way—and most of them do—it is because their desire cannot be accomplished without a struggle."[139] While this framework could not have held up indefinitely without itself becoming mundane, indeed did not hold up when Boetticher tried to return to Western filmmaking after a hiatus of almost a decade, it does give his Westerns, especially those with Randolph Scott, a peculiar appeal and power. Many of his exterior compositions are as fine as those in a John Ford Western, although, as Ford, Boetticher tended to be too restrained in his use of outdoor locations. Only in COMANCHE STATION did he come close to approaching Anthony Mann's deep probing into the psychology of human evil and never did he achieve the comic tone to be found in Howard Hawks' Westerns. His use of the Justice/Revenge Theme allies his film work with that of Henry Hathaway, but Hathaway, less intent on ritual than either Ford or Boetticher, was always able to see more possibilities in human nature than they could. Equally to the point, because Boetticher's view of women was so limited, his Westerns remain chiefly a masculine entertainment, which is to say "masculine" as that term is defined in Boetticher's prescriptive view of life. Only rarely, when the precision of his structure combines with unusually intriguing characters and exceptional landscape compositions, as it does in RIDE LONESOME, did he approach true cinematic artistry.

8

Sam Peckinpah

I

In Peckinpah's early work there is a disturbingly primitive emotional force. Yet in his films from the late 'Seventies this quality has all but vanished from the versions assembled for release, although it was still somewhat in evidence in the film elements he showed me while the films were in production or post-production. In distinct contrast to Howard Hawks, and even more so than was the case with John Ford, Peckinpah has never been really articulate about his films. His personality, as opposed to some rational intention, is most often the driving force in his film work. Therefore, before coming to discuss specifically Peckinpah's Western films, it would perhaps be illuminating to make reference, at least in part, to a visit we had while Peckinpah was in Portoroz, Yugoslavia, filming CROSS OF IRON (Avco-Embassy, 1977).

Sam telephoned me from his villa shortly after we arrived at the Hotel Metropol, where the cast and crew were staying; and, when he heard that Vicki Piekarski, then my secretary, had accompanied me, he suggested lunch, sending a car for us. We met at an outdoor restaurant located on a cliff overlooking the sea. Sam was with Lucky, a native Serbian who was acting as his guide and interpreter. Dressed in blue jeans with a jean jacket, despite where he was, Sam claimed he was just an old, broken-down cowboy. It was sunny, but Sam, for once, was not wearing sunglasses.

Vicki handed him the packet of mail which had accumulated for him at the hotel. Sam began tearing open envelopes. There was a letter from one of his daughters—his four children, three daughters including Kristen who was in Yugoslavia with him, and one son, are all from his first marriage to Marie Selland—telling him how she was doing at school. She addressed him as "Dear Father."

"That's a nice letter," he said, putting it aside.

The next letter was from one of the many children he had adopted through a

Big Brother program. The third letter was from his Los Angeles attorney advising him that he was being sued for battery he allegedly committed when he got into a fistfight boarding a commercial flight to Hawaii.

"How long are you over here?" I asked.

"I'm not over here, Jon. I'm in exile." He squinted his gray eyes at me. "Have some wine. It's good Yugoslavian white wine."

"Mr. Sam is right," Lucky assured us.

"See," Sam said, holding out a hand that trembled with a quiet palsy, "if you drink to a certain point in your life, you don't get the shakes any more." He grinned.

"You're looking better than you did in the States."

"Yeah," Sam replied, "but I got a little gut now."

He patted his midriff. We had lunch and Sam ordered fish. He asked Lucky to keep the head and tail for the cat.

"You still have the cat?" I asked. He had had a cat as a pet when we had last seen him on the M-G-M lot in Culver City.

"Yeah," Sam said, "only it's a different cat. I find it good company. When we're done shooting here, Lucky, who by trade's a sailor—he quit the merchant service to work with us—is going to take me scuba diving all through the Adriatic. Then I would like to make a porn flick. I've always wanted to make a porn flick."

We had cognac. After several rounds, Sam suggested we go down to the seashore to the edit shack so we could watch rushes. He had the car brought around. On the way there we passed the garden patch Sam was using for a battlefield.

"James Coburn says this new picture is about the violence men commit on themselves," I said.

"That's right in part," Sam said. "This is Jim's third picture with me. CROSS OF IRON is about a group of German soldiers retreating from the Eastern front. They're finished and they're running, but they don't stop fighting. Coburn is the leader. You can see what a job Wolf Hartwig is doing financing this picture just by looking at that exterior." Hartwig, formerly the porno king of Munich, was making his debut as a producer of commercial films with CROSS OF IRON. "You've got to meet him while you're here. I can't tell you what it's been like: delays, halts in shooting, no rushes, no film sometimes. Wolf says it's all due to trouble at the border. He's a Prussian. He was on the Eastern front and has lead in his butt, so you know what direction he was going."

Sam cackled.

At the edit shack, the coffee was a day old, but we drank it anyway. Sam sat on an editor's stool and had rushes run. There were battle scenes and battle scenes.

"Ach, excuse me," a man said, standing in the doorway. He was of medium height, wearing a red shirt and red trousers, with a white belt, and he had a bullet-shaped head.

"This," said Sam, punching me in the shoulder and grinning, "is our producer, Wolf Hartwig."

Sam introduced me as Hartwig goose-stepped into the room.

"*Ja*, I know you," he said accusingly. "You're just like Pauline Kael."

"He's not like Pauline Kael," Sam corrected him. "He only writes about pictures after they're made, and he never reviews them."

"Ach, *ja*, an historian. I tell you I know him."

Wolf began pacing back and forth, his head pressed down against his chest, hands clenched behind him.

"Vell, I'm glad you're here. I don't vant you writing about dis picture unless I am included."

"Oh, he'll be sure to include you, Wolf, won't you?" Sam said, punching me again in the shoulder.

"Sure."

"*Ja*," Wolf said, standing and nodding his head.

"Hello, Sam," Veronique Vendell said from the doorway. She was dressed in a tight red sweater that clung to her ample breasts and matched her red stretch pants. She entered the room, smiling. In the picture her part was biting off Arthur Brauss' penis, which was among the sequences edited from the American release version in order to give CROSS OF IRON an "R" rating.

"This," Wolf introduced her to us, "iss my former secretary, then the star of my sex films, and now my vife."

She rubbed the flat of her hand against her mound of Venus and more teeth came into her smile. "Hello," she said to everyone in the room.

"Vell, now to get back," Wolf said, resuming his pacing, "I know dat Sam has probably toldt you of the difficulties ve'ff been haffing on dis picture."

"No difficulties, Wolf," Sam said, "just minor things like running out of film, or not getting paid. Another of the crew just quit."

"*Ja*, qvidt! Vell, I tell you Sam, anybody who vants to can qvidt, budt not you. *You* can't qvidt. I own you, Sam, until you finish dis picture. You and I are like brudders, like dis." Wolf wound his arms around himself and gave himself a tight squeeze. "You are my property, Sam. I own you." Wolf paused suddenly in his pacing and glared at me. "Und vot do you tink of dis picture so far?"

"I haven't seen enough of it to tell."

"*Ja*, vell I vill tell you von ting, it had better be very gudt. Do you know vhy? Because I got die great Sam Peckinpah to direct it for me. It had better be gudt. Do you hear dat, Sam? It had better be gudt!" Wolf started pacing again. "Ve haff a story to tell here, die story of how die German soldier feldt vhen die var vas lost. Dere haff been no pictures sympathetic to die Germans in die last var. Vell, dis vill be a first. A first!" He stopped to stare at me. "I haff to go now, budt I vant you to put in vot I haff said, exactly die vay I haff said it. Understand? Exactly!"

"Don't worry, Wolf," Sam said, "he will."

Hartwig said *Auf Wiederseh'n* all around and shook my hand, and then Sam's.

"I luff dis man," he said, holding onto Sam's hand and looking at me. "He'd better make a gudt picture, dat's all I got to say."

"I'll make your fucking picture, Wolf," Sam said.

Once he was gone, and Veronique with him, Sam clapped me on the back and recommended that we all go to the hotel for a drink. Again he sent for the car.

"I get this fucking Mercedes," Sam remarked as we came out of the edit shack, "but Wolf drives an American Cadillac. The streets are too narrow and there's a lot of places he can't go with it, but it's the only car he'll drive, just so everyone knows it's Wolf Hartwig driving through."

At the hotel bar, we were joined by most of the cast and crew who were congregating for dinner prior to ascending to the casino on the roof to gamble. Katie Haber, Sam's secretary since making STRAW DOGS (Cinerama, 1971), was among them and she came over to join us. Arthur Brauss, playing the Nazi party man assigned to the morale of Coburn's unit and whom Veronique does in, strolled up. Sam introduced him to Vicki.

"When are your bosoms going to grow?" he asked, leering and scratching his crotch. "Turn around and let me see your ass." Vicki turned around. "You've got a beautiful ass." He was scratching again. "I should apologize, but the uniforms Wolf got us to wear are full of crabs. We're all scratching."

"I'll bet it was the uniforms," Vicki quipped.

"Just one Polish joke," Sam said to Vicki. "Come on. I'm the only one here other than Katie who doesn't have trouble pronouncing your last name."

"Okay, but just one."

"Ah," Sam sighed with pleasure. "Do you know what a Polish air conditioner is like?"

"No," Vicki said.

"It's one Polack sitting on top of a high stool flapping his arms while four other Polacks turn him around and around, each holding onto a leg of the stool."

Arthur slapped the bar, laughing. Vicki smiled.

"All right, Jon, now I have one for you," Sam said, turning to me. "Did I ever show you how to masturbate a dinosaur?"

"No."

"Okay," Sam shouted down the bar, "clear the way."

He held his hands together and formed a large circle with his arms. He then ran, holding his arms in this position, to the very end of the long barroom and disappeared out the door. In a moment he returned, still running and holding his arms in a circle. He stopped where we were standing, puffing.

"That's how," he wheezed. He was grinning happily. "I thought you'd like it. Now let me have another of those Irish cigarettes you're smoking."

I gave him the box.

"Let me send you a carton when I get back to London," I said.

"You're on."

Sam ordered all of us triple whiskeys. He was dispensing with the polite drinking. For every drink we had, Sam had three.

"Did you guys finally get the interview finished?" Katie asked.

"I don't give any fucking interviews any more," Sam said.

"No," I told her.

"My God," she said, "how long is it going to take?"

"Probably the next twenty-five years," I replied.

Sam tipped his head back and thought for a moment.

"Yup," he said then, picking up his drink, "that's just about right."

The more he drank, the angrier he became. Finally he decided he wanted to work on the script. Katie said she had not typed the new changes yet, and Sam began cursing. He wanted to make more changes right away. He said he was very pissed off. He did not get into the elevator at once, but stood in front of it talking with us; Katie did, and she was crying.[140]

With the affection I have come to feel for this man over the years, it is not the easiest thing to write critically of his Western films, yet it must be done. As Budd Boetticher before him, Peckinpah set out to make Westerns that constituted a radical departure from the sentimental romanticism of John Ford while laying an extremely heavy emphasis on the atmosphere of violence. As Boetticher and Hathaway, he dealt with the theme of isolation, but for Peckinpah it became disorientation and, finally, rejection. His principal characters, increasingly, came not to belong to the time in which they found themselves in his films and, ultimately, can do nothing about it except die. Following the release of CONVOY (United Artists, 1978), Peckinpah went to Montana and, with the help of neighboring ranchers, built himself a log cabin. When he was in the Valley of Fire in Nevada filming THE BALLAD OF CABLE HOGUE (Warner's, 1970), Sam would occasionally at night go out and stay in Hogue's cabin. Less than a decade later that style of living had become a reality. After a five year hiatus, he returned to direct THE OSTERMAN WEEKEND (20th-Fox, 1983), but it was a confusing film and, in many ways, a caricature of what had once been his best work.

II

THE DEADLY COMPANIONS (Pathé-American, 1961) was Peckinpah's first theatrical Western after working some years on television Western series. It was produced by Charles B. FitzSimons, brother of the film's female star, Maureen O'Hara. It is a Justice/Revenge story with the hero, a Civil War veteran, played by Brian Keith, on the trail of a Confederate renegade who at Chickamauga seven years earlier tried to scalp him. Keith, whose character name is Yellow-leg, has a scar across his hairline and his gun arm is crippled. Very early in the picture, in trying to stop a bank robbery, Keith's trick arm throws off his aim and by accident he kills Maureen O'Hara's young boy. She is a prostitute and determines to journey across the desert to bury her son next to his father at

Siringo. Yellowleg saves Turk, played by Chill Wills, from a scrape caused by his cheating at cards, knowing that Turk is the man he has been hunting. Turk has a protegé, a gunslinger named Billy, played by Steve Cochrane. The three accompany O'Hara in her trek to Siringo, Billy lusting after O'Hara. The script called for Turk to kill Billy at the end and for Keith, giving up his *idée fixe* of revenge, to ride off into the sunset with the heroine-whore. Peckinpah wanted to change this, to let Yellowleg have the satisfaction of vengeance, at least by displacement, and kill Billy. FitzSimons vetoed the idea. Had he been able to film it this way, THE DEADLY COMPANIONS would have incorporated the same essential plot ingredients as THE BALLAD OF CABLE HOGUE, with the exception of still having the more conventional happy ending.

What the film does have in common with later Peckinpah Westerns is the notion of redemption as a consequence of a physical ordeal and trial by violence. During the trip across the desert, once Turk and Billy have dropped back from the buckboard driven by Kit, the character played by Maureen O'Hara, she and Yellowleg see a stagecoach on a high crest, silhouetted against the sky, careening at full speed. The stage comes closer into the frame and then tips over, so that the viewer sees that within it are Indians dressed in shawls and bonnets, being chased by other braves, a drunken parody imitating their recent act of brigandage. From the very beginning, the only use to which Peckinpah put Indians was to further his dramatic purposes. They are non-persons.

Yellowleg steals an Indian's horse. The brave sets out after him, the pursuit being a matter of personal honor. I suppose it is ironic that, in terms of the thematic concerns of the film, Yellowleg, the hunter, becomes Yellowleg the hunted; but, mostly, the episode is used to create a savage, lustful, primeval image. Hiding in a cave, Kit is terrified when the figure of the brave towers over her, and she shoots him down. This reinforces the ideology that, under the proper circumstances, women are as capable of violence as men, and that through violence Kit herself is somehow cleansed.

What peaks the lust directed toward Kit is her decision, midway through the film, to bathe in the nude. A female in a Western environment is viewed, according to the screenplay, as a distraction, a danger, and an object, if sufficiently attractive and physically well endowed, likely to arouse almost uncontrollable sexual heats. Peckinpah is not entirely to be blamed for this image, since he was prohibited from making any changes at all in the Kit character—O'Hara, once production began, refused so much as to speak to him save when it was absolutely necessary—but, notwithstanding, she serves as a prototype for all the subsequent heroine-whores who consistently populate Peckinpah's films, not just his Westerns, and who in their ways embody Peckinpah's ideal of woman: extraordinarily good-looking prostitutes who can perform domestic functions, come to prefer sexual relations with the hero (whom they genuinely enjoy servicing), but who are finally irrelevant in the life of the hero since the ritual ideology of the story prohibits a hero from ever developing a permanent relationship with anyone of the opposite sex. Peckinpah later disowned THE DEADLY

COMPANIONS as "unworkable." Just how little Peckinpah had to do with the screen story becomes more apparent when it is contrasted with the films that followed.

RIDE THE HIGH COUNTRY (M-G-M, 1962) cast Joel McCrea and Randolph Scott in the lead roles. It was the first picture Scott made after his series, produced by Harry Joe Brown and directed by Budd Boetticher, ending with COMANCHE STATION (Columbia, 1960). I have already quoted Boetticher saying, "In every one of the Scott pictures, I felt that I could have traded Randy's part with the villain." That is precisely what Peckinpah did in casting RIDE THE HIGH COUNTRY. In the script, as originally written, both McCrea and Scott are former lawmen who are hired to transport a gold shipment; the Scott character was to try and steal the shipment; and, at the end, he was to die. Peckinpah altered that. The Scott character still tries to steal the gold shipment, still fails, but in the shootout at the end it is the McCrea character who dies and, in dying, inspires the Scott character to transport the gold shipment the rest of the way, his honor restored by upholding the McCrea character's code of honesty. Had McCrea lived and Scott proved himself and regained his integrity, the plot would have been as dozens of others: reform and redemption through the example set by the hero. Had the Scott character proved himself and regained his integrity, but died in the process, it would have been a severe judgment: do not fall from grace even for a moment if you hope to be among the elect. Had it been a Boetticher plot, the Scott character would have been an outlaw who would decide in the course of the journey either to do the right thing, because of the hero's example, or the wrong thing and be killed by the hero. But this is a Peckinpah ending. He was not about to let Scott, at the end, ride off toward Mexico with the gold. He was not then sufficiently bitter and disillusioned. McCrea says at one point: "All I want is to enter my house justified." He does; and, as Peckinpah intended, so does the Scott character.

On their way to Coarsegold to pick up the shipment, McCrea, Scott, and Scott's protegé, Heck Longtree played by Ronald Starr, stop over at the Knudsen ranch. When a child, Peckinpah had been taught passages from the Bible by rote by his father. In casting R.G. Armstrong as Knudsen, Peckinpah initiated the prototype of the religious fanatic who runs as a thread through all of his Westerns. Peckinpah's marriage to Marie Selland—she was in her fourth pregnancy—had become a concentrated torment for him. He put his own frustrations into the mouth of Judge Tolliver, the Justice of the Peace in Coarsegold, played by Edgar Buchanan: "People change . . . the glory of a good marriage doesn't come in the beginning . . . it comes later on . . . it's hard work." Neither the judge's sermonizing nor Knudsen's quoting of the scriptures means a damned thing: what matters is personal loyalty to an ideal, the sense of one's own honor and integrity. They can even make a bad man good.

Mariette Hartley was cast as Knudsen's daughter. She wants to escape from her father's tyranny, run off to Coarsegold, and marry one of the Hammond brothers, Billy, played by James Drury. She joins up with McCrea, Scott, and

Starr. On the trail, she comments to McCrea: "My father says there's only right and wrong, good and evil, nothing in between. It isn't that simple, is it?" "No, it isn't," he replies. "It should be, but it isn't." Jean-Louis Rieupeyrout in LA GRANDE AVENTURE DU WESTERN, who saw in this film "a perfect and very personal synthesis of the moral instruction dispensed by the best part of the contemporary Western, films directed by Ford, Mann, and Aldrich," after quoting this dialogue between McCrea and Mariette Hartley, found he had to add: "Isn't that a response worthy of being applied to this contemporary Western so rich in intentions as in contents? We surrender to the evidence: the course that since 1950 we have traveled via successive stages of the genre has already marked the truth of these words . . . . "[141] As willing as I am to concede this point, I would have expected it to have been made with reference to THE WILD BUNCH (Warner's, 1969). What makes the statement particularly impressive is that Rieupeyrout made it in 1964, fully five years before THE WILD BUNCH and, therefore, saw RIDE THE HIGH COUNTRY continuing a tendency toward moral ambiguity which for him already had been discernible in Westerns for a long time.

Mariette Hartley and Heck fall in love. There is fulfilled romance, therefore, and restored honor, but the tone is sad. McCrea and Scott are old men; most of the gold mined in Coarsegold ends up at the brothel; the amount they are to transport is less than it might have been and, in a way, Scott is a fool, since, although his honor is saved, he will likely return to the artificial life of being a showman, pretending to be someone he is not, where he was when the viewer first met him. Peckinpah obstinately retained a fantasy. He was paid $15,000 to direct this film while its stars, whatever their roles, from investments they made with money earned playing heroes were multi-millionaires, Scott indeed being one of the ten wealthiest men in the State of California. There was an irony in this, a greater irony than Peckinpah's romantic vision permitted him to show.

If THE DEADLY COMPANIONS and RIDE THE HIGH COUNTRY share certain parallels and plot ingredients with a Boetticher/Scott Western, in terms of theme and structure much of MAJOR DUNDEE (Columbia, 1964) resembles Hawks' RED RIVER (United Artists, 1948), Ford's FORT APACHE (RKO, 1948), Mann's THE LAST FRONTIER (Columbia, 1955), and most of all Ford's version of a military filibuster into Mexico in pursuit of Apaches, RIO GRANDE (Republic, 1950). Charlton Heston, as Major Dundee, heads up a mission during the Civil War to pursue Charriba and his Apache renegades and to destroy them. Among his recruits are a group of Confederate prisoners, led by Richard Harris, who give their word to remain under Heston's command until the Apaches are taken. When O.W. Hadley, played by Warren Oates, deserts and is brought back, Heston orders him off his horse—"I don't want to have to look up to him."—which is what John Wayne as Tom Dunson says in RED RIVER when confronted by deserters who are brought back to face him. Dundee is filled with bitterness over being stationed at a distant Western outpost as a disciplinary measure and his inner sense of humiliation fires his ambition, just as similar experiences affect Henry Fonda's Colonel Thursday in FORT APACHE and Robert Preston's Colonel Marston in THE LAST FRONTIER. Unlike either, however, Major Dundee is ultimately successful, as is John Wayne's Lieutenant Colonel Kirby Yorke in RIO GRANDE.

Paul Seydor in an uncharacteristic moment in a book that is often an extraordinary exercise in the art of apologetics, PECKINPAH: THE WESTERN FILMS (1980), remarked that in filming MAJOR DUNDEE what got Peckinpah "into trouble [was] that too many elements and aspects of the materials, especially their historicity, resisted being developed in the way he wanted to develop them; and the one element that was needed to unify them all, the character of Dundee, both caused many of the problems and suffered most from them."[142] Black troopers were not used by the Union to fight Indians during the Civil War, but Peckinpah ignored this and included several under Dundee's command to raise a racial issue with the Confederates. Peckinpah's expeditionary force treats a village of Mexican peasants as callously as do the French and the Juaristas who are fighting between themselves for control of Mexico.

In the midst of his pursuit, in fact shortly after O.W. Hadley is executed, Dundee has sexual intercourse with Teresa Santiago, played by Senta Berger, a woman who prior to this time in the film was an object sought after by both Dundee and Harris' Captain Benjamin Tyreen. Following the episode, Dundee rides into Durango alone, despite Teresa's warning that the French are "*tres fort*" there, and goes on a long drunk. Peckinpah, as Ford and Hawks before him but even more emphatically, presents lovingly scenes of brawling and carousing, but they do nothing for the film story other than tediously illustrate Dundee's degradation. Just before Tyreen rescues him so the company can get back to business, Dundee does avail himself of an opportunity to express his contempt for women in a scene with Teresa and a prostitute with whom he has spent some time. In its way, it is an anticipation in fantasy of what Sam did while filming STRAW DOGS, when he arranged for his first wife, Marie, and his second wife, Begonia, to join him in London, only to take up with Joie Gould in front of them. A year later he married Gould in Juarez, Mexico.

"We still haven't isolated exactly what this picture's *about* . . . ." Charlton Heston recorded in his diary at the time, parts of which he reproduced in his autobiography, THE ACTOR'S LIFE (1978), "maybe because we can't agree, or just don't know . . . but we have to decide."[143] Nor did matters improve during production. Jerry Bresler, the producer on the picture, wanted thirty-five pages of the script cut, which Peckinpah, on location in Mexico, refused to do. When Columbia Pictures, which was financing the picture, sent a field man to Mexico to close down the set, Sam stripped his clothes off at the airport and sent him packing. Heston became so caught up in the project that he agreed to forgo his salary if the production were permitted to continue. Bresler and Columbia waited until the film was completed and then, systematically, in the editing process, managed to cut the requisite pages of script from the film before its release. As a consequence, Peckinpah's critics, such as Paul Seydor, or Jim Kitses in HORIZONS WEST, have undertaken to reconstruct the film as Peckinpah originally intended it, and to judge it on the basis of what it might have been rather than what it is, albeit even so avid a supporter as Seydor had to admit that "if the film in its present form suggests that Peckinpah may have been unprepared at the conceptual level to tackle a project of this size and scope when he did, it is nevertheless an impressive demonstration of his ability to handle, so relatively early in his career, the logistical side of a really *big* production." [144] Kitses, on the other hand, was far more positive: "The recurrent features of this form are familiar: an undermanned company (or settlement), while torn by internal conflicts, functions as the heroic unit in achieving the group objective, the defeat of the faceless hostile. If the form has been brilliantly inflected by both Ford and Mann . . . to make deeply ambiguous statements, nowhere has it been so relentlessly undermined as in Peckinpah's hands." [145]

I think Kitses was absolutely right. MAJOR DUNDEE's chief characteristic is to undermine the very idea of an heroic fighting unit. "What Sam had in mind was, I think, THE WILD BUNCH," Heston recorded in his autobiography, "and what the studio had in mind was a film that made a lot of money and was about cowboys and Indians." [146] Peckinpah himself once commented: "They cut it in DUNDEE. I did it in THE WILD BUNCH." [147] What was it Peckinpah tried to do in MAJOR DUNDEE? In Kitses' words, MAJOR DUNDEE depicts "the blood-bath from which America is born." [148] So much, really, for those who are inclined to feel that Peckinpah made THE WILD BUNCH in reference to the Vietnam War. That war may have helped the popularity of THE WILD BUNCH at the box office, but the underlying vision in the later film was already being worked through in MAJOR DUNDEE before the Vietnam War had become truly an issue of national dissension. Present also in DUNDEE was the Peckinpah stock company, R.G. Armstrong as a Bible-thumper, Warren Oates, Ben Johnson, L.Q. Jones, Slim Pickens, and, as the detached and worldly scout Samuel Potts, James Coburn. Michael Pate was cast as Sierra Charriba, the Apache leader, and, in the graphic spirit of Ford, the trap set by the ragtail whites and blacks under Dundee's campaign, once it is sprung, brings about a virtual blood-bath for the Indians. And there is another blood-bath when Dundee's troops try to cross the Rio Grande, hacking and butchering their way through a company of French lancers, a battle in which Tyreen loses his life but not his honor and in which Dundee supposedly both saves his life and regains his honor.

If there is a theme in all of this violence, it is not a new one, just one more vividly realized in terms of on-camera bloodshed: the old foolishness about redemption through violence; and this is also the principal theme of THE WILD BUNCH.

William R. Meyer in THE MAKING OF THE GREAT WESTERNS included a cast-breakdown chart for Howard Hawks' Westerns in which the chief roles are: hero, second lead, young man, female, old man, and villain. In RED

RIVER, for example, the hero role is played by John Wayne who also played the villain role (just as there is a duality in Heston's role in MAJOR DUNDEE). The second lead is played by John Ireland, a part cut down considerably during production because of Ireland's drinking on the set. The young man is played by Montgomery Clift, the female by Joanne Dru, and the old man by Walter Brennan. In RIO BRAVO, the hero is John Wayne, the second lead Dean Martin, the young man Ricky Nelson, the female Angie Dickinson, the old man Walter Brennan, and the villain John Russell. In MAJOR DUNDEE the second lead is Richard Harris, the young man Jim Hutton, the female Senta Berger, the villain Michael Pate, and Coburn's portrayal of Potts functions in the role of the old man who is, as in a Hawks film, at the center of the action, even a participant, while never himself an initiating force. In THE WILD BUNCH, the hero is William Holden cast as Pike, leader of the bunch; the second lead is split between Ernest Borgnine, as Dutch, who still rides with the bunch and Robert Ryan, as Thornton, who used to ride with the bunch but who has sold out to the Establishment and leads the pursuit; the female—an extremely limited role in any Peckinpah Western with the exception of THE BALLAD OF CABLE HOGUE—is played by Aurora Clavel: she is an unfaithful wife who had an affair with Pike and was killed by her cuckolded husband, an event which leaves Pike with a painful memory; the young man is Jaime Sanchez cast as Angel; the old man is Sykes, played by Edmond O'Brien; and the villain is Emilio Fernandez as Mapache, the leader of a band of cutthroat Mexican revolutionaries. Beyond such character similarities, whole scenes and many specific camera set-ups and shots in MAJOR DUNDEE adumbrate nearly identical scenes, camera set-ups, and shots in THE WILD BUNCH. What in particular is different—different from traditional Westerns with outlaws as heroes, from Westerns with similar themes such as THE PROFESSIONALS (Columbia, 1966) directed by Richard Brooks, and from MAJOR DUNDEE—is that the violence is so intensified that the ''heroes'' as well as the ''villains'' are consumed in the final bloody holocaust.

There are two Mexicos in THE WILD BUNCH, the Mexico of the *Mapachistas* and the *Méjico lindo* to be found in Angel's village which the bunch visits in the course of the film. The latter, Peckinpah felt at the time, was a viable alternative to the United States and in his PLAYBOY (August, 1972) interview commented: ''My second wife was Mexican . . . . Everything important in my life has been linked to Mexico in one way or another. The country has a special effect on me . . . . In Mexico it's all out front—the color, the life, the warmth. If a Mexican likes you, he'll touch you. It's direct. It's real . . . . Here in this country, everybody is worried about stopping the war and saving the forests and all that, but these same crusaders go out the door in the morning forgetting to kiss their wives and water the flowers. In Mexico they don't worry so goddamned much about saving the human race or about the wheeling and dealing that's poisoning us. In Mexico they don't forget to kiss each other and water the flowers.''[149] More of a disavowal of THE WILD BUNCH as an antiwar film would be difficult to imagine. Just as some Westerns—RUN OF THE ARROW (RKO, 1957) directed by Sam Fuller being a prime example—show Hollywood Indians living in a serenely beautiful paradise to which they return after all the blood and thunder of raiding and warring, so in THE WILD BUNCH Angel's village as *Méjico lindo* is a place so pastoral and calm that even the Gorch brothers, played by Warren Oates and Ben Johnson, dangerous rapists normally, help an attractive señorita draw water rather than attacking her. *Méjico lindo* is another Peckinpah fantasy. As a fantasy, it is pleasant; whereas, as a realistic statement, if it had been so intended (and I doubt that it was), it could only be considered patent nonsense.

"Scorpions struggle in a sea of killer ants, children gaily watching," Kitses wrote of the opening image of THE WILD BUNCH. " . . . While dramatically preparing us for the action to follow, the image also describes the relationship between Peckinpah's characters and the society through which they move. And we must not forget the children: above all, the moment introduces a network of detail that is crucial in the film, a structure in which innocence and cruelty, laughter and barbarity, idealism and blood-lust, exist side by side."[150] This is perhaps the most basic fantasy in Peckinpah's vision of the American West and of Western society in the broadest sense: individual criminals are supplanted by a society that is itself criminal.

When Tector Gorch (Ben Johnson) wants to get rid of old Sykes, Pike tells him: "You're not getting rid of anybody. We're going to stick together, just like it used to be. When you side a man you stay with him, and if you can't do that you're like some animal. You're finished. *We're* finished. All of us." Of course, Pike does not quite live up to this code, which is how Thornton ended up on the other side. He has fallen short of his ideal on more than one occasion, but, it is seen, the bloody carnage at the end holds the balm of salvation. Pike also abandoned Aurora long ago to her husband. Maybe it is for this reason that he is shot twice in the back, once by a whore—women are still not be trusted—and once by a child in military regalia, which is a reference back to the children at the opening of the picture, children who have a natural blood-lust which is channeled into either socially acceptable manifestations, the military, or manifestations which are the opposite, outlawry. Angel, too, learns about women when his village sweetheart gives herself sexually to Mapache because Mapache has money and power. Angel shoots her and this triggers his capture, torture, and, finally, execution by Mapache and the bunch's revenge. Women may not have a big role to play in this film, as in this vision of the world, but they cause most of the trouble, at least indirectly. As the Scott character in RIDE THE HIGH COUNTRY, however much Pike has failed to live up to his own code, the path to redemption opens for him; while, unlike the Garrett character in PAT GARRETT AND BILLY THE KID (M-G-M, 1973) who sells out to the Establishment and loses a part of himself, Thornton is "saved": at the end he joins Sykes and a band of revolutionaries.

The racial implications of THE WILD BUNCH are very clear. When the bunch succeeds in its theft of arms and ammunition coveted by the *Mapachistas*, their front man, Herrera, played by Alfonso Arau, meets them on the trail and, as Arthur G. Pettit put it in his essay "The Polluted Garden: Sam Peckinpah's Double Vision of Mexico" in SOUTHWEST REVIEW (Summer, 1977), "insisting that he brings love and affection from his generals, points to the *Mapachista* troops that line the horizon and declares: 'We are friends—*all* of us.' Pike, lighting a fuse and threatening to blow up the shipment, along with the bunch and Herrera, cuts the odds from six Americans and several hundred Mexicans to a personal face-down between himself and Herrera. Screwing his dark, toothy face into the comical grimace of a cakewalk darky, Herrera whines: 'Ple-ee-ze, cot de foose.' Pike cuts the fuse and the perspiring Herrera retreats in disgrace, showing once again that Mexican cowardice and treachery are no match for the straight-talking, fast-acting bunch." [151] The scenes of carnage and butchery when the bunch destroys Mapache and all his followers, so striking at the time because of the slow-motion photography of gushing blood and shattered bodies intercut into the choreography of slaughter, carry a clear message. The four remaining members of the bunch, even though it means their own death, show the power and glory of their race as they kill hundreds of the brown-skinned foe. "The Wild Bunch is America," Jim Kitses wrote. [152] The film is an exaltation of racism and this undoubtedly contributed to its popularity at the time of its release and many people today still rank it as one of their favorite Westerns. It is also an angry film, and killing becomes a form of final release, a romantic immolation in blood and bullets and torn flesh. Nor is it really possible to enjoy THE WILD BUNCH without to some extent accepting its racial ideology. The film represents the logical extension of white supremacy which has traditionally informed so much of the Western mythos. Peckinpah was not objectifying the phenomenon. By returning to a final image of the bunch riding out triumphantly from Angel's village, he was providing them and what they did with legendary status. His apologists argue that he was treating racial genocide with irony, his critics that he was indulging a fascist fantasy. My own view is that he was doing both, and more: he solved the problem, in Paul Seydor's words, of "winning an audience's assent to a vision in which violence is part of the very essence" [153] by getting audiences to watch his film.

ARIZONA NIGHTS (1907) by Stewart Edward White is a collection of short stories and short novels, framed as tales supposedly told around a campfire. In Chapter Two, "The Emigrants," Windy Bill tells the story about Texas Pete who "happened to discover a water hole right out in the plumb middle of the desert. He promptly annexed said water hole, digs her out, timbers her up, and lays for emigrants. He charged two bits a head—man or beast—and nobody got a mouthful till he paid up in hard coin." [154] After a number of instances where Texas Pete manages to gouge thirsty emigrants, Gentleman Tim, a cowpoke, takes a hand. He helps a woman and child take a drink, keeping the drop on Texas Pete, and then forces Texas Pete to dig a grave for the horse which he shot protecting his water hole. The grave is not on Texas Pete's property and, after leaving Texas Pete tied up all night, Gentleman Tim returns the next day with his fellow cowpunchers and they sink a well just adjacent to Texas Pete's claim. When they hit a spring, Gentleman Tim puts up a sign:

Public Water Hole. Water Free.

" 'What did Texas Pete do after that?' asked the Cattleman.
" 'Texas Pete?' chuckled Windy Bill. 'Well, he put in a heap of his spare time lettin' Tim alone.' "[155]

In THE BALLAD OF CABLE HOGUE, Jason Robards, Jr., as Hogue, is left out in the desert to die by his two partners, Taggart and Bowen, played respectively by L.Q. Jones and Strother Martin. Wandering around the desert, nearly dead, Hogue discovers water. He meets a preacher, played by David Warner, goes to town and files on his claim, tries without success to interest R.G. Armstrong, as the local manager of the stage line, in a half interest, borrows a hundred dollars from a friendly banker to make improvements, and sees Hildy, the town prostitute, played by Stella Stevens, toward whom he is strongly attracted. When Hildy is driven out of town by the "good people," she comes to stay with Hogue at his water hole before continuing on to San Francisco. Hogue wants revenge and Hildy wants to marry a rich man. Their idyll lasts three weeks before Warner returns, in flight from Gene Evans whose wife Warner has seduced. The next day, Hildy goes on her way, Hogue waiting for Taggart and Bowen to show up. The stage line has given him a contract to function as a way station and over the next few years he accumulates a fair amount of money. When Taggart and Bowen do show up, Hogue tricks them into digging what may well be their own grave, throws snakes in the hole after them, and plugs Taggart when Taggart refuses to strip down to his long-johns and to head out into the desert, instead going for his gun. Bowen begs for mercy and Hogue makes him a partner. Hildy then returns, in an automobile driven by a black chauffeur, and asks Hogue if he is ready to join her. Hogue is ready, but he is run over by the automobile, pushing Bowen aside when the car begins rolling down an incline. Warner returns in time to read an eulogy over him.

The picture has been called one of Peckinpah's gentler moments, and that it is, although no less a fantasy than THE WILD BUNCH. In a dozen ways, Peckinpah gave tribute to John Ford's West, in the love shown the American flag (recalling a similar moment in Ford's DRUMS ALONG THE MOHAWK [20th-Fox, 1939]), the yellow ribbon Susan O'Connell, the woman seduced by Warner, wears in her hair (reminiscent of Ford's SHE WORE A YELLOW RIBBON [RKO, 1949]), the attitude of the townspeople toward Hildy (harking back to the scene in STAGECOACH [United Artists, 1939] when Claire Trevor's Dallas is forced to leave town), and a reversal from nearly all Westerns, and especially Ford's, in showing a compassionate banker willing to take a chance and make a character loan. In a way, the wild bunch are social outcasts whom, in the spirit of Bret Harte and John Ford, we come to care about; but here the intimations are even stronger, with Hildy being an extremely attractive prostitute with a capacity for monogamous love:

Hildy: You've been awful nice to me, Hogue. Ain't it never bothered you none, what I am?

Hogue: No, it never bothered me. I enjoyed it. Well, what the hell are you? A human being. We try the best we can. We all got our own ways of living.

Hildy: And loving?

Hogue: Gets mighty lonesome without it.

The implication here is plain. Hildy is a prostitute because it is her way of living *and* loving. Hogue tells her he lives in the desert because in the desert he is someone. It would be different if he lived in town. "In town," he says, "I'm nothing. I've been that before. I don't like being nothing."

When Hildy leaves him, Hogue goes about his business. "He affects nonchalance," Paul Seydor wrote, "but Josh [David Warner] puts things in the right perspective once again by pointing out, 'Funny thing. It doesn't matter how much or how little you've wandered around, how many women you've been with. Every once in a while one of them cuts right through, right straight into you.' Confused, his armor pierced again, Cable asks, 'Well, what do you do about it?'; to which Josh answers, 'I suppose, maybe, when you die you get over it.' When Cable makes no move to follow Hildy, Josh realizes his work is finished. He has made his point, issued the warning for one last time, and indicated to Cable the way to salvation. And so he bids the desert rat farewell."[156]

One gets the impression from the foregoing that the "way to salvation" is for Hogue to abandon his hopes for revenge and go off with Hildy. If so, it is an even more absurdly romantic proposition than what Hogue does: remain in the desert until he revenges himself on Taggart and forgives Bowen. While I happen to be entertained by THE BALLAD OF CABLE HOGUE, unlike Seydor and other critics, I cannot take the premises of the film in earnest or discuss them as if they represented some profound perspective on life. I regard it instead as a male reverie. Hildy is an imaginative projection of Peckinpah's definition of a good woman. In the reality of the American West, while there was considerably less violence than Peckinpah would have us believe and while the way Stewart Edward White handled a plot of this kind was another kind of fantasy, greed and power were moving forces and Hogue would not have lasted very long at his water hole when a bullet could have vacated his tenancy. I tend to agree with Charles Silver in THE WESTERN FILM that "a problem with Peckinpah's later and lesser films arises from the uncertainty as to whether he is chronicling decadence or is, in fact, decadent. In THE WILD BUNCH he is able to fall back on the old Hawksian virtues of togetherness, men united by a cause. He freezes the last happy frame, as if to preserve a time when there were causes to unite behind. Peckinpah's THE BALLAD OF CABLE HOGUE . . .

contains a hopefulness of a kind, embodied in its lyrical theme song, 'Tomorrow.' Jason Robards striking it rich represents the ultimate, if all too brief, triumph of the grizzled sidekick. His success is the success of all the Walter Brennans of the West who have lusted in frustration after all the Stella Stevens types. Peckinpah is aware of the decadence inherent in Robards' redemption through hedonism, and he must finally kill him off.'' [157]

Redemption through hedonism, therefore, leads to the same result as redemption through violence. The viewer is assured of Hogue's virility when, in his eulogy, Warner remarks "But, Lord, he was a man," with Hildy chiming in, "Amen to that!" Warner also says—it *is* a moving eulogy, however ridiculous—"He built his empire, but was man enough to give it up for love when the time came." This would imply that there was a "right" time, an appeal to ritual behavior; but if this is the "right" time, Hogue has only time enough to die.

In those scenes where Hogue captures snakes with his bare hands and makes a stew from toads, grasshoppers, rabbits, squirrels, gophers, and prairie dogs (with wild onions for seasoning), the metaphor of turning a desert into a garden is newly invoked, and the wasteland is seen to be bountiful. The values are those of *Méjico lindo*, Hogue and Hildy "don't forget to kiss each other and water the flowers."

Peckinpah shot a sequence in which Gene Evans battled with David Warner, Hogue stepping in and getting an injured wrist, which is why he still has a bandage on in the scene which directly follows this. Sam deleted the scene because he felt it did not work. It was his own decision and THE BALLAD OF CABLE HOGUE is more or less intact as he filmed it, which cannot be said of MAJOR DUNDEE, THE WILD BUNCH, or PAT GARRETT AND BILLY THE KID—this last will be a subject for discussion in the chapter on Billy the Kid. "If we want to have complete control," Henry Hathaway remarked in the interview with Rui Nogueira, "we must put up the money ourselves." [158] Peckinpah obviously never felt that way. Since critics, for the most part, have accepted his position, much of their "critique" is directed toward versions of Peckinpah's intentions rather than the released films. My own feeling is that this controversy too easily permits one to ignore what is in fact on the screen. It also obfuscates—and there is no way to put this charitably—the circumstance that in certain of Peckinpah's Westerns, such as THE WILD BUNCH and PAT GARRETT AND BILLY THE KID, there is a dimension of almost alcoholic despair—to use consciously an oxymoron: a blurred clarity—a depth of disquiet, a sorrowful, resigned, fated inevitability. It is as intrinsic to them as the variously barren and luxuriant Mexican landscape.

1. Tom Mix about to send his horse, Tony, for help in RIDER OF DEATH VALLEY (Universal, 1932). *Unless otherwise noted, illustrations are from the author's collection.*

2. Fred Thomson as Carson, Dorothy Janis as Sings-in-the-Clouds, from KIT CARSON (Paramount, 1928).

3. Alan Ladd and Van Heflin as they appeared in SHANE (Paramount, 1953).

4. *From left to right, in the foreground,* John Wayne, Howard Hawks, Montgomery Clift, Paul Fix *(in uniform shirt),* Hal Taliaferro *(sitting on ground),* and Walter Brennan on the set of RED RIVER (United Artists, 1948).

5. For John Ford, Monument Valley *was* the American West. It was filled with menacing Indians who could be shot down in spectacular chase sequences, such as these from STAGECOACH (United Artists, 1939).

6. *From left to right,* Harry Carey, Randolph Scott, and Raymond Hatton, the triad hero in Henry Hathaway's THE THUNDERING HERD (Paramount, 1934).

7. Screenwriter Marguerite Roberts added this scene of John Wayne and Kim Darby at the Ross family plot for Hathaway's TRUE GRIT (Paramount, 1969).

8. Arthur Kennedy and James Stewart in a scene from THE MAN FROM LARAMIE (Columbia, 1955), in that milieu Mann loved, ''la montagne et les torrents, les sous-bois et les cimes neigeuses.''

9. Gary Cooper and Julie London in a tender moment excised from MAN OF THE WEST (United Artists, 1958); director Anthony Mann is beside the camera.

10. Budd Boetticher on horseback directing Randolph Scott in the memorable Scott series for Columbia.

11. Karen Steele forced to the extremity of having to fight her husband's battles (played by Michael Dante) in WESTBOUND (Warner's, 1959).

12. Randolph Scott and Joel McCrea as aged Westerners in Sam Peckinpah's RIDE THE
HIGH COUNTRY (M-G-M, 1962).

13. The photograph Billy the Kid had taken of himself at Fort Sumner in 1880. It was in the possession of the Maxwell family for years. Paulita Maxwell told Walter Noble Burns, "I don't think it does Billy justice. It makes him look rough and uncouth. The expression of his face was really boyish and very pleasant."

14. Johnny Mack Brown as he appeared playing the Kid in BILLY THE KID (M-G-M, 1930).

15. Sam Peckinpah's version of Billy the Kid, with *(from left to right)* Matt Clark as J. W. Bell, Kris Kristofferson as the Kid, R. G. Armstrong as Bob Olinger, and James Coburn as Pat Garrett in PAT GARRETT AND BILLY THE KID (M-G-M, 1973).

16. Sam Peckinpah directing Stella Stevens, his conception of a frontier prostitute, and Jason Robards, Jr., in THE BALLAD OF CABLE HOGUE (Warner's, 1970).

17. "Wild Bill" Hickok as he appeared when he arrived in Deadwood, Dakota Territory in 1876.

18. William S. Hart and Kathleen O'Connor in WILD BILL HICKOK (Paramount, 1923).

19. Gordon Elliott, who starred in THE GREAT ADVENTURES OF WILD BILL HICKOK (Columbia, 1938). Typically, it is the white man who must instruct the Indians, even in their own sign language.

20. Jean Arthur *(left)* as Calamity Jane welcomes Helen Burgess as Louisa Cody to the West in THE PLAINSMAN (Paramount, 1936).

21. Wyatt Earp in a photograph taken circa 1885.

22. Jesse James in a photograph taken circa 1879.

23. Lieutenant Colonel George Armstrong Custer in a photograph taken in 1872.

24. *Center*, Tyrone Power as Jesse James, Arthur Aylesworth next to him, during the Northfield bank robbery as depicted in JESSE JAMES (20th-Fox, 1939).

25. Henry Fonda as Wyatt Earp and Victor Mature as Doc Holliday in MY DARLING CLEMENTINE (20th-Fox, 1946).

26. William Wellman *(leaning forward alongside camera)* directing Warner Baxter and Ann Loring in THE ROBIN HOOD OF EL DORADO (M-G-M, 1936).

27. Two views of Custer. *Above*, a lobby card from THE FLAMING FRONTIER (Universal, 1926); *Below*, Richard Mulligan as Custer in LITTLE BIG MAN (National General, 1970).

28. Ella Watson, later called "Cattle Kate" after she was hanged by cattlemen in 1889.

29. Jane Fonda in an exploitation shot from CAT BALLOU (Columbia, 1965).

30. Hollywood's conception of the frontier prostitute from the made-for-television film, THE CHEYENNE SOCIAL CLUB (NBC-TV, 1967).

31. A series of tableaux from THUNDER MOUNTAIN (RKO, 1947), with Tim Holt

and Martha Hyer, which says it all. *Photographs courtesy of Richard Bann.*

32. Betty Miles posing with Ken Maynard *(left)*, Robert Tansey (producer/director), and Hoot Gibson *(right)* from the Trail Blazer series, released by Monogram, in which she often acted against "type."

33. Peggy Stewart and Sunset Carson in a publicity still from ALIAS BILLY THE KID (Republic, 1946). Despite its title, Billy the Kid is *not* in the picture.

34. Julia Thayer as the "Indian" rider who leads the Indians in THE PAINTED STAL-
LION (Republic, 1937), a chapter play with Ray Corrigan.

35. Ronald Reagan and Barbara Stanwyck in CATTLE QUEEN OF MONTANA (RKO,
1954).

36. The Pocahontas stereotype. *(Left)*, Debra Paget with Robert Wagner in WHITE

FEATHER (20th-Fox, 1955); *(right)*, Sarita Montiel having her "red" skin touched up in RUN OF THE ARROW (RKO, 1957).

37. Jim Thorpe, All-American, standing next to Carl Laemmle, head of Universal Pictures, and Lucile Browne. Thorpe's life as a Hollywood Indian was not told in the idealized screen biography, JIM THORPE—ALL AMERICAN (Warner's, 1951), in which he was portrayed by Burt Lancaster.

38. The Hollywood Indian. *(Above)*, a view of Indians massing for an onslaught from THE FLAMING FRONTIER (Universal, 1926); *(below)*, Indians committing depredations against white technological civilization from UNION PACIFIC (Paramount, 1939).

39. Hollywood's version of "the truth at last" in SOLDIER BLUE (Avco-Embassy, 1970).

40. Burial of the dead at Wounded Knee, New Year's Day, 1891. *Photograph courtesy of the Nebraska State Historical Society.*

PART III
FRONTIER LEGENDS

With no love of knowledge for its own sake they have no wish to discover whether their beliefs are false. If you tell them that "Wild Bill" was not the great civilizer of the West, and as a pistoleer was only an average shot, that Wyatt Earp was largely an imposter and braggart . . . , they will want to run you out of town.

—Vardis Fisher[1]

9

Jesse James

Jesse James was born in 1847 and died in 1882. Jesse's father left the family farm in Clay County, Missouri, when Jesse was three, heading for the California gold fields where he died. Jesse's mother, Zerelda, remarried soon after that, but this marriage proved short-lived because she objected to the way their new stepfather treated Jesse and his older brother, Frank. Zerelda then married Dr. Reuben Samuel and this marriage, apparently, was successful. When the Civil War began, the family declared itself for the Confederacy. Frank joined up with William Clarke Quantrill's raiders. The family was misused on a number of occasions by Federalists. In the summer of 1863, the local militia came out to the Samuel farm, tied a rope around Dr. Samuel's neck, and hoisted him four times in an effort to pry information out of him, presumably about Quantrill's activities. They next abused and insulted Jesse's mother, who was pregnant at the time, and sought out Jesse in a field where he was plowing, whipping him as he ran through corn rows trying to escape. A few weeks later Mrs. Samuel was arrested and imprisoned with one or more of her children at St. Joseph. This determined Jesse to join Frank in the ranks of the guerrilla bands.

"Bloody Bill" Anderson broke away from Quantrill and by the time Jesse joined up he and George Todd were the leaders of the raiders in Missouri. "Not to have any beard," "Bloody Bill" is reputed to have said about Jesse, "he is the keenest and cleanest fighter in the command."[2] On 27 September 1864, Anderson led a raid on Centralia, holding up the train from St. Charles. Among its passengers were twenty-five unarmed Union soldiers on furlough. They were forced to strip out of their uniforms—the guerrillas intended to wear them as a disguise—and then, with the exception of Sergeant Thomas Goodman, they were all shot down. That afternoon Major A.V.E. Johnson arrived in Centralia with a mounted infantry and gave pursuit of the raiders. When Anderson and his men were located, Johnson foolishly gave the order to dismount. The guerrillas charged on horseback and annihilated the Federalists. The shooting of Major

Johnson was attributed to Jesse, who was then seventeen, and his brother, Frank, confirmed this in an interview with a Columbia newspaper many years later. A month hence "Bloody Bill" was killed when he led his men into an ambush set by Major S.P. Cox, Jesse being among those who escaped. Five days earlier, at Independence, George Todd had been killed. Frank undertook to rejoin Quantrill; Jesse presumably became a member of a group of raiders led by George Shepherd who took his men to winter in Texas.

After the war, Jesse, having returned from Texas, was among a group of raiders who rode into Lexington to surrender where, despite the flag of truce, Union soldiers opened up on them. Jesse was wounded in the chest, the bullet entering close to where he had previously suffered a chest wound in August, 1864. Jesse made his way to the farm on which his mother was living in Nebraska and he stayed there for about eight weeks. Convinced he was going to die, he pleaded with his mother to take him back to Missouri. Jesse was transported by riverboat to Harlem, now North Kansas City, and put up at a boardinghouse owned by his uncle, John Mimms. Jesse was nursed there by his cousin, Zerelda Mimms, and before he left for the family farm near Kearney, in Clay County, he and Zee, as she was known, were betrothed.

For the next four years Frank and Jesse lived at the family farm and, when they were there, worked in the fields. Jesse joined the Baptist church in Kearney and was baptized. "The extent to which Frank and Jesse James were involved in several bank robberies that occurred in the area in 1866, 1867, and 1868 is difficult to determine," William Settle, Jr., wrote in JESSE JAMES WAS HIS NAME (1966). "No contemporary evidence has been found to indicate they were even suspected in the earliest of these, but their known friends were involved, and in time Frank and Jesse came to be acknowledged as the leaders of the band that started its depredations at Liberty, Missouri, on 13 February 1866."[3]

On the afternoon in question a group of ten or twelve men rode into Liberty. Most posted themselves in strategic places while two men, dressed in blue soldiers' overcoats, entered the Clay County Savings Bank. The bank was deserted except for the cashier and his son. The two men drew their revolvers and told the bank employees to make no noise if they did not want to be shot. William Bird, the cashier's son, made no move until one of the men hit him in the back with his revolver, forced him into the vault, and insisted that he transfer the contents of the vault into a cotton wheat sack. The other bandit gathered up the currency and government bonds and, when joined by his accomplice, put them into the sack. The two bank employees were then herded into the vault and the bandits closed the door. The lock did not catch. The bandits had almost $60,000 in the sack. No attention was attracted by the robbery while it was taking place, but as the bandits were riding away, one who had been in the bank suspected a passerby, S.H. Holmes, and George Wymore, who happened to be on the street, of wanting to raise an alarm and began shooting at them. Then the band generally began firing into the air as they rode out of town. Holmes was not hit, but Wymore was killed outright. A posse was got up but it lost the trail in a blinding snowstorm.

The principal associates of the James brothers in the series of bank robberies which followed were the Younger brothers, Cole, who had been a lieutenant under Quantrill, James, Bob, and John. If he was not the leader from the beginning, Jesse in time emerged in this role as the years passed. There is no way of knowing precisely which banks the James-Younger gang robbed, but there were numerous shootings in the course of these depredations resulting in the deaths of bank officials and innocent bystanders such as George Wymore.

Popular reaction to the robberies tended to be neutral. Banks, usually controlled or owned by Yankee money, charged exorbitant interest rates and so did not inspire sympathy. A journalist named John Newman Edwards played a significant role in being the first to mold public indifference into passive endorsement through a series of inflammatory editorials which began with an editorial in the KANSAS CITY TIMES on 27 September 1872 after a daring robbery at the Kansas City Fair; the editorial was titled "The Chivalry of Crime." "Although Edwards' editorial on the robbery at the fair did not refer specifically to Frank and Jesse James, it showed his attitude toward the band of outlaws of which they were said to be members," Settle wrote in his book. "Soon he was denying their guilt while at the same time justifying their crimes and lauding their bravery and valor. His effusive defense and glorification of the James band continued until his death in 1889 and constituted a major influence in transforming Jesse James' public image from a ruthless robber and murderer into a modern Robin Hood."[4] To a very marked extent, the James brothers became the creation of the publicity given their crimes by Edwards, just as Pat Garrett would "create" Billy the Kid, Eastern journalists "Wild Bill" Hickok, popular writers Wyatt Earp and Joaquín Murieta, and Elizabeth Custer would perpetuate the memory of her husband as a hero and martyr.

In 1873 the James-Younger gang branched out into train robbery. This excited no greater social reaction since the railroads were also controlled by Yankee money and charged exorbitant rates. The move, however, caused the railroad companies to enlist the help of the Pinkerton Detective Agency. On 23 April 1874 Jesse married Zee Mimms and thus began his dual life: by day he lived openly in a community under an assumed name, a devout, practicing Christian, and, in time, the father of a son and a daughter; by night, or when away from home on business, he pursued his life as a bandit, committing numerous robberies and being implicated in several murders. After each important robbery, in addition to an editorial defense from Edwards, there was usually a letter from Jesse James, also run in newspapers, claiming innocence and offering to furnish proof that he was not involved. After John Whicher, a Pinkerton detective, was killed while in pursuit of the James gang, on the night of 26 January 1875 a band of Pinkerton detectives staged a raid on the James farm. Dr. and Mrs. Samuel were awakened during the night by a noise outside and discovered a ball of cotton blazing on the floor in the kitchen. As they put it in the fireplace, another ball was thrown through a window. Using a poker and shovel, the Samuels pushed this ball, too, into the hearth, only for it to explode. A large fragment of the device tore a hole into the side of Archie Peyton Samuel, the nine-year-old half-brother of Frank and Jesse; he died within an hour. Mrs. Samuel's right hand was so badly mangled that it had to be amputated. A black servant was also injured. Obviously the detectives outside suspected that the James brothers were inside and hoped, with the fire balls, to cause a fire and force them out of the house. Placing the fire balls into the fireplace caused an unintended explosion. The detectives had been careless and desperate. But the incident, especially when it was taken up by the newspapers, became another issue to be used in behalf of the James gang and against the Pinkertons.

The James gang and their robberies also became a political cause, uniting behind them certain ex-Confederates and Democrats, with the Radical Republicans and the Jayhawkers opposed to them. After the fire bombing of the Samuels, a movement began to grant the gang amnesty. On 17 March 1874 Jefferson Jones of Callaway County introduced into the Missouri House a joint resolution which read in part: "Whereas, under the outlawry pronounced against Jesse W. James, Frank James, Coleman Younger, Robert Younger, James Younger, and others, who gallantly periled their lives and their all in defense of their principles, they are of necessity made desperate, driven as they are from the fields of honest industry, from their friends, their families, their homes, and their country, they can know no law but the law of self-preservation; can have no respect for and feel no allegiance to a government which forces them to the very acts it professes to deprecate and then offers a bounty for their apprehension, and arms foreign mercenaries with power to capture and kill . . . " and so on.[5] The "foreign mercenaries" were the Pinkertons. It was a Civil War issue: the Jameses and Youngers were only continuing the war and it was society that was to blame. Such an argument might not have worked in another state less divided than Missouri had been during the Civil War; and, as for Eastern journalists, they were mostly swayed by what they read in editorials such as those written by Edwards. When a vote was taken on 23 March, there were 58 ayes and 39 nays—an insufficient number, two-thirds being required for joint resolutions. Fifty-six Democrats and two Republicans voted for the measure, twenty Democrats and nineteen Republicans opposed it.

Notwithstanding, many people continued to believe that the Jameses and the Youngers did not need amnesty, that they were totally innocent of all of the charges brought against them. Then came 7 September 1876. Eight members of the James-Younger gang rode into Northfield, Minnesota, to rob the First National Bank. Three stayed at the edge of town, two remained outside the bank with horses, and the other three went inside. When cashier Joseph L. Heywood refused to open the safe, one of the bandits slashed his throat and then shot him. A.E. Bunker, a teller, ran out of the building and, on the way, was winged in the shoulder. He raised an alarm and the citizens hurriedly put up a resistance. The street guards of the gang shot and killed Nicholas Gustavson, a Swede who was unable to understand English even when it was shouted at him. As the firing between the three coming out of the bank and the two outside with the horses and the citizens intensified, the three men at the edge of town rode in to help. Two of the band—William Stiles and Clell Miller—were killed, as was one of the horses. Bob Younger was severely wounded. The citizens believed that the James-Younger gang had attempted the robbery and organized a large posse to give pursuit. According to Cole Younger, Jesse wanted either to abandon Bob or shoot him, since he was slowing them up. Cole, naturally, rejected both ideas, and so the two groups separated. Samuel Wells, who stayed with the Youngers, was killed when the posse overtook them; Cole, Bob, and Jim Younger were captured. The Youngers did not implicate the James brothers; but, at their trial, rather than face hanging, they pleaded guilty in the murder of Gustavson, Cole being charged, Bob and Jim convicted as accomplices, and received the maximum sentence which was life imprisonment. Bob Younger died in prison in 1889 of tuberculosis; Jim, who lost most of his jaw as a result of a wound incurred during the Northfield robbery, committed suicide while in prison. Cole Younger was pardoned in February, 1903, after which he joined with Frank James in a tour of several months' duration with the James-Younger Wild West Show, went on lecture tours—a typical theme was "Crime Does Not Pay"—and wrote an autobiography, THE STORY OF COLE YOUNGER BY HIMSELF (1903). There is nothing new in the United States about criminals later becoming national celebrities.

Frank James eloped with a Kansas woman in late 1876, Annie Ralston, who two years later bore him a son. For the next few years Frank and Jesse lived with their respective families in Tennessee under aliases, before moving back to Missouri in 1881. Also in 1881 Thomas T. Crittenden, a candidate for the railroad companies and their friends, a Unionist, and a Democrat, was elected governor of Missouri and he declared his determination to rid the state of outlaws, the James gang in particular. Since the Northfield fiasco, the James brothers had been keeping a low profile, and there were rumors that Jesse was dead. Then, on 11 July 1881, four men robbed the Davis and Sexton Bank at Riverton, Iowa, with the *modus operandi* of the James gang; it was followed, four days later, by a robbery of the Chicago, Rock Island, and Pacific Railroad near Winston, about sixty-five miles from Kansas City. The Chicago and Alton train, which Jesse James was accused of holding up in October, 1879, was held up again in the same place in September of 1881. The engineer, Jack "Choppey" Foote, was forced by armed outlaws to break into the express car and H.A. Fox, the messenger, was compelled to open the safe. The bandits, unhappy that the loot was not more, beat Fox into insensibility with their pistol butts and then systematically robbed the nearly one hundred passengers. The next train, reportedly, was carrying a shipment of $100,000, and perhaps this was what the bandits had been after. The leader of the gang, tall with a black beard, was the only one who wore no mask. He announced that he was Jesse James and that this robbery was his form of protest against the Chicago and Alton's participation in financing Governor Crittenden's reward of $5,000 each for the arrest of Frank and Jesse James. During the earlier robbery near Winston, William Westfall, a conductor, in coming upon a tall man with a heavy black beard while collecting fares had been asked at gunpoint to raise his hands. Westfall had tried to escape and the man had shot him twice, killing him. The leader now waved his revolver at Foote and told him that he had best cooperate since it was the same gun that had been used to kill Westfall. After the passengers were robbed, the leader escorted Foote back up to the engine. "You are a brave man and I am stuck on you," he told Foote. "Here is two dollars for you to drink the health of Jesse James with tomorrow morning." He placed two silver dollars in Foote's hand and then offered to have his men remove the stones which had been piled up on the tracks in order to stop the train. "I was so tickled to get out of the scrape so smoothly," Foote later explained, "that I told him not to mind the stones, we could take them off ourselves if he would only take himself and party off. He laughed and said, 'All right, Pard, good night,' and started up the bank with his men behind him."[6]

In November, 1881, Jesse moved with his family to St. Joseph where he lived under the name of Thomas Howard. Charles Ford had helped in the second Chicago and Alton train robbery and he now introduced his brother, Bob, to Jesse, as a new recruit for the gang. Jesse in April 1882 was planning the robbery of a bank in Platte City. Charles and Bob, however, had opened secret negotiations with Governor Crittenden and had been promised both amnesty for any crimes they might be charged with as well as a part of the reward money being offered, should they kill Jesse. After breakfast on the morning of 3 April, Charles and Bob, who had been staying with Jesse for a few days, adjourned with him to the living room. Jesse removed his guns, laid them on a bed, and mounted a chair to straighten and dust a picture which hung on the wall. Bob drew his pistol and shot Jesse in the back of the head. Zee rushed into the room and broke into grief upon seeing her husband's dead body. The Fords ran out of the house, wired the governor that they had killed Jesse, and surrendered themselves to the St. Joseph authorities. It is not known how much of the reward they ever collected, but when they were sentenced by a grand jury in St. Joseph to hang for first degree murder, Governor Crittenden pardoned them. Jesse's body, after a funeral procession aboard a special train provided by the Hannibal and St. Joseph Railroad, was buried under a coffee bean tree in the yard of the Samuel home.

On 11 April 1882 the NEW YORK DAILY GRAPHIC devoted its entire front page to a monument to Jesse James on which was inscribed:

HIC JACET

Jesse James

The most renowned murderer and robber of his age. He quickly rose to eminence in his gallant and dangerous profession and his exploits were the wonder and admiration and excited the emulation of the small boys of the period. He was cut off in the prime of his strength and beauty, not by the hands of the hangman but by the shot of a base assassin of whom the Governor of the State of Missouri was the accomplice. He was followed to his grave by mourning relatives, hosts of friends, officers of the law, and the *reverend clergy*, who united in paying extraordinary honors to his memory. Go thou and do likewise.

When other Eastern newspapers did not take this attitude, they tended to use Jesse's death as an excuse to air a feeling of contempt toward the West, alleging, as did the NEW YORK ILLUSTRATED TIMES, that "Missouri is under the bloody sway of a band of cut-throats, outlaws, and assassins and has been for the last fifteen years or more."[7] There is one truth in all this: for virtually sixteen years Jesse James had been at large. His success as a bandit was due not only to the daring of his exploits but to the many people who, out of loyalty or fear, covered for him and for his gang.

On 4 October 1882, with John N. Edwards working behind the scenes, Frank James walked into Governor Crittenden's office, took off his guns, and surrendered. "Governor Crittenden," he said, "I want to hand over to you that which no living man except myself has been permitted to touch since 1861, and to say that I am your prisoner."[8] Newsmen were present by prior arrangement along with other officials, all of whom accorded Frank a cordial welcome. After a series of trials and legal manipulations to keep him out of the hands of Minnesota authorities, Frank was successively acquitted of the Missouri charges against him; and, after a trial in Alabama, he was released from custody in February, 1885. He held various odd jobs, was occasionally a race starter, and except for the years 1907–11 when he lived on a small farm near Fletcher, Oklahoma, which he owned and stocked, after 1901 he maintained his residence on the family farm in Missouri until his death in 1915. He voted for Theodore Roosevelt in 1904 and when Roosevelt organized the Bull Moose party in the election of 1912 Frank was hired by him to be his personal body guard.

Already by the end of the 1870s a series of dime novels had been launched celebrating the "heroic" deeds of the James gang. The Postmaster General in 1883 threatened Frank Tousey, one of the most active publishers of these lurid and sensational books, with cancelling his second class privileges if he did not withdraw some of the more inflammatory titles. Yet, by 1901, both Tousey and Street and Smith, another pulp publisher, had inaugurated separate series of books devoted to the fictitious adventures of the James brothers. Over the next two years a total of 277 novels appeared in Tousey's JAMES BOYS WEEKLY and Street and Smith's JESSE JAMES STORIES. Public clamor became such by 1903 that the U.S. government brought renewed pressure to bear on these publishers and both firms discontinued the publications.

The first films to deal with the Jessie James legend were a brace of pictures produced by Mesco Pictures in which the James family had a financial interest and which starred Jesse's son,Jesse James, Jr., who played both his father and himself in them. JESSE JAMES UNDER THE BLACK FLAG (Mesco, 1921) is concerned with Jesse's joining Quantrill's raiders and details how, after the war, he receives kind treatment from a judge and falls in love with a woman he calls Zee with whom he hopes to spend a peaceful life. It was not to be, for reasons shown in JESSE JAMES AS THE OUTLAW (Mesco, 1921) where it is revealed how Jesse, falsely accused of a bank robbery, is forced into living the life of the outlaw he is branded, how many crimes are committed by others and blamed on him, how members of his family are maimed and killed, how he performs acts of charity while pursuing a philosophy of "a life for a life," until he is finally assassinated.

Fred Thomson, then a popular movie cowboy, made JESSE JAMES (Paramount, 1927) directed by Lloyd Ingraham. The plot has Thomson as Jesse meet Nora Lane, cast as Zerelda Mimms, a Northern girl living on her uncle's Southern plantation during the Civil War and the two fall in love. Thomson's usual sidekick, William Courtright, was cast as Parson Bill, and, after the war, Bill tells Jesse that his mother has been maimed by fanatic Unionists. Jesse becomes wanted as an outlaw. Bob Ford, played by Harry Woods, is also in love with Zee and, although Jesse once saved his life, he turns on him. In one spectacular scene Thomson and his horse Silver King lead thirty men in boarding a passenger train moving at thirty-five miles per hour by jumping their horses through open windows. After foiling Woods' plot to snare him, Jesse escapes with Zee and the two of them are married by Parson Bill.

Thomson was a former Presbyterian minister but little of his Presbyterianism is apparent in a scene where he, James Pierce, a quondam screen Tarzan cast as Frank James, and Harry Woods go swimming naked in a creek only to catch sight of Nora Lane, clad in a bathing suit reaching down to her ankles. In Missouri, where feelings about the James gang were sensitive, the state censor ruled that Paramount had to delete the title card from the film in which Parson Bill says, "If this is justice, durned if I'll be a preacher any longer." "That a bad man can be a good man only when he's a dead man," VARIETY reported upon the film's release, "may be Paramount's excuse to turn out JESSE JAMES as the reason to charge more for Fred Thomson as a Western actor than F.B.O. did when Fred Thomson made Westerns without a disguise . . . . He [Jesse] was probably the first gangster in America following the Civil War, having aptly graduated from a band of cut-throats . . . . The James brothers were known thirty or forty years ago, with but little difference between the two in their evilness, although Jesse was looked upon as the leader of his brother and their band of robbers and murderers."[9]

The late 'Twenties was a bad period for Westerns. JESSE JAMES cost too much to book into theatres, but many in Hollywood attributed its poor showing as much to content as to marketing and so more than a decade passed before another James film was attempted.

Nunnally Johnson, who did the screenplay for JESSE JAMES (20th-Fox, 1939) directed by Henry King, claimed that he had read in a Missouri newspaper how Jesse James' mother was killed by a fire bomb and he based his screen story, supposedly, on similar old newspaper accounts. When shown Johnson's first treatment, Henry King became excited about the project and urged Johnson to take the script to Darryl F. Zanuck. King told me much later that once the film was in preproduction, he personally flew to the James farm in Missouri and talked to Robert F. James, whom he referred to as Joe Francis James, Frank James' son, a retired lawyer. They sat in the backyard and talked. From what King learned, the Jameses had been a good family; their father had been a minister. He said he saw the window where the bomb was thrown during the trouble between the family and the railroad, but almost forty years after the film had been made, at the time of our interview, King could not recall why, save for dramatic reasons, Mrs. James was shown to have been killed in the explosion, rather than maimed. Frank James was buried next to a cherry tree, he said, but tourists had chopped away the head stone.

Despite King's insistence, both at the time the film was being made and subsequently, about how historically authentic the treatment is, JESSE JAMES is a pastoral fantasy, totally misrepresenting all of the major issues and personalities, while small details, such as the kind of wooden water buckets used, are true to the period. With Tyrone Power cast as Jesse, Henry Fonda as Frank, and Jane Darwell as their mother, the film opens with Brian Donlevy as a railroad man buying up land for less than it is worth. Donlevy's gang roughs up Mrs. Samuels (sic), but Jesse and Frank interrupt them. Jesse tries to organize the farmers against the railroad. Donlevy gets himself and his gang deputized. The James boys flee. Donlevy and his gang show up at the Samuels' farm and Donlevy throws a bomb which kills the boys' mother. Jesse settles the score by shooting Donlevy in a fair fight. The St. Louis-Midland Railroad, for which Donlevy worked, terms the killing murder and brands Jesse an outlaw. In a brilliant set-up, Jesse boards a moving passenger train at night, silhouetted as he runs along the tops of the lighted cars (cardboard figures were backlighted inside to give the illusion of being passengers). The train and passengers are held up, Jesse advising the passengers to sue the St. Louis-Midland to get their money back. Henry Hull played the Major, a lawyer turned newspaper editor whose niece, Zee, played by Nancy Kelly, is in love with Jesse, while Hull is Jesse's champion. Randolph Scott, cast as Will Wright, is the marshal; he is also in love with Zee. King emphasized horse action: Jesse and Frank on horses plunging over a cliff into a lagoon, Jesse crashing through a plate-glass window during the Northfield raid. Although social and economic conditions are clearly blamed for forcing the James brothers into brigandage, by the end of the film Marshal Wright (!) tells Zee that Jesse is no longer the same man she married; he has changed—in the film, Jesse is gone most of the time, robbing and looting. Zee leaves him at one point, but near the end of the film, Jesse, badly wounded, makes it to the cabin where Zee used to live and finds her there. He sees his son for the first time! Jesse promises that he will give up his life of crime and they will go to California. The Ford brothers, Charles, played by Charles Tannen, and Bob, played by John Carradine, show up, and Bob shoots

Jesse in the back. "I don't think even America dislikes Jesse," the Major says over his grave. "His times produced him." It was certainly not accidental that Nunnally Johnson also scripted THE GRAPES OF WRATH (20th-Fox, 1940) directed by John Ford and that in the later film Jane Darwell was cast as Ma Joad, Henry Fonda as her son; both films deal with farm families disenfranchised by big business.

JESSE JAMES, as might be expected, was a success at the box office. It led to several more films on the James brothers, foremost among them, at least in terms of immediate sequence, DAYS OF JESSE JAMES (Republic, 1939) directed by Joseph Kane, RETURN OF FRANK JAMES (20th-Fox, 1940) directed by Fritz Lang, JESSE JAMES AT BAY (Republic, 1941) directed by Joseph Kane, and JESSE JAMES, JR. (Republic, 1942) directed by George Sherman. In DAYS OF JESSE JAMES, Roy Rogers plays a detective who goes undercover, joins the James gang to catch Jesse, only for him and his sidekick, Gabby Hayes, to learn that Jesse, played by Don Barry, is an upstanding family man framed for a robbery by a crooked banker. They set about to raise money to help put Jesse through medical school, but the burning of the family homestead sends Jesse off the deep end. In RETURN OF FRANK JAMES, Henry Fonda, as Frank, decides to let the law take care of Bob Ford. However, after Ford is pardoned, Frank goes on the vengeance trail. Charles Ford falls to his death while being chased by Frank. Jackie Cooper, playing Clem—Jesse's son!—joins in the vendetta. When his servant is framed for murder, Frank determines to return home and stand trial. He is backed by the Major and falls in love with Gene Tierney, cast as a newspaper woman who helps Frank keep his faith in the ultimate justice of due process. When Frank is on trial, Bob Ford shows up. After the jury acquits Frank, Frank races out of the courtroom in pursuit of Ford. Historically, Bob Ford died of a shotgun wound on 8 June 1892 in Creede, Colorado, where he operated a saloon. He accused Ed O. Kelly of stealing a diamond ring and had him thrown out of his saloon. Kelly got a shotgun, came back, and blasted Ford. In this film, as Ford is running from Frank, Clem shoots him, and is shot himself. Ford, wounded, runs into a livery stable, but he dies before Frank can get to him. Jesse's death is thus avenged and Frank receives a full pardon from the governor—although he supposedly did nothing to warrant one.

In JESSE JAMES AT BAY Roy Rogers was himself cast as Jesse with Gabby Hayes still on hand as his sidekick. Jesse joins with Missouri settlers in battling against crooked landgrabbers working with the railroad. Committing a series of daring train hold-ups, Jesse distributes the money among the embattled settlers and the film ends with a dramatic scene showing the completion of an irrigation project. JESSE JAMES, JR., was, if such a thing is imaginable, even more asinine, with Don Barry cast in the title role, most of the best scenes in the picture going to Barry's sidekick, Al "Fuzzy" St. John.

Republic followed up this inauspicious beginning with three chapter plays devoted to the Jesse James legend. JESSE JAMES RIDES AGAIN (Republic,

1947) directed by Fred C. Bannon and Thomas Carr cast Clayton Moore as Jesse and did not feature Frank James or any of the by then familiar ingredients. Jesse intends to go straight and settles down on his Missouri farm only to be warned by his friend Steve, played by John Compton, that he has been accused of the Northfield bank robbery, of which he is totally innocent. Jesse and Steve head into the South and, riding through Tennessee, come upon Peaceful Valley which is being harassed by a band of hooded raiders. Jesse decides to get to the bottom of the trouble, at one point even joining the raiders until he is exposed, and in the final chapter battles it out with Roy Barcroft who, as Lawton, is the leader of the raiders and has been after the rich oil deposit which lies under Peaceful Valley.

Clayton Moore was back as Jesse with Steve Darrell cast as Frank for AD-VENTURES OF FRANK AND JESSE JAMES (Republic, 1948) directed by Fred Bannon and Yakima Canutt. This plot has it that Jesse and Frank want to pay back all the people they have robbed. Jim Powell, played by Stanley Andrews, has the answer for them. He is convinced that with a little more work one of his mines will yield enough gold for the James boys to do their good deeds and still become rich. A gang of crooks does not want this to happen; they want the mine for themselves; and so Frank and Jesse have a battle on their hands, which they win by the thirteenth episode.

Keith Richards played Jesse and Robert Bice played Frank in THE JAMES BROTHERS OF MISSOURI (Republic, 1950) directed by Fred C. Bannon. Of the three the cheapest in production values, the story has Jesse and Frank, using the aliases John Howard and Bob Carroll respectively, help Noel Neill save her freight business from the schemes of Patricia Knox and Roy Barcroft. At the end of the serial, the marshal, aware of the real identities of the James boys, congratulates them on their good work and wishes them well.

In the promotional literature for JESSE JAMES RIDES AGAIN Republic publicists wrote: "JESSE JAMES . . . . The dreaded name that haunted a thousand lawmen . . . NOW . . . strikes terror into the hearts of the lawless!" Both this serial and its sequels caused a number of complaints, inspired mostly by the attempt to continue the trend to whitewash Jesse. By the time the studio came to film STRANGER AT MY DOOR (Republic, 1956) directed by William Witney, the plot, as originally written, called for Jesse James to fall in love with a preacher's young wife while the preacher sets out to convert Jesse to the path of the righteous. The legal department suggested that any and all references to Jesse James be removed from the film.

"I'll make it very brief about Mr. Robert Ford," Sam Fuller told Eric Sherman and Martin Rubin in an interview for THE DIRECTOR'S EVENT. "I happen to like Robert Ford, because he did something which should have been done quite a bit earlier in the life of Jesse Woodson James. Jesse James was a half-assed homo who impersonated a girl for Quantrill's raiders when he was fifteen. Acting as a hooker, he enticed soldiers into a little shack called 'The House of Love,' where these bastard raiders would kill the soldiers and rob them. When he was eighteen, Jesse and his brother held up a hospital train, wherein they killed all the casualties and robbed them.''[10] Fuller had his version down pat since he said almost the identical things to me when I interviewed him myself in 1975. The plot of I SHOT JESSE JAMES (Lippert, 1949) which he directed begins with Bob Ford, played by John Ireland, watching Jesse, played by Reed Hadley, taking a bath; then, after Jesse dresses, Ford plugs him in the back. Ford does it for the reward money, so he can marry Cynthy, played by Barbara Britten. However, he gets only a fraction of the reward and finds the townspeople are firmly against him. John Kelley, played by Preston Foster, then woos Cynthy. Ford, in order to raise money, takes a job re-enacting the murder. Becoming disgusted with this, he turns to gold prospecting instead. Tom Tyler, cast as Frank James, tracks down Ford and is ready for a showdown, but it is Kelley who draws against Ford and kills him in a fair fight. ''The last line in the picture is my story,'' Fuller went on. ''Ireland tells the girl, 'I'll tell you something I haven't told anyone. I'm sorry I killed Jesse. I loved him.' I wanted that type of an association. Robert Lippert, the man who financed the picture, didn't catch that. He just thought it was a kind of Damon-Pythias relationship, and let it remain.''[11]

Fuller's film was a solid financial success. Jesse is not really much of a character in it; nor is he present very much in the earlier BADMAN'S TERRITORY (RKO, 1946) directed by Tim Whelan where Jesse, played by Lawrence Tierney, and Frank, played by Tom Tyler (hence, perhaps, Fuller's subsequent casting of Tyler in this role), rescue their henchman, Gabby Hayes. The Daltons, Belle Starr played by Isabel Jewell, and Sam Bass are also on hand, but the real conflict is between Randolph Scott, a sheriff, and Morgan Conway, a captain of the Texas State Police and a bigger crook than any of the others.

KANSAS RAIDERS (Universal, 1950) directed by Ray Enright went back to Jesse's days with Quantrill's raiders, a subject Henry King avoided completely. Jesse, played by Audie Murphy, Frank, played by Richard Long, Kit Dalton, played by Tony Curtis, and ''the Younger brothers,'' played by James Best and Dewey Martin, join up with Quantrill's band of cut-throats during the war. Brian Donlevy was cast as Quantrill. The plot has it—a commonplace since THE DARK COMMAND (Republic, 1940) directed by Raoul Walsh—that Quantrill is a profound egoist, strictly out for himself, and he plunders Kansas, murdering and burning, to acquire wealth. Jesse is the natural leader of the group of five, and tough, but he draws the line at killing innocent women and children, a squeamishness which repels Quantrill. In time, Unionists successfully surround Quantrill, shooting down his rabid followers—''Bloody Bill'' Anderson is played by Scott Brady and he is shown as one of the worst; but Quantrill does one last, almost redeeming act: he covers the escape of Jesse and his friends so they can continue robbing and looting!

THE GREAT MISSOURI RAID (Paramount, 1951) directed by Gordon Douglas cast Wendell Corey as Frank James and Macdonald Carey as Jesse. Anne Revere, cast as their mother, opens the picture by narrating the ''true story'' of how her sons were forced to become outlaws. During the Civil War, Union soldiers are run off the James farm and the provost marshal's brother is killed in the process. Ward Bond, cast as the provost marshal, sets out for vengeance. He double-crosses the Jameses when they seek amnesty at the end of the war and thwarts their efforts to settle down to peaceful lives. Joining with "the Younger brothers," played by Bruce Bennett and Bill Williams, again a twosome, they become fugitives. Bond pursues them relentlessly, firing their barns and homes and even cripples Anne Revere by throwing a fire bomb into her house. Compelled to commit a number of suspenseful robberies, Jesse in the meantime marries Bee Moore, played by Ellen Drew, and Frank marries Lois Chartrand. After retiring from the army, Bond starts a detective agency and is hired by the Bankers' Association to capture the James gang. The gang, to retaliate, only robs banks protected by Bond's agency. Eventually Frank quits and settles down. Ellen Drew wants Jesse to do the same and, finally, he gives in, only to be shot down by one of his men secretly in league with Bond. HARRISON'S REPORTS, in keeping with the philosophy that morality is more important than truth, claimed that KANSAS RAIDERS "is ethically unsound, for at the finish the desperadoes, although deserving of punishment for their misdeeds, ride off into the hills scot-free."[12] whereas THE GREAT MISSOURI RAID was "unobjectionable morally."[13]

In BEST OF THE BAD MEN (RKO, 1951) directed by William D. Russell, Robert Ryan was cast as a former Union officer forced by circumstances to join up with the James-Younger gang during the Civil War, Bruce Cabot cast as Cole Younger, Lawrence Tierney and Tom Tyler back again as Jesse and Frank. Unlike the others, Ryan is sickened by crime and by the fade he willingly gives himself up to the authorities. It is a poor film, but nowhere as wretched as JESSE JAMES' WOMEN (United Artists, 1954) directed by Don Barry and starring him as Jesse and Jack Beutel as Frank. The James gang arrives in Mississippi. All the women are crazy about Jesse, one after another swooning over him; in fact, two of them even have a hair-pulling fight over him. The most insulting ingredient, perhaps, is to make "Cattle Kate" one of the crooked women whom Jesse swindles in the course of the film, not once but twice, leaving her the second time behind bars.

Almost as bad is JESSE JAMES VS. THE DALTONS (Columbia, 1954) directed by William Castle. Barbara Lawrence, the heroine, is being hanged for a murder she did not commit. Brett King, the hero, saves her and they ride off. Lawrence's father used to ride with the James gang and King suspects not only that Jesse is still alive but that he is Jesse's son. The two seek out Bob Dalton, played by James Griffith, who arranges a meeting between King and Jesse, only for Bob Ford, and not Jesse, to show up. Ford tells King that Jesse is dead and that King is not his son. The two then form a coalition to capture the Dalton gang!

Nicholas Ray, when he came to direct THE TRUE STORY OF JESSE JAMES (20th-Fox, 1957) with a screenplay based on Nunnally Johnson's script for the

Henry King version, changed the emphasis somewhat. Robert Wagner was cast as Jesse, Jeffrey Hunter as Frank. Jesse is portrayed as a distraught juvenile who rejects the values of the older generation and its obsession with material gain. Hope Lange's father is more interested in whether or not Jesse will be able to support her, not how much he may love her. When Jesse, forced by the materialism of the community to resort to robbery, comes to claim Hope, he leaves her father with a bag filled with loot to satisfy him. In terms of theme, the film is more a replay of the conflicts and tensions in Ray's earlier REBEL WITHOUT A CAUSE (Warner's, 1955) than it is a serious attempt to explore the psychology of the James brothers or to depict the peculiar character of their times. In a way this is regrettable, since Ray concentrated more than any director hitherto, if not to significant advantage, on the contradiction between Jesse's clandestine life as an outlaw and his day-to-day existence as an upright family man living a seemingly "normal" life, albeit under an alias.

Wendell Corey was back for ALIAS JESSE JAMES (United Artists, 1959) directed by Norman McLeod, this time cast as Jesse. Jim Davis was cast as Frank. Bob Hope, cast as a bungling insurance salesman, sells Jesse, posing as T.S. James, a policy. When the error is discovered, Hope is ordered to find Jesse and return his premium. The train on which Hope is riding is held up and Hope is robbed of the premium by Jesse. At the end there is to be a shootout with Gary Cooper, Roy Rogers, Ward Bond, Jay Silverheels in his Tonto role from the Lone Ranger television series, Fess Parker, and James Arness making cameo appearances, offering Hope their help. Jesse and his band are finally led off to jail.

John Lupton was cast as Jesse in JESSE JAMES MEETS FRANKEN-STEIN'S DAUGHTER (Embassy, 1966) directed by William Beaudine. When Jesse's pal, played by Cal Bolder, is wounded, Jesse takes him to an ancient mission. Narda Onyx and Steven Geray are there, doctors and grandchildren of Dr. Frankenstein. Onyx, who plans to turn Jesse in for the reward, is attracted to Bolder and wants to make him into a robot by means of a brain operation. Jesse avoids the trap set for him by Onyx, but he is not in time to prevent Geray being strangled to death by Bolder. Onyx next wants to experiment on Jesse, but she, too, is strangled to death by Bolder who, in turn, is shot down by Jesse's girl friend, played by Rosa Turich. The girl friend tells Jesse she will wait for him as he is carted off by the sheriff. There may be those who will feel that this film represents the blending of two "mythological" themes. It does not. It is just a bad picture.

Don Graham in his essay "THE GREAT NORTHFIELD MINNESOTA RAID and the Cinematic Legend of Jesse James" in THE JOURNAL OF POPULAR FILM (Winter, 1977) quoted the director, Philip Kaufman, as having written to him that his purpose in making THE GREAT NORTHFIELD MINNESOTA RAID (Universal, 1972) was to show the "sense of Jesse James as a hero who came out of movies" and to expose the "bogus history we're generally given in movies."[14] One would like to say, therefore, that this is precisely what

Kaufman did; but, not at all—instead he filmed a reversal into the opposite. Take, for example, that folk tale long told about Jesse. One time, right after a robbery, Jesse and his gang stopped at the ranch of a widow. The widow gave them a hearty meal and then, unable to control herself, broke down. She told a considerate Jesse that she was about to lose her ranch that very day. The banker was coming out from town to repossess it. Jesse asked her how much was owing on the mortgage and, once she told him, gave her the money. The banker arrived, all ready to foreclose, but was paid off instead, to his disgruntlement. However, on his way back to town, he was held up by Jesse and robbed of the payment. In Kaufman's film, Jesse, true enough, gives the mortgage payment to a kindly old grandmother, but then he kills the banker who collects the money and leaves a clue so that the crime can be traced to the kindly old grandmother.

Robert Duvall was cast as Jesse, John Pierce as Frank, and Cliff Robertson as Cole Younger. When the gang spends a night in a brothel, Jesse abstains and Cole ridicules Jesse's virility, implying that it is non-existent. Jesse is depicted as a maniacal killer who still thinks he is fighting a guerrilla war against the Yankees. But there is a hero of sorts in all this nonsense, one to take the place of the neurotic Jesse—namely, Cole Younger—and, typically, as played by Robertson, he is the only character the viewer comes to know at all well. The reason given for robbing the bank in Northfield is to get enough money to bribe legislators back in Missouri to grant the Jameses and Youngers amnesty, a counterbribe for monies already paid out by the Pinkertons to defeat the measure.

"It should be clear by now that Kaufman's revisionist study of bogus history as purveyed in Jesse James movies is not itself free of bogus elements," Graham concluded. "This is as it should be, for the Western movie has never purported to be history, only to use it and interpret it."[15] My objection is to the last sentence. In the first place, hundreds of Hollywood Westerns have claimed to be the "true story," to be history, to be factual. In the second place, how can a Hollywood movie "use" and "interpret" history when nowhere in the course of the film—or, for the vast majority of viewers, in anything they have read—is the historical reality purveyed so it can be used and interpreted?

Let me, at this point, make a distinction between what I have called an historical construction and an historical reconstruction. While an historical construction, ideally, should contain no statement not necessitated or supported by factual evidence, an historical reconstruction, because it is fiction and not history, can embellish details based on the evidence *but it ought not at any point contradict the factual evidence*. Notwithstanding assertions to the contrary by filmmakers and others, none of the films about Jesse James—or, for that matter, the other historical personalities dealt with in this part of the book—has respected this rule; and, until this rule *is* respected in the scripting of Western films about historical personalities or events, it is folly to talk about using or interpreting history. What is being used, even exploited, is the ignorance of history on the part of the audience in order, not to interpret, but to distort. It is also needlessly insensitive to believe that when history is so consistently and systematically distorted that the motivation is either accidental or non-existent. I shall address this issue directly later on, but for now suffice it to be pointed out that images of Jesse James in the films made about him are basically of three kinds: of a man all good, of a man who is good who becomes bad, and of a man all bad.

The most recent film about him is THE LONG RIDERS (United Artists, 1980) directed by Walter Hill. James Keach was cast as Jesse, Stacy Keach as Frank, David Carradine as Cole Younger, and his actual brothers, Keith and Robert, played his screen brothers. There is a preposterous episode in a brothel with attractive Pamela Reed cast as Belle Starr, a high-priced whore! The Northfield raid is more accurately staged than in previous versions. Afterwards, Jesse and Frank cut out for themselves, leaving the three Youngers—and, inaccurately, one of the Miller brothers—behind because Cole will not agree to abandon the seriously wounded Bob Younger, or to shoot him. From this point on, however, the film plunges back into fantasy, with the Ford brothers going to the Pinkertons and negotiating $15,000 to kill Jesse. They both shoot Jesse. Frank turns himself in to a Pinkerton on the condition that he can bury his brother. Jesse is treated as a martyr, much as he was in many films over the decades since the family financed the first entries.

10

Billy the Kid

Although there has been much speculation about it, the truth of the matter is that it cannot be said with certitude where the man known later in life as Billy the Kid was born. It is known that his given name was Henry McCarty and that in 1866 he was living in Marion County, Indiana, with his mother, Catherine McCarty, and his elder brother, Joseph McCarty. It was at this time that Catherine McCarty became acquainted with the man she was eventually to marry, William H. Antrim, of the town of Huntsville, located between Indianapolis and Anderson. Catherine McCarty suffered from tuberculosis and this may have prompted her to move farther West. In 1873 the Kid and his brother were present when their mother married William H. Antrim at the First Presbyterian Church in Santa Fe, New Mexico. The Kid's most familiar alias in later years was his stepfather's praenomen and middle initial and the surname Bonney. The family settled in Silver City where Mrs. Antrim opened a boarding house. She died there, of consumption, in September, 1874. The Kid, at maturity, was 5'7" with scrubby blond hair; he made friends easily. Shortly after his mother's death, he took to wandering and spent two years as a general laborer, cowboy, and teamster in eastern Arizona and it was there, in the area near Camp Grant, that in 1877 he killed his first man.

Since only four killings can be documented against the Kid throughout his lifetime, they perhaps deserve mention in some detail. Frank P. "Windy" Cahill, the man the Kid shot at Camp Grant after a brawl in a saloon, made a deathbed statement that he had called the Kid—who was then known as Kid Antrim—a "pimp" and that Antrim had called him a "sonofabitch." He attacked the Kid, wrestling him to the floor. When the Kid was pinned, he pulled Cahill's gun and shot the older and heavier man through the body. The TUCSON CITIZEN reported on 1 September 1877: "Henry Antrim shot F.P. Cahill near Camp Grant on the 17th inst., and the latter died on the 18th. Cahill made a statement before death to the effect that he had some trouble with Antrim during which the shooting was done . . . . The coroner's jury found that the shooting 'was criminal and unjustifiable, and that Henry Antrim, alias Kid, is guilty thereof.' ''[16] It should be mentioned that the jury was made up of men partial to Cahill. The Kid escaped from custody and returned to New Mexico.

The Kid spent the winter of 1877 hunting with a man named George Coe, at least until late January, 1878, at which time he was hired by John H. Tunstall, an Englishman who owned a ranch in Lincoln County, then an area about the size of the state of Ohio. The biggest rancher in the district was John Chisum. The smaller ranchers, fearing Chisum's economic grip, allied themselves with Major Lawrence G. Murphy, a former Army officer who was notorious for his dishonest dealings at Fort Stanton and supplying the Mescalero Indian reservation nearby. He established the House of Murphy, a store and saloon, and maintained a monopoly on the beef and flour contracts for the reservation, though most of the beef (which was actually rustled from Chisum's herds) never reached its intended destination and the flour was black and of poor quality. Murphy formed a political alliance with Thomas B. Catron, U.S. district attorney for New Mexico Territory and head of the Santa Fe Ring, and through Judge Bristol and District Attorney Rynerson of the Third District court and Lincoln County Sheriff William A. Brady controlled the local governmental bureaucracy. Tunstall, in alliance with a Lincoln attorney, Alexander A. McSween, opened a store and bank in Lincoln, which was the county seat for Lincoln County, and went into competition with Murphy. James J. Dolan, long a business associate of Murphy, bought out L.G. Murphy & Co. His success depended on monopoly and, therefore, Tunstall and McSween had to be removed. Dolan accused McSween of embezzlement and Judge Bristol set bond at $8,000. Sheriff Brady sent a posse to foreclose on Tunstall's cattle—Brady claimed the cattle were also partly McSween's—and Jesse Evans and his cattle rustling gang went along with the posse as did Dolan as special deputies.

On 18 February 1878 Tunstall left his ranch, heading for Lincoln. With him were Dick Brewer, Tunstall's foreman, John Middleton, a cowhand, Robert Widenmann, a clerk in Tunstall's store, and Billy Bonney. Widenmann and Brewer broke away from the group when they spotted some wild turkeys. This left Tunstall out front, with the Kid and Middleton trailing behind him at about five hundred yards. Jesse Evans, Billy Morton, and Tom Hill, as advance guard of the posse, swept down on Tunstall. Morton shot Tunstall through the chest. After Tunstall pitched forward to the ground, Evans came up and shot him through the head with his own pistol, claiming that the bullet had been fired when Tunstall had tried to get away. The head of the corpse was then beaten with a rifle butt. The Kid and the others hurried to McSween and told him what had happened. Justice of the Peace Wilson swore out warrants for the arrest of members of the posse who had murdered Tunstall and the Kid and several others were declared "Regulators," riding under the command of Dick Brewer, who was made a special constable.

In early March, the Regulators arrested Frank Baker and Billy Morton and proposed to take them back to Lincoln. On the way, Morton and Baker were shot, presumably while trying to escape. Governor Axtell, who was in debt to J.J. Dolan, declared the Regulators outlaws and they were thenceforth hunted. Probably while preparing to ambush McSween when he came in to Lincoln for his hearing, on 1 April 1878 Sheriff Brady and his deputy, George Hindman, were mortally wounded by the Kid and five other Regulators.

Three days later, on 4 April 1878, the Kid was with a large party of Regulators putting up for a meal at Blazer's Mill. Presently "Buckshot" Roberts, a heavily armed bounty hunter for the Dolan forces, rode into their midst. Roberts was shot and mortally wounded by Charles Bowdre, one of the Regulators, and, maneuvering himself into a better position, Roberts blew off the top of Dick Brewer's head. The Kid and the other Regulators rode off, leaving Roberts to die of his wound.

The decisive battle of the Lincoln County War, as it was later called, was fought during a five-day shoot-out in Lincoln itself with the Kid and several Regulators trapped in McSween's house in Lincoln. Sniping went on for four days. On the fifth day, McSween's home was set on fire after the Cavalry arrived from Fort Stanton to support the Dolan forces. The Kid, after nightfall, led a rush out of the burning house, hoping to distract the gunfire from McSween and the others who were to follow him. The Kid managed to escape from the fusillade. McSween, however, and several others were riddled with bullets.

Along with what was left of the Regulators, the Kid was outlawed for good. Chisum had nominally supported the Tunstall/McSween faction, but after the five-day battle he decided to pull up stakes and to move his cattle operation to the Texas Panhandle. The Kid staged a raid on Chisum's cattle in Texas and Chisum sent his brother and some men to reclaim the herd. It was probably James Chisum, John's brother, who hired Joe Grant, a roustabout, to kill the Kid. On 10 January 1880, while celebrating in Bob Hargrove's saloon at Fort Sumner—albeit, the Kid himself never drank—Grant pulled his gun and started shooting bottles on the back bar. The Kid proposed to join him in the fun. Grant, however, turned his gun on the Kid. The shell beneath the hammer misfired. Grant did not get a second chance. The Kid pulled his own gun and shot him down.

After Brady was killed, he was succeeded as sheriff by John N. Copeland, whom Dolan did not like and whom he had Governor Axtell replace by George Peppin who was sheriff during the five-day battle. When Peppin quit in a dispute over wages, George Kimball was appointed. Dolan and Chisum by this time had become allies in wanting the Kid out of the way and they nominated Patrick Floyd Garrett for sheriff. Garrett was a petty cattle thief from Fort Sumner who won their support because he promised to put all other business behind pursuing and killing the Kid.

"There seems to be no doubt that he knew Billy the Kid," Leon Metz wrote in PAT GARRETT: THE STORY OF A WESTERN LAWMAN (1974). "It has been claimed that Pat Garrett often rode with the Kid and sometimes helped him rustle cattle, but no documentary evidence exists to support such claims.''[17] If further demonstration would be needed that Garrett knew the Kid but vaguely, one need look no further than THE AUTHENTIC LIFE OF BILLY THE KID (1882) which Ash Upson wrote under Garrett's name and based in large part on what Garrett told him. It is a book riddled with fantasy and misinformation, while the image of the Kid is such as to justify Garrett's method of hunting him down.

On 19 December 1880, waiting in ambush with a posse at Fort Sumner, Garrett opened up on the Kid and his followers when they rode in under the cover of darkness. Tom O'Folliard, a close friend of the Kid, was killed as a result of the shooting. The Kid and the others escaped.

Charlie Bowdre wrote a letter to Governor Lew Wallace, who had been appointed by President Hayes to replace Governor Axtell, confessing to the shooting of ''Buckshot'' Roberts but asking for amnesty. Shortly thereafter, the Kid with Bowdre and three others, while hiding out in a rock house at Stinking Springs, was surrounded by Garrett and a posse. Garrett ordered his men to kill the Kid on sight. When Bowdre emerged from the rock house in the dawn light, Garrett gave the signal to fire. Bowdre reeled with the bullets, finally slumping down before Garrett and some of the others. Later that day, the Kid and the other fugitives surrendered.

There were two federal indictments open against the Kid. The first was for the shooting of ''Buckshot'' Roberts, the second for the death of the clerk on the Mescalero Indian reservation, Morris J. Bernstein. Bowdre had been responsible for the former. As for Bernstein, the Kid had been almost a mile away when the shooting occurred. ''Bernstein had been killed by a shot from the gun of Atanacio Martinez [Lincoln constable] under justified circumstances,'' the LAS VEGAS GAZETTE reported on 14 September 1878. THE MESILLA INDEPENDENT supplied more information: ''It is positively asserted that Bernstein was killed by a Mexican who was in a party bound from San Patricio to Tularosa to assist in recovering a lot of stolen stock in possession of Frank Wheeler and others at San Nicholas. When the Mexicans reached the water alongside the road of the Agency, they stopped to water their horses. Bernstein saw them and probably supposing them to be a party of Regulators, attacked them with a party of Indians; he rode upon one Mexican and fired two shots at him, the man took shelter behind a tree. Bernstein still advancing rode close to the tree and fired again at the man who returned the fire and killed Bernstein. The Mexican says he acted strictly in self-defense and will at any time deliver himself up for trial. His name is Atanacio Martinez.''[18]

The prosecution decided both charges were so insubstantial as to make acquittal probable and so it was decided to try the Kid for the murder of Sheriff Brady. The trial was held on 6 April 1881, Judge Warren Bristol presiding. The judge told the jury that only two verdicts would be allowed, murder in the first degree or acquittal. He ruled further that the prosecution only needed to prove that the Kid was in the vicinity of the shooting to demonstrate his guilt, not that he had actually done the shooting (which he had not). After the evidence had been heard, Bristol explicitly instructed the jury, before they retired to decide on their verdict, that "there is no evidence before you showing that the killing of Brady is murder in any other degree than the first."[19] The Kid's defense lawyer was Colonel Albert Jennings Fountain, a lodge brother in the Masonic order with T.B. Catron, James J. Dolan, the principal witness against the Kid, and S.B. Newcomb, the prosecuting attorney. The financial powers in the Territory wanted the Kid hanged and the jury found him guilty as charged. On 15 April Bristol ordered that the prisoner be delivered to the custody of Sheriff Pat Garrett and that on 13 May 1881, William H. Bonney, alias the Kid, alias William Antrim, "be hanged by the neck until his body is dead."[20]

James J. Dolan took up a collection for Garrett and with this windfall he became, comparatively, well-to-do. Newspapers controlled by the Sante Fe Ring lauded him and Eastern newspapers were quick to pick up some of these editorial tributes. Subsequently, after Garrett shot the Kid, Dolan raised $1,100 in recognition of his services and John Chisum, reportedly, gave Garrett an additional $1,000.

The Kid "was to be hanged as a convicted lawbreaker," Metz wrote. "Yet beside him [as he was being transported from Mesilla, where he had been tried, to Lincoln where he would be executed] sat John Kinney, one of the worst cattle rustlers and killers in the Territory, and squatting on the opposite end of the seat was Billy Mathews, a deputy in the posse that murdered Tunstall . . . . Hunkered on the seat facing him grinned Bob Olinger, a locally well-known manslayer who liked to flex his muscles and stroke his double-barreled shotgun. Several times along the trip, Olinger patted his weapon and asked Billy whether he would like to make a run for it."[21]

Incarcerated in the two-story courthouse in Lincoln—the former Dolan store which had been sold to the county; Dolan now owned and operated the Tunstall store and owned Tunstall's ranch, both acquired at public auction—the Kid's guards were J.W. Bell and Bob Olinger. The morning of the Kid's escape—28 April 1881—Olinger took the other prisoners across the street to eat at the Wortley Hotel, leaving Bell alone with the Kid. The Kid had been informed by a partisan that a gun had been left for him in the outhouse and he now asked Bell for permission to go to the outhouse. On the way back, the Kid pulled out the revolver and told Bell to raise his hands. Instead, Bell turned and fled, the Kid shooting him. Then, grabbing Olinger's shotgun, the Kid, who wore leg irons, hobbled to a window just as Olinger came rushing across the street. He shot down Olinger. After working at his leg irons with a small pick, he was only able to free one leg. Arming himself and borrowing a horse, which he would send back to Lincoln, the Kid said good bye to a number of the local citizens who came to wish him farewell and then rode leisurely out of town.

Garrett was away, in White Oaks. When he learned of the break, he began a second manhunt for the Kid. The Kid was in love with Paulita Maxwell,

younger sister of Pete Maxwell who managed the Maxwell ranching interests
for his mother and the rest of the family around Fort Sumner—Pete Maxwell's
father had bought the fort from the U.S. government in 1875—and the Kid remained hidden around the Fort Sumner area. Pete disliked this romance and so
he notified John Poe, one of Garrett's deputies, of the Kid's whereabouts. On
the night of 14 July 1881 Garrett, Poe, and Tip McKinney rode into Fort Sumner to confirm this message from Pete. The hour was late and Pete was asleep.
Garrett entered his bedroom, while the other two stood guard. The Kid, who
was visiting Jesus Silva, a Maxwell employee, wanted a beefsteak and, unarmed except for a butcher knife, came over to Pete's to cut a steak off a newly
butchered yearling. Seeing the two deputies standing near Pete's bedroom, the
Kid called out: "¿Quien es? ¿Quien es?" [Who is it?]. The deputies did not
answer and the Kid, concerned perhaps as much for Maxwell as for himself,
stepped into Maxwell's bedroom to ask the rancher about the men outside. As
soon as he entered the room and spoke, Maxwell identified him to Garrett and
Garrett, who had drawn his gun, shot him, firing two bullets. Then, followed
by Maxwell who clutched his bedcovers around him, Garrett ran from the room
outside onto the porch.

Everyone was too terrified to re-enter Maxwell's bedroom until Jesus Silva
and Deluvina Maxwell, an old Navajo woman who had adopted the family name,
crossed over the threshold and identified Billy's dead body. Deluvina burst out
of the room and ran through the crowd that was collecting, confronting Garrett.
"You piss-pot!" she screamed at him. "You sonofabitch!" She would have
clawed his face had others not held her back.

Garrett himself in the Garrett/Upson account claimed that the Kid had a pistol. His intention was obviously to make himself appear as much of a hero as
he could, but the real significance of THE AUTHENTIC LIFE OF BILLY THE
KID was that, as John N. Edwards' editorializing about Jesse James, it publi-
cized Billy the Kid. Basically, the Kid shot four men, was involved in the losing side of a mercantile war, and was, in the final analysis, less spectacular
than many of the hired killers associated with the Dolan forces and the Santa
Fe Ring. But for the fact that Pat Garrett needed the Kid to make a name for
himself, I firmly believe the Kid would have been readily forgotten. Only one
truly notable dime novel had been issued about the Kid prior to his death, Ed-
mund Fable's BILLY THE KID, THE NEW MEXICO OUTLAW: OR, THE
BOLD BANDIT OF THE WEST (1881). Fable, after the fashion of the Jesse
James dime novels, emphasized the audacity of Billy's deeds, but, unlike many
entries in the James series, no effort was made to justify the Kid. This, in fact,
remained for a number of years the way with which the Kid was dealt. Don
Jernado's THE TRUE LIFE OF BILLY THE KID (1881) characterized him as
"a fiend incarnate"; J.C. Cowdrick's SILVER-MASK, THE MAN OF MYS-
TERY: OR, THE CROSS OF THE GOLDEN KEYS (1884) called the Kid "a
common cut-throat"; and Francis W. Doughty's OLD KING BRADY AND
"BILLY THE KID": OR, THE GREAT DETECTIVE'S CHASE (1890) termed

him "the bloodthirstiest little cowpuncher who ever straddled a horse." Legends sprang up about him. He was reputed to have killed twenty-one men in as many years—although the Kid was probably closer to twenty-four when he died.

On 29 February 1908, near Las Cruces, New Mexico, Garrett was seated in a buggy driven by Carl Adamson. Alongside on horseback rode Wayne Brazel who had leased a tract of land from Garrett who now wanted to break the lease. Garrett's reputation as a dangerous man—in 1884 he had been hired by the Panhandle Cattleman's Association *to kill* rustlers, not bring them in—had increased in the years since the Kid's death. This gave special poignance to Garrett's words to Brazel: "Well, damn you. If I don't get you off one way, I will another." Garrett had the buggy stop so he could climb out to urinate. He went around behind the buggy and, as he was standing there, his head bent over, a slug from Brazel's gun slammed into the back of his skull, tearing out his right eye, and a second bullet caught him in the middle as he fell. Brazel pleaded not guilty on grounds of self-defense and was acquitted.

Walter Woods in his play, BILLY THE KID (1903), was the first to treat the Kid as a hero; and the Kid lives through the end of the play to ride off with his sweetheart. Walter Noble Burns in his fanciful THE SAGA OF BILLY THE KID (1926) made the Kid a hero in the first part of his book and in the second half, after McSween is killed and Garrett becomes sheriff, the principal villain.

Using Burns' book as their basis, in 1930 Laurence Stallings and King Vidor wrote a screenplay about the life of Billy the Kid. They took the story to Irving Thalberg, then head of production at Metro-Goldwyn-Mayer, and described the whole thing to Thalberg in the tonneau of his limousine as Thalberg and his assistant, Eddie Mannix, were *en route* to Mabel Normand's funeral.

Vidor began the conference by saying that Billy shot his first victim because of an insult to his mother. Louis B. Mayer was vice president at M-G-M and he liked at least one reference to motherhood in every film the studio released. "This bit of historical half-truth was emphasized in the hope of convincing Thalberg that all of the Kid's murders were understandable, if not entirely excusable," Vidor later asserted. "Then I took Billy through scenes of murder in self-defense, and murders on the side of justice if not on the side of law."

"Too many murders," was Thalberg's whispered assessment as the four of them sat dutifully in a pew near the flower-draped coffin. On the way back to the studio lot in Culver City, Thalberg broke in with a question.

"Was Sheriff Pat Garrett his friend during the time of those last five murders?" he asked.

Stallings and Vidor gave their assent. They were both convinced that the screen was ready for what they termed a more truthful presentation of violence. Thalberg finally agreed with them.

In his book, FROM HOPALONG TO HUD: THOUGHTS ON WESTERN FICTION (1978), C.L. Sonnichsen told the following anecdote about Mrs. Sophie Poe, wife of John Poe who was present at the Kid's death, and her being hired as a consultant to King Vidor during the filming of BILLY THE KID

(M-G-M, 1930). Disgusted by what she was seeing, she remarked to Vidor, "Sir, I knew that little buck-toothed killer, and he wasn't the way you are making him at all." "Mrs. Poe," Vidor responded, "I understand your feelings, but this is what the people want."[22] She was soon removed from her consulting position by the M-G-M publicity department and replaced by movie cowboy William S. Hart.

"One of the grips saw it first," Johnny Mack Brown, who had been cast in the role of the Kid, recalled for me once as we talked together. "A small cloud of swirling dust far off in the distance. It kept coming closer. We could make out that it was a rider. We were on location filming the cave scene on the desert where Billy gets starved out. The rider was nearer now. We could finally recognize him. It was William S. Hart."

"He acted as technical adviser on that picture, didn't he?" I asked.

"Yes," Brown agreed, "and I'm proud to say that we became friends afterward. You know, he wrote books and would give me autographed copies. He taught me a great many things. How to crouch, for instance, and to turn your left side away, to protect your heart. 'Diminish your target,' he told me. 'Diminish your target and keep your heart as far away as you can from an enemy's bullet.' I followed his advice when I had a gun battle in the picture. He even gave me one of Billy the Kid's guns. I still have it."

The presentation of the gun to Brown by Hart became part of the promotional campaign for the picture as did an open letter from then New Mexico governor, R.C. Dillon. The letter appeared right after the credit crawl and endorsed the film. The scenario called for Billy to be portrayed as the victim of repeated injustice, Brown's warm characterization minimizing the terror that had once been attached to the person of the real-life Kid.

BILLY THE KID opens to a trail herd led by two Englishmen, Tunston and McSween, played by Wyndham Standing and Russell Simpson. They want to settle in the Pecos. William Donovan, the local land baron played by James Marcus, tells them to push on. Donovan is the law in New Mexico. He is seen to seize a homesteader's ranch and have both the homesteader and his wife shot. The two Britishers try to organize resistance to Donovan's rule. Factions develop, Donovan and Bob Ballinger, played by Warner Richmond, and Ballinger's gang on one side, Tunston and McSween and Billy the Kid and the Kid's supporters on the other side. After a shoot-out in town, Billy is offered amnesty if he will only make peace. Wallace Beery, cast as Pat Garrett, threatens to come after Billy if he will not agree. Billy rejects the offer. Garrett and a posse made up of Ballinger's men starve out Billy when he hides in a cave. Billy is taken to Lincoln and put in jail. Claire Randall, played by Kay Johnson, originally in love with Tunston until his death, has now transferred her affections to the Kid. Billy is sentenced to hang and Ballinger is made his jailer.

The Kid gets hold of Garrett's gun and locks Pat in a closet. He shoots the gun which causes Ballinger, who is across the street, to run out into the street where the Kid guns him. Billy goes to hide at the home of Santiago, played by Chris-Pin Martin, where Claire joins him. Garrett sneaks up. The Kid and Claire ride off across the border, Garrett shooting after them, deliberately missing and smiling.

After this whitewash, the Kid was left alone until BILLY THE KID RE-TURNS (Republic, 1938) directed by Joseph Kane, the second entry in Republic's new Roy Rogers series. Rogers played a dual role, both the Kid in a prologue and himself during the rest of the film. The prologue shows the Kid to be feared by crooked cattle ranchers and a friend of the settlers. Wade Botiller, cast as Pat Garrett, shoots the Kid. The next morning, Rogers is arrested when he rides into town because of his resemblance to the Kid. In due course, he is deputized to help the settlers, impersonating the Kid. Smiley Burnette was cast as Rogers' sidekick and in the course of the film's time of 58 minutes seven songs are sung.

It was not too long afterward that Producers Releasing Corporation began its Billy the Kid *series*, Bob Steele cast as the Kid in the early entries, Buster Crabbe later on. The first picture was BILLY THE KID OUTLAWED (PRC, 1940) directed by Sam Newfield under a screen pseudonym, Peter Stewart, with a screenplay by Oliver Drake. In it, the Kid avenges the murders of two friends and cleans up a crooked town at the same time. While in history, the Kid's brother, Joe Antrim, was reputed to be out to revenge Garrett's killing of the Kid until, dispelling all such rumors, Antrim and Garrett met for a couple of hours' quiet conversation in the lobby of the Armijo Hotel at Trinidad, shaking hands afterwards; in BILLY THE KID IN TEXAS (PRC, 1940) directed Sam Newfield under his Peter Stewart pseudonym, Bob Steele, as the Kid, now with a $5,000 reward on his head from the earlier film, again cleans up a crooked town, being sworn in as sheriff, his brother shown as being in with the crooks.

This series did not improve when Buster Crabbe replaced Steele. In BILLY THE KID'S SMOKING GUNS (PRC, 1942), the Kid is joined by his two pals, played by Dave O'Brien and Al "Fuzzy" St. John—Sam Newfield directed, this time under the pseudonym Sherman Scott. They escape across the county line and come upon a wounded rancher and find out that the district is dominated by a crooked ranchers' co-operative association led by Milton Kibbee, a country doctor, and Karl Hackett, cast as the sheriff. The boys help the honest ranchers wipe out the crooked association.

Sam Newfield had reverted to using his own name by the time he directed BLAZING FRONTIER (PRC, 1943), the last entry in the series. Villains Stan Jolley and Frank Hagney are behind a crooked land company attempting to promote a real estate boom so that the railroad will have to pay inflated prices for land. What a distortion this was! The villains hire Al "Fuzzy" St. John to work as a detective for them, but he helps out the Kid instead to get the goods on them. Buster Crabbe, commenting once on the picture, recalled how it was such a low-budget production that the villain, in the chase sequence, rode his horse past the camera, rode around in a circle behind the camera, let Crabbe mount the *same* horse, and then Crabbe rode past the camera, supposedly chasing the villain.

One thing that Garrett in his memoir, George Coe and John Poe in theirs, and Frank M. King in PIONEER WESTERN EMPIRE BUILDERS (Trail's End Publishing, 1946) all agreed upon is the fact that Billy the Kid was right-handed. The error about his being "left-handed" was derived from the manner of producing tintypes in which the sides can become transposed. The one full-length tintype we have of the Kid was (and still is) frequently reversed in this way and, accordingly, when it is, the Kid appears to have been left-handed. It is perhaps a minor point—in view of the gross inaccuracies to be found in all the films about the Kid—but in BILLY THE KID (M-G-M, 1941) directed by David Miller it was added to his screen image. Miller, and screenwriter Gene Fowler, wanted to make a romantic and tragic tale out of the Kid's life. The picture was filmed in Monument Valley. It was given the benefit of Technicolor and, when Nature fell short, the M-G-M artists took over and painted in mesas and picturesque cloud formations.

Pat Garrett is not even in this version. Robert Taylor, cast as the Kid, is hired by Gene Lockhart to help his gang eliminate Ian Hunter, cast as an English cattle rancher, from the district. The Kid's boyhood chum, played by Brian Donlevy, works for Hunter. They meet during a cattle stampede—and because Louis B. Mayer was still running the studio, Donlevy recalls how Billy loved Donlevy's mother's pies and had been wont to take them without asking. This was apparently the beginning of Billy's life of crime. Billy's first meeting with Ian Hunter is just as sentimental. Hunter plays the piano for him, tells him little parables about why it is better to be good than bad, and announces that he does not wear a gun because he is protected by the Kid's code never to shoot an unarmed man. It is, supposedly, a code upheld by *all* Western bad men.

When one of Hunter's wranglers dies, the Kid is so moved by the wrangler's sobbing wife that he quits Lockhart's gang and comes to work for Hunter. Lockhart's men then kill Billy's sidekick, Pedro, played by Frank Puglia, but Hunter persuades the Kid to hold off while he writes a letter to the governor. The governor responds by making Hunter a U.S. marshal, Billy paroled into his custody. Hunter is shot down by Lockhart's men and the Kid, locked up in jail for his own good until Lockhart can stand trial, breaks jail and takes off after Lockhart's hired killers. He shoots them down one by one before the posse, led by Donlevy, catches up with him. The Kid cannot resist the temptation of shooting Lockhart, who is with the posse, in the back. Knowing he deserves to be punished for this foul deed, the Kid reverses his holster to his right side, goes up against Donlevy, and, his draw slowed because of the switch, is gunned down.

Walter Woods' play BILLY THE KID was the first time in print, and surely well in advance of Vidor's film, that the Kid was permitted to slip across the border alive at the end of the story. Howard Hughes in directing his own version, THE OUTLAW (RKO, 1943), not only went back to this ending, but he added Doc Holliday, played by Walter Huston, to the cast of characters. With the music of Tchaikovsky's *"Pathetique"* symphony playing under the credits, the picture opens with Pat Garrett, played by Thomas Mitchell, declaring that Doc Holliday is his best friend. Doc and the Kid, played ineptly by Jack Beutel, get into a fight over Doc's horse which the Kid stole. When Garrett and Doc get the drop on the Kid, he gets out of his dilemma by telling Doc how much he has admired him ever since he was in short pants! Doc's mistress, played by Jane Russell, takes a shot at the Kid; she bears him a grudge because he killed her brother in a gunfight. When Garrett tries to arrest the Kid, the Kid bolts and Garrett wings him. Doc hides the Kid at his ranch where Russell undertakes to nurse him back to health. She finds him sexually appealing, and the two have sexual intercourse—according to the screen shorthand of that era. "I'll give you your pick," the Kid says to Doc, referring to a choice between Russell and Doc's horse. Doc chooses the horse. "I like that horse!" the Kid sighs. "They're all alike," Doc advises the Kid about women. "There isn't anything they wouldn't do for you . . . or *to* you."

The truth of his words are borne out when Garrett arrives on the scene and Doc and the Kid flee: Russell puts salt into their canteens. Garrett overtakes the two in the desert and in an almost homosexual frenzy shoots Doc. The Kid gets away, kidnaps Russell, and then lets her go free. Garrett continues his pursuit of the Kid and the Kid again eludes him, this time Russell voluntarily joining up with the Kid as he rides for the border. An afterword implies that Garrett lived to be a worried old man because he had a reputation he did not deserve.

According to Jane Russell, Hughes filmed two versions, one for commercial release and one for private viewing by himself and his close circle. The latter featured Russell naked from the waist up, whereas the commercial version showed Russell's ample bosom piled into a "heaving" brassière of Hughes' own design. It was Russell's erotic contribution to the film which caused the censors to rise up in arms, and, certainly, not the distortions of history. When the film was later reissued in 1946, Hughes, to satisfy the censors, had a line dubbed in near the fade implying that Russell and the Kid were to be married.

Audie Murphy was cast as the Kid in THE KID FROM TEXAS (Universal, 1950) directed by Kurt Neumann. New Mexico is in turmoil because of a range war with Dennis Hoey on one side, Albert Dekker and Shepperd Strudwick on the other. When four of Hoey's men raid the offices of Dekker and Strudwick, the Kid saves the two men by disarming the attackers and routing them. Strudwick likes the Kid and gives him a job at the ranch. Dekker, on the other hand, does not like the Kid—who wears two guns in the film—and particularly resents him when Gale Storm, cast as Dekker's wife, begins to take a romantic interest in the Kid. When Hoey's men raid the ranch and kill Strudwick, Dekker sends the Kid and his other hands after them. The range war becomes so serious that Robert Barrat, military governor for the Territory, becomes alarmed. Dekker shifts all the blame onto the Kid and even offers a reward for his capture, dead or alive. The Kid decides to live the life of an outlaw and attracts a gang to follow him. One day, pulling in at Dekker's ranch, Pat Garrett, played by Frank Wilcox, and his deputies who have laid a trap open up and kill every member of the Kid's gang. Dekker, too, falls in the fray. The Kid alone escapes. He has gone to find Gale Storm. Coming up outside a window while she is playing the piano inside, the Kid stands there listening until Garrett finds him. The Kid refuses to draw his gun and Garrett plugs him.

The Kid is nowhere in evidence in CAPTIVE OF BILLY THE KID (Republic, 1952) directed by Fred C. Bannon—the plot is a quest for treasure the Kid once buried—but Scott Brady was on hand to play him, much too old for the part and wearing a typical 'Fifties-style haircut, in THE LAW VS. BILLY THE KID (Columbia, 1954) directed by William Castle. Paul Cavanaugh was cast as Tunstall, a man who does not believe in violence and who treats Billy as a son. When Tunstall is shot by one of the crooked sheriff's posse, the Kid henceforth takes the law into his own hands. The Territorial governor appoints Pat Garrett, played by James Griffith, sheriff and offers amnesty to the Kid, but Brady tells him: "You stick to legal, Governor, and I'll stick to right and wrong." The Kid—it is really inappropriate to refer to the aging Brady by this moniker—is in love with Tunstall's daughter, played by Betta St. John. Garrett tries to talk the Kid out of his vendetta against Tunstall's murderers, is unsuccessful, and has to shoot him down. However, after the deed, he throws down his gun in disgust.

In STRANGE LADY IN TOWN (Warner's, 1955) directed by Mervyn LeRoy, Greer Garson is a doctor from Boston who comes to New Mexico in 1880 to practice medicine. In a brief vignette Billy the Kid comes to see her with another man long enough to establish the fact that he is nineteen and has killed nineteen men. He is obviously doomed, which is just the opposite from THE PARSON AND THE OUTLAW (Columbia, 1957) directed by Oliver Drake which tells of what happened to the Kid after Garrett let him escape across the border. Turning over his guns to Garrett at his (supposed) gravesite, the Kid, played by Anthony Dexter, promises to start homesteading. Soon after, he saves Jack Slade, played by Sonny Tufts, from Indians and learns that Slade is on his way to find out if he can outdraw the Kid. Now going by the name Bill Antrim, the Kid and Slade team up after Antrim tells Slade about how the Kid was presumably shot by Pat Garrett. They come to where Bill Antrim's homestead is located and find the district dominated by Colonel Morgan, played by Robert Lowery, and his gang. Bob Steele, who had once played the Kid, in this film is one of Morgan's heavies and is shot down by Slade who himself goes to work for Morgan. Steele had been squatting on Bill's homestead and his former girl friend, played by Marie Windsor, becomes interested in Bill. Buddy Rogers, cast as the parson of the title, recognizes the Kid and asks his help in wiping out Morgan and his gang so the community can be rightfully God-fearing. The Kid refuses. He changes his mind, however, when Slade shoots the parson who falls over a hitching rail and appears properly Christ-like. The

Kid shoots down Slade, then he shoots down Morgan and four of his men, suffering a minor wound in the process. At the fade, the Kid rides off with Marie
Windsor.

The next year saw two more additions to the cycle, both from the same company. In BADMAN'S COUNTRY (Warner's, 1958) directed by Fred F. Sears,
the Kid is already dead and Pat Garrett, played by George Montgomery, quits
his job and wants to marry and lose his reputation. Neville Brand, as Butch
Cassidy, has no intention of letting him do this and summons forty of the Wild
Bunch to lay siege to the Territory. Wyatt Earp, played by Buster Crabbe, comes
along to assist Garrett in battling against this crime wave. In THE LEFT-
HANDED GUN (Warner's, 1958)—guess who is left-handed?—directed by
Arthur Penn, Paul Newman, who had played the Kid previously in the PHILCO
PLAYHOUSE production of THE DEATH OF BILLY THE KID (NBC, 1955)
by Gore Vidal, was again cast in the role for the film adaptation of the teleplay.
The scenario, consistent with Vidal's interpretation of the Kid as a manic-de-
pressive with an Oedipus complex, has the Kid befriended by a Scottish rancher
named McSween, played by John Dierkes. When McSween is killed by four
toughs, the Kid sets out to avenge him, killing not only the four responsible
but three others as well. Given Vidal's sexual preoccupations, it is not surprising that the Kid's homosexuality comes very much into play in his rough-housing with his friends, played by James Congdon and James Best, and in his search
for a father figure, a role which Pat Garrett, played by John Dehner, seems best
suited to fill. A huckster played, by Hurd Hatfield, disillusioned that the Kid is
not more of a hero, turns him in to Garrett—who has become alienated from
the Kid because the Kid disrupted his wedding—and Billy forces Garrett to draw,
himself packing an empty holster. The screenplay, to be sure, has the Kid unarmed, but the rest is nonsense. Penn's obvious interest was elsewhere. "The
character of Hurd Hatfield," he is quoted as saying in his interview for THE
DIRECTOR'S EVENT, "was constantly confronted with a myth he had formed
in his own mind about Billy the Kid. His grave disappointment when he found
out what Billy actually was, and his inability to reconcile these two, caused
him to betray Billy. The need to have heroes be genuinely heroic seems to me
to be an absurdity and a foolish intention, and when somebody like the Hatfield
character is let down, his revenge has no limit."[23] THE NEW YORK TIMES
perhaps best summed up the film in commenting that "very little of it makes
sense and the whole thing is so laboriously arty that it hurts . . . . The picture
moves self-consciously, at a snail's pace . . . ."[24]

When Charles Neider's THE AUTHENTIC DEATH OF HENDRY JONES
(Harper's, 1956) was reissued in paperback in 1972 by Harrow Books, Wirt
Williams, in an Introduction, after claiming this novel "may be the greatest
'western' ever written" and divining, presumably, that it was based on the life
of Billy the Kid, determined to set the reader straight concerning the known
facts about the life of the Kid: "He was born William Bonney in New York
City, probably illegitimate. His mother moved to the Southwest and at an early

age he was thrown on his own. He survived and made a name for himself, as they say, but the report that he had killed twenty-one men by the time he was twenty-one was probably apocryphal. He was a devoted follower of an English rancher in the Lincoln County Wars in New Mexico, and emerged as one of the conflict's 'heroes.' Subsequently, he and a band of young men lived off the land by rustling cattle, and a drinking companion, Pat Garrett, was hired by the ranchers with the specific objective of killing Billy."[25] There is very little about the foregoing obviously that is accurate; Williams was simply disinclined, for whatever reason, to learn the facts about which he proposed to write. Neider did not know the facts about the Kid, either, but in his case this is somewhat excusable since all the names of the characters in his novel were changed and even the setting was altered to California.

In Neider's novel Dad Longworth goes after Hendry Jones and shoots him in the dark of night in Hijinio's adobe. "There was a sixshooter in the Kid's right hand and a long knife lying beside his left. Longworth's ball had struck him just above the heart, a good shot. It had left a neat hole where it had entered, with only a trickle of blood . . . . "[26] There is then a discussion about cutting off the Kid's trigger finger.

Marlon Brando brought his version of all this to the screen in ONE-EYED JACKS (Paramount, 1961) which in Brando's cut ran almost five hours. The severely edited version that was released may or may not be less execrable, but at the end Brando, playing Rio, shoots Dad Longworth, played by Karl Malden, and then rides off into the sunset. What is of interest about ONE-EYED JACKS, when it comes to the Kid, is that Sam Peckinpah worked on the screenplay for a time and had occasion to read Neider's novel. Nearly all of Peckinpah's own notions about the Kid were derived from Neider and, hence, in PAT GARRETT AND BILLY THE KID (M-G-M, 1973), there is the small, clean bullet hole in the Kid's corpse and the squabble between Poe and Garrett when Poe wants to cut off the Kid's trigger finger.

What is at play here is not the growth of legend or the emergence of myth: it is rather a question of human indolence and what results from depending on unreliable secondary sources. In his novel—which, in my opinion, Williams highly overrated—Neider wanted to explore the mythic qualities of his subject, and so, with the names and places changed, he did so. Most of the time, however, this is not the case. In BILLY THE KID VS. DRACULA (Embassy, 1966) directed by William Beaudine, Chuck Courtney was cast as Billy. A reformed outlaw, Billy is foreman of Melinda Plowman's ranch and engaged to her. When Dracula, played by John Carradine, shows up, he poses as Plowman's uncle. As Plowman falls increasingly under Dracula's spell, the Kid reads up on vampire lore. Finally, at the end, tracking Plowman and Dracula to a mine on her property where they are hiding, the Kid finishes off the vampire. There are those, I am certain, who might say that a film such as this combines the popular folklore of Europe with that of America. In my view, like the companion film about Jesse James, it is just a silly hodge-podge.

In CHISUM (Warner's, 1970) directed by Andrew McLaglen, John Wayne was cast as John Chisum, Geoffrey Deuel as the Kid, and Glenn Corbett as Pat Garrett. At the outset Wayne and Ben Johnson, as Wayne's close friend and employee, Mr. Pepper, talk about the West, their beginnings, and how the times are changing. "Well," says Chisum, surveying his land and cattle empire, "things generally change for the better." Forrest Tucker, cast as Murphy, is intent on taking over the town and Sheriff Brady, played by Bruce Cabot, is his right hand. The Indians on a nearby reservation are not Mescaleros, but Comanches. Wayne gets in his line from HONDO (Warner's, 1953) about Indians—"It was a good way of life."—and Wayne's Chisum is paternalistic toward them as he is toward everybody. The Kid is supposed to have killed twelve men, his first at twelve. He works for the mild-mannered Tunstall who preaches the Bible to him and in one scene the Kid—significantly, very significantly—balances the Bible in one hand, his gun in the other. Both the Kid and Garrett fall in love with Chisum's niece. When Tunstall is killed, Chisum is deputized to bring back the killers and arrests Morton and Baker. On the way back to Lincoln, the Kid rides up and shoots them in cold blood. Next, also in cold blood, he guns down Sheriff Brady in the street. Garrett, at this point, presses his suit with Chisum's niece, instructing her that just as there is a difference between infatuation and love, so there is a difference between Chisum and the Kid: the Kid wants revenge, Chisum wants justice.

CHISUM affirms that political structures are frequently inadequate, if not downright crooked, and in some cases gun law is the only way to invoke justice. However, it must be done in Chisum's way, not the Kid's. When the Kid and his gang are cornered in McSween's store, Chisum and his men ride to town for a showdown. Stampeding a herd of cattle through a barricade, Chisum's wranglers rout Murphy's men, Chisum crashing through a window atop his horse in the best Tom Mix fashion, tackling Murphy, and fighting with him to the death. The Kid rides off alone at the end and Chisum has Garrett *appointed* sheriff. When Ben Johnson comments to Chisum's niece that there is no law West of Dodge and no God West of the Pecos, the line rings all the way back to a wry statement made by Gary Cooper as "Wild Bill" Hickok in THE PLAINSMAN (Paramount, 1936). Chisum, however, has a different answer than Hickok did: "Wherever there are people who come together, the law is not far behind and they'll find, if they look around, that God has already been there."

When DIRTY LITTLE BILLY (Columbia, 1972) directed by Stan Dragoti was first released, critics hailed it as the truth at last. "The present vogue for realistic portraits of the Old West has turned up several very satisfying films . . . ," the INDEPENDENT FILM JOURNAL reported on 13 November 1972, "but now Stan Dragoti and his co-writer Charles Moss have come up with what must be the ultimate in Old West authenticity in DIRTY LITTLE BILLY . . . ."[27] In this opus, Billy Bonney, played by Michael Pollard, arrives in Kansas from New York with his mother and stepfather and the family takes up residence on an old dilapidated farm. Billy does not like working in the fields, so he runs away and meets up with the wild Goldie, played by Richard Evans, and Goldie's trouble-making girl friend, a whore named Berle played by Lee Purcell. Very little happens really, except that the Kid loses his virginity and learns how to use a gun.

At the same time that Peckinpah was in Durango, Mexico, filming his version of the Kid's life and death, John Wayne was about a mile away filming CAHILL, U.S. MARSHAL (Warner's, 1973) directed by Andrew McLaglen. The cast and crew of both films mixed freely during their off hours—except for Wayne and Peckinpah; Wayne had an antipathy for Peckinpah so strong that he refused so much as to meet him. Dub Taylor, a character actor in the Wayne picture, had evidently read the script of the Peckinpah film, since he confided to me the morning I arrived: "I'll tell you this. After Sam gets through nobody will ever make a pitchur about Billy the Kid again. *This is it*! They'll never touch Billy again." Rudolph Wurlitzer provided Peckinpah with the screenplay and, in another example of the blind instructing the blind, Paul Seydor in PECKINPAH: THE WESTERN FILMS informed the reader that "Wurlitzer chose to confine his original screenplay to the last three months of Billy's life because they offered him the freest area for invention and imagination: no one knows what Billy did then, only that he was told to clear out of the territory or face execution."[28] Who, supposedly, told this to the Kid? In the Peckinpah/Wurlitzer version, Garrett himself! For Seydor, "one of the subtlest yet most impressive of Peckinpah's and Wurlitzer's achievements [was] the depiction of the casualness of frontier violence and of its ready acceptance by its perpetrators, victims, and spectators alike as a fact of their lives."[29]

Peckinpah had been working out of an office on the Samuel Goldwyn lot and living in a house trailer on Malibu beach, supervising the editing of THE GETAWAY (National General, 1972), when the deal was set for him to direct PAT GARRETT AND BILLY THE KID. He had watched Penn's THE LEFT-HANDED GUN three or four times and felt that now his opportunity had come to treat the Kid as the character in Charles Neider's novel: a neurotic and callous murderer. Once on location in Durango, using Chupaderos, a former Pancho Villa fort refurbished to look like Fort Sumner, New Mexico, Peckinpah was determined to tell the story of the Kid's clash with Garrett as if it were a Bible story, where everyone knew how the story ended and the emphasis, therefore, could be placed on *why* it had to end that way. With Kris Kristofferson cast as the Kid and James Coburn as Garrett, Peckinpah wanted their story told in *tableaux*, as stations of the cross in a medieval passion play, each scene bringing the Kid nearer his death and Garrett nearer his own self-crucifixion. Peckinpah wanted the film to open in 1908 with Garrett as an old man being shot down at the instigation of the same forces that had once hired him to murder the Kid and the Kid's gang, ostensibly in a dispute over the land which Chisum, played by Barry Sullivan, had given Garrett after he successfully dispatched the Kid. As the bullets tear into Garrett's body, there is a flashback to

1881, showing a chicken's head being shot off at Fort Sumner where the Kid and his gang are engaged in some target practice.

There is no celebration of capitalism in PAT GARRETT AND BILLY THE KID as there is in CHISUM, no new frontier as in so many Westerns, only a vast wasteland, a desert punctuated by silvery, surrealistic lakes and streams. Much of the film is photographed in shadow, at dusk, in hazy light, or after nightfall. There is a hopelessness in the terrain, an agonized loneliness in the principals, a frustrated quest for identity, a bitter confrontation with futility, and, moving through it all, desperately erupting, a sustaining violence, a lewd intimacy with death.

Garrett comes to Fort Sumner to tell the Kid that Chisum and the others in the Sante Fe Ring, who had once hired the Kid to be sheriff of Lincoln County, have now hired Garrett. The Kid and Garrett have ridden together for years; now Garrett wants the Kid out of the Territory.

"Why don't you kill him?" one of the Kid's henchmen asks Billy as Garrett leaves.

"Why?" the Kid returns, gulping whiskey. "He's my friend."

Cut to the Kid and two cronies—supposedly Bowdre, played by Charles Martin, and Tom O'Folliard, played by Rudolph Wurlitzer—in a shack at dawn surrounded by Garrett and a flock of deputies. The two cronies are shot to pieces, but the Kid surrenders, holding out his empty arms sacrificially. The Kid is sentenced to hang. He plays poker in a room above the jail with Garrett and Matt Clark, cast as J.W. Bell, while a scaffold is being erected outside. R.G. Armstrong is on hand to play Bob Olinger as a religious fanatic who, right-eously holding a shotgun to the Kid's heart, demands, "Repent, you sonofabitch." Garrett leaves to collect some taxes, but, before he goes, he presumably places a gun in the outhouse so that the Kid can make his escape. Billy shoots Bell and Olinger—"How does Jesus look to you now, Bob?"—and rides off.

When Garrett gets back to Lincoln, he hires Jack Elam as a deputy to help him hunt for the Kid. Before he takes to the trail, Garrett stops briefly to see his Mexican wife; a parallel scene shows the Kid following after Marie, played by Rita Coolidge, a loose woman, if not an outright whore, at Fort Sumner, while a group of children heckle him. Stopping at the military governor's mansion, Garrett refuses an additional reward offered for the Kid's capture by two capitalist investors. Jason Robards, Jr., cast as Governor Wallace, is sympa-thetic with Garrett's position. The Kid, in the meantime, attempts to collect the twenty head of cattle Chisum supposedly still owes him from when the Kid was sheriff. This move outrages Chisum and he has John Poe, played by John Beck, who will eventually lure Garrett to his own death by ambush, assigned to ride with Garrett to insure that Garrett will capture the Kid. "This country's gettin' old," Garrett tells Poe, "an' I aim to get old with it. The Kid don't want it that way, an' maybe he's a better man for it."

This is Garrett's refrain throughout the picture. He says the same thing to

Slim Pickens, cast as a deputy sheriff, when he wants to enlist Pickens to join him in killing some of the Kid's gang. Pickens is fatally shot in the attempt. When he is first seen, Pickens is building a boat—rather a clumsy symbol—behind the jail and intends to leave the Territory in it.

Garrett kills more of the Kid's gang. The Kid decides to go to Mexico to hide but when Chisum's men kill his friend Paco, played by Mexican director Emilio Fernandez, and rape Paco's wife, the Kid decides to return to Fort Sumner to organize a showdown with Chisum. Garrett and Poe meet Chisum at Chisum's ranch and Chisum makes Garrett the offer of property which the viewer already knows will lead to Garrett's death at Poe's hands. Garrett accepts the offer and, after spending some time with the Kid's whore and three other hookers, Garrett, Poe, and Tip McKinney ride out toward Fort Sumner. The Kid knows Garrett is coming, but he relaxes his vigilance to make love with Marie—women are dangerous and they can distract a man. On his way to Pete Maxwell's shack where the Kid and Marie are together in bed, Garrett happens upon Will, the coffinmaker, played by Sam Peckinpah. Will is putting the finishing touches on a coffin and claims that when he is finished with it, he will put his belongings in it and leave the Territory for good. "Finally figured it out, eh?" Will asks Garrett, turning down a drink. "Well, go get him. You don't even trust yourself any more, do you Garrett?"

Garrett shoots the Kid, who is barechested but armed with his gun which he does not fire, pistol-whips Poe when he would cut off the Kid's trigger finger, and the next morning, in an ironic reference to the conclusion of SHANE (Paramount, 1953), rides off alone, a child following after him, throwing stones. Cut to Garrett riding in his buggy in 1908, an old man met on the trail by John Poe, and again the viewer is taken through Garrett's assassination. It was all a flashback in Garrett's last fleeting moments alive.

Kris Kristofferson was drinking two quarts of whiskey a day while playing the Kid. Peckinpah, on location, was "pissed off" because gossip columnist Rona Barrett had said Sam had a drinking problem. Through every scene of PAT GARRETT AND BILLY THE KID, the drinking had been constant and intense, with at least Kristofferson preferring the real thing. In this way the film itself became a descent into alcoholic despair, in which life could be reduced to a state of permanent depression punctuated by sudden violence. James Aubrey, then head of M-G-M, had the film edited extensively before release, claiming that viewers could not follow the director's cut. The editing did not make the screen story any more accurate.

As is the case with Jesse James, the films about Billy the Kid portray him in three basic ways: as a man all good, as a man who is good but who becomes bad, and as a man all bad. No one of these images is confined to any particular decade, but rather recurs consistently throughout the films, depending on the ideology of the specific film. Even the most recent films provide contradictory images, DIRTY LITTLE BILLY portraying him as a worthless delinquent, PAT GARRETT AND BILLY THE KID as a killer among killers and a martyr to a freer way of life. Having studied Peckinpah's *oeuvre* in an earlier chapter, it ought also be apparent just how much his version of the Billy the Kid story is an embodiment of his themes and his perspectives and how the Kid is used to "sell" these notions to the viewer, as opposed to any other predominant influence on the picture's composition or treatment of its subject.

11

"Wild Bill" Hickok

He was born James Butler Hickok in 1837 at Homer, later renamed Troy Grove, Illinois, and died at Deadwood, Dakota Territory, in 1876. According to his own testimony, a woman during the Civil War first called him "Wild Bill," and the moniker stuck. Hickok's father was a farmer and a merchant who also established a way station for the Underground Railroad. His young son frequently helped in hiding out fugitive slaves from their pursuers. As he grew up, Hickok became adept with firearms and his fists and in 1855 he fled the area after a vicious fight with a teamster, believing, erroneously, that he had killed him. He drifted into Kansas—torn into factions over slavery—and joined the Free-State militia of General Jim Lane. Tiring of what he found a dull life, he quit and was elected constable of Monticello, tired of this, and moved on to Leavenworth, Kansas, where he secured a job as a teamster on the Santa Fe Trail. It was also at this time that he made the acquaintance of William Frederick Cody, later better known by his show business name of "Buffalo Bill."

In March, 1861, Hickok was employed at the Pony Express and Overland Stage and Express station at Rock Creek then in Jones County, Nebraska Territory. Dave McCanles, who owned the property on which the station was situated, had come West in 1859 with a woman calling herself Sarah Shull but whose name seems to have been Katherine Shell. McCanles had originally deserted his wife and family in North Carolina, but eventually he sent for them, albeit retaining Sarah as his mistress. Soon after "Wild Bill" arrived, Sarah transferred her affections to him and this caused a rift between the two men, McCanles calling Hickok "Duck Bill" because of his facial features and accusing him, because of his supposedly "effeminate" manner of dress, of being a hermaphrodite. On 12 July, upset because the express company owed him money, Dave showed up at the station with his young son, Monroe, his cousin James Woods, and James Gordon, an employee. Horace Wellman, the station manager, Wellman's common-law wife, and Hickok, who was the stock tender, all refused to come outside. McCanles, in edging around the side of the building, spotted Hickok hiding behind a curtain partition. "Come out and fight fair," he demanded. Then he threatened to drag Hickok outside. "There will be one less sonofabitch when you try that," Hickok warned. McCanles stepped inside and was shot to death by Hickok. Hickok had already cocked his revolver before McCanles entered. McCanles' son, Monroe, ran up and cradled his father's body in his arms. Woods and Gordon were a short distance behind Monroe. Hickok shot Woods twice and then turned to wing Gordon. The two wounded men tried to flee, but Wellman, armed with a hoe, and Doc Brink, a stable hand armed with a shotgun, gave pursuit. Wellman caught up with Woods and hacked him to death with the hoe. Brink killed Gordon with a shotgun blast. At a preliminary hearing on 18 July, Hickok, Wellman, and Brink, who argued that they were only defending private property, were released from custody on the ground that they had acted in self-defense.

Hickok left the area and on 30 October 1861, at Sedalia, Missouri, he enlisted in the Union Army as a civilian wagon master. Although both "Wild Bill" and later fabulists embellished Hickok's role as a scout during the Civil War, the next gunfight he was in that can be documented occurred on 21 July 1865. Hickok was by then living in Springfield, Missouri, and he clashed with Davis K. Tutt, Jr., over the affections of one Susannah Moore. The two confronted each other in the town square before a crowd of witnesses. "Don't come any closer, Dave!" Hickok shouted to Tutt when the man was seventy-five yards away. Tutt brought up his pistol and fired at Hickok, missing. Hickok, taking aim and steadying his revolver with his left hand, shot Tutt dead. He gave himself up and was acquitted; his defense attorney was ex-Brevet Brigadier General John S. Phelps, former U.S. military governor of Arkansas and later governor of Missouri.

Lieutenant Colonel George Ward Nichols of the Union Army and a correspondent of HARPER'S NEW MONTHLY MAGAZINE came to Springfield in September, 1865, and, fascinated by all the lies Hickok told him, wrote a fictitious biography of Hickok for HARPER'S which marks the real beginning of his frontier legend. Losing the election for Chief of Police at Springfield, Hickok moved on to Fort Riley, Kansas, where he met the Custer family for the first time. Custer was acting regimental commander of the newly created Seventh Cavalry. Hickok shared an affinity for poker with the "General" and with his younger brother, First Lieutenant and later Captain Thomas Ward Custer, although the latter, in 1869, would have a falling out with Hickok in an argument over a prostitute in Hays City, Kansas. Hickok tried his hand at buffalo hunting. Once he was surrounded by a Sioux war party intent on keeping the white men away from the buffalo, but his life was saved by a Sioux peace chief known to the whites as Whistler. On 1 January 1867 Custer persuaded Hickok to sign on with the Seventh as a scout, but he was never Chief of Scouts as was often claimed. In his off-hours, Hickok was usually to be found gambling or wenching at Leavenworth. In April and May of 1867, at Fort Harker,

Kansas, Hickok was interviewed by then war correspondent Henry M. Stanley from the NEW YORK HERALD who was on the Plains covering the hostilities between the Plains Indians and the War Department. In the April interview Hickok went so far as to tell the credulous Stanley that he had killed more than a hundred men.

Defeated in the election for sheriff of Ellsworth, Kansas, in November, 1867, Hickok, having left the army, went to work instead as a deputy U.S. marshal under U.S. Marshal Charles C. Whiting. In his capacity as a deputy and with the aid of William F. Cody, Hickok arrested eleven renegade soldiers who had been stealing horses in the Solomon River country. To supplement his earnings he also was involved in a freighting venture at Hays City. Then on 18 August 1868 he went back to work as a civilian scout for the army, this time under Brevet Major General Benjamin H. Grierson at Fort Hays, commander of the Tenth Cavalry, a regiment of black Buffalo soldiers.

In the spring of 1869, Hickok returned home to Troy Grove to visit his family, but by July 1869, he was back at Hays City. By special election in August, 1869, he was elected interim sheriff at Hays City, hiring Peter Lanihan as a deputy to do most of the leg work and all of the paper work while Hickok spent his time playing cards in Tommy Drum's saloon or frolicking at Ida May's sporting house where he had his run-in with Tom Custer. On 24 August Hickok tried to arrest a man named Bill Mulrey and when Mulrey resisted Hickok shot him down. On 26 September Samuel Strawhim led a band of drunken teamsters through Hays City and about an hour after midnight they began tearing up a beer parlor. Hickok and Deputy Peter Lanihan arrived at the scene. Strawhim went for his gun and Hickok shot him in the head. A little more than a month later, Hickok ran in the regular election for sheriff on the Independent ticket, Peter Lanihan, running as a Democrat, opposing and defeating him, 114 to 89. Hickok was permitted to remain in office until his term expired on 11 January 1870, after which he hung around Hays City, on and off. On 17 July 1870, Hickok became involved in a drunken brawl at Drum's saloon with five equally drunken troopers from the Seventh. It was later whispered that Tom Custer had put them up to it, but whatever the truth, when Hickok was thrown to the floor and roundly kicked about, he drew a gun and started shooting. Privates Jeremiah Lanigan and John Kile fell, severely wounded, Kile dying the next day. Hickok left town in a hurry.

Until April 1871, when he was sent for by the town council of Abilene, Kansas, and made city marshal, Hickok was hiding out, mostly at Ellsworth and Topeka. At the time Abilene was the leading railhead for Texas cattle with thirty-two places licensed to sell liquor and sixty-four gambling houses. Although this may be considered its most tempestuous period, there were only three violent killings, two of them by "Wild Bill" and one attributed to Western bad man John Wesley Hardin. In TRIGGERNOMETRY (1941) Eugene Cunningham recorded one old cowboy named Brown Paschal who remembered seeing Hickok in 1871 when he was city marshal at Abilene; eschewing holsters, Hickok carried his ivory-handled guns in his belt or in a silk sash butts-forward for a "twist" or "Cavalry" draw. "When I came along the street," Brown recalled, "he was standing there with his back to the wall and his thumbs hooked in his red sash. He stood there and rolled his head from side to side looking at everything and everybody from under his eyebrows—just like a mad old bull. I decided then and there I didn't want any part of him."[30]

Some question has arisen about just what it was that came to impair Hickok's vision during his Kansas years. Mari Sandoz in THE BUFFALO HUNTERS (1954) declared that it was incurable glaucoma. Joseph G. Rosa in THEY CALLED HIM WILD BILL: THE LIFE AND ADVENTURES OF JAMES BUTLER HICKOK (1964) took exception to this, but, as he noted, "lack of documentation does not eliminate the probability that something was wrong with Wild Bill's eyes. His brief affairs with the Cyprian sisterhood, both in the East and in the West, may have been in part responsible. Medical evidence suggests that gonorrhea, if transferred to the eyes, can produce a condition known as gonorrheal ophthalmia."[31] In HEROES OF THE PLAINS (1882) J.W. Buel recorded that early in 1876 Hickok returned to Kansas City where "he remained for some time inactive owing to an attack of ophthalmia superinduced no doubt from the exposure he underwent while in the Black Hills. Dr. Thorne treated him for several months with such success that his eye-sight, which was for a time entirely destroyed, was partly restored, but he never again regained his perfect vision."[32]

On the subject of Hickok's womanizing while he was city marshal at Abilene, Dale T. Schoenberger noted in THE GUNFIGHTERS (1976) that "with several deputies to do his leg and paper work, 'Wild Bill' whiled away his time playing cards at his favorite haunt, the Alamo Saloon on Cedar Street, and consorting with the ladies of the night. Abilene's strumpets seem to have occupied as much of 'Wild Bill's' time as card playing. His favorite mistress was Jessie Hazel, whom he kept in a room at the three-story, eighty-four room Drover's Cottage on South Main. Later in the summer Jessie was employed as a semi-nude dancer at Billy Mitchell's Novelty Theatre. Hickok kept two other women in a small cabin down in 'McCoy's Addition' (Abilene's red-light district which was formerly called the 'Devil's Half Acre'). These two women were Susannah Moore, his old flame, who had come to Abilene from Springfield, Missouri, and Nan Ross, a local prostitute."[33] In a letter from Charles Gross to J.B. Edwards, dated 15 June 1925 and in the Manuscript Division of the Kansas State Historical Society, Gross wrote: "The many talks I had with Bill I do not recall any remarks or reference to any women other than those he made to the one he lived with in the small house and he did not ever show before me any special affection for her . . . . He always had a mistress. I knew two or three of them, one a former mistress of his was an inmate of a cottage in McCoy's Addition. . . . She [Susannah Moore] came to Abilene to try and make up with Bill. He gave her $25, and made her move on. There was Nan Ross but Bill told her he was through with her. She moved on . . . . "[34]

Hickok's trouble with Phil Coe, owner with Bill Thompson of the Bull's Head Saloon in Abilene, came to its climax over Jessie Hazel. Coe, who had been living with a woman named Alice Chambers, threw her over for Jessie and Jessie became Coe's mistress. This infuriated Hickok to the point where he interrupted them one night at the Gulf House Hotel, kicking Jessie in the face with his boot and beating Coe badly. Coe was no gunman. A few nights later, on 5 October 1871, while making the rounds of Abilene saloons with a group of Texans, Coe, when outside the Alamo Saloon, was attacked by a vicious dog and fired a wild shot at it. Hickok, who was standing before the Novelty Theatre where Jessie had put on her semi-nude show, was talking with Mike Williams, a close friend and a special policeman assigned to help keep order. Hickok crossed over to the Alamo Saloon and confronted Coe, still holding his six-gun. Coe claimed he had shot at a dog, whereupon Hickok went for his own guns. Coe fired hastily, his bullet hitting Hickok's coattails. Hickok, only eight feet away, took better aim and his bullet tore through Coe's stomach, coming out his back. "I've shot too low," Hickok grumbled. Mike Williams, trying to come to Hickok's aid, broke through the crowd. Hickok saw the sudden movement, whirled, and shot Mike twice in the head, Williams dying instantly. Three days later Coe died. Hickok paid for Williams' funeral expenses.

In February, 1872, Abilene voted to bar the Texas cattle trade from the county and Hickok, there no longer being any need for him, was relieved of his official position. He began to wander again. In the fall of 1872, while Hickok was buffalo hunting with Newt Moreland, the peace chief Whistler visited his camp. "They made the signs of hunger and were given a little cold fried buffalo steak that they ate with their knife points, munching dry hardtack with it," Mari Sandoz wrote in THE BUFFALO HUNTERS, "while the two white men sat together at the other side of the fire, silent. Then Whistler spoke his few words for coffee, and when no one seemed to understand, he motioned toward the coffee pot of hospitality that had been filled very well for him the time he charged in to save Bill's camp and his life five years ago. But today the white men seemed unfriendly, perhaps not understanding, so the old Sioux arose and went to the pot and started to make the sign of pouring and of lifting the grub box lid, as for a tin cup perhaps, or for sugar. Swift as in a barroom brawl 'Wild Bill' drew and shot Whistler down."[35] Moreland plugged the sub-chief who was with Whistler and Hickok finished off the remaining Indian, Whistler's nephew.

Just prior to this shooting Hickok had been in the East, at Niagara Falls, where he appeared in late August and early September, 1872, with Sidney Barnett's Wild West Show. On 8 September 1873 he made his debut at Williamsport, Pennsylvania, in Fred G. Maeder's THE SCOUTS OF THE PLAINS, billed third behind "Buffalo Bill" Cody and John B. "Texas Jack" Omohundro. After touring with this show, Hickok quit on 14 March 1874, and returned to wandering in the West. He was not in good health; his sight was failing him; and he was balding. He took to wearing eyeglasses at times to aid his vision.

Originally Hickok had met Mrs. Agnes Lake, a circus owner eleven years his senior, when he was city marshal at Abilene; he met her again in the East in 1874; and, meeting her a third time in Cheyenne, Wyoming, where Hickok more than once had been jailed for vagrancy, he married her there on 5 March 1876. The couple spent their honeymoon in Agnes' home town, Cincinnati, Ohio, but in the spring Hickok left her behind while he set out for the gold fields of Deadwood. Mrs. Hickok was to follow as soon as her husband made his "strike." She never saw him again.

In July, 1876, Hickok was at Fort Laramie, Wyoming, where he joined a wagon train headed for the Dakota Territory. At the fort Hickok met for the first time Martha Jane Cannary, a camp-follower of rough ways known as "Calamity Jane." She was also reputed to be a drunkard and a trouble-maker and the military authorities at the fort put her on the wagon train to insure that she would leave. During the trip she became mistress to Steve Utter, brother to "Colorado Charlie" Utter, an old friend of Hickok, who was also with the train. Jane drank with Hickok, but there is no record that they were intimate and, in fact, Hickok seems to have developed an antipathy for her.

Once in Deadwood, Hickok did almost no mining, holing up instead at Carl Mann's and Jerry Lewis' Number Ten Saloon. On the afternoon of 2 August 1876, Hickok became involved in a poker game with Carl Mann, one of the proprietors, Charles Rich, a gambler, and Frank Massie, a riverboat pilot. Massie, sitting opposite Hickok with his back to the wall, was asked twice by Hickok to exchange seats, and both times refused. Hickok was completely cleaned out after half an hour and borrowed fifty dollars from Mann in order to stay in the game. At 4:10 P.M. Jack McCall, a drifter, entered the saloon, drank a shot of whiskey, and, drawing a .45 Colt, walked up behind Hickok. Hickok had just drawn a queen and two pairs, aces and eights. McCall's slug hit him in the back of the head, coming out under his right cheekbone and embedding itself in Massie's left forearm. As Hickok slumped to the floor, dead but still holding onto his cards, McCall shouted: "Take that!" He later told federal authorities that he was hired by Deadwood gambler John Varnes, who had had a dispute with Hickok over cards in Denver, to kill Hickok. After unsuccessful appeals to President Grant and the U.S. Supreme Court, McCall was hanged at Yankton on 1 March 1877. Hickok's remains were buried at Ingleside with money raised from selling his possessions; on 3 August 1879 they were removed to Deadwood's Mount Moriah Cemetery. In view of how much Hickok disliked "Calamity Jane," it was either frontier malice or frontier humor that must have prompted her body, when she died on 1 August 1903, being buried some twenty feet from Hickok's grave which, by that time, sported a huge headstone, in keeping with his posthumous, and mostly spurious, fame as a law man and a "town tamer."

Even while he was still alive, Hickok was made the subject of dime novel adventures, and this trend, with books such as Prentiss Ingraham's WILD BILL, THE PISTOL DEAD SHOT: OR, DAGGER DON'S DOUBLE (1882), increased as the years passed. William S. Hart not only starred in WILD BILL HICKOK (Paramount, 1923) directed by Clifford S. Smith, but he also wrote the screen story. He must have gotten his plot directly out of these dime novels. According to Hart's film, Hickok gets his nickname "Wild Bill" in recognition of his courage in foiling the attempt of a gang of road agents to hold up a stagecoach. Next, Hickok is told to move on by a nasty group of heavies and, accepting this as a challenge, he saves himself and his horse through an astonishing display of marksmanship. Because of actions such as this, he is personally commended by President Lincoln. Hickok then goes to Dodge City and agrees to put up his guns. However, he finds the city filled with so many recalcitrants, he rides to the fort to get permission from General Custer to use his guns in taming the town. Permission received, Hickok returns to Dodge and in a spectacular gunfight in the street, with the bad elements hiding behind barrels while Hickok stands alone and exposed in the center of town, he outshoots all of them. "Calamity Jane," played by Ethel Grey Terry, is on hand in Dodge as a faro dealer and she and "Wild Bill" become friends; but Hickok's deepest affections in true William S. Hart fashion are reserved for heroine Kathleen O'Connor. Jack McQueen, played by James Farley, is Hickok's sworn arch enemy. When Hickok feels his career as a law man is about to be terminated because of the onset of blindness, McQueen interprets this as a loss of nerve and begins to badger him. In a lightning swift gun battle, Hickok settles McQueen's hash. It has been obvious from the beginning that everything Hickok has been doing to make Dodge a safe and law-abiding community has been done for the sake of impressing Kathleen O'Connor. Having dispatched McQueen, he now feels he must make not only his intentions known to her but must tell her of his failing eyesight. In a highly sentimental moment, O'Connor gives Hickok the bad news: *she is married.* Brushing back the tears, Hickok gets on his horse and rides off.

In their rather cavalier style, George N. Fenin and William K. Everson wrote in THE WESTERN: FROM SILENTS TO THE SEVENTIES (1973) that "Hart's regard for the truth of the old West on the screen could, in fact, be affected by only one thing—a sincere wish not to hurt anyone's feelings. A case in point was his film, WILD BILL HICKOK. Although he had not known Hickok personally, he knew a great deal about him from his father, and from others who had been contemporaries of the famed frontiersman. Thus Hart was able to construct a reasonably accurate, although artistically sentimentalized version of Hickok's life, this accuracy even extending to the little known fact that in his later life, Hickok began to go blind. (Hart achieved some interesting effects at this point in the film by having his camera go out of focus.) One of the legendary stories concerning Hickok is his gun battle with the McCanless [*sic*] boys, who jumped him at a relay station. What really started the fracas was never recorded, but it is an established fact that Hickok killed at least four [*sic*] men in the battle. When it was known that Hart was going to incorporate this incident into his picture, relatives of the McCanless clan wrote him, asking that their family name not be dishonored. Hart, realizing that there were undoubtedly two sides to the story of that battle, and not wanting to cause distress to any McCanless descendants, willingly changed the names in his film."[36]

Hart in his autobiography, MY LIFE EAST AND WEST (1929), recounted a talk he gave before the Lamb's Club in New York City in April, 1925, in which, among other biographical facts about Hickok, he told of his having to kill Phil Cole (*sic*), a hired gunman, in Abilene, Kansas. Following this shooting, according to Hart, "the bad element, in darkness across the street, were quickly mustered; . . . they must get Hickok at once, or leave town, whipped and beaten, their power gone forever; . . . they watched Hickok re-enter the saloon—[the] eight gunmen, bad men, all followed—there was no back door; . . . Hickok stood with his back to them, yet such was the instinct and courage of this wonderful man that not one of the eight men made the first move . . . . When his twelve shots had been fired and the smoke had cleared away, eight men were dead or dying on the floor of the Bull's Head saloon . . . ."[37] After citing this and a number of similar passages from Hart's talk, Ramon F. Adams in his book, BURS UNDER THE SADDLE: A SECOND LOOK AT BOOKS AND HISTORIES OF THE WEST (1964), observed that "all this was told to a believing audience, yet there is not one word of truth in it from beginning to end . . . . Coe (whom Hart calls 'Cole') was not imported from Texas to kill Hickok. He was a businessman of the town, owning half interest in the Bull's Head Saloon the author mentions . . . . The tale of Hickok's killing eight men in a saloon is ridiculous. He killed only two men during his entire stay in Abilene, as we know . . . . And to show how little attention the motion picture people pay to authenticity, here is a quotation from Mr. Hart's book about his picture, WILD BILL HICKOK: 'One of the principal sets of WILD BILL HICKOK was *Dodge City, Kansas.*' But we know that Hickok was not in Dodge City."[38]

It is specifically in this context that it should be noted that Fenin and Everson titled the chapter on Hart in their book, "Hart and Realism," because they felt that he "loved the truth of the West and the Western with a passion and a devotion rarely shared later by other human beings"[39] and, accordingly, set up his films as a standard of value for historical realism against which were judged all other Western films!

THE PLAINSMAN (Paramount, 1936) directed by Cecil B. DeMille was based in part on Courtney Ryley Cooper's short story, "The Prince of the Pistoleers," and, if anything, made more claims about historical accuracy than had Hart's film. The picture opens with Lincoln discussing with his cabinet the idea of sending returning soldiers to the West. In the meantime, arms manufacturers, having become rich during the Civil War, hire Charles Bickford to sell munitions to the Indians. Gary Cooper was cast as Hickok and in his watch case he has a picture of himself and "Calamity Jane," played by Jean Arthur. "Wild Bill" meets "Buffalo Bill" Cody, played by James Ellison, and they get on a riverboat where Porter Hall, cast as Jack McCall, introduces himself to Hickok. When Jane sees Hickok again, she hauls off and kisses him. Hickok is a misogynist. General Custer, played by John Miljan, asks Cody, who has just married, to lead forty-eight troopers and an ammunition train through hostile Indian country. Hickok, on his own hook, goes to see Yellow Hand, played by Paul Harvey. Some nasty Cheyennes speaking gibberish take Jane prisoner and sing *à la* a Hollywood conception of African natives as they march toward their camp. Hickok joins them, remarking to Jane: "Indians'll sell anything. They might sell you." At camp, when he is dragged off to be tortured, Hickok confesses to Jane that he loves her. Under pressure to save her beloved's life, Jane tells Yellow Hand the route Cody intends to take. The Indians let the two of them go and Hickok rejects Jane completely for having given in. Hickok heads to warn Cody while Jane rides off to tell Custer of the planned attack. Since this is a Cecil B. DeMille picture, there are easily a thousand Indians on hand to swoop down on Cody and his forty-eight men—a symbolic number!—but the forty-eight successfully hold them off until Custer arrives.

Jack McCall joins Bickford and the gunrunners. Bickford bribes three Cavalry soldiers to assassinate Hickok. Hickok shoots them down and makes it clear, afterwards, that he only fights in fair fights. Custer misinterprets Hickok's action and sends Cody to bring in Hickok, dead or alive. *En route*, Cody meets an Indian played by Anthony Quinn—at the time DeMille's son-in-law—and Quinn tells Cody of Custer's defeat, a flashback showing the expiring Custer clinging to the flag as he breathes his last. Cody then teams up with Hickok to prevent Bickford from selling munitions to Sitting Bull. Hickok arrives in Deadwood. Jane is there before him and tells him she will gladly cook for him, if he has changed his mind about her. Hickok, who for his own part is having second thoughts about being a gunman, puts all this aside when he sees Bickford. He shoots him down. He holds Bickford's gang prisoner at gun point at a poker table in a saloon where Jack McCall is the bartender. While playing cards with the gang, Hickok has his back to McCall, who creeps up and shoots him. Hickok dies in Jane's arms. Cody fortuitously arrives with the Cavalry and together they round up McCall and Bickford's gang. The film concludes with a patriotic message that reads in part: "It shall be as it was in the past . . . a nation molded to last."

VARIETY said of THE PLAINSMAN when it was released that it was "a big and good Western . . . not a COVERED WAGON, but realistic enough."[40] When it was remade—THE PLAINSMAN (Universal, 1966) directed by David Lowell Rich—Judith Crist in TV GUIDE called the remake "a prime example of Hollywood's pointless (and perpetual) attempts to remake its classics . . . . Even discounting the predecessor, this oater stands on its own as a prairie dog."[41] I think she got the sentiment a little wrong. The predecessor was no classic.

However, the predecessor did inspire Columbia Pictures as to the appropriate subject matter for its first Western chapter play, THE GREAT ADVENTURES OF WILD BILL HICKOK (Columbia, 1938) directed by Mack V. Wright and Sam Nelson and starring Gordon Elliott as Hickok. The plot has it that Abilene

is a lawless, wild town. The entire district is being terrorized by a band of marauders called the Phantom Raiders. Others would challenge the Phantom Raiders' control: the Kansas-Pacific railroad, which is in the process of completing
its railhead at Abilene; a huge herd of Texas cattle being led on its way to Abilene by Colonel Cameron, played by Monte Blue. Federal authorities in Washington, D.C., alarmed at the situation assign U.S. Marshal "Wild Bill" Hickok
to the district. The Phantom Raiders are not above turning loose bands of wild,
screaming Hollywood Indians to raid the Cameron herd and, in the final episode, the Raiders and the Indians unite in an all-out battle with Cameron and
his men. Hickok saves the day when he rides in leading the Cavalry which makes
short work of the Raiders and the Indians while Hickok himself kills the leader
of the Raiders in a gun duel.

Henceforth, as his namesake, Elliott became known as "Wild Bill." He was
identically attired, however, no matter whom he was playing: Hickok, Kit Carson in OVERLAND WITH KIT CARSON (Columbia, 1939), a grandson of
Boone in THE RETURN OF DANIEL BOONE (Columbia, 1941), or THE SON
OF DAVY CROCKETT (Columbia, 1941). Elliott made a series of "Wild Bill"
Saunders adventures in 1938–1939, but for the next season he was mostly "Wild
Bill" Hickok, beginning with THE RETURN OF WILD BILL (Columbia, 1940)
directed by Joseph H. Lewis. One example from this series should certainly
suffice to show how Hickok is portrayed.

In PRAIRIE SCHOONERS (Columbia, 1940) directed by Sam Nelson, the
year is given as 1874, a time of drought in Kansas. Kenneth Harlan is a loan
shark driving indebted farmers off their lands. The heroine, Evelyn Young, for
some reason is better off than the farmers and she shares her food with them.
Her foreman is Dub "Cannonball" Taylor, Elliott's usual sidekick. When we
first see "Wild Bill" in Butte, Colorado, he tells a blacksmith that he does not
need his guns to quiet the town heavy: he uses a bull whip on him. Three times
in as many minutes he repeats the refrain used throughout the series: "I'm a
peaceable man." Riding up to Young and Cannonball, he is compared to a tor-
nado. Young informs the farmers that "Wild Bill" is "the hardest ridin' peaceable man I know." In the meantime, the viewer learns that Harlan and his partner Ray Teal are playing the Indian tribes—the Sioux against the Pawnees—in
order to trade furs for beads with the Pawnees and furs for guns with the Sioux.

"Wild Bill" organizes a wagon train. All the farmers are going to relocate
to Colorado. In stock footage from THE BIG TRAIL (Fox, 1930) directed by
Raoul Walsh, they cross a river in a rain storm. Harlan in an effort to stop
them—he is convinced their migration will ruin his fur business—sends Jim
Thorpe and his Pawnees against the wagon train. "Indians!" "Wild Bill" says,
pointing. "Pawnees." Then there is a stock footage clip of Cheyennes crossing
the Powder River from END OF THE TRAIL (Columbia, 1932) directed by D.
Ross Lederman. Young is separated from the wagon train and is taken captive
by Harlan. "Are you in cahoots with those savages?" she demands. Pawnees
are shot down right and left, and finally they retreat. "You folks turned out to

be first-rate Indian fighters," Elliott tells the homesteaders. Next "Wild Bill" goes to talk to Jim Thorpe, only to find Harlan and Teal there and Young tied up. "Wild Bill" talks to Thorpe in pidgen English: "These people no steal your hunting grounds." It turns out that when Ray Teal traded guns with the Sioux, they made him a blood brother and he has a scar on his chest to prove it. "Wild Bill" exposes him. Young is released. The wagon train is allowed to proceed. The Pawnees will deal personally with Harlan and Teal.

In the 'Fifties, Guy Madison took over the role of "Wild Bill," first on radio, beginning in 1952, and then in the television series WILD BILL HICKOK (Syndicated, 1952–1954, CBS, 1954–1957, ABC, 1957–1958). In Madison's case, as in Elliott's before him, Hickok was portrayed as a hero. In films, however, made in the same decade, a viewer could take his choice. In PONY EX-PRESS (Paramount, 1953) directed by Jerry Hopper, Charlton Heston was cast as "Buffalo Bill" and Forrest Tucker as Hickok. The film showed one heroic episode after another. The two—in what might well be regarded as an unoffi-cial remake of THE PLAINSMAN—are commissioned to set up the Pony Ex-press to California. Hickok is definitely second fiddle when it comes to the women, both Rhonda Fleming and Jan Sterling vying for Cody's affections. Porter Hall was cast as frontier scout Jim Bridger. When Sterling is killed in the terrific shoot-out with which the film ends, Cody is no longer perplexed as to which one of the two he will marry.

In JACK McCALL, DESPERADO (Columbia, 1953) directed by Sidney Salkow, the story is a combination of the Hollywood version of the Billy the Kid/Pat Garrett stand-off and an example of the Outlaw Story plot setting. George Montgomery, cast as McCall, is "Wild Bill's" deputy in Deadwood. He out-draws Hickok face to face at the very opening of the picture. After shooting him down, McCall is put on trial and he tells of how he and Hickok were in the Cavalry together during the Civil War. Hickok was his sergeant. McCall was falsely accused of being a spy and, while supposedly searching for Mc-Call, Hickok and McCall's cousin shoot down McCall's mother and father and take over the McCall plantation. Douglas Kennedy was cast as Hickok. Later, in Deadwood, Hickok's sole reason for taking the job as town marshal is to get rich gold fields away from the Sioux led by Chief Red Cloud, played by Jay Silverheels. Secretly, Hickok raises an army of cut-throats to prey upon the Sioux as part of his scheme to convince Silverheels to sell out. He even persuades McCall that he is honest, until he leads McCall and Silverheels and a party of Sioux into ambush. Then McCall learns the truth. Hence, the gunfight. McCall is acquitted and, joined by heroine Angela Stevens, decides to return to the McCall family plantation.

"Calamity Jane" did not fare much better. In THE PLAINSMAN among the things Jane tries in order to attract "Wild Bill" is to switch from wearing pants to wearing a dress. I will have more to say about this dress code in a later chapter, but it is a sub-theme in most of the Jane films. In CALAMITY JANE AND SAM BASS (Universal, 1949) directed by George Sherman, Yvonne

DeCarlo was cast as Jane and throughout she projects the image of a frontier Mae West in britches. "Wild Bill" is nowhere in evidence; the heart-throb is Howard Duff as Sam Bass. Dorothy Hart, the other heroine also in love with Bass, is saved from total perdition when Jane breaks Bass out of jail and rides off with him, character actress Ann Doran cooling Hart's ardor by telling her that now Bass is "gallivanting around with that 'Calamity Jane' person"—one more wrong choice on Bass' road to ruin.

Instead of that old chestnut of how Jane pined away for Hickok, asking on her deathbed to be buried next to "Wild Bill," a new flame is provided for her in THE TEXAN MEETS CALAMITY JANE (Columbia, 1950) directed by André Lamb. Evelyn Ankers is Jane. The film opens with her kneeling at "Wild Bill's" grave, sobbing. She claims that Hickok was the only man she ever loved. She runs the Prairie Queen saloon which is coveted by heavy Jack Ingram. James Ellison, cast as a frontier lawyer, comes to town and takes Jane's side in the dispute. We know when she falls in love with Ellison because she changes from pants to a dress.

In CALAMITY JANE (Warner's, 1953) directed by David Butler, Doris Day is Jane. In this version, she cannot make up her mind whom she loves more, Phil Carey, a Cavalry lieutenant, or "Wild Bill," played by Howard Keel. The maid of an opera singer from Chicago helps both Jane and Hickok make up their minds once she convinces Jane to surrender her buckskins for dresses. The film ends with Jane and "Wild Bill" getting married.

Equally absurd is the storyline of THE WHITE BUFFALO (United Artists, 1976) directed by J. Lee Thompson, to say nothing of the mechanical buffalo which does all the menacing. But Charles Bronson, cast as Hickok, portrays him much as he must have been, which is to say a haunted, nearly psychotic killer. If Mari Sandoz was right, and Hickok suffered from glaucoma rather than gonorrheal ophthalmia, glaucoma can be induced by syphilis, as suggested here in the screenplay. In fact, the view of Hickok is closest to Sandoz' own. Hickok makes friends with Crazy Horse, played by Will Sampson, and hunts for the white buffalo. Once the monster is killed, Crazy Horse tells Hickok: "You have lost a friend . . . and found one." But they must part company forever because Hickok shot down peace chief Whistler. Bronson's Hickok wears dark glasses much of the time, as the historical Hickok did, and the interior saloon sequences are among the most convincing in any Western film. Unfortunately, none of this can really compensate for the foolish plot.

"I was raised in a little town of which many of you may never have heard," Dwight D. Eisenhower said in a speech at Washington, D.C., on 23 November 1953. "But out in the West it is a famous place. It is called Abilene, Kansas. We had as our marshal a man named 'Wild Bill' Hickok. Now that town had a code and I was raised as a boy to prize that code. It was: Meet anyone face to face with whom you disagree. You could not sneak up on him from behind, or do any damage to him, without suffering the penalty of an enraged citizenry.

If you met him face to face and took the same risks as he did, you could get away with almost anything, as long as the bullet was in front."[42]

The delusion, created by image-makers, lives on. Wyatt Earp was in an even more advantageous position than Hickok because he lived into the age of the motion picture, made friends with movie cowboys Tom Mix and William S. Hart—they were both pallbearers at Earp's funeral—and with John Ford. Earp, during his last years, wanted Hart to film his life; it was not to be. Of the men Earp knew personally, it was John Ford who filmed the story of his Tombstone years.

12

Wyatt Earp

Although he lived a long and eventful life—having been born in Monmouth, Illinois, in 1848 and dying in Los Angeles in 1929—Earp is remembered primarily for the brief period when he and his brothers were in Tombstone and with Doc Holliday took part in the shoot-out near the O.K. Corral. In 1871 he jumped bail and fled a charge of horse-stealing. For most of his life, he was occupied with owning and operating saloons, devising and pulling off various confidence games, and gambling. In 1877 he met Doc Holliday at Fort Griffin and Doc became his closest friend as long as Doc lived. In his series of articles, "Famous Gunfighters of the Western Frontier" which ran in HUMAN LIFE MAGAZINE in 1907, Bat Masterson, who knew both men, wrote that Doc's "whole heart and soul were wrapped up in Wyatt Earp and he was always ready to stake his life in defense of any cause in which Wyatt was interested."[43]

Earp was married for the first time to Irilla H. Sutherland on 10 January 1870, but the marriage lasted less than a year, when Irilla died, probably of typhoid fever. By the time Earp met Doc Holliday, Celia Ann (Mattie) Blaylock was living with him as his wife. On 1 December 1879 Wyatt and Mattie arrived in Tombstone, Arizona Territory. While *en route*, Wyatt had stopped off at Prescott and talked to his brother, Virgil, who on 27 November 1879 had been appointed a U.S. marshal for Yavapai County, Arizona Territory, persuading him to come to Tombstone. Presently Wyatt's other brothers, Jim and Morgan, followed him to Tombstone, the youngest, Baxter Warren Earp, coming last from the family home at Colton, California. Wyatt speculated in several mining operations, selling one claim with his partner, Harry Finaty of Dodge City, for $30,000. Wyatt also found employment as a shotgun messenger for Wells, Fargo, and Company, at which Morgan Earp succeeded him when Wyatt accepted a job as a deputy under Sheriff Charles A. Shibell, Tombstone then being part of Pima County. On 28 October 1880, Wyatt may have assisted Virgil in jailing the outlaw, William Graham, known as "Curly Bill Brocius," after the latter had shot down City Marshal Fred White. Morgan and Wyatt did assist Virgil in arresting several of "Curly Bill's" associates. In the interim before an election could be held, Virgil Earp was appointed assistant city marshal. Fifteen days later, he was defeated at the polls by Ben Sippy in a special election, and defeated by him again in the municipal election held on 4 January 1881. It was not until 6 June 1881, after Sippy had left Tombstone, never to return, that the town council appointed Virgil city marshal.

While this was going on, Wyatt was dismissed by Shibell and replaced by John H. Behan, formerly sheriff of Yavapai County. When Cochise County was formed from part of Pima County in early 1881, both Wyatt and Behan applied for the office of sheriff. Former Major General John C. Frémont, then Territorial governor of Arizona, decided on Behan. Wyatt and Behan became bitter enemies and the situation was worsened when Josephine Sarah Marcus, Behan's mistress, was thrown over by Behan only for her to take up with Wyatt even though Wyatt was still living with Mattie.

In exchange for protection, Wyatt acquired a gambling interest at the Oriental Saloon and installed Morgan, Doc Holliday, who had shown up, and ex-Dodge City cronies Bat Masterson and Luke Short as dealers at the Oriental. The Oriental was owned by Milton E. "Mike" Joyce and his association with Earp was anything but cordial, Wyatt at one point having to slap him down. It was in this atmosphere that the chain of social and economic events began which resulted in the famous shoot-out.

The initial incident centered around the theft of six U.S. government mules. First Lieutenant Joseph H. Hurst and a detail of four troopers were assigned to recover the mules. Hurst enlisted the assistance of Virgil, who was still a deputy U.S. marshal, and Wyatt and Morgan accompanied Virgil. The mules were traced to the ranch of Thomas and Robert F. (Frank) McLaury, a short distance from the township of Charleston. The McLaury brothers refused to come outside but said they would surrender the mules if the Earps were sent back to Tombstone. The Earps went back and the McLaurys reneged, instead making threats against the lives of the Earps. A few weeks later when Wyatt met the McLaurys at Charleston, they tried to pick a fight with him. It was not Wyatt's way to grandstand when he was alone. He refused to fight and they promised to kill him if they ever came across him again.

Then, on the night of 15 March 1881, the Benson stage was held up about a mile outside Contention City, near Tombstone, and the driver, Eli (Budd) Philpot, was shot by one of the hold-up men. The horses bolted and the stage with its reputed $26,000 was brought to safety by Robert H. Paul, the shotgun messenger. Several eye-witnesses implicated Doc Holliday in the hold-up. Many people in and around Tombstone were convinced that Marshall Williams, the Wells, Fargo agent, the Earps, and Doc Holliday had been behind a whole series of stage robberies. The clinching piece of evidence came from Kate Elder, Doc's mistress (who claimed to be his wife). After a quarrel, she signed an affidavit that Doc had been involved in the murder of Philpot and on 5 June

John Behan arrested him. Earp then went to see Kate and, after talking with her, got her to swear that the affidavit was false, that Behan had got her drunk, and that she had had no idea of what it was she was signing. Doc was released for want of evidence.

N.H. "Old Man" Clanton owned a ranch near Tombstone where he was assisted by his youngest son, Billy. His two elder sons, Ike and Phineas, operated a freight line. Together with the McLaury brothers, the Clantons would stage frequent raids across the border into Mexico to rustle cattle, and then bring them back and sell them in Arizona. When "Old Man" Clanton died unexpectedly as a consequence of wounds received from a recent foray into Mexico, Ike took over as the leader of the Clanton-McLaury faction. William F. "Billy the Kid" Claiborne, born in 1860, became a hanger-on with the Clantons.

Billy Clanton and Wyatt had a heated exchange over a horse Wyatt claimed to own. Then, on the night of 8 September 1881, the Bisbee stage was robbed of $3,100 by Deputy Sheriff Frank C. Stilwell of Cochise County and Peter Spence. Wyatt and Morgan Earp, Marshall Williams, the agent, and Frederick J. Dodge, a Wells, Fargo detective, helped arresting officer Deputy Sheriff William A. Breakenridge escort Stilwell and Spence to Tombstone after their arrest at Bisbee. Stilwell and Spence were friends of Ike Clanton and Frank McLaury and McLaury later threatened the life of Morgan Earp and his brothers for the role they had played in the apprehension. Accusations flew back and forth, the Earps and Doc blaming Ike Clanton for somehow being implicated in the Benson stage hold-up. On the night of 25 October, Wyatt, Morgan, and Doc confronted Ike and Doc three times tried to get Ike to go for his gun. Ike insisted that he was unarmed. Later that night, having in the meantime armed himself, Ike confronted Wyatt and said he was now armed and would be ready to have it out in the morning. Then Ike sat in a poker game with Virgil Earp, John Behan, and Tom McLaury; the game broke up with Ike and Virgil hurling insults at each other.

The next day, Wednesday, 26 October 1881, the showdown came. Virgil Earp, acting in his official capacity as city marshal, pistol-whipped and then arrested Ike for carrying weapons within the city limits. Virgil and Morgan took Ike to police court and, after Ike was fined, he berated Morgan and Morgan offered Ike a gun right there, daring him to make something out of it. Tom McLaury, on his way to the police court, collided with Wyatt who was just entering himself. Wyatt slapped McLaury with one hand and pistol-whipped him with the other. Later that same day, Wyatt engaged Frank McLaury in a round of verbal abuse. At 2:30 P.M. the Earps and Doc Holliday decided jointly on a show of force. Virgil Earp told Sheriff Behan: "I will not arrest them, but will kill them on sight." Behan pleaded with Virgil not to start any shooting. When he saw this was not going to get him anywhere, he went to the Clantons and McLaurys and asked them to give up their weapons. Frank McLaury and Billy Clanton refused. Tom McLaury threw open his coat to show he was not carrying a weapon and Behan searched Ike and found no gun. Billy Claiborne, who was standing on the sidelines, told Behan that he was not involved. Behan then went again to remonstrate with the Earps, but was told it was too late.

The Earp party—Wyatt, Virgil, Morgan, and Doc—met the McLaury brothers, Ike and Billy Clanton, and Claiborne on the South side of Frémont Street, a short distance east of Third Street, in a vacant lot between the boarding house of Camillus S. Fly, a photographer, and a private dwelling. The lot had open stalls which were used by the O.K. Corral stable. Sheriff Behan tried to intervene, but both sides ignored him. "Throw up your hands!" Virgil Earp shouted. "You sonofabitches have been looking for a fight and now you can have it!" Wyatt said. As Wyatt reached into his right overcoat pocket for his pistol, Frank McLaury cried, "We will!" "Let them have it," Morgan Earp said. "All right!" Doc Holliday said. Shooting began. Morgan shot Billy Clanton. Wyatt pumped lead at Frank McLaury, hitting him in the stomach.

Billy Claiborne broke from where he was standing behind the Clantons and McLaurys and ran toward Fly's boarding house. Ike Clanton, still unarmed, rushed over to Wyatt. "The fighting has commenced," Wyatt snapped at him, "go to fighting or get away." Clanton fled into the photography studio in front of the boarding house. Claiborne, by this time, was right behind him, heading for cover. As soon as one of Wyatt's bullets hit Frank McLaury, Frank's horse reared and bolted. Tom McLaury made a try for the Winchester slung in the boot of Frank's mount and missed it. Doc brought up a sawed-off shotgun and plugged Tom in the chest and the right side. Tom pitched forward, dead. Frank McLaury snapped off a shot at Doc, the bullet ricocheting off Doc's holster and ripping across Doc's back. A second later a bullet fired by Morgan Earp hit Frank in the head, killing him instantly. Billy Clanton, reeling backwards from the bullet fired by Morgan Earp, was hit again in the wrist by a bullet from Virgil Earp's gun. Using his left hand, he was able to draw his gun and fired, hitting Morgan Earp near the base of the neck and felling him. Billy then fired at Virgil and hit him in the calf of the right leg. By this time, Billy was down, crawling along the ground toward Frémont Street. Billy wanted to fire again, but he was very weak and C.S. Fly, the photographer into whose studio Ike Clanton and Billy Clairborne had fled, came over and took the gun out of his hand. The shooting was over. It had lasted thirty seconds.

Billy Clanton was picked up to be carried away. He asked where he was hit. Told he was dying, he said, "Get a doctor and put me to sleep." As he was being carried off, he whimpered: "Pull off my boots. I always told my mother I'd never die with my boots on." Once he was set down, he began to call out: "They've murdered me! Clear the crowd away from the door and give me air. I've been murdered." A physician came and injected morphine alongside an abdominal wound while Billy was restrained. Fifteen minutes later, after muttering again about the crowd, Billy Clanton died.

"Almost everyone, in a kill situation, is reluctant to shoot," Western fiction author E.B. Mann wrote in a letter to Joseph G. Rosa quoted in Rosa's THE

GUNFIGHTER: MAN OR MYTH? (1969). "I would expect most of today's fast gunmen to draw, see that they had the opponent hopelessly beaten, and stop, expecting him to accept defeat. Whereupon Hickok (or Hardin, or Earp, or Breakenridge, et al.) would proceed to kill him! Because I don't believe those men *had* much, if any, such reluctance!"[44]

The McLaury brothers and Billy Clanton were dressed in fine clothes and placed in the window of a hardware store with a sign stating that they had been murdered in the Streets of Tombstone. "Murdered in the streets of Tombstone" was also written on their headstones. To an extent, this was not just an expression of bias. The gunfight could scarcely be called "fair" insofar as neither Ike Clanton nor Tom McLaury was armed—as surely they would have been if they had been convinced that the confrontation were to lead to a shoot-out. Wyatt and Doc were arrested. Warrants, although issued, were not served on Morgan and Virgil because they were bedridden. On 29 October Virgil was relieved of his position as city marshal by the city council. Testimony was heard before Justice of the Peace Wells Spicer for most of the month of November and on 1 December he ruled that Wyatt and Doc be released from custody on the grounds "that the defendants were fully justified in committing these homicides."[45] A grand jury then reviewed the evidence and upheld Spicer's decision.

The vendetta continued. On 28 December Virgil Earp was gunned while crossing Allen Street in Tombstone; his arm was left partially crippled as a result of the wounds he received. On 18 March 1882, Morgan Earp was assassinated while playing billiards with Robert S. Hatch in Hatch's saloon and billiard hall. Wyatt, who was watching the game, narrowly missed being hit by the bullets. After investigation, a coroner's jury ruled that Morgan had been killed by Frank Stilwell and Peter Spence along with Florentino "Indian Charlie" Cruz, a *mestizo* woodcutter working for Spence, and a faro dealer named Fries who had replaced Morgan as a dealer at the Oriental Saloon when Wyatt sold out his interest there. Morgan was Wyatt's favorite brother. Wyatt and Warren Earp, along with Virgil Earp and his wife, Doc, and two other Earp cronies, accompanied Morgan's body on its way back to Colton, California, via rail as far as Tucson, where Wyatt, Warren, Doc, and the other two detrained, cornered Stilwell, who was in town that night, in the railroad yard, and shot him to death. Wyatt got in the first shot—using a shotgun which Stilwell tried to push aside but which wounded him anyway—before the others let loose. Murder warrants were sworn out for the two Earps, Doc, and the other two men, but this did not stop them. They went hunting Peter Spence at his wood camp near Tombstone, found Spence gone, but "Indian Charlie" Cruz was there and they riddled him with five bullets. Spence turned himself in to John Behan for safe-keeping, was eventually tried, and released. In April, 1882, Wyatt and Warren Earp fled the Territory, winding up in Gunnison, Colorado, while Doc went to Pueblo, Colorado. On 8 November 1887 Doc died at the sanitarium at

Glenwood Springs, Colorado, his final comment being: "This is funny . . . . "
It was just about the last thing this alcoholic dentist, turned gambler and gunfighter, had expected—dying quietly in bed.

Wyatt Earp's career continued for nearly five decades after he left Arizona
and, so far, the best account we have of it is to be found in I MARRIED WYATT
EARP: THE RECOLLECTIONS OF JOSEPHINE SARAH MARCUS EARP
(1976) as collected, edited, and annotated by Glenn G. Boyer. From about 1905
on, Wyatt tried to publish his own account of his life, but he was unsuccessful
in finding anyone willing to take it on. He urged William S. Hart to use his
influence to get a biography published written in collaboration with a close family
friend, John Flood, Jr., but not even Hart could overcome Flood's writing style
which an editor at Bobbs-Merrill termed "stilted and florid and diffuse."[46] The
manuscript continued to make the rounds, but with similar results.

In his book, THE WAR, THE WEST, AND THE WILDERNESS (1979),
Kevin Brownlow recorded a conversation he had with film director Allan Dwan
in which Dwan told him of how Wyatt Earp had happened on Dwan's set one
day when Dwan was directing Douglas Fairbanks, Sr., in THE HALF-BREED
(Triangle, 1916) and Dwan put Earp in a crowd scene. " 'When I knew him,' "
Dwan told Brownlow, " 'he was no longer a marshal, and there was no longer
a West, and he couldn't be the symbol that he'd been. He looked for what anybody would look for. And the first person that got hold of him said he was a
natural for show business. Well, he was and he wasn't. Our suspicion, because
of the people that came around the set with him, was that he was looking for a
place in law and order. He would have loved to have been Chief of Police of
Los Angeles, or the marshal of the county. I think he was timid about being
photographed, about acting and pretending. He knew inside himself that he wasn't
an actor and had nothing to offer. I remember he saw Fairbanks bouncing around
in the trees, and said, 'Oh no, I'd not like to do that.' and I think for that
reason he just finally took one last look and left."[47]

In 1926, Walter Noble Burns, who had done so much to distort the facts
about Billy the Kid and who would likewise deal with Joaquín Murieta, happened on the scene, announcing to the aged Earp that he wanted to tell his story.
Earp declined and so Burns switched gears and declared that he was writing a
biography about Doc Holliday. Wyatt agreed to assist in this project but became suspicious when so many of Burns' questions centered around Wyatt and
the other Earps rather than Doc. William S. Hart only aggravated the situation
when he told Earp that Burns had plagiarized Charlie Siringo's book on the Kid
in writing about him. Unfortunately, Hart was unaware that Siringo himself had
copied much verbatim for his THE HISTORY OF "BILLY THE KID," which
was privately printed in 1920, from Pat Garrett's book which Ash Upson wrote:
fantasy perpetuating fantasy. Nor was Burns unduly dismayed. He had now met
and talked with Wyatt Earp and that, seemingly, was enough for the gullible to
believe true the image of the heroic gunfighter he projected in his characterization of Wyatt in TOMBSTONE: AN ILIAD OF THE SOUTHWEST (1927).

In fact, knowing Burns' *modus operandi*—in his THE SAGA OF BILLY THE KID he fabricated all manner of conversations with people, including one between himself and Pat Garrett—not even talking to Earp would have been necessary for him to write the book he had had in mind all along.

W.R. Burnett, who is better remembered for his gangster novel, LITTLE CAESAR (1929), followed in Burns' wake with SAINT JOHNSON (1930), a fictionalized version of the Wyatt Earp legend in which he changed the names of the characters involved. Yet the *piéce de résistance* was Stuart N. Lake's WYATT EARP: FRONTIER MARSHAL (1931) dedicated "in acknowledgment to Wyatt Berry Stapp Earp who lived and relived this book."[48] By the time Lake's account was re-issued for the second time in paperback in 1959, the publisher's hype called Lake "the man who knew Wyatt Earp best" and, on the back cover, informed the prospective reader that Lake "spent six years in close association with Wyatt Earp. It is from Earp's spoken words and living recollections that Stuart Lake created this account of the almost legendary life and times of the man whose icy courage and relentless deliberation made him known, feared and respected throughout the Southwest in its most lawless and violent era."[49]

The truth of the matter is that Wyatt Earp's first communication with Lake was a letter dated Christmas, 1927. Lake wanted to write Wyatt's biography and in late summer, 1928, he met with Wyatt and Josephine and a regular correspondence began between them. "This writer took over the Flood manuscript and sought to professionalize it, starting with several personal interviews with Wyatt," Glenn G. Boyer noted in an editorial epilogue in I MARRIED WYATT EARP. "The old law man may not have learned caution from the Burns experience, but Josephine had. She made sure that all her husband's meetings with Lake were monitored by herself and John Flood, who took down what was said in shorthand. By the winter of 1928 the manuscript was nearing completion. At this stage, with Wyatt still living, the work was quite likely a realistic biography as the former marshal wished it to appear. But Wyatt Earp died on 13 January 1929, without having read a single word of it. With his controlling collaborator gone, Lake was now free to liven up the story."[50] Also, as Boyer observed, "the preface stated that the entire story was Wyatt's first-person account as told to Lake, a statement which he himself later admitted was untrue."[51] On 9 January 1941 Lake wrote to Burton Rascoe that " . . . your suspicions are well founded . . . . As a matter of cold fact, Wyatt never 'dictated' a word to me. . . . He was delightfully laconic, or exasperatingly so."[52]

Ramon F. Adams perhaps put it best in BURS UNDER THE SADDLE when he wrote of Lake's book that it "leaves out all of the shady incidents of Earp's life and does everything possible to glorify him. One wonders if such a man is human: a fabulous and invincible hero, a man who could do [no] wrong, a man who never lost a conflict, a man without fear or fault, a man who could make notorious gunmen quake with fright."[53] Adams then set about to correct Lake's many, many errors of fact, but this was many years later. While he was alive,

Lake considered Wyatt Earp his own personal creation and he guarded it vigorously. He even went to the extreme of initiating several legal moves in an effort to suppress THE EARP BROTHERS OF TOMBSTONE: THE STORY OF MRS. VIRGIL EARP (1960) by Frank Waters on which Waters began work in 1935 and which had to wait many years to see the light of print. In it, Waters treated, among other issues, Wyatt's desertion of his second wife, Celia Ann (Mattie), for Josephine, and Mattie's tragic last years and suicide. Unwisely, Waters included in his condemnation of the Earps in general Virgil Earp. Allie Earp, Virgil's widow, whose story Waters was ostensibly telling, took umbrage, repudiated the book, and, more effectively than Lake, held up its publication.

W.R. Burnett's SAINT JOHNSON made it to the screen first under the title LAW AND ORDER (Universal, 1932) directed by Edward Cahn. As THE VIRGINIAN (Paramount, 1929) directed by Victor Fleming, LAW AND ORDER centered around a pathetic hanging. Walter Huston, as Frame Johnson, is the hero, supported by Harry Carey as Ed Brandt, Raymond Hatton as Deadwood, and Russell Hopton as Luther Johnson. They are a closely knit group, Frame known as "Saint" Johnson because of his reputation as a lawman. Opening to stock footage from such Universal Westerns as THE INDIANS ARE COMING (Universal, 1930), the standard serial chase music playing on the track, the four principals are seen, sitting in a saloon. Richard Cramer tries to cheat Harry Carey at cards before Walter Huston breaks up the game. The four are on their way to Tombstone. Fin Elder, played by Alphong Ethier, is running for re-election as sheriff. He is backed by the Northrups, played by Ralph Ince, Harry Woods, and Dick Alexander. The decent element, outraged by the lawlessness of the Northrups, hires Huston to be deputy marshal.

Andy Devine is placed in Huston's custody. Devine has shot a man. There is a gang after him, intent on a lynching. Huston and the others protect Devine, backing down a mob with shotguns. When, after a fair trial, Devine is sentenced to hang, Huston glibly tells Devine that he should be quite pleased to be the first man to be hanged legally in Tombstone's history. Devine becomes rather effusive in his avowals of gratitude, in contrast to the stark grimness of the public hanging itself, with the camera panning many faces amid the sounds of women screaming.

Huston invokes a gun-toting ordinance. The Northrups object. Russell Hopton shoots Dick Alexander in a fair gunfight. The decent element, however, begins to think that Huston and the others are trying to take over the town for themselves. The Huston faction, in a predictably dumb play, takes off its guns, only for Harry Carey to be shot down in a dark street by the Northrups. In the Huston faction's hotel room, Carey dies, after having given away his belongings. There is a wake until dawn. Huston then quits as deputy marshal and vows vengeance. He tells the others to strap on their guns and they meet the Northrups at the O.K. Corral—the name painted on a livery stable on Mauser Street which ran through Universal's Western town set. The shooting begins. Raymond Hatton is killed. Russell Hopton is shot. Huston closes in on Ralph Ince, chasing him through a barn and finally dropping him. As a church bell tolls, Huston mounts his horse and rides out of town, alone. In A PICTORIAL HISTORY OF THE WESTERN FILM (1969), William K. Everson declared that this film has "the finest reconstruction yet of the famous gun duel at the O.K. Corral." [54]

The picture was remade three times, first as the serial WILD WEST DAYS (Universal, 1937) directed by Ford Beebe and Cliff Smith, and then as LAW AND ORDER (Universal, 1940) directed by Ray Taylor and LAW AND ORDER (Universal, 1953) directed by Nathan H. Juran. Johnny Mack Brown starred in both the serial and the first of the two feature versions. WILD WEST DAYS owed virtually nothing to the novel and employed a triad hero and a white master villain leading a band of Indians. In the feature Brown comes to a town— still the Universal Western town set—to find it controlled by the villainous Daggetts, played by Ted Adams and Ethan Laidlaw. With the help of James Craig, a reformed gambler, and comedian Fuzzy Knight, Brown restores order and is eligible to marry heroine Nell O'Day. In the second feature remake Ronald Reagan was cast as Frame Johnson, Alex Nicol as Luta Johnson, and Russell Johnson as Jimmy Johnson. Dorothy Malone was added to the cast for the purpose of romance. In view of his subsequent career, it is interesting to watch Reagan put forward his belief in gun law as a final mediator in a world where there is only right and wrong—black and white even in Technicolor.

Stuart N. Lake's novel was adapted for the screen the first time as FRONTIER MARSHAL (Fox, 1934) directed by Lew Seiler. Josephine made such a fuss about what she felt to be the lies in Lake's book that Fox fell back to the same ruse Universal had necessarily used in filming Burnett's fictional account. Wyatt Earp's name was not used in the film; instead the character played by star George O'Brien was called Michael Wyatt. The plot has it that in Tombstone a crooked mayor, played by Berton Churchill, and his gang are behind a series of daring stage robberies as well as running the gambling casinos and dance halls. Churchill murders his partner, played by Oscar Reid, just as O'Brien arrives in town. O'Brien rejects Ruth Gillette, cast as Queenie La Verne, a role played in a poor imitation of Mae West, and instead takes up with Irene Bentley, cast as the murdered man's daughter. With the help of Doc Warren, played by Alan Edwards, a desperado who steals from the rich to give to the poor, O'Brien manages in just over an hour to bring the villains to the bar of justice.

After the success of Henry King's JESSE JAMES (20th-Fox, 1939), the studio decided to make a series of such "biography" films about Western personalities. In time, THE RETURN OF FRANK JAMES (20th-Fox, 1940) directed by Fritz Lang and BELLE STARR (20th-Fox, 1941) directed by Irving Cummings would be added to the list, but the picture Darryl Zanuck wanted the studio to make right after JESSE JAMES was the definitive version, under its rightful title, of WYATT EARP, FRONTIER MARSHAL. Again, Josephine put up a fuss. Stuart N. Lake had insisted from the beginning that she was hopelessly insane. Zanuck was not so sure, but he was adamant that the lead character in the film would have to be called Wyatt Earp. The studio paid Josephine $5,000. When the film came out and Wyatt, played by Randolph Scott, was depicted as having had a romance with a made-up character named Sarah Allen, played by Nancy Kelly, Josephine threatened a suit against the studio, claiming that this relationship was a misrepresentation of the truth. What ultimately held her back, however, in this proceeding, as in others, was her fear that the real truth about *her* background would be brought to light. There are several instances of this reticence in her autobiography which Boyer had to amend or expand.

FRONTIER MARSHAL (20th-Fox, 1939) directed by Allan Dwan—it was Dwan's first sound Western—cast Cesar Romero, at the time playing the Cisco Kid for the same studio, as Doc Holliday, a gambler in poor health who loses his girl friend, Sarah Allen, to Wyatt in the course of the story. John Carradine was cast as a crooked saloon owner. The musical numbers performed by Binnie Barnes and Eddie Foy, Jr., the latter cast as his famous father, are almost, but never quite, enough for a viewer to forget the resurrection of the 1934 plot.

When John Ford returned to commercial filmmaking after the Second World War, Zanuck told him he wanted FRONTIER MARSHAL made again, this time the right way. Josephine had died in 1944 and so the studio did not anticipate any interference from relatives, or anyone for that matter who might be said to know the facts. In the course of the second make of FRONTIER MARSHAL, Holliday is saved by Wyatt when he is seized by a fit of coughing during a standoff with a couple of heavies. Doc is a surgeon, not a dentist; he wins the sympathy of the audience by performing an operation on a small boy; and at the conclusion of the film he is killed during the shoot-out at the O.K. Corral. These romantic and sentimental ingredients were irresistible to Ford.

Once, when I talked to him about his version, MY DARLING CLEMENTINE (20th-Fox, 1946), he made the point that during his early days as a director at Universal, Wyatt Earp would occasionally stop by the set and tell him about events from his past life, such as what really happened at the O.K. Corral. This led me to raise the question as to why the gunfight was misrepresented in his film. His reaction was one of *hauteur*. "Did you like the film?" he demanded. When I told him I did, *as a film*, he responded: "What more do you want?" He felt he was providing Americans with a tangible heritage of heroism in which to believe. I mentioned to him that Zanuck had told me that the final shot in the picture, of Henry Fonda as Wyatt Earp saying good bye to Clementine Carter, played by Cathy Downs, and then riding off into Monument Valley was one of the moments in film in which Ford clearly proved himself a visual artist of the first rank. "I'm not surprised that he told you that," Ford snapped, "since that shot was his idea and *not* mine. I wanted to end the picture with Fonda settling down." J.A. Place in THE WESTERN FILMS OF JOHN FORD wrote that "the story and characters in MY DARLING CLEMENTINE might seem limiting and restrictive, but Ford uses the viewer's already established awareness of the legend to enhance the myth he is creating."[55] This statement is too pretentious for anything either Ford or Zanuck felt when the film was being made. Historical reality simply meant nothing to them. Their commitment was to a fantasy world that, even if populated by characters with the names of real persons who once had lived, was nonetheless to serve as an embodiment of certain accepted moral and political values, constructed according to definite cinema story conventions, a prescription favoring certain social attitudes. MY DARLING CLEMENTINE is as a Bible story; it has a definite moral message to transmit; and, also just as a Bible story, if history does not support the moral message, then history must be altered.

"About CLEMENTINE, the only story I know is—," John Ford recalled, "Wyatt Earp moved out here and lived some place beyond Pasadena, and his wife was a very religious woman, and two or three times a year, she'd go away on these religious conventions, and Wyatt would sneak into town and get drunk with my cowboys. Along about noon, they'd sneak away and come back about 1:15 swacked to the gills—all my cowboys *and* Wyatt—and I'd have to change the schedule around. And he told me the story of the fight at the O.K. Corral. And that was exactly the way it was done, except that Doc Holliday was not killed. Doc died of tuberculosis about eighteen months later. And that's the only story I know about CLEMENTINE—except that the finish of the picture was not done by me. That isn't the way I wanted to finish it."[56]

In MY DARLING CLEMENTINE, Ford concentrated on the two families the screenplay created, the Earps, Fonda as Wyatt, Tim Holt as Virgil Earp, Ward Bond as Morgan Earp, Don Garner as James Earp, and the Clantons, with Walter Brennan as Clanton, John Ireland as Billy Clanton, Grant Withers as Ike Clanton, Mickey Simpson as Sam Clanton, and Fred Libby as Phin Clanton; and he emphasized the mutual respect between Wyatt and Doc Holliday, played by Victor Mature, the two meeting for the first time in Tombstone, a town set built in Monument Valley. Doc is still a surgeon and in the obligatory Ford scene he studies himself reflected in the glass framing his medical degree and does some soul searching. The film opens with the Earp brothers herding their cattle into Monument Valley. Clanton and his son Ike drive up in a buckboard and Clanton offers to buy the herd for less than it is worth. Wyatt rejects the offer. That night, as Wyatt, Morgan, and Virgil head into town, leaving James to guard the camp, the Clantons murder James and rustle the cattle. When the Earps discover what has happened, there is the obligatory Ford scene of Wyatt sitting beside James' grave, vowing to make things right. Wyatt returns to Tombstone and is sworn in as town marshal.

Doc and Wyatt meet and become friends. Doc is dying of consumption. Doc's fiancée, Clementine Carter, comes to Tombstone. He will have nothing to do with her and tells her to go back East. Linda Darnell, cast as Chihuahua, the stereotypical hot-blooded Mexican hellcat, becomes jealous of what she perceives as Doc's attachment to Clementine and takes up with Billy Clanton. When

Wyatt discovers that Billy Clanton was involved in James' death, there is some shooting, and Billy flees town. Virgil takes off after him. Billy dies. Clanton shoots Virgil and drops his body off in front of the jail as a challenge to the two remaining Earps to meet for a showdown at the O.K. Corral. Doc performs an emergency operation on Chihuahua, but she dies. He joins the Earps for the finish and is shot down. The Clantons are shot down. Wyatt rides off at the fade, leaving Clementine behind to become Tombstone's schoolteacher.

While THE LIFE AND LEGEND OF WYATT EARP (ABC, 1955–1961) with Hugh O'Brian was playing on television, John Sturges brought the Wyatt Earp story to the screen in THE GUNFIGHT AT THE O.K. CORRAL (Paramount, 1957), directly in the wake of MASTERSON OF KANSAS (Columbia, 1955) directed by William Castle. In the latter, which stars George Montgomery as Bat Masterson, when Doc Holliday, played by James Griffith, is patching up Virgil Earp, heroine Nancy Gates says to him: "I see you haven't forgotten how to be a doctor . . . " to which Doc responds: "There are some things a man never forgets . . . . " In Hollywood, at least, Doc consistently forgot he was a dentist. Kirk Douglas was cast as Holliday in THE GUNFIGHT AT THE O.K. CORRAL, Burt Lancaster as Wyatt. In an extremely episodic story, Wyatt, who is marshal of Dodge City, shows up in town, looking for Ike Clanton, played by Lyle Bettger, and Johnny Ringo, played by John Ireland. Wyatt meets Doc for the first time and Doc is antagonistic toward him because Wyatt's brother, Morgan, marshal of Tombstone, ran him out of town the previous year and impounded $10,000 of his money. Doc flings a knife at Lee Van Cleef and kills him. He is arrested on no charge and Wyatt saves him from a lynch mob. Wyatt returns to Dodge City. Doc shows up and Wyatt wants him to leave town. When Wyatt arrests lady gambler Laura Denbow, played by Rhonda Fleming, for disturbing the peace, Doc convinces Wyatt to let her go.

In another episode, Wyatt deputizes Doc for a manhunt. Doc saves Wyatt's life by shooting at three men who creep up on their camp. Doc's prostitute girl friend, disgusted with Doc, takes up with Johnny Ringo. Wyatt, in the meantime, is attracted to Laura. He tells Doc he is going to marry Laura and go to California. Ringo taunts Doc to go for his gun, but Doc refuses, because he gave his word to Wyatt that he would not resort to gunplay. Then a message comes from Virgil Earp, played by John Hudson, for Wyatt to come to Tombstone to help out. Laura will not go with Wyatt; she rejects him, albeit tearfully. Wyatt and Doc head for Tombstone. Wyatt is appointed U.S. marshal. Ike Clanton has been rustling Mexican cattle by the thousands and he wants now to take over the town. The Earps close the city to him. James Earp, played by Martin Milner, is shot down by the Clantons, who mistake him for Wyatt. This means there is going to have to be a showdown. Doc reminds Wyatt he will be throwing away a lifetime as a lawman if he makes this a personal fight. Doc is sick and thought to be dying, but, rallying for the shoot-out, he remarks: "If I'm going to die, I'm going to at least die with the only friend I've ever had." Wyatt, Virgil, Morgan, played by Forest Kelley, and Doc march down the street to meet Ike Clanton, Johnny Ringo, and five others. The fight lasts a full five minutes. Doc nails Ringo and the youngest Clanton, the latter because Wyatt is squeamish about killing one so young. Wyatt drops his badge next to the boy's corpse after the fight and Doc reminds him that Laura will be waiting for him.

WARLOCK (20th-Fox, 1959) directed by Edward Dmytryk and based on Oakley Hall's retelling of the Earp legend in a novel by the same title starred Henry Fonda in the title role as Clay Blaisdell and Anthony Quinn as the Doc Holliday character, here called Morgan, as in the novel. What is interesting about the film is that neither Blaisdell nor Morgan is regarded as a hero, but rather honest cowhand Richard Widmark who is made deputy sheriff. Clay kills Morgan and leaves town at the end. In this film, the O.K. Corral gunfight is handled by just Blaisdell and Morgan. It is a somewhat more intriguing film than John Sturges' second try at the story in HOUR OF THE GUN (United Artists, 1967).

Sturges cast James Garner as Wyatt and Jason Robards, Jr., as Doc Holliday. Here the film begins with the O.K. Corral gunfight, differently but still inaccurately staged. Robert Ryan, cast as Ike Clanton, continues to dominate Tombstone even after the shootout. When one of Wyatt's brothers is crippled by Ike's men and another killed, Wyatt swears vengeance and Doc goes along for the ride. The tension of THE GUNFIGHT AT THE O.K. CORRAL depends on the initial antagonism between Wyatt and Doc transforming itself into a deep personal friendship. HOUR OF THE GUN introduces a clash in values, Wyatt using the law to make his revenge legal, Doc delighting in exposing Wyatt's hypocrisy. The picture concludes with Doc in a sanitarium, having given up his life of violence but not his drinking, facing the inevitable, and Wyatt resolving never to be a law man again.

With all of these films as a preamble, Frank Perry, a New Yorker, decided he was going to tell the story of the gunfight as it really happened when he came to direct DOC (United Artists, 1971). However, after consultation with Pete Hamil of Brooklyn, the screenplay which emerged was neither more truthful nor less ridiculous. Stacy Keach was cast as Doc, Harris Yulin as Wyatt. Doc—at last!—is a dentist dying of tuberculosis. Wyatt is a coward who feels his guns can even the score no matter what adversary he is pitted against. Faye Dunaway was cast as Kate Elder, the whore who lives with Doc. Doc befriends Denver John Collins, cast as the Kid. At the final shoot-out, when the Kid cannot draw on Doc, Doc guns him anyway. The film is heavy with significant symbolism, but there is little in the way of psychological motivation. Kate Elder becomes possessive of Doc; Wyatt increasingly becomes a gun-crazed lunatic: "You'd be surprised what you can solve with a bullet"; Doc becomes committed to some profound internal quest the nature and purpose of which remain enigmatic. "Why the Kid?" Wyatt asks Doc at the end of the picture. "I guess he reminded me of too many things," Doc replies, and rides off alone.

Perhaps the retelling of the O.K. Corral confrontation since 1932 charts at least one trend in Western film production. From the situation of a confrontation pulling men together into mutual inter-reliance, later versions seem to show greater human separation, depicting men increasingly closed off from one another and imprisoned by themselves and their pasts, amid oppressive social and economic conditions. The friendship between Wyatt Earp and Doc Holliday changed from the assurance of the value of human relationships to an occasion to despair in the permanence of any kind of relationship. The general public and critical response to MY DARLING CLEMENTINE was very positive, somewhat less so to THE GUNFIGHT AT THE O.K. CORRAL, while HOUR OF THE GUN proved disappointing at the box office and DOC was a commercial failure. Critics who would point to these later films and draw conclusions from them about the decay of American beliefs in a certain kind of social order should perhaps be counselled that the more recent films did not meet with popular endorsement and are really a commentary on nothing except how to make an unsuccessful Western.

However, it need not have been this way. Will Henry romanticized Wyatt Earp in his novel, WHO RIDES WITH WYATT (1955). Yet, when it was adapted for the screen as YOUNG BILLY YOUNG (United Artists, 1969) directed by Burt Kennedy, the screenplay, also by Kennedy, preserved the incidents while making the characters wholly fictitious; and, contrary to W.R. Burnett's novel, Kennedy made sure none of the incidents he did include were such as could be linked with the activities of the Earps in Tombstone. The result was an interesting film, enjoyable in its own right, not a deliberate attempt to distort historical reality.

Notwithstanding, it is significant, I think, that the movie images of law men such as Hickok and Earp are quite the same as those assigned to bad men such as Jesse James and the Kid: they are portrayed as all good, as good men who become bad, or as bad men. I do not believe this to have been merely coincidental.

13

Heroes in Defeat

JOAQUÍN MURIETA

On 13 May 1846 the United States declared war on the Republic of Mexico. The Anglo-Americans claimed that this war was precipitated by a boundary dispute and a failure on the part of the Mexican government to pay monies presumably owed certain American citizens. The truth of the matter was that the United States wanted to acquire the North Mexican provinces—Andrew Jackson had opened negotiations with Mexico as early as 1835 to purchase California—and, when the Mexicans consistently refused to sell, the decision was made to seize these lands by force. The California Territory was acquired, along with other lands in the Southwest, by the Treaty of Guadalupe Hidalgo on 2 February 1848. The Anglo-Americans apparently were somewhat uneasy about how this seizure would look since in exchange the United States paid Mexico $15,000,000 for the ceded lands and assumed financial claims charged by Americans against Mexico in the amount of $3,250,000. "It seems worth noting," W.H. Hutchinson wrote in his book, CALIFORNIA: TWO CENTURIES OF MAN, LAND, AND GROWTH IN THE GOLDEN STATE (1967), " . . . that payment by a conqueror for what it has acquired by force of arms is not common practice in international relations."[57]

About the time this treaty was signed, or a little before, gold was discovered in California. It caused an international sensation. Literally thousands of Mexicans rushed to the site and in the first year of mining, even though the government had changed hands, half the gold mined from the mother lode was done by Mexicans. The Anglo-Americans already in California could see no reason why such a situation should persist and they were supported by thousands upon thousands of 'Forty-niners flooding the Territory. The Greaser Act of 1850—its official title—and the Foreign Miners Tax accomplished legally what until this time had been possible only through vigilante violence: to impose on the Mexican population of California the same solution John Sherman, U.S. Senator from Ohio and brother of General William Tecumseh Sherman, had recommended with regard to all Indians who eluded being killed outright: they must be reduced to "a species of pauper."[58] The Spanish-Americans and the Mexican-Americans in California reacted to this new policy with as much perplexity and lack of enthusiasm as did Native Americans.

It is against this background that the legendary horseman, called the "Ghost of Sonora" after a town in California named this because of the number of Mexicans from the province of Sonora who lived there, Joaquín Murieta emerged to play out his role of *El Patrio* [The Patriot] to his people by becoming a revolutionary rebel chief opposed to Anglo-American rule. John Rollin Ridge articulated the legend in THE LIFE AND ADVENTURES OF JOAQUÍN MURIETA, THE CELEBRATED CALIFORNIA BANDIT (1854). Ridge was a mixed-blood and his Cherokee name was Yellow Bird. For him, the Murieta legend was a prescription against certain basic attitudes he perceived in American society. In an expansive concluding statement, he commented that Murieta "leaves behind him the important lesson that there is nothing so dangerous in its consequences as *injustice to individuals*—whether it arise from prejudice of color or from any other source; that a wrong done to one man is a wrong to society and the world."[59]

Another account, THE LIFE OF JOAQUÍN MURIETA, appeared in the CALIFORNIA POLICE GAZETTE in 1859 and began the trend toward sensationalizing Murieta's life and exploits. Joseph E. Badger, Jr., in writing seven of the eight dime novels published about Murieta, passed through the full gamut of postures. In his first book in the series, THE MANHUNTERS: OR, THE SCOURGE OF THE MINES (1871), he began on a negative note, calling Murieta a "famous and desperate highwayman, a demon incarnate." By the late 1870s Badger began to imitate Edward L. Wheeler's dime novel Deadwood Dick series in which banditry was seen as a response to injustice and persecution and the new attitude was apparent in the title of the last entry in his series, JOAQUÍN, THE TERRIBLE: OR, THE TRUE HISTORY OF THE THREE BITTER BLOWS THAT CHANGED AN HONEST MAN TO A MERCILESS DEMON (1881).

Walter Noble Burns, having had a go at Billy the Kid and Wyatt Earp, turned his attention to Murieta in THE ROBIN HOOD OF EL DORADO (1932) in which the California bandit was portrayed as a combination of the Jesus in St. Luke's Gospel, the medieval Robin Hood as depicted in legend, and the glamorous figure of the Cisco Kid as played by Warner Baxter in the films IN OLD ARIZONA (Fox, 1929) directed by Raoul Walsh and Irving Cummings and THE CISCO KID (Fox, 1931) directed by Irving Cummings. Western fiction author Dane Coolidge followed with GRINGO GOLD (1939), but in his account, as in Burns', the characters, including Murieta and Juan Tres Dedos, never become more than two-dimensional and only in the final chapters is the narrative permeated by a tone of sadness which itself had become a convention by that time in telling the story of Murieta's life.

One is justified in calling Joaquín Murieta legendary because there is no documentary evidence whatsoever to indicate that this was the proper, or even assumed, name of the man killed by the California Rangers in July, 1853, and whose severed head was then immersed in alcohol to preserve it inside a glass jar so it could be placed on public display and admission charged to anyone who wanted to see it enough to pay for the privilege. In any event, the California legislature, in establishing the Rangers, had so little idea who was responsible for all the pillage charged against a bandit named Joaquín, they named five different Joaquíns, of which the closest to Joaquín Murieta was one Joaquín Muriati.

THE AVENGER (Columbia, 1931) directed by Roy William Neill was based on a story by Jack Townley. Part of Columbia's "B" series with Buck Jones, it is the first film devoted to the life of Joaquín Murieta. Neill's camera set-ups and imaginative direction, along with the unusual lighting on the part of cinematographer Charles Stumar, make for at least a visually stimulating film. The story opens with Buck as Murieta serenading blonde heroine Dorothy Revier in a lurching stagecoach, Jones' voice obviously dubbed. It was generally axiomatic in Hollywood at this time that Mexicans must sing and so rarely does a Mexican appear without a guitar or mandolin. When Murieta enters a saloon looking for his brother Juan, played by Paul Fix, the recording equipment adroitly mixed his queries of the bartender with the schemings of three rough Anglo-American prospectors who are plotting to steal the Murieta gold mine. Murieta is seized once he arrives at the mine. He is tied to a tree and forced to watch his brother hanged as a horse thief. Neill managed one stunning shot of Buck as Murieta, a black silhouette against a clouded horizon behind which the setting sun blazes, riding off into a diffused haze. Disguised as "The Black Shadow," Murieta becomes a road agent, holding up ore shipments which he feels rightly belong to him. By the end of the film, he exposes the three crooked prospectors, gets back his mine, and wins the girl.

Burns' book was filmed under the same title, THE ROBIN HOOD OF EL DORADO (M-G-M, 1936) directed by William Wellman. Warner Baxter, in his Cisco Kid outfit, played Murieta, J. Carrol Naish was cast as Three-Fingered Jack. Filmed on location in the Sierras at Strawberry Flats, near Sonoma, Wellman later admitted that he was dissatisfied with the picture, not on factual or historical, but on artistic grounds: "Baxter was old enough to play Murieta's father. I liked him, but I couldn't make a picture with him. I knew all the tricks. I had dancers around the fire, and all kinds of fights, and everything else you can imagine, but the minute you got with Baxter and his girl, in the love scenes, it was really embarrassing. The whole story was embarrassing."[60] The screenplay was written by Joseph Calleia, an opera singer who became an actor in the late 'Thirties, and Wellman, as an added precaution, took along screenwriter Robert Carson to do standby dialogue. A set painter on the crew painted Carson a sign: "Dialogue written while you wait. Curb service." Baxter, despite his experience in Westerns, was still afraid of horses, and so veteran stunt man Yakima Canutt doubled him during almost all of his riding sequences.

On the credits, Joaquín's surname is spelled "Murrieta." Gold is discovered in California and men flock to mine it. Paul Hurst and his gang beat up Joaquín, murder his wife Rosita, played by Margo, and knock out his blind mother. Joaquín goes on the vengeance trail after Hurst and his gang. Naish, once he is introduced in his role, grotesquely overacts. Bruce Cabot was cast as a sympathetic friend of Joaquín. Harry Woods, familiar from many heavy roles, leads a mob in town which hangs Joaquín's brother and Joaquín is given thirty-nine lashes. This makes him more spiteful than ever. Three-Fingered Jack kills Chinese and keeps their ears on a string. Joaquín organizes Jack and a large gang. On a raid, Harry Woods is shot down.

In an interesting double-exposure California is pictured as a globe, Joaquín and his raiders riding at the top of the frame as the globe turns. Of course, Joaquín and his whole gang sing and continually make music. The women dance. Ann Loring, whose father once owned the land on which Joaquín was a peon, joins Joaquín because the Americans have robbed her of everything. She is very attractive in her tight-fitting riding suit. When Cabot's brother's fiancée is accidentally killed by Jack during a stage hold-up, Cabot turns against Joaquín and leads a big posse to his hide-out. Ann Loring wants Joaquín to quit and go to Mexico with her; he decides now is the time to do it. Suddenly they are attacked. There is a pitched battle with hundreds of extras. Loring is shot. Cabot chases after the wounded Joaquín who lives just long enough to make it back to Rosita's grave before he expires.

MURIETA (Warner's, 1965) directed by George Sherman was an effort to update the Murieta story, especially by adding the ingredients of excessive bloodletting and violence typical of European Westerns of this period—it was filmed in Spain. Jeffrey Hunter was cast in the title role. When his wife is savagely murdered by three crooked prospectors, he takes to the vengeance trail, posing as a saloon card sharp. He finds the killers eventually and guns them down. Arthur Kennedy was cast as the sympathetic law man who lets Murieta go free, realizing that his case would not receive justice in the prejudiced courts and that he was right to take the law into his own hands. However, Murieta, instead of going straight, becomes a bandit leader and Kennedy at the end leads a posse to capture him, the film concluding with a terrific shoot-out in which Murieta loses his life. Sherman employed a number of Spanish and Spanish-American actors and in this version, whatever else might happen, they do not sing.

It is worth mentioning in this connection an incident which occurred in 1983 while I was conducting my course titled "Images of the American West" for teachers in the Portland public school system. We customarily met in a sixth grade classroom in a middle school. One day, before class, I asked the sixth grade teacher who was not taking my course what history, if any, was being studied in the sixth grade? She responded that it was the history of Canada and Latin America. I then asked her if any mention was made of the fifty-five times between 1865 and 1972 we had militarily intervened in the political affairs of Latin American nations? No, she assured me, the history being taught included nothing so controversial. Rather, it was concerned with the culture of the various countries and on one day at least someone from one of the Latin American countries would be invited to come to class in his native dress and sing for the students some of the songs of his nation.

GEORGE ARMSTRONG CUSTER

Custer, who was born in 1839 and who died in 1876 in what many at the time considered a blaze of glory, has now been deleted from mention in many elementary and secondary school textbooks used in American schools and replaced, if at all, by Sitting Bull. A native of Rumley, Ohio, he entered West Point and distinguished himself by being a disciplinary problem. He accumulated a total of ninety-seven demerits, whereas one hundred would have resulted in expulsion. Attached to the Fifth Cavalry in the Army of the Potomac during the Civil War, Custer attracted attention to himself by his daring recklessness in battle and his spectacular showmanship in manner and dress and personal deportment. In 1864 he married Elizabeth Bacon. When the war ended, Custer held the rank of major general, but this reverted to the rank of captain in 1866 following the cessation of hostilities. By this time, however, the U.S. War Department was committed to carrying out the federal government's policy of genocide toward the remaining Indian nations and Custer saw this as a personal opportunity to win new acclaim. He was appointed lieutenant colonel and attached to the newly formed Seventh Cavalry. In 1867 the regiment played a significant role in the Hancock campaign, the objective of which was to remove the Sioux and Cheyennes from the pathway of the transcontinental railroad. Due to a number of military excesses, such as harsh treatment of deserters and overly long and cruel forced marches, Custer was court-martialed and suspended from rank for one year. General Phil Sheridan commuted this sentence before it expired because, he said, he needed Custer to fight Indians; and it was Custer's victory at the Battle of the Washita where he surrounded the Cheyenne village of peace chief Black Kettle and wiped out most of the "enemy" that initiated the glorious reputation which henceforth was associated with his command. Despite controversy in the press inspired by the wholesale slaughter of a tribe that was under truce with the United States, Custer continued his operations against non-reservation tribes in the Oklahoma Territory.

Custer spent the summer of 1869 at Fort Hays, Kansas, where he began his autobiography, MY LIFE ON THE PLAINS (1874), which was first published as a series of magazine articles. The principal purpose behind the book was to consolidate in the public's mind Custer's own estimation of himself as a national hero. Curiously, Kent Ladd Steckmesser in his book, THE WESTERN HERO IN HISTORY AND LEGEND (1965), while supposedly endeavoring to explicate the Custer legend, praised Custer's memoir for having struck "a realistic note" in one respect, that being Custer's "views of the Indians."[61] What was this realistic note? Custer wrote: "It is to be regretted that the character of the Indian as described in James Fenimore Cooper's interesting novels is not a true one . . . . Stripped of the beautiful romance with which we have been so long willing to envelope him, transferred from the inviting pages of the novelist to the localities where we are compelled to meet with him, in his native village, on the war path, and when raiding upon our frontier settlements and lines of travel, the Indian forfeits his claim to the appellation of the '*noble* red man.' We see him as he is, and, so far as knowledge goes, as he ever has been, a *savage* in every sense of the word: not worse, perhaps, than his white brother would be similarly born and bred, but one whose cruel and ferocious nature far exceeds that of any wild beast of the desert . . . . In him we find the representative of a race . . . between which and civilization there seems to have existed from time immemorial a determined and unceasing warfare . . . . ."[62]

By writing persuasively in this fashion, Custer was clearly in the tradition of those propagandists who were intent on replacing the equally false notion of the Native American as a noble child of Nature with the image of the savage which as early as 1676 Sir William Petty, physician and member of the Royal Society, articulated in THE SCALE OF CREATURES when he assigned "savages" an intermediate, or "midle," ground between human beings and animals in the great chain of being and, of course, thereby mitigated any culpability in their extermination. Three years after Custer's MY LIFE ON THE PLAINS appeared, Sitting Bull remarked to his own people about relations with the whites: "We cannot dwell side by side. Only seven years ago we made a treaty by which we were assured that the buffalo country should be left to us forever. Now they threaten to take that away from us. My brothers, shall we submit or shall we say to them: 'First kill me before you take possession of my Fatherland . . . . ' "[63] Following the discovery of gold in the Black Hills in 1875, the United States government ordered the Sioux to leave their Powder River hunting grounds which had been guaranteed to them forever in the treaty of 1868—a treaty which in the late 1970s again became the subject of much heated litigation in federal court. It was in connection with this removal order that Custer and his command lost their lives in the battle of the Little Big Horn.

Black Elk in BLACK ELK SPEAKS told John G. Neihardt, referring to Custer by his Lakotah name, Pahuska (Yellowhair), that on the Little Big Horn battlefield "there were not many of our own dead there, because they had been picked up already; but many of our men were killed and wounded. They shot each other in the dust. I did not see Pahuska, and I think nobody knew which one he was."[64] A national memorial shrine now marks the battlefield, but the tributes are only to Custer and his men; there are no memorials to the Native Americans who lost their lives in the encounter. Custer's defeat, while it was only a momentary victory for the Indian nations, made Custer a hero in nearly everyone's eyes and the decimation of the Indians became a national *cause célèbre*. Elizabeth Custer, because her pension was inadequate, began writing books which canonized her husband's memory, but even she had been anticipated in this practice by Frederick Wittaker's POPULAR LIFE OF GENERAL GEORGE

A. CUSTER (1876) which portrays Custer as a misunderstood hero, a victim to both Indian cunning and white political corruption.

While historians began to attack the Custer legend soon after Elizabeth Custer died, it was not until the mid Twentieth century with the publication of novels such as Ernest Haycox' BUGLES IN THE AFTERNOON (1944) that the legend began being questioned in Western fiction. Even so, as Haycox explained in a letter dated 14 July 1943 to Ray Everitt, his editor at Little, Brown, "this whole Custer thing is not in the hands of scholars. It is in the hands of partisans who started with a conviction and thereafter spent years hunting for facts to justify their view." [65] Notwithstanding, Haycox himself made no effort to characterize the Native American point of view in his fictional account.

Mari Sandoz, in her BATTLE OF THE LITTLE BIGHORN (1966), stressed Custer's political ambitions for the presidency as one of his primary motives. Against a counterpoint of the many novels about the battle still partial to Custer, Thomas Berger in LITTLE BIG MAN (1964) reduced the conflict to parody and pictured Custer as a frantic, almost comic, lunatic.

C.G. Jung, writing about the trickster figure as an embodiment of the shadow in THE ARCHETYPES AND THE COLLECTIVE UNCONSCIOUS (1969), reflected that "the figure works, because secretly it participates in the observer's psyche and appears as its reflection, though it is not recognized as such. It is split off from his consciousness and consequently behaves like an autonomous personality. The trickster is a collective shadow figure, a summation of all the inferior traits of character in individuals. And since the individual shadow is never absent as a component of personality, the collective figure can construct itself out of it continually. Not always, of course, as a mythological figure, but, in consequence of the increasing repression and neglect of the original mythologems, as a corresponding projection on other social groups and nations." [66] If in the pro-Custer fiction, the Indians incarnate projections of the shadow, in LITTLE BIG MAN the polarities are reversed and the shadow is projected on the white men and the Indians are transformed into the innocent victims. There is, however, no substantial change; it amounts to no more than a reversal of roles.

From the very beginning, in CUSTER'S LAST STAND (Chicago Film Exchange, 1909), Custer was depicted in film as a hero and a martyr. In CUSTER'S LAST FIGHT (New York Motion Picture Company, 1912), directed by Thomas Ince, a very ambitious three-reeler, the story opens with two naturalists, after an exhausting day spent in exploration, sitting by a water hole smoking their pipes. Before morning they are dead and a Sioux brave is shown making his way back to his tribe to boast of his bloody deed. Eight months later the brave is arrested and sent to prison. He escapes and returns to his people. With the help of Sitting Bull, he convinces the tribe to rise up against the white man. Despite the direct order from the U.S. government not to leave their reservation, the Indians leave to go on a buffalo hunt. The Cavalry is ordered to force them back to the reservation and, trying to implement this order, Custer and his courageous men meet their deaths, literally engulfed by hundreds of shrieking "redskins."

Similarly, in a comedy from the same period, COLONEL CUSTARD'S LAST STAND (Frontier, 1914), when a fort is besieged by Indians, Molly, Colonel Custard's daughter, sneaks out to go for help. She is followed by Indians and trapped in a cabin which they start on fire. Her comic lover hides in a mortar cannon and is shot through the air, landing on the roof of the cabin. He begins immediately killing Indians, saves Molly, and, going back to the fort, routs the Indians there, thus saving both the girl and the troops.

DODGE CITY (Warner's, 1939) directed by Michael Curtiz was the first of Curtiz' collaborations with Errol Flynn in making Westerns. Henry O'Neill, as Colonel Dodge, sums up the railroad as "a symbol of American progress—iron horses and iron men" and, for him as ostensibly for the viewer, "the West stands for honesty, courage, and morality." After Flynn cleans up Dodge City, saving it from the machinations of Bruce Cabot and Victor Jory, Colonel Dodge enlists Flynn's help in performing the same service for another town, VIRGINIA CITY (Warner's, 1940), the second film joining Curtiz and Flynn. SANTA FE TRAIL (Warner's, 1940) was the third. This film opens at West Point in 1854. Flynn was cast as J.E.B. Stuart, Ronald Reagan as George Armstrong Custer. They are cadets, as is Van Heflin, cast as Rader, who has a fight with Stuart and is drummed out of the academy. Stuart and Custer are sent to Fort Leavenworth. John Brown, the abolitionist, played by Raymond Massey, is portrayed as a murderous fanatic with a rabble of familiar movie heavies for his followers. Brown holds up a wagon train to get rifles. His son is captured and tells of what a butcher he is. When the boy dies, heroine Olivia de Havilland is told by her screen father that it is just as well since he would probably have grown up to be a killer as Brown. Brown's freed slaves, on the other hand, are shown to be bewildered victims. "If dis is freedom," one of them says, "then Ah want ta go back ta Texas where Ah can set and set until Kingdom come." Rader, who has joined Brown's gang, turns on him and Brown is defeated while trying to capture a powderhouse. De Havilland's screen father in another pithy line remarks that "the end of John Brown is our beginning."

Theodor Reik in THE SECRET SELF: PSYCHOANALYTIC EXPERIENCES IN LIFE AND LITERATURE (1952) wrote about Shakespeare's comedy, THE MERCHANT OF VENICE (1596): "I do not doubt any more that behind Antonio and Shylock are hidden the great figures of their gods. Here are two small people in Venice, but the shadows they cast are gigantic and their conflict shakes the world. There is the vengeful and zealous God of the Old Testament and the milder Son-God of the Gospels who rebelled against His father, suffered death for His revolt and became God himself, afterwards. The two Gods are presented and represented in this play by two of their typical worshipers of the playwright's time."[67] In SANTE FE TRAIL, Raymond Massey's make-up, after the fashion of a Puritan elder, makes him resemble Yahweh, and he and what he represents stand judgment and execution at the hanging with which the film ends. The son-god is split into Stuart and Custer. An old Indian woman, who is a fortuneteller, predicts that in the future they will be enemies.

Errol Flynn was the star and so the viewer's sympathies are naturally with him, but the ground-work was laid for Flynn's next Western in which he would take over the role of George Armstrong Custer. Whereas Cecil B. DeMille's film, THE PLAINSMAN (Paramount, 1936), as so many before it, concentrated on Custer's last days, THEY DIED WITH THEIR BOOTS ON (Warner's, 1941) directed by Raoul Walsh undertook to narrate Custer's life from the time he joined West Point until he valiantly lost his life at the Little Big Horn serving his country and serving honesty, humanity, and morality. Cast opposite Flynn as Custer was Olivia de Havilland, this time as Elizabeth Bacon Custer. Anthony Quinn played Chief Crazy Horse, according to the screenplay the man who personally kills Custer.

The film opens at West Point in 1857, Custer riding up in a cavalier's uniform. He claims to want glory and that is why he has joined the army. His behavior at the Point is reprehensible. He has the lowest marks and highest demerits of any officer candidate in the history of the school. Interestingly, however, unlike SANTA FE TRAIL where Moroni Olsen as Robert E. Lee presided over the Point, here John Litel as General Phil Sheridan is the commanding officer. Custer makes a date with Elizabeth but he has to break it because the Civil War has begun and he is graduated early so as to be sent into combat— hence, nothing about the trip to Fort Leavenworth and the problem with John Brown depicted just a year earlier! Warner Bros. obviously felt viewers had a short memory. Custer deploys his troops spectacularly during the war, marries Elizabeth, and emerges a brigadier general and a national hero. Bored with civilian life, he enters into the frontier service, becomes friends with Crazy Horse, and champions the Indians' cause. Unfortunately Crazy Horse and the Sioux are too stupid to realize that Custer is a true friend and, misled through the schemings of crooked businessmen and evil political appointees, they blame Custer and massacre him and all of his men. At the very root of all the trouble are Arthur Kennedy and his father who are profiteering in whiskey and guns.

Subsequently, just the slightest reference to the Custer legend was thought to be enough to attract viewers. LITTLE BIG HORN (Lippert, 1951) directed by Charles Marquis Warren is about two officers, played by Lloyd Bridges and John Ireland, and their psychological conflicts as they embark on a desperate 250-mile trek to warn Custer that the Indians are coming. Or Custer might be just a sub-plot as he is in WARPATH (Paramount, 1951) directed by Byron Haskin, a Justice/Revenge story. Edmond O'Brien is the hero, searching for three men who accidentally killed his wife while committing a bank robbery. He kills one of them—"He died too easy!"—and then enlists in the Seventh Cavalry—the picture is dedicated "to the memory of the glorious Seventh"— because the other two men are now in the army. When a detail comes upon a burned-out wagon train, Wallace Ford comments that General Sheridan has the right idea about Indians: "Every last Indian should be killed." In due course, O'Brien becomes a prisoner of the Indians and they want him to tell them of Custer's whereabouts; they know he is somewhere in the area! Custer, played by James Millican, must be warned that the Sioux are uniting to ambush him. The two men O'Brien has been searching for, played by Forrest Tucker and Dean Jagger, as well as Jagger's daughter, are also prisoners of the Indians. Tucker sacrifices his life so the other three can escape. O'Brien and Jagger's daughter, played by Polly Bergen, ride to join Major Reno. Jagger joins Custer, but his warning comes too late. HARRISON'S REPORTS of 2 June 1951 wrote of this film: "Suitable for the family."[68]

BUGLES IN THE AFTERNOON (Warner's, 1952) directed by Roy Rowland and based on the Haycox novel skirts the Custer issue completely by playing up Haycox' numerous sub-plots. Here, Forrest Tucker was cast as a sympathetic Irish sergeant, recently demoted, who saves hero Ray Milland's life so Milland can get through the Indian lines to tell Major Reno of Custer's fate. "God be with you," Milland says to Tucker, before escaping across a cliff. "He's never left me," Tucker assures him. "We've been partners for years." Custer is on screen for all of thirty seconds, but one thing is accurate: he has short hair as he leads his men out in pursuit of hostiles.

SITTING BULL (United Artists, 1954) directed by Sidney Salkow is a preposterous film. Iron Eyes Cody, whom the late Colonel Tim McCoy regarded as a complete fraud, to the extent that one so-called Indian "expert" can so term another "expert," was the technical advisor. Sitting Bull opens the picture, presenting the Indian point of view. The Indian agent is a rabid Indian-hater; Custer, played by Douglas Kennedy, is little better. Dale Robertson, cast as an idealistic Cavalry officer, becomes a friend of the Sioux after defeating Crazy Horse, played by Iron Eyes Cody, in a dagger duel. Sitting Bull demands that President Grant come for a parley or there will be an uprising of all the nations. Grant comes! But it is too late. Custer distrusts the Indians and orders his regiment to attack them as a warning not to continue their war preparations. Indian warriors, with saddles under their blankets, stage a well-executed massacre. Sitting Bull remarks that they will not scalp brave men. The ending becomes maudlin. As a consequence of his pro-Indian activities, Robertson is summarily court-martialed and sentenced to be shot. Only Sitting Bull, riding up to the fort and talking personally with President Grant, gains him a stay of execution. Jack DeWitt, who master-minded the idiocy of A MAN CALLED HORSE (National General, 1970) directed by Elliott Silverstein and MAN IN THE WILDERNESS (Warner's, 1971) directed by Richard C. Sarafian, co-wrote the screenplay with Salkow.

The battle footage was so good—or at least Salkow and others felt it was so good—that it could not be permitted to go unused a second time. Salkow also directed THE GREAT SIOUX MASSACRE (Columbia, 1965), this time with Michael Pate as Sitting Bull, Iron Eyes Cody as Crazy Horse, and Phil Carey as General Custer. Joseph Cotten, cast as Major Reno, is depicted as being drunk all the time. Custer actually is a champion of the Indians. So what's new? Well, in this film Custer is told by Senator Blaine that if he wants to be popular with the people he *must* hate Indians. Historically, when Custer's body was found, there were two small wounds: a bullet hole through his left breast and another in his temple. In THE GREAT SIOUX MASSACRE, Custer's pretended Indian-hating goes to such extremes that his men begin to desert. The final showdown with the Sioux is largely footage from SITTING BULL, except for some medium shots of Carey as Custer, standing beside the flag and shooting. He is felled by an arrow. "The army is worthy of the nation it defends," the viewer is told just before the fade.

In SEVENTH CAVALRY (Columbia, 1956) directed by Joseph H. Lewis, hero Randolph Scott is a captain in the Cavalry. "General Custer was a great human being," he says. Scott is assigned a detail to collect the bodies after the massacre. When they come upon the battlefield, Sitting Bull's coup stick marks Custer's grave! The detail is surrounded by what is supposed to seem a thousand Indians. "Custer's bravery and spirit now lives in our people," Young Hawk says. Harry Carey, Jr., cast as a scout, is riding Custer's horse, the horse he did not take into battle with him. He is bushwhacked by an Indian and the riderless horse comes galloping onto the scene. The Indians are terrified. "Let them go in peace," Sitting Bull says. "The spirit of Yellow Hair has spoken." Scott and his men are then allowed to remove the bodies for Christian burial.

"The bodies were all in similar condition on this third day of heat," Mari Sandoz wrote in THE BATTLE OF THE LITTLE BIGHORN. "Most of the dead were completely naked, many scalped and hacked, although it was no longer always possible to distinguish the wounds of actual combat from later mutilations. Custer's stripped body had been found in a sort of sitting position between two troopers in the low pile of dead behind the breastwork that was a tangle of still horse legs sticking out, and great bloated bellies, the gases stewing and whistling in the climbing heat of the sun, the rushing sound of maggots busily gnawing, great dark flies crawling heavily over it all . . . . There were 42 bodies and 39 dead horses on Custer Hill. Altogether . . . they [the burial detail] buried 212 bodies, bringing the dead, with the missing and those of Reno, to 265, including sixteen officers, seven civilians, and three Indian scouts."[69]

No film that has bothered to give numbers about those lost in the battle has ever got them correctly, and CUSTER OF THE WEST (Cinerama, 1967) directed by Robert Siodmak even got it wrong about Captain Myles Keogh's horse, Comanche, being the only survivor: in this film, it is Custer's white charger that survives. "I want action!" Robert Shaw, cast as Custer, tells Lawrence Tierney, as General Phil Sheridan, early on. "You are paying the price for being backward," Custer tells the Indians. He also explains that the whites are no different than the Cheyennes when, because of a superior number of Cheyennes, they destroyed in the past an inferior tribe and seized their lands. Just before the final, decisive battle, Custer is out palavering with Chief Dull Knife, played by Kieron Moore, when against his express orders a charge is called. Custer is spared to the very last and is even offered a chance to escape, which he gallantly refuses. All of this notwithstanding, Judith Crist in her review of the film for NEW YORK wrote that "Shaw's interpretation of Custer gives substance to both story and history and elevates the inevitable Cavalry vs. Indians clichés. The result is an engrossing adventure film that puts the emphasis on character and, perhaps wisely, avoids putting the final word on an historical controversy." [70]

In the foregoing, I neglected to mention one of the most elaborate Custer films made during the silent era, THE FLAMING FRONTIER (Universal, 1926), because it has become the source of some controversy among critics and points up again how film reviewers and critics attribute historical accuracy to Westerns which have none whatsoever. THE FLAMING FRONTIER was directed by Edward Sedgwick and opens with scenes of the Indians growing restless and jealous of the merciless advance of the white man, a typical tableau in most would-be epic Westerns. On the Plains settlers and soldiers blaze away at the Indians while in Washington politicians and profiteers bargain to sell whiskey and arms to them. Hoot Gibson was cast as Bob Langdon, a Pony Express rider and a close friend of General Custer. Dustin Farnum was cast as Custer. Through the agency of Senator Stanwood, played by George Fawcett, Langdon gets an appointment to West Point. There he meets Lawrence Stanwood, the senator's son played by Harold Goodwin, and Stanwood's sister, Betty, played by Anne Cornwall. Grant is president. Custer seeks to bring about peace in the West but his efforts force him into an open clash with profiteers and the latter succeed at disgracing the general in Grant's eyes. In order to get at Senator Stanwood, the profiteers involve his son with a disreputable woman at the Point. There is a scandal and Langdon, to shield the senator, takes the blame and is expelled. He returns to Custer's command. The Indians, prodded by dishonest whites, unite under Sitting Bull to mount an attack on settlers. Custer, misled as to their numbers, campaigns against them on the Little Big Horn. He has four hundred men with him! The Indians number in the thousands. Custer sends Langdon through the enemy lines with a message to Major Reno to come to the rescue. Reno cannot and Custer and his command are slaughtered after an heroic resistance. The profiteers are joyous, but the emotion is short-lived. The settlers, learning of the chicanery of a crooked Indian agent, set upon him and burn a whole town to the ground, photographed in sweeping panorama shots, smoke billowing from the many buildings; there are even a few aerial shots. Just before the fade, Lawrence Stanwood, dying during the fracas, writes his sister Betty a letter exonerating Langdon. The two are happily reunited.

Fenin and Everson in THE WESTERN FROM SILENTS TO THE SEVENTIES wrote of THE FLAMING FRONTIER that "the political and historical backgrounds were sketched in with general accuracy . . . ." [71] "This statement must be challenged . . . ," Brian W. Dippie responded in his book, CUSTER'S LAST STAND: THE ANATOMY OF AN AMERICAN MYTH

(1976). "Apparently the Indians were incited to take the warpath by renegade whites greedy for their lands. President Grant, duped by his political advisers, was unable to extricate himself from the web of intrigue and corruption they had woven around his administration. Left to his own devices, and hoping to prevent an Indian war, Custer set out after the hostiles. He found them, and in numbers that even he, for all of his legendary rashness, should have known enough to avoid. For, according to THE FLAMING FRONTIER, every Indian tribe in North America was represented in the camp on the Little Big Horn. Sitting Bull alone commanded a following of ten thousand. With only a touch of imagination, one can picture the scene: Indians lined up a hundred deep along the entire length of the Little Big Horn, waiting turn for a shot at Custer." [72]

Dippie concluded his discussion of this film and Fenin and Everson's claim for its historical accuracy by citing Leonard Jennewein's article, "Big Horn Battle Subject for Much Controversy," which appeared in the RAPID CITY JOURNAL on 20 January 1957. "It is better," Jennewein wrote, "to look at Western movies for recreation than for historical edification." [73] For my part, I have rather strong feelings. If the habituation to falsehood is to be equated with recreation, then something is either profoundly amiss with the society making that equation or the equation itself is an incontrovertible demonstration of that society's unwillingness or inability to find recreation in reality. In this context, the portrait of Custer as a crazed lunatic in LITTLE BIG MAN (National General, 1970) directed by Arthur Penn is not a break-through. It is a reversal into the opposite in which merely the exteriors of stereotyped polarities are exchanged. It is not really a reference to the historical Custer, but a clumsy attempt to poke fun at previous films which exalted his stature to that of a hero. But Penn's film does illustrate that, as in the case of outlaws or law men, legendary heroes in defeat can be men who are all good, men who are good but who become bad, or men who are all bad.

14

Legendry and Historical Reality

Before detailing what I regard as a workable methodology in treating frontier legends in relationship to historical reality, I ought to mention some of the curious aberrations which inquiry into this subject has produced in recent scholarship. The most persistent and, at the same time, the most ridiculous proposition one repeatedly encounters is what I have already termed the Henry Nash Smith thesis. Dippie in his book wrote that "to succeed as entertainment, movies must be attuned to and rather closely reflect the public's changing moods and interests. The Custer films always have."[74] If that was Dippie's impression, the films he noted in CUSTER'S LAST STAND: THE ANATOMY OF AN AMERICAN MYTH certainly did not bear him out. However, Dippie made this remark nearly at the end of his study and it can be said in his behalf that he did not write his book as an effort to prove this thesis.

The same cannot be said for Stephen Tatum's INVENTING BILLY THE KID: VISIONS OF THE OUTLAW IN AMERICA, 1881–1981 (1981) which is the only full-length attempt I know of to try to demonstrate this thesis. Beyond the Henry Nash Smith thesis, Tatum also called upon two other strange notions, derived from the writings of John G. Cawelti, which seem to appear and reappear when trying to deal with frontier legends: the idea of the "epic moment" and the feeling that somehow Zane Grey's Western fiction was significantly related to William S. Hart's films. The origin of Cawelti's notion of the "epic moment" is to be found in Frederick Jackson Turner's essay, "The Significance of the Frontier in American History" (1893). "This perennial rebirth," Turner wrote, "this fluidity of American life, this expansion Westward with its new opportunities, its continuous touch with the simplicity of primitive society, furnish the forces dominating American character. The true point of view in the history of this nation is not the Atlantic coast, it is the Great West. . . . In this advance, the frontier is the outer edge of the wave—the meeting point between savagery and civilization."[75] At this "meeting point" *who* was savage, who civilized? Richard Drinnon answered this question in FACING WEST: THE METAPHYSICS OF INDIAN-HATING AND EMPIRE-BUILDING when he observed that "Turner's 'meeting point between savagery and civilization' . . . was the supreme expression by an historian of all the other expressions before and since by novelists, poets, playwrights, pulp writers, painters, sculptors, and film directors. It separated the cowboys from the Indians by making the latter easily recognizable dark targets, especially if they had war paint on to boot. It unmistakably shaped national patterns of violence by establishing *whom* one could kill under propitious circumstances and thereby represented a prime source of the American way of inflicting death."[76] Yet, for Cawelti in his book, THE SIX-GUN MYSTIQUE (1975) as in Tatum's book on the Kid, Turner's racist ideology is posited to have been an historical fact! "The Western story," Cawelti insisted, "is set at a certain moment in the development of American civilization, namely at that point when savagery and lawlessness are in decline before the advancing wave of law and order, but are still strong enough to pose a local and momentarily significant challenge. In the actual history of the West, this moment was probably a relatively brief one in any particular area."[77]

More bluntly, without resorting to this brand of "newspeak," to invoke George Orwell's term, this so-called "epic moment" is merely an occasion for "Two Minutes Hate"—as Orwell employed this idea in NINETEEN EIGHTY-FOUR. Robin Moore, in GREEN BERETS (1965), described the reaction of a South Vietnamese strike force during the showing of a Western at Nam Luong. It did not matter that the film was projected against the side of a building and was probably a cinemascope print so that the figures appeared elongated. " . . . The strikers loved the action and identified themselves with it. When the Indians appeared the strikers screamed 'VC,' and when the soldiers or cowboys came to the rescue the Nam Luong irregulars vied with each other in shouting out the number of their own strike-force companies."[78] Perhaps because French critics have not been so profoundly indoctrinated by the imagery of Western films as American critics, someone such as Jean-Louis Leutrat could easily recognize that "l'indien été, bien évidemment, la principale victime de l'imagerie raciste" [the Indian, quite obviously, has been the principal victim in this business of making racial images].[79]

In his book, ADVENTURE, MYSTERY, AND ROMANCE: FORMULA STORIES AS ART AND POPULAR CULTURE (1976), Cawelti asserted that Zane Grey and William S. Hart "produced what was unquestionably the most effective and successful work of the period 1910–25" and that "their works have so many points in common that it seems reasonable to view them as exponents of the same essential version of the formula."[80] Hart made sixty-two Western films; Cawelti cited two, HELL'S HINGES (Triangle, 1916), the plot of which he described, and THE RETURN OF DRAW EGAN (Triangle, 1916) which is only mentioned by title. For Zane Grey, who wrote more than sixty novels with a Western setting over the years from 1910 to 1939, Cawelti cited

only four of them. There is scarcely enough substance in such a limited sample
to establish any kind of significant relationship between them. Hart was virtually finished as a leading box-office attraction by the end of 1921. His sentimentality and pseudo-religious fervor were more typical of Harold Bell Wright
than they were of Grey's fiction. Indeed, the Western fiction Hart himself wrote
most resembles that of Wright. This, of course, is not the place to probe deeply
into this question of relationship and I would not have brought it up at all if
Tatum in his book on the Kid had not, in turn, tried to extend this significant
relationship between Hart and Grey to apply equally to visions of the Kid. In
terms of the Western film, what is much more significant is that the Kid did
not make his cinematic appearance until 1930 when Hart could no longer find
screen work and when Zane Grey's popularity was definitely on the wane.

"This study's success," Professor Tatum wrote, " . . . rests on its demonstration that discovering, inventing, and understanding the Kid is in large
measure discovering crucial aspects of ourselves and our cultural history."[81]
For much of his book, Tatum then proceeded to carry through the Henry Nash
Smith thesis, although to do so he was required to declare that Walter Woods'
stage play, BILLY THE KID (1903), despite its initial success and subsequent
twelve-year tour beginning in 1906, because of its image of the Kid as a hero,
actually belonged in the period of the 'Twenties rather than chronologically where
it occurred in American cultural history, and that BILLY THE KID (M-G-M,
1941), because of its image of the Kid as a reprobate rather than a hero, also
was an anomaly. He had to avoid mention of at least a third of the Kid's motion picture appearances for the same reason, whereas in Michael McClure's
stage play, THE BEARD (1965), the Kid's realization of his erotic fantasy of
having oral sex with Jean Harlow paralleled "the ideological fragmentation of
American society during the Vietnam and Watergate years' political and social
upheavals."[82] The Kid was first conceived as a reprobate because, "as John
Cawelti has stated , . . . the significant point about the Western formula is its
dramatization of that epic historical moment in our national past when the opposing forces of civilization and wilderness confronted each other and shaped
the course of American history."[83] What changed all this in the 'Twenties, so
that "the Kid was eventually accepted as something other than a misfit and
murderer," were the "writings of Zane Grey and the films of William S. Hart."
According to Tatum, who relied on Cawelti's assertion rather than reading Grey's
novels or viewing Hart's films, "the Grey and Hart good-badman was typically
domesticated by marriage, or was last seen in the heroine's company as the duo
entered a secret, idyllic landscape in which violence had no place."[84] Almost
as often as Hart ended up with the heroine, he did not. This has already been
seen to be the case in WILD BILL HICKOK (Paramount, 1923), but—to cite
a few other examples—it is true also of WAGON TRACKS (Paramount, 1919),
THE TOLL GATE (Paramount, 1920), O'MALLEY OF THE MOUNTED
(Paramount, 1921), and TRAVELIN' ON (Paramount, 1922). Further, Zane Grey
used the idea of a duo entering "a secret, idyllic landscape" in RIDERS OF

THE PURPLE SAGE (1912) and not in his many subsequent novels; and violence *did* have a place there, since we learn in the sequel, THE RAINBOW TRAIL (1915), that the Mormons came to the "secret, idyllic landscape" and forcibly and brutally took young Fay Larkin away with them. This "decades" approach, as should be obvious now in view of the preceding chapters, is never supportable when successive productions are studied in depth and only seems possible when they are not. As for films about the Kid made, presumably, during the time of American "ideological fragmentation," such as DIRTY LITTLE BILLY (Columbia, 1972) which did so poorly at the box office that it has never been sold to network television for domestic showing, was never put into syndication, and never made it to the foreign television market, or PAT GARRETT AND BILLY THE KID (M-G-M, 1973) which cost $4,345,000 to make and grossed $2,754,218, I find it altogether preposterous to assert, as Tatum did, that these pictures can somehow provide us with an insight into what most Americans were thinking and feeling during these years. Nor is it a meaningful statement to write that "the Kid's exploits do not serve to integrate him into society" in King Vidor's BILLY THE KID (M-G-M, 1930), "unlike earlier good-badman figures like William S. Hart's Draw Egan," and that therefore Vidor's film has something to tell us of special significance about how the feelings of Americans had changed by 1930 because Hart's exploits in his films of a decade or more prior to Vidor's film often do not result in his good-badman being integrated into society. What all this amounts to is trying to force the Billy the Kid material into the Henry Nash Smith thesis; it is not an observation that becomes self-evident after studying the history and development of the varying images of the Billy the Kid legend.

The second chapter of Tatum's book is devoted to a brief account of the historical Billy the Kid. There are twelve errors of fact in it of varying seriousness, but it would not bother Tatum greatly to have such errors pointed out to him. First, this is true because, for Tatum, the Kid "historian is a symbolic 'outlaw' when he delivers truthful visions that invalidate current beliefs, and when he complains that his vision is unacknowledged"; and, second, because Tatum would have us "view myth and legend not as distortions or perversions of the truth—but rather as in fact different forms of reality and different forms of the truth."[85] Now, I must confess from the very outset in this book I have made the assumption that there is such a thing as past historical reality and that we are capable of constructing a comprehensible model of it which approximates what it once was. For Tatum, "no matter how plainly-written, no historical narrative duplicates reality."[86] Quintilian said that history is written to narrate events and not to prove something. For Tatum, history cannot narrate events, it can only be written in order to prove something. "Whereas one viewer," he wrote, " . . . posits the Kid's boyhood spent on the lawless frontier as the cause for his violent acts, another might emphasize the Kid's yearning for a father figure like Tunstall as the motivating force behind the Kid's actions. The point is not that one explanation is more true, but that each explanation offers a different truth using the same data, that each, in short, distorts the field to tell a story." Accordingly, since there is no such thing as an immutable historical reality, or even a close approximation to it, "the question becomes not whether Ramon Adams' style is more truthful than Walter Noble Burns' style; rather, the question is why, at that particular time, each author's stylistic techniques gained a following."[87] By means of this kind of reasoning, all we have, all we can ever have, is the Henry Nash Smith thesis. I suspect that this is one of the reasons this thesis is so popular among a certain group of scholars. By using it, these scholars can at last achieve the situation in NINETEEN EIGHTY-FOUR: the historical past is whatever we wish at a given time to believe it to have been.

In THE WESTERN HERO IN HISTORY AND LEGEND, Kent Ladd Steckmesser opined that "people . . . have a right to know whether they are reading fact or fiction, and the historian has a responsibility to draw the line which separates the two."[88] His *modus operandi* was to provide, first, an accurate, albeit brief, historical account of the four historical personalities he chose for study—Kit Carson, Billy the Kid, "Wild Bill" Hickok, and General Custer—and then to trace the growth and diversification of their legends. It is basically the method I have employed myself in the preceding pages. But, sadly, Steckmesser was also lured by the attractions of the Henry Nash Smith thesis. In treating of Kit Carson, for example, he proposed that Nineteenth-century "mountain-man biographies reveal less about frontier life than they do about the literary techniques and moral ideas of the period in which they were written."[89] In his favor, Steckmesser did not use this notion to the point of historical solipsism; but I think it is more to the point to understand that the legends about frontier historical personalities reveal almost nothing about the "period" in which they were composed and a great deal about the "moral ideas" of those who worked in manufacturing the legends. What is ultimately most at fault with the Henry Nash Smith thesis is the emphasis it mistakenly places on the public receiving the media action. Presumably, so the thesis goes, the public gets only what it wants and what it wants is to be reassured of what it already believes, that the most successful "popular" notions are always those which reflect and reinforce what the public wants. This is by far a much too static concept for an interchange as essentially dynamic and interactive as the relationship between media and the public. The "moral ideas" embodied in media projections of frontier legends are moral ideas prescribed for the receiving public. Popular literature, newspaper editorials, and, in this century, radio, films, and television are all components of *emotional* media, i.e., media seeking to persuade through the manipulation of emotions. As Gerda Lerner stressed in THE MAJORITY FINDS ITS PAST: PLACING WOMEN IN HISTORY (1979), "the pitfall in such interpretation . . . is to confuse prescriptive literature with actual behavior."[90] In these terms, Nineteenth-century mountain-man biographies, as fictions about any legendary personality, act primarily as indicators of what certain individuals, namely their authors, wanted the public to believe concerning certain moral ideas. John Ford's version of the Wyatt Earp legend embodies what he wanted his viewers to think, as Sam Peckinpah's version of the Kid's legend embodies how he wanted a viewer to view the Kid's life. Juxtaposing historical reality with fantasy thus allows us to distinguish between prescription and actual behavior, between what people actually did and what their actions are being used to prove.

Steckmesser was the first, to my knowledge, to recognize that "the first tentative step toward a heroic interpretation [of the Kid] occurred when newspaperman Ash Upson in 1882 wrote a biography of the Kid under Pat Garrett's name."[91] To be a hero, Steckmesser insisted, an outlaw must have his story told in such a fashion that his outlawry is seen to "result from social injustice rather than from any defect of character."[92] This principle is certainly borne out in the films about Jesse James or the Kid in which they are depicted as heroes. Steckmesser also cited Walter Woods' BILLY THE KID as the first full statement of the heroic image of the Kid in that he survives the end and leaves to wander with his sweetheart. "From being a symbol of malicious criminality," Steckmesser wrote, "the Kid now is viewed as a victim of circumstances who deserved a better life."[93] The Kid, Steckmesser concluded, as one whose side loses "endows his career with the same fascination that surrounds the Confederates at Gettysburg, the Texans at the Alamo, and Custer's troopers at the Little Big Horn."[94] Steckmesser further refined this notion until he felt that the Kid, Hickok, Custer, and by extension any other frontier historical personality whose life terminates in unexpected death, in the heroic aspect of their legends could be compared to the tragic heroes in Greek drama "moving inexorably toward death by treachery."[95] This strikes me as too much of an abstraction because I cannot find among the fictional narrative structures devoted to the historical personalities who have become and have been made into frontier legends one that actually follows this course, although there are many parallels with a medieval passion play which would portray these deaths as varieties of martyrdom. It is a subtle distinction, perhaps, but an essential difference between the perspective of classical Greece and the Judaeo-Christian tradition. In Greek tragedy, a human being is reconciled to the nature of the universe through the *praxis*, the progress, the movement, the action of the drama, whereas in the Judaeo-Christian tradition one's death can be a form of protest against the injustice of a social order and an appeal to a higher, divine order. Those romantic historical reconstructions which present historical personalities as heroic victims belong, in terms of their ideological content, to the latter tradition: the meaning of such a death is not reconciliation but protest. It is also worth noting that Steckmesser made no allowance in dealing with the Outlaw Story plot setting in romantic historical reconstructions for the Janus-figure capacity of this plot structure: a frontier legend can be both a hero and a villain, even within the context of a single narrative, as, for example, the Kid is in Walter Noble Burns' THE SAGA OF BILLY THE KID. This capacity allows a good man to become a bad man or, more rarely, a bad man to become good.

In his essay, "The Western Bad Man as Hero" in MESQUITE AND WIL-
LOW (1957), Mody Boatright suggested that there are certain common ingredients in the folk lore efforts to transform Western bad men into modern-day
heroes. I would take exception, however, with his initial requirement which "is
that he belong to the dominant Anglo-American majority. Indians and half-breeds
and Latins are excluded. A Joaquín Murieta might become a hero to the Latin-
American in California and elsewhere, and even to Joaquín Miller, who appro-
priated his name; but never to a considerable number of Argonauts and their
descendants. The chief repository of the Murieta saga is Chile."[96] This statement overlooks the tremendous popular success of the Cisco Kid who was, after
all, a variation on the Joaquín Murieta saga, not merely in the early films but
throughout the entire film series which spanned the years 1929–1950 and on
into the 139 episodes of the television series. In point of fact, O. Henry's original short story about the Cisco Kid, "The Caballero's Way" (1904), featured
an Anglo-American named "Goodall," a surrogate for William H. Bonney. The
films changed this to a Spanish-American bandit fighting in the cause of righteousness and justice. In the late 'Thirties and throughout the Second World
War the State Department urged Hollywood to make more Westerns featuring
Latin-American heroes to assist in projecting a positive image with which
American youth, as well as youth in Latin-American countries, could identify
and thus serve the political objectives of the Pan-American convention.

Boatright's other ingredients seem to me to have more cogency. First, such
a good bad man must come "from a respectable but not wealthy family."[97]
This is true of the James family as it is featured in films about Jesse James and
for the Kid as well in films such as DIRTY LITTLE BILLY which show his
family. A second requirement "is an unfortunate childhood."[98] This, too, is
true for both Jesse and the Kid and, as concerns his early manhood, Joaquín
Murieta. Third, "the youth from a respectable but unfortunate family . . .
commits his first crime under extreme provocation."[99] This has been more or
less consistently the case for Jesse James as it is true for Murieta, but it has
been less true for the Kid who has most often been depicted either as an outright do-gooder or a young man who is emotionally disturbed. "A fourth requirement is that the bad man hero fight the enemies of the people. This does
not mean that the people wholly approve the methods of warfare."[100] Curiously, this has come to mean that in a film such as CHISUM (Warner's, 1970)
the Kid sides with a big rancher and in a film just three years later, such as
PAT GARRETT AND BILLY THE KID, the Kid fights against that same big
rancher: in both he is a pawn in the film's ideology. The ideology as to who
belongs properly to the Establishment has remained somewhat more consistent
in the films about Jesse James, although in his case, as in Murieta's, the ideology of the plot structure tends to condemn the means of evening the score.
"A fifth requirement is that during the career of outlawry, the hero performs
acts of tenderness and generosity."[101] This remains true in all films which portray either Jesse or the Kid to be in some sense a hero, even recent films such

as THE LONG RIDERS (United Artists, 1980) and PAT GARRETT AND BILLY THE KID.

"The outlaw," Boatright concluded, "must, of course, atone for his misdeeds. For the lesser ones like Frank James and Emmett Dalton a penitentiary sentence followed by a quiet, law-abiding life is sufficient." However, historically, in Frank James' case, he was acquitted; Emmett Dalton served only fourteen years of a life sentence before he was released and, among other things, produced and starred in a picture about himself and his brothers, titled THE LAST STAND OF THE DALTON BOYS (Dalton, 1912), lived to star in the commercial remake, BEYOND THE LAW (Southern Feature Films, 1918), and he almost lived long enough to see his autobiography brought to the screen, WHEN THE DALTONS RODE (Universal, 1940). For others, such as Jesse, Murieta, and the Kid, "the outlaw can attain the highest heroic stature only by an atoning death. That death must be as a result of treachery and must have in it an element of martyrdom."[102]

"We were told . . . ," Mark Twain wrote in ROUGHING IT, "that the dreadful 'Mountain Meadows Massacre' was the work of the Indians entirely, and that the Gentiles had meanly tried to fasten it upon the Mormons; we were told, likewise, that the Indians were to blame, partly, and partly the Mormons; and we were told, likewise, and just as positively, that the Mormons were almost if not wholly and completely responsible for that most treacherous and pitiless butchery . . . . All our 'information' had three sides to it, and so I gave up the idea that I could settle the 'Mormon question' in two days. Still, I have seen newspaper correspondents do it in one."[103]

What, in my opinion, a legend about an American frontier personality *must* have about it is *three* sides. This kind of flexibility is a vital first step in the legendary process. For this reason I have not found it coincidental that every one of the frontier personalities we have surveyed, in terms of their legendry, have had this Janus-figure quality: that each has been portrayed as all bad, all good, or as good becoming bad. The historical Jesse James, Billy the Kid, "Wild Bill" Hickok, Wyatt Earp, George Armstrong Custer, and the possibly fictitious Joaquín Murieta have all been used as illustrations, depending on the intention of the individual fabulist and what he has wanted to prove by means of them. Each has been variously reduced to exemplify various moral parables and it is just part of the total process that the same individual, in order to be truly legendary, must be able to illustrate totally different kinds of parables. Of course, I have not mentioned *every* Western film made about Jesse James, the Kid, Hickok, Earp, or Custer, but rather enough of them and over a broad enough time span to demonstrate that the particular decade has nothing whatsoever to do with *how* a particular legend is interpreted so much as that his image can be seen as a direct reflection of what the filmmaker wanted the viewer to think and feel about him, the kind of parable he wanted to use the legend to illustrate by means of which to instruct the viewer as to what is and what is not, in his opinion, acceptable behavior. However, by contrasting an individual mutation of a legend with the historical reality one is able to isolate where the particular distortions occur and, from this, arrive at what, precisely, a filmmaker wanted or hoped a film's viewers would think or feel seeing his film.

Having said this much, we are ready, I think, for the final one of my four approaches to the Western film, by means of which we shall be able to discern what behavior is prescribed for women by the American patriarchy as acceptable and what punishments will be meted out to women who defy these prescriptions; and, equally as important, *who* must be hated, *who* can be exterminated, and how those who have meted out this violence against those shown to be deserving of it not only escape with impunity but are even rewarded with success, wealth, social prestige, those things which are prescribed as having the most value in the society being depicted. In this investigation, how the body is clad will help us, as well as the color of the skin: by these manifestations we shall know who is redeemed and who is damned.

PART IV
TYPES AND
STEREOTYPES

Much of our criticism, obsessed with pleasure-values and blind to influence-values, seems to me frivolously irresponsible (with eccentric exceptions like Tolstoy) towards the vital effects of books in making their readers saner or sillier, more balanced or more unbalanced, more civilized or more barbarian.

—F.L. Lucas[1]

15

Women

Because, until quite recently, men have written history, women with very few exceptions have been almost invisible. This has not meant, however, that women were not participants nor even, as in the case of the American Westward expansion, women did not leave behind a mass of personal documents. "Much of what traditional sources tell us about women," Gerda Lerner pointed out, "has come to us refracted through the lens of men's observation. The historian of women must question her sources for androcentric bias and must seek to counteract such bias by seeking primary sources which provide women's points of view."[2] This, it would seem, is precisely what Sandra L. Myres did in WESTERING WOMEN AND THE FRONTIER EXPERIENCE: 1800–1915 (1982). In the course of her book, Myres had constant recourse to the voluminous first-hand documents by women currently stored in numerous American archives. It was on the basis of contrasting these primary sources with male fantasies about women on the frontier that Myres came to the conclusion that over the years women have become "the protagonists of a stereotyped version of the West as false as that of the Hollywood Indian."[3]

What one also finds, in reading her excellent book, is that the prescription process has been with us from the very beginning of American history. To take only one example, Myres noted how, as war between the United States and Mexico approached, "newspapers and popular periodicals, especially in the Midwest and the South, besieged their readers with anti-Mexican propaganda. Much of the flavor of these articles was continued throughout the 1840s and 50s. Even the guidebooks warned prospective immigrants of the defects in the Mexican character . . . . Thus by the time American women came into contact with Mexican-Americans in any substantial numbers, there was a good deal of literature which had shaped their thinking and which presented anything but a positive or reassuring picture. Given what they had read, it is hardly surprising that westering women tended to view their first contacts with Mexicans with much the same mixture of fear and curiosity with which they viewed their first Indians."[4]

When it comes to women in Western films, it may be recalled that Budd Boetticher remarked that "what counts is what the heroine provokes, or rather what she represents. She is the one, or rather the love or fear she inspires in the hero, or else the concern he feels for her, who makes him act the way he does. In herself the woman has not the slightest importance." Women have changed externally in Western films during the last eight decades, with the trend always in the direction of revealing more and more of their bodies until total nudity was achieved; male attitudes concerning them, however, have changed very little. Sebastian Cabot, playing a heavy in BLACK PATCH (Warner's, 1957), beats women and such behavior is condemned in the film. Yet it is only a matter of degree. The heroine in Will Cook's novel, THE PEACEMAKERS (1961), kisses Lieutenant Jim Gary and then whispers, " 'You've always felt that a good lick across the britches would have done wonders for me. And of course you were right.' "[5] Spanking heroines was a precedent long established in "B" Westerns such as GOLD MINE IN THE SKY (Republic, 1938) starring Gene Autry or OUTLAWS OF THE DESERT (Paramount, 1941) starring William Boyd before Audie Murphy spanked Kathryn Grant in THE GUNS OF FORT PETTICOAT (Columbia, 1958) or John Wayne ritualized spanking Maureen O'Hara into an erotic fantasy in McLINTOCK! (United Artists, 1963).

What Boetticher was addressing and what has not changed is the *role* assigned to the heroine in Western films. A good demonstration of this reification process can be had by contrasting THE RETURN OF DRAW EGAN (Triangle, 1916) directed by and starring William S. Hart with HEAVEN'S GATE (United Artists, 1981) directed by Michael Cimino. In DRAW EGAN, Hart played an outlaw who goes into hiding after the impression has been widely circulated that "Draw" Egan was killed in a shoot-out. Mat Buckton, played by J.P. Lockney, is head of the reform committee at Yellow Dog and, seeing Egan in a saloon, he proposes "Draw" take the job of sheriff without knowing, of course, Egan's real identity. Egan is amused by the idea and regards it a capital cover for resuming his outlaw activities. What he had not counted on was meeting Buckton's daughter, played by Margery Wilson, described on the title card following a close-up of Hart's thunderstruck, anguished countenance as "the kind of woman he didn't think existed." The heroine does nothing; but her appearance on the scene marks the crisis moment in the film after which everything changes. In order to be worthy of her, Hart decides that he must reform, that he must truly stamp out the evil element in Yellow Dog, and that whether or not he should lose his life he will make himself morally fit to love the heroine. Near the end, he is exposed, but he makes up for his past by his courage during a duel with a former crony and the town forgives him his transgressions, reconfirms him as sheriff, and the heroine welcomes him with open arms.

In commenting on the relationship between motion pictures and society, Andrew Tudor in his book, IMAGE AND INFLUENCE: STUDIES IN THE SO-

CIOLOGY OF FILM (1975), commented that "one article of faith must inform such a task: do not make premature assumptions about the direction and nature of the links between movies and society. The one thing we should have learned from the history of such studies is that we are dealing with interaction and not with simple cause and effect."[6] However, whatever the shifting reality of women's roles in American society, when it comes to women in Western films the prescriptions have been unrelentingly the same. HEAVEN'S GATE, touted as a "realistic epic" and according to the hype from United Artists "based on a little-known incident in American history," takes place during the Powder Valley War of 1892. This "little-known incident" is actually quite famous in the annals of the history of the American West since it involved the hanging of a woman for alleged cattle-stealing. While men named Buchanan and DeCory tried to prevent the lynching, nooses were dropped about the necks of Jim Averill and Ella Watson, the latter called after her death "Cattle Kate." In Mari Sandoz' words in THE CATTLEMEN: FROM THE RIO GRANDE ACROSS THE FAR MARIAS (1958), Buchanan, DeCory, and the others were driven behind some rocks by gunfire, the lynch mob throwing "the rope end over a long limb of a twisted tree hanging out over the gulch. Then Bothwell shoved the slight Averill off. While he jerked and swung in the air, the contemptuous and defiant Kate was pushed out, too, mainly by Henderson. The arms and legs of both jigged what seemed a long, long time, the young woman's moccasins flying off, her skirts blowing and ballooning in the updraft and the slow dying. Sickened, the men in the rocks tried to crawl closer, DeCory vomiting as he moved forward, yet was compelled to see, to know for certain just who such men were. Finally the two bodies hung still in the cooling shade of the old tree, with the sad and desolate forward-tipped heads of the hanged."[7] Do not expect to find anything this dramatic in Cimino's film; in fact, do not even expect to find the hanging, because in Cimino's version Isabelle Huppert, cast as Ella Watson, is shot at the end while Kris Kristofferson, cast as Jim Averill, is trying to rescue her. Watson dies and Averill lives on. The plot shows the rich cattlemen organizing a vigilance committee to deal with immigrant rustling. The immigrants are very poor, but not so poor that they cannot afford rollerskates for a roller derby. The committee prepares a list of those who must be removed from the area and Ella, who is a prostitute and who is seen frequently in the nude in bed with Averill, is on the list. Most of what happens in the picture is confused and illogical, but one thread remains easy to follow: Averill's determination to save Ella's life. That he is ultimately unsuccessful is not as important, upon reflection, as that Ella's rescue is indeed his primary motivation and that therefore she is *primum mobile* of virtually all that happens in the film. For "Draw" Egan, the heroine was his motivation; for Jim Averill, Ella Watson's safety is his all-consuming motivation.

A commonplace in Zane Grey's novels is that the heroine does not know for a long time—usually for the better part of the story—that she is really in love with the hero. One of the consequences of her being so mentally retarded when it comes to her own emotions is that anybody reading about her, or watching such a heroine on the screen, must feel superior to her because what she will do eventually, what the structure of the plot will compel her to do, is so obvious. Occasionally the heroine is so much out of touch with herself as to think she is in love with the villain; this is a cue to the viewer that she will have to undergo an ordeal to learn her lesson, since the heroine *a priori* must love the hero. This is decidedly the case in THE COVERED WAGON (Paramount, 1923) directed by James Cruze and, at one tense moment, a marriage ceremony is almost performed between the heroine, played by Lois Wilson, and the villain, played by Alan Hale. It was not until well into the sound era that the heroine actually went ahead and married the villain, but with predictable consequences: (1) the villain dies, thus freeing the heroine to marry the hero, as in THE DARK COMMAND (Republic, 1940) directed by Raoul Walsh; or (2) there is a second heroine to marry the hero and the first heroine is forced to suffer for her folly, as in MAN IN THE SADDLE (Columbia, 1951) directed by Andre de Toth. If the heroine is so foolish as to be married to one villain and in love with another, she will pay the price: death, as in THE VIOLENT MEN (Columbia, 1955) directed by Rudolph Maté. If the heroine consorts with villains but does not marry them, then she, too, as the villains, must die at the end of the picture, as in DESTRY RIDES AGAIN (Universal, 1939) directed by George Marshall.

The "B" Western very early made it clear that in the celluloid West there are two distinct types of women who, as hero and villain, can be told apart by how they are dressed. In THE TWO GUN MAN (Tiffany, 1931) just before the fade Ken Maynard is embracing heroine Lucille Powers and a dance hall girl is about to rush over to him. She is stopped by Maynard's sidekick, Lafe McKee, who says: "Can't you see there would be a crowd over there?" Even more frequently sidekicks in "B" Westerns are misogynists, as in UNDER MONTANA SKIES (Tiffany, 1930) when Slim Summerville tells hero Kenneth Harlan, "Where there's women, there's trouble," or in IN OLD SANTA FE (Mascot, 1934) when Gabby Hayes, holding up his good luck horseshoe, tells Ken Maynard, "This has kept me shy of the ornery sex for nigh onto twenty years, but I'm thinkin' you need it right now more than I do." In CATLOW (M-G-M, 1971), the racial stereotype concerning Mexican women created during the 1840s is still in force, but another dimension is added to the selection and a new resolution. Dahlia Lavi is a hot-blooded, sexually passionate Mexican señorita who makes nothing but trouble for hero Yul Brynner whereas JoAnn Pflug is a white Anglo-American woman who has an independent streak: "God gave women minds, too, you know." At the end, Brynner chooses neither, leaving instead in company with his men.

In GUN FURY (Columbia, 1953) Donna Reed comes West to marry Rock Hudson but is kidnapped by Phil Carey and his gang. Leo Gordon, one of the gang, warns Carey: "As far as I'm concerned, all women are alike. They just got different faces so you can tell them apart." Lee Marvin and Neville Brand are also members of Carey's gang and they, too, lend their voices to the mounting chorus, Marvin remarking to Carey, "I told you that woman would be trouble," with Brand chiming in, "We should have dumped her in the desert." Carey does not listen. He leaves the recalcitrant Gordon behind, tied to a corral post. Before the abduction, Hudson was a pacifist, a man sick of violence who believes in peaceful negotiation. Ultimately, vengeance is more important than a woman, to Carey who swaps her for Gordon (whom Hudson released and who then accompanies Hudson on his quest) and also to Hudson who leaves Reed behind once Carey shoots Gordon because Hudson is not about to let Carey get away with such a heinous act. However, it is the Indian accompanying Hudson who does most of the actual killing in the film, including finishing off Carey. In the era when heroes only rarely were permitted to do their own killing— from THE COVERED WAGON to GUN FURY—the sidekick usually ended up having to do it, or what was felt to be a member of a more primitive race.

ARIZONA (Columbia, 1940) is a pseudo-epic in which, in addition to the Apaches slavishly taking their orders from white villain Warren William, Jean Arthur was cast as Phoebe Titus, the only white woman in Tucson, whose becoming figure is set off by her tight leather pants and who runs a pie business. She starts a freight company with William Holden and once she is in a dress and sees the beautiful home her capitalist enterprise has paid for Holden can hit her with the pregnant line: "You got to admit it's worth fightin' for."

In THE LADY FROM CHEYENNE (Universal, 1941) the title card tells the viewer that this is the story of how women changed the West. Loretta Young was cast as a schoolteacher with water rights coveted by chief villain Edward Arnold. She goes to the legislature to introduce a bill calling for women's suffrage, to which William Davidson, a legislator, responds that a woman's place is in the home. "He sure said a mouthful," a black janitor remarks and proceeds to give Young other unwanted political advice. A group of prostitutes shows up and they teach Young how to dress and wheedle, so that she can successfully lobby her bill at the governor's ball. The bill is passed. Edward Arnold is tried before an all-woman jury; and Young proposes to hero Robert Preston, promising, now that she can vote, to be a dutiful wife and stay at home!

One of the interesting changes that came about in "B" Westerns in the early 'Forties was that the heroines were not always the damsels in distress that they had been in former years. A good example would be the roles Betty Miles played. In THE RETURN OF DANIEL BOONE (Columbia, 1941), Bill Elliott as "Wild Bill" Boone was the hero but Betty Miles, as the heroine, far from being dependent on anything he might do was capable herself of wrestling a gun out of heavy Lee Powell's hand when he was foolhardy enough to draw on her. True, she had an attractive face and her figure was exploited, but in Westerns such as WILD HORSE STAMPEDE (Monogram, 1943) instead of being the fragile daughter of a widowed father, as so many heroines continued to be, she was seen to manage her own ranch, as she also did in WESTWARD BOUND (Monogram, 1944). In SONORA STAGECOACH (Monogram, 1944) she did her own stunting, leaping about on a runaway stage.

To a degree, it would be legitimate to say that heroines behaving in this fashion were acting less as truly "feminine" women and therefore more "masculine," as these terms were then defined in Western films. In part, of course, heroines were dressed in pants and blouses to call attention to their figures. Peggy Stewart, under contract at Republic Pictures, once confided to me that she resented working in Westerns because her backside was to the camera more often than her face. "Although they [women] dressed 'appropriately' most of the time," Myres reported, "some continued to wear pants when doing outside chores." [8] The Western film took this historical reality and subtly distorted it to establish a dress code for heroines. This dress code was not related to practical realities, but rather to the prescription for women. In THE DESPERADOES (Columbia, 1943) heroine Evelyn Keyes wears extremely tight-fitting leather pants when she works in a stable and, when she has hard riding to do or has to appear titillating, this remains her apparel; but when Glenn Ford falls in love with her, she changes into a dress.

THE RENEGADES (Columbia, 1946), again with Evelyn Keyes, is another primary example of this code. In COMANCHE TERRITORY (Universal, 1950) Maureen O'Hara is a fiery Irish redhead who runs a bank and wears pants, but at the end, when she wants hero MacDonald Carey to return to her, she switches to a dress. "Hurry back," she says. "I'll need a lot more help now." "Not looking like that, you won't," Carey quips. In A BULLET IS WAITING (Columbia, 1954), Jean Simmons wears incredibly contoured jeans, but at the end when she wants to be kissed by the hero she wears a dress. As late as SCALP-LOCK (Columbia, 1966), pilot film for the television series THE IRON HORSE (ABC, 1966–1968), hero Dale Robertson, having to choose between two heroines, selects Sandra Smith who has always worn pants but who now wears a dress (save for one bit of *gaucherie*: beneath the dress she has on riding boots). Herbert J. Yates, head of Republic Pictures, might exploit contract players such as Peggy Stewart, but when it came to starring his wife, Vera Hruba Ralston, in a Western, as in DAKOTA (Republic, 1945), she wore *only* dresses—even when walking overland.

In BACKLASH (Universal, 1956) Donna Reed enters upon the scene looking very svelte in black riding pants. She is a widow searching for $60,000 in gold. When she wants to get information out of a man, she changes into a dress. In STREETS OF LAREDO (Paramount, 1949) William Holden, MacDonald Carey, and William Bendix are all involved in a stage holdup. While on the run, they save Mona Freeman's cattle from the schemes of a gang of assessors led by Alfonso Bedoya, an actor responsible for probably the most degrading portrayals of Mexicans in Westerns. There is much fuss made about Freeman wearing pants. In time, Holden and Bendix become Texas Rangers—the film is dedicated to the Texas Rangers—while Carey remains on the owlhoot trail.

Freeman falls in love with Carey, but after he kills Bendix she shoots Carey, changes over to a dress, and is now ready to begin married life with Holden. Since the point being made in this and many other Westerns is that women not only must endorse the use of violence in solving social dilemmas but must even become violent themselves at times, it is worth keeping in mind that Sandra L. Myres found on the basis of her research that "women armed themselves with rifles, revolvers, and knives and stood ready to defend themselves and their families when they felt it was necessary. Occasionally, women's ire was aroused by Indians who annoyed them with their incessant begging or whose curiosity invaded their privacy, and they struck out in anger with brooms, hot pokers, boiling lard, or anything else close at hand. Despite such occasional flares of temper, women usually eschewed violence and sought peaceful solutions to their Indian problems."[9] The attempt to masculinize women in Western films is more apparent, I think, in their willingness to resort to violence with firearms than in their occasional masculine dress. Ideologically women are made to feel that violence is the *only* solution, just as, obviously, the male filmmakers so often thought women *should* think.

Sometimes the whole *raison d'être* of a Western film is to reinforce the circumstance that women come to knowledge through emotion and intuition, while men must have physical proof and logical demonstration. Audie Murphy is falsely accused of cowardly desertion from a wagon train he was leading when it was attacked by Yaqui Indians in TUMBLEWEED (Universal, 1953) and heroine Lori Nelson is told she must decide in her heart whether or not Murphy is guilty. The sheriff, however, needs better proof than this and gets it at the end of the picture when the Yaqui chief, played by Ralph Moody, makes a death-bed confession in English exonerating Murphy. At other times ideological continuity is stressed through the men who shape women's thinking as in UTAH BLAINE (Columbia, 1957) where the heroine is attracted to the hero because of his similarity to her father: "My father thought about things the same way. Utah, you and I will get along just fine."

In a number of Westerns in the 'Fifties it became fashionable for women to undergo something of a transformation, most notably Barbara Stanwyck's portrayals in CATTLE QUEEN OF MONTANA (RKO, 1954), FORTY GUNS (20th-Fox, 1956), and THE MAVERICK QUEEN (Republic, 1957), Marlene Dietrich's role in RANCHO NOTORIOUS (RKO, 1952), and Joan Crawford's performance in JOHNNY GUITAR (Republic, 1954). Women in these Westerns dressed in men's clothing that called attention to their figures and behaved even more as male heroes than had formerly been the case. At the beginning they ride roughshod over men, owning and operating successful ranches or saloons; only for them, by the fade, to have to be saved by a man, or at least come under the spell of a man and have to admit that they are somehow still the weaker sex. In FORTY GUNS, when near the end Barbara Stanwyck is grabbed and held as a shield by the villain so that Barry Sullivan cannot get a clear shot at him, Sam Fuller, who directed the picture, told me it was his intention to have Sullivan fire a shot right through Stanwyck, killing both her and the villain. This, he claimed, he was not allowed to do; and so, instead of dying, Stanwyck is reduced to having to run after Sullivan, properly humbled. The prescriptions as to what is acceptable female behavior were no less stringent in these films than the dress code continued to be. Because Barbara Stanwyck defies this code in THE MAVERICK QUEEN, she must die; and because Joan Crawford narrowly escapes violating it in JOHNNY GUITAR, she is allowed to live past the fade and plan a future life with the hero. Whenever someone dies in a Western, one must ask: why? the reason invariably has to do with the ideological prescription embodied and illustrated in the film.

In THE STRANGER WORE A GUN (Columbia, 1953) Randolph Scott is enmeshed in a plot in which he must choose between two heroines, the daughter of a stage line owner and a gambler. Recalling the conclusion of William S. Hart's HELL'S HINGES (Triangle, 1916) and numerous other films, the villain meets his death in a blazing saloon and Scott, in view of his own moral ambiguity, decides in favor of the gambler. A DISTANT TRUMPET (Warner's, 1964) is about the U.S. Cavalry's pursuit of War Eagle, the last renegade not on a reservation. War Eagle's Apaches wear Sioux warbonnets and are finished off by the end. During the course of the picture, the hero falls in love with a married woman, a situation complicated by the arrival at Fort Delivery of his fiancée. The skirmish with the Indians makes the married woman a widow and so the fiancée can be sent packing. An equally tough decision faces George Montgomery in FORT TI (Columbia, 1953). Here an Indian maiden, played by Cicely Browne, is in love with Montgomery who is a captain in Rogers' Rangers. Joan Vohs is the blonde heroine. "There is death all over the forest," Montgomery tells Vohs. "Men can live with it. Women can't." Maybe, for this reason, because Vohs has such a problem with death and Browne does not, Montgomery chooses Vohs, whereupon Browne suicides; but I suspect that the color line had as much to do with it. Whenever a hero is confronted with this choice between two heroines, the one he chooses usually is a sure indication of the ideology being prescribed.

In THE CHARGE AT FEATHER RIVER (Warner's, 1953) the Cheyennes are "irrationally" objecting to the coming of the railroad and hence are on the warpath. Besides learning a little Indian lore—Guy Madison remarks that Indians do not like to fight at night because, if they are killed, it will always be dark in their happy hunting grounds—Madison and his troopers rescue two white women who have been held captive for the last five years. Madison reassures Helen Westcott that she ought not worry about what the "prim and proper white women" will say because he likes what he sees. Unfortunately, Vera Miles wants to return to living with the Cheyennes. She tries to run away when they are under siege, shoots her brother in the process, and falls to her death. When more troops come to the rescue, Madison tells Westcott: "Those are the men who will dance at your wedding." Vera Miles, conversely, illustrates by her example what will happen if a woman dares to defy the color line once she has been rescued.

The plot and ideology of THE WHITE SQUAW (Columbia, 1956) are somewhat more complex. David Brian is poisoning the Indians' waterholes because he claims to have come to the area before the Indian reservation was created. May Wynne is a mixed-blood living among the Indians, the illegitimate daughter of a wealthy white rancher. Accompanied by the tribal chief, May makes a down-payment to buy William Bishop's cattle so the Indians can go into the cattle business. When May's white father dies, his will leaves half of his holdings to May, but his legitimate white daughter does not want to split with her and Brian takes her side. At the end Brian is killed and May gets her patrimony. The tribal chief tells Grant Withers that he is glad that Brian is dead. "We try not to judge the other fellow," Withers pontificates. "I Sioux Indian," the chief says. "I glad."

One might conclude from this film that mixed-bloods such as the character played by May Wynne could make the difference, starting Indian nations on the white man's road. ARIZONA RAIDERS (Columbia, 1965) goes even further in this direction when the Yaquis join the Texas Rangers in protecting a gold shipment, spurred on to do so by Gloria Talbot, cast as a Yaqui maiden. But the ideologies of these particular films have a deeper message. May Wynne may receive her patrimony, but she is to stay with the Sioux. At the fade of ARIZONA RAIDERS, Audie Murphy rides off with the ranger captain while Talbot enters a convent to become a Roman Catholic nun. The prescription states that Indian mixed-bloods and Indian women may accept the white man's road, but such acceptance is not to be interpreted as changing the fundamental fact that they are, notwithstanding, less than completely white and that they must therefore be prepared to settle for less in life because of it. Conversely, when the ideology differs from this, as in THE OREGON TRAIL (20th-Fox, 1959) where Gloria Talbot was cast as a mixed-blood, the resolution can be different. Surveying the carnage after an Arapaho attack on Fort Laramie, Talbot tells the hero: "It is because of this that I renounce my people." She is rewarded for this renunciation: she joins the hero aboard a wagon bound for Oregon. Once there, of course, in the historical reality of the American West, the Oregon miscegenation law prohibiting whites from intermarrying with inferior races would have prevented such a marriage from taking place.

The distinction Lafe McKee makes between the two kinds of women in THE TWO GUN MAN was no less true later in a picture such as THE WILD AND THE INNOCENT (Universal, 1959) in which the title serves as a direct reference to the two images of women presented. Audie Murphy, on his way to Casper, is accompanied by Sandra Dee. Dee's father has been trying without success to sell her off. When they arrive at Casper, Murphy meets a prostitute, played by Joanne Dru, and is at once attracted to her. Dee has been too much of a bumpkin for him, but this all changes as soon as she puts on a fancy dress: she becomes the image of refinement. Gilbert Roland was cast as the sheriff and the owner of the local brothel. He tells Dee, who is being groomed to work in the brothel, that he runs it because of what women have done to him, what a cheating woman did to his father. Murphy does not like the idea of Dee, whom he now recognizes as a true innocent alongside the tainted, wild Dru, working at such a place and he has a shoot-out with Roland over it. "You can't die," Murphy tells Roland. "I can't kill no human being." Roland dies! Dee heads back into the mountains with Murphy.

A similar point is made in KLONDIKE KATE (Columbia, 1943), filmed three years prior to DETOUR (PRC, 1946) directed by Edgar G. Ulmer, a memorable *film noir* with the same principals, Ann Savage and Tom Neal. In KLONDIKE KATE, Neal hires a group of prostitutes to work in his dance hall only to learn that Savage, the "good" girl, holds the deed to the place. By the fade, he has learned the difference in women.

In contrast to films such as these, the Bret Harte stereotype of the prostitute with a heart of gold persisted in the ideologies of even such more recent Westerns as THE CHEYENNE SOCIAL CLUB (National General, 1970), THE BALLAD OF CABLE HOGUE (Warner's, 1970), and McCABE AND MRS. MILLER (Warner's, 1971). Peckinpah was scarcely alone in THE BALLAD OF CABLE HOGUE in picturing Western prostitutes as extraordinarily beautiful women, untouched by the arid land, the harsh weather, or the nature of their work. While "Squirrel Tooth" Alice in Dodge City and Julia Bulette in Virginia City, Nevada, in the last century might well be called attractive, they were really no match for Julie Christie's Mrs. Miller, Stella Stevens' Hildy, or Shirley Jones and her bevy of beauties in THE CHEYENNE SOCIAL CLUB. In a sense, this notion of the merry, comely prostitute, perfectly happy in her profession and proud of it, constitutes what is probably the most vicious of patriarchal stereotypes because it is the most inaccurate and callous, not only on the frontier but no less since then.

The dialogue given to Pernell Roberts in RIDE LONESOME (Columbia, 1959) was already anticipated in THE TALL STRANGER (Allied Artists, 1957) when Joel McCrea tells Virginia Mayo that she's a "man's woman" and hence he cannot understand why she is traveling alone with a wagon train. The answer to McCrea's perplexity may well have been in the dialogue given to Richard Webb in THE NEBRASKAN (Columbia, 1953). When Jay Silverheels' Sioux attack a trading post in stock footage of an Apache attack, Webb, who is in love with the heroine, is fatally wounded. "You can't always pick a winner," he tells her before he dies, thus leaving her free to marry the hero.

In THE BURNING HILLS (Warner's, 1956), Natalie Wood was cast as a tempestuous Mexican. Tab Hunter, overlooking the color line, comments to her: "I've never met a girl with such spunk. You've got a heap of Yankee." Spunk also seems to be what Alexis Smith has in MONTANA (Warner's, 1950). She owns a large ranch and is opposed to Errol Flynn moving in with his sheep herd. At the end she shoots Flynn, only grazing him, regrets herself, and then runs into his arms.

Early on in ACROSS THE GREAT DIVIDE (Warner's, 1951), Kirk Douglas complains about Virginia Mayo wearing pants. Mayo becomes chattle in this picture and, after Douglas proves her father innocent of a murder charge,

Mayo switches to a dress, Douglas getting her for a wife and the feisty old man as a father-in-law. Douglas does his own killing in ACROSS THE GREAT DIVIDE, which is more than Audie Murphy does in THE QUICK GUN (Columbia, 1964). In the latter, a town is about to be raided by a gang of outlaws. The minister convinces the sheriff to try to reason with the outlaws, a foolish ploy which results in virtually everyone getting annihilated except for Murphy, two other men, and the peace-loving schoolteacher. In a scene right out of HIGH NOON, where a Quaker woman takes up firearms, the schoolteacher guns one of the outlaws in order to save Murphy's life, adding her vote to the anti-appeasement ideology of the film.

Only rarely is the "black widow" stereotype from *film noir* to be found in a Western, but a good example is THE HARD MAN (Columbia, 1957). The film opens to Guy Madison, as a Texas Ranger, pursuing and killing Myron Healy. Once Madison learns that Healy was framed, he gives up his badge and goes after the real culprit who, he suspects, is Lorne Greene, a ranching mogul married to Valerie French. French will do whatever is necessary to have her way. She tries to have an affair with Madison, urging him to kill her husband. In the final scenes, French herself kills Greene and is jailed for that murder as well as for framing Healy.

In APACHE DRUMS (Universal, 1951), Coleen Gray says: "I want what every woman wants. A home, a place in town, and an honest husband." Although she is attracted to Stephen McNally, he is a gunfighter and she refuses to marry him. All of the town's whores are rounded up and shipped out on the stage. McNally, too, is asked to leave. He comes upon the overturned stage. All the woman have been raped, killed, and scalped by the Apaches—a fitting end?—and a black retainer, who was accompanying them, tells McNally that the Indians plan next to attack the town and then dies. McNally goes back to warn the town, but the residents will not believe him. "The Indians are God's children," the local minister pontificates. When the Apaches strike, everyone hides in the church. A Cavalry officer who happens to be present passes on a bit of lore: the Apaches are attacking because their women are barren and they believe that if they die they will breed ghost warriors. In view of the enforced sterilization program the Bureau of Indian Affairs has continued to conduct throughout this century to keep the Indian population under control, this remark is doubly ironic. When the minister and an Apache scout for the Cavalry lead the others on their knees in prayer, the call is answered and Cavalry troops arrive to finish off the dwindling Apaches. Coleen Gray, too, realizes her mistake: a woman cannot do better than to have a man around who is good with a gun.

In THREE HOURS TO KILL (Columbia, 1954), Donna Reed also wants only an honest man; or rather, she did want an honest man, but she became pregnant out of wedlock with Dana Andrews' child. He was framed for a crime he did not commit and fled. Now Reed is married to a banker who has accepted her, despite her sin, and her small son. Andrews returns to clear himself. Reed confides to Andrews that she still loves him, but in answer to his confusion as to why things have worked out as they have she responds: "Maybe because of what I did." If a woman becomes pregnant, in the ideology of this film it is entirely her fault. Andrews does clear himself. Reed stays with the banker. Dianne Foster, a prostitute, is also in love with Andrews and she rides off with him at the fade reminding the viewer *à la* John Ford that his character has not been such that he deserves a virgin.

Most Westerns from the very beginning have repeated this idiocy *ad nauseam*: that if a man deports himself properly, in a word if he *performs* as he is expected to perform, his reward will be a beautiful, virginal female. This ideology reflects, as it perpetuates, a profound sickness in American society. It is as ultimately destructive in its way as the ethnocentrism in a film such as CALIFORNIA CONQUEST (Columbia, 1952) in which Teresa Wright, an American woman in riding pants, tells Cornel Wilde, a Spanish-American, "I wonder if we Americans will ever understand your people," and Wilde comforts her with the sentiment: "It is more important we learn to understand you." When the two are on the trail after Wright's father has been killed, she says: "I talk too much." "How else," Wilde responds, "would I know you are a woman?" In the final reel, Wright herself shoots the Mexican bandit chief, and then reverts to type, telling Wilde that all she wants is fourteen children. A similar lesson is prescribed for Maureen O'Hara in THE REDHEAD FROM WYOMING (Universal, 1953). She runs a saloon. She is attracted to Alex Nicol. After O'Hara tames a spooky horse, one of the dance hall girls who works for her remarks to Nicol: "I bet she'd be real handy on a homestead." In the final shoot-out, O'Hara plugs the villain and then confesses contritely to Nicol: "I cried because when I met you I realized I was all the things I never wanted to be."

OUTLAW STALLION (Columbia, 1954) is a primary example of the cliché where the heroine, a widow, refuses to marry the hero because he encourages her son to ride and work with horses and to do other masculine things, only to be persuaded forcefully of the error of her ways by the villain. Here again, men must learn that they are to perform; and women, should they be mothers, are to encourage them, and, should they also be heroines, are to love them—provided that the men perform *well*.

In terms of the images of women, Jane Fonda's two contributions to the genre are rather a disappointment. CAT BALLOU (Columbia, 1965), whatever may be its attractions as a comedy, exploits Fonda's physical attributes at the expense of everything else in her characterization and so it was fitting to find a full shot of her callipygian figure in tight jeans used throughout the promotional literature. In COMES A HORSEMAN (United Artists, 1978), it was apparently impossible for Fonda to play a "liberated" female rancher without confusing independence of spirit with just plain bad temper.

ROUGH NIGHT IN JERICO (Universal, 1967) has Jean Simmons cast as a twice-widowed owner of a stage line who gets drunk with George Peppard, but there is no romance for her in this film and she is shown to be at an utter loss without a man in her life. The same message is conveyed to Jane Alexander and Karen Black in A GUNFIGHT (Paramount, 1971) when they discover to their dismay that they are of the least importance to gunfighters played by Kirk Douglas and Johnny Cash who are most concerned with preserving their reputations.

Are there no positive images of women in Western films? Two portrayals of this kind do come to mind. In THE HIRED HAND (Universal, 1971) Verna Bloom was cast as a frontier woman of character, integrity, and grit, a woman who does not want to be alone, but who nonetheless is alone; and the man who comes back to her at the end is not the man she loves. Women on the frontier had to endure endless hardships and the kind of personal fortitude it required has rarely been represented so well. The same might be said for the female photographer, played by Jackie Burroughs, in THE GREY FOX (United Artists, 1982). The film, a fantasy based on the life of Bill Miner, an actual bandit well portrayed by Richard Farnsworth, is notable for the way it treats the relationship between Farnsworth, a man in his sixties, and the middle-aged Burroughs and it manages, rather adroitly, to avoid most of the clichés found in Western films.

However, the fact remains, as should be obvious from almost any Western film, that the roles assigned to women have been invariably prescriptive. All we can learn about women from the vast majority of Western films is what roles the patriarchy felt they ought to play, and nothing at all of the roles they actually did play on the frontier.

16

Images of Indians

There seem to be two widely divergent views about Native Americans in Western films. The first I have already cited, Jean-Louis Leutrat commenting that "l'indien été, bien évidemment, la principale victime de l'imagerie raciste," in brief the view that American Indians have been the principal victims of racial stereotyping. The alternative view was embodied in Robin Wood's remarks in an article titled "Shall We Gather at the River?: The Late Films of John Ford" which appeared in FILM COMMENT (Fall, 1971). In an effort to justify the way in which Wyatt Earp pacifies a drunken Indian in MY DARLING CLEMENTINE (20th-Fox, 1946), Wood wrote that "Earp knocks him around a bit and wants to know why he's been let out of the reservation; in racial terms the scene is obviously very unpleasant, but in mythic terms very meaningful, civilization conceived as demanding the rigorous suppression of the untamed forces Indian Joe represents." [10] I must decline Wood's position. I do not find it critically responsible to exalt a racial stereotype to the level of mythology. To put it bluntly, what apologists really mean by a "mythic" dimension in a Western film is that part of it which they know to be a lie but which, for whatever reason, they still wish to embrace.

One afternoon while visiting the late Duncan Renaldo at his home in Santa Barbara, I was introduced to Jack DeWitt who had written the screenplay for A MAN CALLED HORSE (National General, 1970) based on a short story by Dorothy M. Johnson. I asked DeWitt why he had changed so much of the original story, turning the Crows into Sioux, showing the Sioux sun dance ceremony as being the *okipa* ceremony of the Mandans (the Sioux did not practice elevation the way the Mandans did), and why he had Horse, played by Richard Harris, teaching the Sioux British military tactics. In response to this last, he had based the teaching episode on LAWRENCE OF ARABIA (Columbia, 1962) and as for the rest: at this late date, who cares? When I repeated this conversation to Dorothy M. Johnson, she replied that if I thought A MAN CALLED HORSE was a bad film, I should see the sequel!

"Rather than a tale of Indian life," Dan Georgakas wrote in an essay titled "They Have Not Spoken: American Indians in Film" (1972), A MAN CALLED HORSE is "really about a white nobleman proving his superiority in the wilds. Almost every detail of Indian life is incorrect. An angry Sioux writing to the VILLAGE VOICE complained . . . that the Sioux never abandoned widows, orphans, and old people to starve and freeze as shown in the film." [11] This criticism was well intentioned, but I would have to amend it somewhat. "Some old people, unwanted and without relatives, had no place to go," Royal B. Hassrick wrote in THE SIOUX (1964). "These were forced to live alone at the edge of the encampment. Here they were given food and supplies by the generous young men who thereby gained prestige . . . but at best theirs was a tragic lot, too often filled with insecurity and despair." [12] Notwithstanding, being reduced to beggary is not the same thing as being abandoned to starve and freeze to death. Criticism of this kind, which at times amounts to investigative reporting, is preferable to that of the "mythic" variety because it involves an *ethical* inquiry into the prescriptions and ideologies illustrated by Western films.

In the early days Thomas H. Ince was one of the very few producers to use actual Native Americans to play Indians in his films. Since he persisted in this practice throughout the 'Teens, either he did not read or, if he did, was unmoved by the chapter on "The Dangers of Employing Redskins as Movie Actors" in Ernest Alfred Dench's book, MAKING THE MOVIES (1915). "The Red Indians who have been fortunate enough to secure permanent engagements with the several Western film companies are paid a salary that keeps them well provided with tobacco and their worshipped 'firewater,' " Dench wrote. "It might be thought that this would civilize them completely, but it has had a quite reverse effect, for the work affords them an opportunity to live their savage days over again, and they are not slow to take advantage of it. They put their heart and soul in the work, especially in battles with the whites, and it is necessary to have armed guards watch over their movements for the least sign of treachery." [13]

The predominant images of Indians were firmly established by pictures such as THE INVADERS (Bison, 1912) directed by Thomas H. Ince, THE BATTLE AT ELDERBUSH GULCH (Biograph, 1913) directed by D.W. Griffith, and THE SQUAW MAN (Famous Players-Lasky, 1914) directed By Cecil B. DeMille. In THE INVADERS, the Indians—no tribe is specified—sign a treaty with a U.S. Cavalry commander played by Francis Ford. Ethel Grandin was cast as Ford's screen daughter. A group of surveyors arrives and violates the terms of the treaty. Sky Star, Chief Eagleshirt's daughter, falls in love with one of the surveyors. When Ford refuses to listen to the Indians' complaints, there is an uprising. The surveyors are massacred. Sky Star makes it to the fort to warn Ford, but dies soon after. Grandin begs Ford to shoot her with his last bullet as the Indians storm savagely around the fort. He is about to do so when reinforcements arrive. Ford pays his final respects to Sky Star for sacrificing her life in the white cause. This is basically the Wild West Show approach to the Indian/Anglo-American conflict. It is what Robert Altman (who once told me that in all his films he has parodied the Greatest Show on Earth: the United States) sought to expose in one of his better Westerns, BUFFALO BILL AND THE INDIANS, OR SITTING BULL'S HISTORY LESSON (United Artists, 1976). In Altman's film, President Grover Cleveland is heard to say about "Buffalo Bill" who did so much to popularize the Wild West Show: "It is men like him who have made America what it is today." Certainly, it was men such as "Buffalo Bill" who made so many Western films what they have been!

THE BATTLE AT ELDERBUSH GULCH is built around a similar situation: a group of whites huddling in a block house with wild Indians circling until, at the last minute, the Cavalry arrives to disperse them. I have already called attention to the scene in this film in which Lillian Gish is about to be shot rather than let her fall into the hands of the savages and how John Ford used quite the same incident in STAGECOACH (United Artists, 1939). In Anthony Mann's WINCHESTER '73 (Universal, 1953) during an Indian attack Shelley Winters, taking a gun from James Stewart, tells him, "I understand about the last one." The only really notable variation on this theme is in Sydney Pollack's THE SCALPHUNTERS (United Artists, 1968). The heroine is once more Shelley Winters; only this time, playing a lusty frontier prostitute, when she is surrounded by a Kiowa war party, Winters shrugs it off with a comment that, after all, they are only men and, far from being afraid, she intends to become the damnedest white squaw in the whole Kiowa nation.

Insofar as the Indians have a legitimate motivation in THE INVADERS—the violation of a treaty—it can be said that the film is more "sympathetic" than Griffith's ELDERBUSH GULCH, but this term is strictly comparative. If their motivation is a cause for compassion, their subsequent behavior is not and the viewer is expected to watch them being killed off with relief. In ELDERBUSH GULCH, the Indians—again no tribe is specified—have a ridiculous ceremony in which they eat their dogs and become delirious. Unfortunately, the chief's son and his friend arrive too late to join in the repast and so they try to steal Mae Marsh's puppies. The whites shoot them and the Indians launch an all-out attack. Anticipating the closing scene of THE BIRTH OF A NATION (Epoch, 1915) when the Ku Klux Klan races to save whites surrounded in a block house by raging blacks, ELDERBUSH GULCH features the Cavalry rushing to the rescue instead. But the end result is the same here as in THE INVADERS: the whites are saved by superior troops and the audience is expected to cheer as the Indians are shot down by the dozens.

The propaganda in THE SQUAW MAN is somewhat different. Based on Edwin Milton Royle's very successful stage play of 1905, the plot of the film concerns an English noble, falsely accused of a crime which his brother actually committed, who ventures into the American West in an effort to clear his name. He falls in love with an Indian maiden of the Pocahontas stereotype variety and they have a child. Years pass and his brother, on his death bed, makes a confession exonerating the hero. In the meantime, the Indian maiden has murdered a man and the sheriff is after her. The hero, now able to return to England and claim his title, accidentally shoots the Indian maiden (in the play she is a suicide); she dies in his arms, happy, because, as she tells him, she knows white culture to be superior and their child need not be held back because of her primitive ways.

The film was so popular that a sequel was made titled THE SQUAW MAN'S SON (Famous Players-Lasky, 1917) directed by Edward LeSaint. In the sequel, the son's marriage to an English woman fails because she is a morphine addict; she dies, whereupon he decides to live among the Indians and marries a native woman. The next year DeMille directed a remake of the original, THE SQUAW MAN (Famous Players-Lasky, 1918), and he even made a subsequent talking version twice as long as the 1918 remake, THE SQUAW MAN (M-G-M, 1931). An Indian actress named Redwing had played the Indian maiden in the original. Ann Little, who was not an Indian but who had played Sky Star in THE INVADERS, had the part in the remake and Lupe Velez essayed the role in the talking version. In all three versions the ideological message is clear and the audience is to be reassured that Anglo-American culture is pre-eminent. Moreover, in vanishing, i.e., dying, the Indians give that culture their whole-hearted blessing and wish it well in a future which cannot include them.

A true *rara avis* among all Western films is AN INDIAN'S BRIDE (Bison, 1909) in which a white woman is in love with an Indian named Little Bear. A Mexican tries to make advances to her, but he is driven away by Little Bear. The heroine's father disapproves of her love and he orders Little Bear away. The heroine befriends Little Bear's sister. The Mexican returns with a gang and abducts the heroine, but not before Little Bear's sister signals him what has happened. Little Bear rescues her. He is rewarded by being allowed to marry her, but he must agree henceforth to wear white man's clothes and behave as a white man. The imposition of one-settlement culture is a curious addition to the Perseus legend!

Due perhaps to the popularity of Thomas Ince's well-produced Westerns as well as some of D.W. Griffith's Western films, the Indian Story plot setting enjoyed what might almost be called a vogue in the early 'Teens. THE VANISHING RACE (American, 1912) focuses on the last remnants of the Hoppe (sic) tribe: father, son, and daughter. This is an interesting variation on the white families in so many Western films: father, daughter, and hero (son-in-law). A white man in love with a white woman finds himself nonetheless attracted to the Indian maiden. The two Indian males object to the maiden's responding to this attraction, but it is mutual and she runs off with the white man. Eventually he leaves the maiden and returns to the white woman who welcomes him with open arms. The maiden's brother goes on the warpath, kills the white man, only to be shot down himself. Next his father comes on the scene, draws a knife, and is also shot down. The two widows find themselves wandering through the sunny fields. The ideology is simple: races should not mix. When they do, the Indians are numerically the biggest losers, while an errant white may pay a penalty no less severe. However, the number of Indians is dwindling and soon this will no longer be a problem.

GERONIMO'S LAST RAID (American, 1912)—which, I suspect, was unofficially based on General Charles King's TWO SOLDIERS (1888)—tells of two Cavalry officers vying for the affection of the major's daughter. Instead of having one of the two suitors die, the plot is varied and one of them is shown to be a scoundrel. Captain Gray fills this role. Geronimo is being held prisoner at Fort Sill. Since this fort was in Oklahoma, built as an agency for the Kiowas and Comanches, one might wonder why Geronimo, an Apache, is there, but that is to anticipate. Captain Gray decides to disgrace his rival, Lieutenant Parker, by letting Geronimo escape and framing Parker for it. In the course of the action Parker and the heroine become Geronimo's prisoners, but they escape and Parker even rescues Gray and his command from certain death. The truth, exonerating Parker, comes out at a court-martial. The ideology informs the viewer that Geronimo is a savage killer of whites with no motivation whatsoever, that he "belongs" nowhere in the West, and that he was the dupe of manipulative whites. This last may have been the reason for setting the film at Fort Sill. Geronimo died there at the military hospital on 17 February 1909. The days of his being placed on exhibition, such as his appearance at the Louisiana Purchase Exposition in 1904 selling the bows he made by hand, were over. He had gone, prior to his death, to Lawton to sell one of his bows, got drunk on the money he made from the sale, and, returning, fell out of his buggy and spent the night in the road in a freezing rain. He had become a farmer, a member of the Dutch Reformed Church, a Sunday School teacher, and a self-promoter. His autobiography, titled GERONIMO'S OWN STORY (1906), had appeared only a few years before and he had ended it with the soulful plea that his people be allowed to return to Arizona. "If this cannot be done during my lifetime—if I must die in bondage—I hope that the remnant of the Apache tribe may, when I am gone, be granted the one privilege which they request—to return to Arizona." [14] GERONIMO'S LAST RAID wrote a new ending to his life and reassured anyone who might question the circumstance of his having been detained at Fort Sill.

Intermarriage was very often a one-way process in these early Westerns. A white man might co-habit with an Indian woman, but the marriage seldom lasted, if indeed marriage it could even be called. Conversely, the squaw man's son, being a mixed-blood, really belonged with the Indians and, despite his mother's belief in the superiority of white culture, when it comes to mixed-bloods the effect proves ephemeral. In James Fenimore Cooper's THE LAST OF THE MOHICANS (1826) when Uncas to attracted to Cora, the dark-hair, the Munro daughter with some Negro blood, whatever her genealogy, as far as Cooper was concerned such a romance was possible only in death.

Cooper's fictional world was first brought to the screen by D.W. Griffith in LEATHERSTOCKING (Biograph, 1909) and in 1911 two different film companies made a version of THE LAST OF THE MOHICANS; but the most impressive early version of this novel was THE LAST OF THE MOHICANS (Associated Exhibitors, 1920) directed by Maurice Tourneur. According to Clarence Brown, Tourneur had only been working on it two weeks before he "fell off a parallel and was in bed for three months. I made the whole picture after that."[15] No matter who directed it, one thing is of importance: this particular version stresses the romance between Uncas, the "last" of the Mohicans, and Cora, and the triangle which is formed when Magua, the renegade savage, would also have Cora for his bride. While in the novel, Magua is driven equally by a desire for vengeance against Cora's father, Colonel Munro, who once had him whipped, in the Tourneur/Brown film the emphasis is almost entirely on his attraction to Cora and she is *primum mobile* of all the trouble. Tourneur/Brown also retained Cooper's dichotomy between Magua and Uncas, the former representing the demonic savage, the latter a noble savage living in harmony with his wilderness environment. In its sentiments, the Tourneur/Brown film supported Cooper's horror of miscegenation and reinforced the belief that the color line is divine in origin and eternal.

Rather than responding to American history or current events, the plots of Western films, as exemplified by the Mohican cycle, this early no less than consistently later became primarily responses to the plots of other Western films. When Mascot Pictures filmed THE LAST OF THE MOHICANS (Mascot, 1932) as a twelve-chapter serial, the romance was non-existent thanks to the adroit casting of juvenile actor Junior Coghlan in the role of Uncas. In fact the plot, while retaining the distinction between infernal and noble savages, was altered to the extent that Uncas' father, Chingachgook, herein called the Sagamore, is killed at the end instead of Uncas and Uncas becomes the youthful companion of Cooper's woodland hero, Hawk-eye. THE LAST OF THE MOHICANS (United Artists, 1936) was next in order of appearance and in it there is a switch of the Munro daughters. Alice, the yellow-hair in the novel and in all the previous films, became the dark-hair and Cora, the dark-hair, became the yellow-hair. Uncas, played by Phillip Reed, is attracted to Alice, not Cora, but the color line is still upheld and in a sentimental tableau the two die holding hands. Hawk-eye, who never marries in the five novels in Cooper's saga, falls in love with Cora and the film ends with them embracing. In the 1932 version, the French general, Montcalm, conspires with the Hurons to massacre the English after the surrender of Fort William Henry; in the 1936 version, the Hurons still attack, but Montcalm begs the dying Colonel Munro's forgiveness and claims that he has been disgraced: "No one could stave the savagery of the Huron."

In LAST OF THE REDMEN (Columbia, 1947), Hawk-eye talks in a thick Irish brogue and is accompanied only by Uncas. There is no romance to speak of, although Uncas does die at the end, as does Alice. In this film her sin is being a weak female, something Cooper regarded as a virtue in his original characterization of her which is why she survives in the novel. "Hawk-eye, you were right," she says in this film. "There isn't any room in North America for weepers.'' Since the fade also finds all the Indians dead including Uncas, there is also apparently no room in North America for Native Americans. It is interesting to contrast this film with THE PATHFINDER (Columbia, 1953). Here, Uncas is a child orphaned after an Iroquois raid on his Mohican village. He is adopted by Pathfinder and Chingachgook. Neither Uncas nor Chingachgook die at the end and Pathfinder winds up with the girl. Chingachgook gives their romance a pleasant send-off by informing Pathfinder about the heroine: ''Much better than horse.'' THE LAST OF THE MOHICANS in the 1936 version has a pro-French, anti-British ideology; in THE PATHFINDER this ideology is altered to anti-French, pro-British, except that Pathfinder disapproves of the way the British—and not the Colonial Americans—are taking away the Indians' lands.

The polarization of Indians typical of Cooper's novels and these films had the status of a long-standing convention when in the 'Fifties a spate of supposedly ''pro-Indian'' Westerns were made which actually only reaffirmed this artificial dichotomy. BROKEN ARROW (20th-Fox, 1950) directed by Delmer Daves was in the vanguard with Cochise, played by Jeff Chandler, representing the noble savages, and Goklia, played by Jay Silverheels, leading the demonic savages. The film was filled with nonsense, for example, borrowing from European secret societies the idea of a blood brotherhood symbolized in a wrist-cutting ceremony (this notion would have a long livelihood in subsequent Westerns); and it also occasioned Debra Paget's debut as the decade's most memorable embodiment of the Pocahontas stereotype. In this film, she marries the hero, but, as the squaw in THE SQUAW MAN, dies before the fade. She was back, however, to play a similar role in both WHITE FEATHER (20th-Fox, 1955) directed by Robert Webb and THE LAST HUNT (M-G-M, 1956) directed by Richard Brooks. In THE LAST HUNT she shucked her soft hide dress to provide a view of her naked derrière. Also the ending of BROKEN ARROW was reversed in both of these pictures: Paget survived the fade in the white hero's arms.

BROKEN ARROW was such a popular success it led to a television special and then to a series by this title. Jeff Chandler was such a hit that he went on to play Cochise in later films, BATTLE AT APACHE PASS (Universal, 1951) directed by George Sherman and TAZA, SON OF COCHISE (Universal, 1954) directed by Douglas Sirk. BATTLE AT APACHE PASS persisted in the absurdity of the wrist-cutting ceremony—this time between Cochise and Geronimo—and even went so far as to deny the Apaches knowledge of making mescal: Mescal Jack, a white scout played by Jack Elam, is warned that he is never to be caught *selling* mescal to the Indians! As in BROKEN ARROW, Cochise wants peace. However, a crooked Indian agent wants to force Cochise and his people to move to the San Carlos reservation and to achieve this end he offers Geronimo guns in order to stir up trouble to be blamed on Cochise. The film concludes with a fight between Cochise and Geronimo—shades of Chingachgook's fight to the death with Magua—and the Apaches are awed by the use of artillery by the U.S. Cavalry. Superior technology usually has this effect, a subject to which I shall return.

In TAZA, SON OF COCHISE, Cochise dies and Taza, played by Rock Hudson, takes over leadership of the tribe. Taza agrees to move his people to the San Carlos reservation if they will be provided with farm implements and are permitted to maintain their own police force. Generally speaking, in Westerns which deal with the subject of agriculture, history is reversed and it is always the Anglo-Americans who are teaching the Indians how to grow food and survive in the New World. Geronimo will have none of this and remains on the warpath. At the end of the film, Taza and his native police force have rounded up or shot down most of Geronimo's followers. Taza has also saved General Crook and his Cavalry detachment and so he asks Crook a favor: will Crook see to it that Geronimo is taken to a reservation in the East for the sake of future peace? "I'll wire Washington," Crook responds. "I'm sure they'll do it." In this way the film manages to get around the wretched way the Arizona Apaches were deported to prison in Florida and even Crook, who refused to see his scouts imprisoned and who had to be replaced by General Miles, is thus made a willing party to what, historically, was first-class betrayal.

In the meantime, Delmer Daves wrote and directed DRUM BEAT (Warner's, 1954) which is a total distortion of the Modoc War. Notwithstanding, the film claims to be a "true" historical account. Captain Jack, played by Charles Bronson, is the demonic savage, Mannik, played by George J. Lewis, the noble, peace-loving savage. Dialogue that historically occurred between Hooker Jim and Albert B. Meacham is given to Captain Jack and General Canby—how else could Captain Jack be made a villain?—and the film ends, instead of showing the removal of the Modocs to Indian Territory, with the sentiment that "among the Indian people, as among ours, the good in heart outnumber the bad." One of Captain Jack's business practices is selling Indian women to white men. Marisa Pavan, among the noble savages, has a crush on the white hero, played by Alan Ladd. Ladd sets her straight: she must marry within her own people. Then he pays court to the white heroine while Pavan, apparently in despair, loses her life trying to save his.

In counterpoint to this "pro-Indian" trend there were such films as APACHE (United Artists, 1954) directed by Robert Aldrich, TOMAHAWK (Universal, 1951) directed by George Sherman, SEMINOLE UPRISING (Columbia, 1955) directed by Earl Bellamy, INDIAN UPRISING (Columbia, 1952) directed by Ray Nazarro, and BRAVE WARRIOR (Columbia, 1952) directed by Spencer Gordon Bennet—which I have ranked according to their degree of imbecility. The theme in all of these films is that the Indians are aware of the superiority of Anglo-American culture and, but for impediments which are duly dramatized, are anxious to enter onto the white man's road. In APACHE the film opens with an Apache carrying a peace pipe—a ceremony which, as wrist-cutting, this people never practiced. Geronimo is on his way to Florida with the other Apaches. One of their number, played by Burt Lancaster, alone escapes. His flight leads him through Indian Territory where he meets a Cherokee farmer, played by Morris Ankrum, who has nothing but praise for the white man's ways. He gives Lancaster a small bag of corn seed—in this opus the white men were the first to cultivate corn—and tells him to go plant it. When Lancaster returns to Arizona, he finds that the Apaches still there—there are some!—are more interested in drinking than in planting. Jean Peters, cast as an Indian maiden, is being courted by an Apache scout played by Charles Bronson, but she loves Lancaster and follows him into the hills. When Lancaster beats her with a club to make her stop following him, she breaks down and says: "I am only a woman. Good for bearing children, cooking, sewing . . . without you I am nothing." Lancaster gives in and together they plant the corn seed. When the Anglo-Americans see the corn field, all is forgiven and Lancaster and Peters are allowed to continue on the white man's road. "This was the only war we had," sighs John McIntyre, cast as scout Al Sieber. "We're not likely to find another."

The narration beginning TOMAHAWK places the story in Wyoming in 1866. Van Heflin is Jim Bridger and, although he is accompanied by an Indian maiden, she turns out to be his sister-in-law, a daughter of Black Kettle, leaving him free to marry Yvonne DeCarlo at the end of the picture. Red Cloud is anxious to put the Sioux on the white man's road, but he needs more time. Alex Nicol, who served with Colonel Chivington at Sand Creek, is an Indian-hater attached to Colonel Carrington's command. Heflin saves DeCarlo from being kidnapped by killing Red Cloud's favorite son. The drums beat for four days. Nicol orders Captain Fetterman to attack the Sioux and Fetterman, of course, is massacred. When Red Cloud attacks the fort, the Sioux are virtually wiped out; but Carrington spares Red Cloud. "We didn't beat him," Heflin tells Carrington. "It was these breech-loaders." The fort is closed up and the narrator proudly informs the viewer that for another thirty years the sun will rise on the Sioux, Red Cloud and Sitting Bull.

In SEMINOLE UPRISING, Karen Booth is taken hostage by a mixed-blood who has stirred up the Seminoles. The mixed-blood is named Black Cat and, when he wants to make war at night, his Seminole followers refuse, claiming that making war at night will make the sun god angry. Shortly after this exchange, Booth makes her grand plea to Black Cat: "Your people could go to school. Will the sons of the Seminoles forgive you for preventing them from becoming civilized?" In DISTANT DRUMS (Warner's, 1951) directed by Raoul Walsh, the subject is also the Seminole wars. The film is not any more accurate historically than SEMINOLE UPRISING, but at least Walsh, unlike Bellamy, did not costume his Seminoles in Apache garb. Instead, Walsh's Seminoles, as quite a number of Indian tribes that were neither Sioux nor Apache, for their motion picture representation were clad in the third kind of movie Indian garb (other than Sioux or Apache): what could be termed "*other* Indian garb."

INDIAN UPRISING is derivative of John Ford's FORT APACHE (RKO,

1948). It was filmed in Monument Valley and used the same fort as an exterior set. Miguel Inclan, who played Cochise in FORT APACHE, was cast as Geronimo. George Montgomery is a Cavalry captain charged with keeping the peace. "Apaches can only stay at peace so long," he reflects. "War is their religion." The opening narration tells the viewer how the Indians have resisted the push of civilization. The heroine has the solution to the problem. She hopes to open a school to teach the Indians, in her words, "to think as we do." When Geronimo is captured in dishonor, Montgomery, who by this time has been branded an Indian-lover, wants to resign his commission in protest, but Geronimo talks him out of it. The time has come for everyone to get on the white man's road; Geronimo can see it, so why cannot Montgomery?

This whole process is taken a step further in BRAVE WARRIOR where Jay Silverheels, as Tecumseh, chief of the Shawnees, admits to Jon Hall: "Your schools, your religion, the way you build towns . . . these things are good." In order to keep the peace, Hall proposes that Tecumseh now set about realizing his childhood dream of building a white man's town at Tippicanoe to prove to the whites that the Shawnees can live the same as white men do and that the United States can offer them this opportunity, whereas the British cannot. Tecumseh, as Hall, is in love with the heroine. The way this situation is resolved is that after Tecumseh and his people move into the town set at the Columbia ranch in Burbank, California, Tecumseh's war-like brother sets it on fire and burns it down, thanks to stock footage from THE MAN FROM COLORADO (Columbia, 1948). "I died when Tippicanoe died," Tecumseh says cryptically to Hall and the heroine. "Here all the Indian nations are buried."

While on the subject of burial, it might be pointed out that in Westerns Indians very seldom pick up their dead, much less bury them—another indication of their lack of civilization; and, sometimes, there are a lot of dead Indians to be buried. In ONLY THE VALIANT (Warner's, 1951), Gregory Peck's detail is out from Fort Invincible and determined to prevent the Apaches from "swarming and killing everything in sight." While on their mission, the detail gets pinned down by Apaches and despite the detail's blowing up a pass which collapses on a large number of them, the Apaches press their attack, only for reinforcements to arrive at the last minute armed with Gatling guns, the Indians then falling by the tens.

This is another instance of the Anglo-American superiority in technology, but in order to work it depends on very stupid Indians in massive, reckless, suicidal numbers. In THE GATLING GUN (Universal, 1971) directed by Robert Gordon, Cavalry officer Guy Stockwell tells another character that Dr. Gatling invented this gun because a terrible weapon will prevent war. Two Knife and his Apaches want the gun and trap Stockwell's detachment and a number of civilians, two women among them, in an old pueblo. The Apaches capture a soldier and burn him alive in front of the others. Stockwell observes: "If we stop now, all those women have to look forward to is rape and murder." The

Gatling gun has not been working, but this is enough to inspire Pat Buttram, who is repairing it, to greater effort. Once it is working, as the Apaches rush the defenders in slow motion the gun mows them down by the hundreds, the camera lingering on their blood-covered corpses, a sequence evidently influenced by Sam Peckinpah's THE WILD BUNCH (Warner's, 1969).

BATTLE OF ROGUE RIVER (Columbia, 1954) directed by William Castle is an updated version of the Rogue War from the way it is presented in CANYON PASSAGE (Universal, 1946) directed by Jacques Tourneur. In the latter, the Rogues go on the warpath because a crooked white man tries to rape two Rogue women. In BATTLE OF ROGUE RIVER the Rogues, still dressed as Sioux as they are in CANYON PASSAGE, are led by Chief Mike and are being stirred up by Richard Deming, leader of the Oregon civilian volunteers. Deming wants to control all the natural resources of Oregon, but his scheme backfires when George Montgomery leads his troopers onto the scene. The troopers fire a cannon into the forest and Rogues by the dozen fall or jump out of the trees in which they have been hiding and run to tell Chief Mike about the "big gun." Chief Mike, wearing his headdress, has been lying down—Rogue Indians did not wear headdresses nor did they live in teepees, but no matter . . . . When Chief Mike hears the news, he negotiates a thirty-day truce. Hostilities almost break out again, but Montgomery beats the truth out of Deming in Chief Mike's presence which inspires Mike to respond in the words of Chief Joseph of the Nez Perce: "From where the sun now stands, we will fight no more with the white man."

Breech-loading guns quite frequently turn the tables. In MASSACRE CANYON (Columbia, 1954) directed by Fred F. Sears, the Cavalry is trying to smuggle Henry repeating rifles to their fort past renegade Black Eagle and his Apaches. In the ensuing confrontation, no white man is even wounded, but the Apaches are virtually all decimated. In THE GUN THAT WON THE WEST (Columbia, 1955) directed by William Castle, it is Springfield rifles which do the trick, with this time Dennis Morgan playing Jim Bridger and the Cavalry beating Red Cloud and his Sioux into abject submission—apparently this Red Cloud had not seen TOMAHAWK from a few years before. Henry rifles are just as effective on Mexicans. In APACHE AMBUSH (Columbia, 1955) directed by Fred F. Sears, a Mexican bandit chief and his gang organize the Apaches to help them attack a wagon train. "Now," says the Mexican bandit chief, "I can do something for my country. Viva Mexico!" When he leads this combined force against San Arturo, the townspeople have Henry rifles and they slaughter the invaders in short order.

In THE COMANCHEROS (20th-Fox, 1961) directed by Michael Curtiz, in addition to getting some Comanche lore from John Wayne—a plume stick held by a white man means: do not attack—the viewer is impressed by the fact that, during an Indian raid, even a little boy, *but* a little boy armed with a blunderbuss, can fell three braves with a single shot. George J. Lewis was back in this picture cast as an Indian, Chief Ironshort, a drunken sot. It ends in a pitched battle with the Texas Rangers arriving just in time to help Wayne finish off all the Comanches and their Comanchero fellow-travelers.

In WHITE EAGLE (Columbia, 1932) directed by Lambert Hillyer, Buck Jones was cast as a full-blood Bannock who works as a Pony Express rider. At the beginning of the picture, a young boy tells Buck that, once he rubs down Buck's horse, "I'll have him shinin' like a nigger's heel." The villains are racially prejudiced against Buck, but this does not faze Buck. He beats up one of them in a fist fight and saves the heroine, who is white, from a mountain lion by wrestling it down and knifing it. "When we learn the way of the white man," Buck tells his Bannock father, "we will all live together in peace." Before the fade, Buck's father tells Buck the truth: he is white! He was stolen from his family as a child. This permits Buck, without violating the color line, to embrace the heroine.

Matters were no different when William Castle directed CONQUEST OF COCHISE (Columbia, 1953) with John Hodiak as Cochise. At the beginning of the film, the "dreaded Apache" and the "savage Comanche" are seen to join forces to butcher and pillage the area around Tucson. Because Hodiak believes "it does no good to attack Americans," the depredations are confined to Mexicans and it is relatively easy for Cavalry officer Robert Stack to negotiate a peace with Hodiak which finds the Apaches uniting with the Cavalry to wipe out the Comanches. Both Hodiak and Stack are in love with the heroine, but Hodiak saves the day for both her and Stack by telling her that Apache law forbids him marrying outside his own people.

Zane Grey originally published his novel, THE VANISHING AMERICAN (1925), as a magazine serial in 1922 in THE LADIES HOME JOURNAL, a Curtis publication as was THE SATURDAY EVENING POST. At the conclusion, Grey had his heroine, a blonde-haired, blue-eyed schoolteacher marry his full-blood Navajo hero. This set off such an outraged reaction among the magazine's readers that, henceforth, Curtis publications made it a stipulation that Indian characters were never again to be characterized and Harper's refused to publish the novel until Grey agreed to have the Navajo die at the end. It is for this reason that I called AN INDIAN'S BRIDE a true *rara avis* among Western films and I cannot think of another Western after its appearance until WINTER-HAWK (Howco, 1975) directed by Charles B. Pierce in which a white heroine voluntarily chooses to marry an Indian and both survive the fade. True, their coming together in the later film occurred only after Woody Strode is burned alive, but then it was probably felt by the producers to be quite enough to express sympathy toward one race without having to express it toward all races.

The budget of a film has had nothing to do with its ideology. In TEXAS STAGECOACH (Columbia, 1940) directed by Joseph H. Lewis, Charles Starrett remarks to an Indian: "Apache, you're a lazy, thieving redskin, but I've got a job for you." In THEY RODE WEST (Columbia, 1954) directed by Phil Karlson, the post doctor says to a Cavalry captain, "I saw some people moving around," to which the captain, the hero of the film, replies, "People? You *mean* Indians!" In the high-budget film, THE UNDEFEATED (20th-Fox, 1969) directed by Andrew McLaglen, the Indians join Union soldiers led by John Wayne and Confederate soldiers led by Rock Hudson in order to kill Mexicans.

One may be uncertain, depending on the ideology of a particular Western film, just how far one should go in hating Indians. ARROWHEAD (Paramount, 1953) directed by Charles Marquis Warren in this regard pulls no punches. The picture opens to a quotation from General Crook praising his chief of scouts, Al Sieber, as being in a class with such heroes as Daniel Boone, Kit Carson, and William F. Cody. This was meant to be taken seriously, although Sieber's character name was changed to Ed Bannon with Charlton Heston cast in the role. Bannon is fired by the Cavalry because the colonel wants peace and Bannon claims peace with Apaches is impossible. When a detail is attacked by Apaches, Bannon is blamed by the colonel for having incited them. Bannon's response to this accusation is to point out the number of men the Apaches have killed who have wanted peace. Bannon has spent some years living with them and he knows that "you have to think like an Apache to understand them." Jack Palance, cast as Toriano, has been to school in the East. He returns, having seen a vision of the Ghost Dance—wrong tribe, wrong ceremony, wrong visionary, but . . . . His first act after getting off the train is to kill the Wells, Fargo agent, his blood brother. The Apaches are coming to the fort because it is their desire to be removed to Florida and the chiefs make a special point of asking if it would be possible for them to be shipped there in box cars! Toriano objects to this submission and speaks for war. Katy Jurado is a mixed-blood spying on Bannon. When he foils her attempt to stab him to death, he promises her as a punishment to have her confined in a cell which will cause the Apache blood in her to drive her insane; she suicides rather than let this happen. Toriano in what I have termed the John Ford/James Warner Bellah racial nightmare summons tribes from all over to join with him in a unified rebellion against the whites. Not a moment too soon, Bannon cuts Toriano's wrist and his own, making them blood brothers, which in this film means one has to kill the other. Bannon kills Toriano and he is reinstated as a scout, put in charge of directing the cleanup of all the remaining Apaches.

In FORT MASSACRE (United Artists, 1958) directed by Joseph M. Newman, Joel McCrea, a sergeant leading C Troop after it has been decimated by Apaches, leads them first to a water hole where in retaliation they have to kill fifty Apaches before they can drink and then on to an old cliff dwelling where they shoot down another bunch of Apaches but without any more casualties. John Russell saves the day by plugging McCrea. Unlike the ideology in ARROWHEAD, here hatred and killing can be carried too far, by McCrea and by his wife before him who killed their two children rather than see them taken captive.

FORT MASSACRE brings to mind another Western with McCrea, TROOPER HOOK (United Artists, 1957) directed by Charles Marquis Warren. Here Barbara Stanwyck played a white woman rescued from Apache captivity together with her mixed-blood son. McCrea is assigned to return her to her white husband. Stanwyck is autistic, almost catatonic, for the first twenty minutes of the film due to shock caused by her ordeal; but on the way back she confides to McCrea that it was the squaws who made her want to die until she finally became one of them, even "smelled like them." Nanchez, Stanwyck's Apache abductor, escapes and pursues her. He arrives on the scene just as Stanwyck is reunited with her less than enthusiastic husband—the Indian child being responsible for his coolness—and Nanchez and the husband kill each other, leaving McCrea in a position to marry her and adopt her son in the bargain. As such, this plot is similar to THE STALKING MOON (National General, 1969) directed by Robert Mulligan, where white Eva Marie Saint is discovered among a band of Indians captured by the Cavalry and Gregory Peck takes her and her son to live with him in New Mexico. As with Nanchez in TROOPER HOOK, the Apache chief who had wived Saint wants to reclaim his family and follows—but with no better results. However, whatever the harrowing moments in these two films, I admit that neither McCrea nor Peck has it as badly as Glenn Ford does in DAY OF THE EVIL GUN (M-G-M, 1969) directed by Jerry Thorpe, when he is forced to endure one terror after the other before he is finally able to rescue his wife and two daughters from Apache captivity.

But then, many victims are not so fortunate. In A THUNDER OF DRUMS (M-G-M, 1961) directed by Joseph M. Newman, the film opens on a vicious raid by Indians on a woman and her children. When the Cavalry arrives, their faces are masked because of the stench from the corpses they are transporting with them after their own run-in with the Indians. The question to be answered is this: are the Indian raiders Apaches or Comanches? Comanches, the viewer is told (James Warner Bellah wrote the story!), prefer horse meat and rape their own women and so do not usually violate white women: thus it is most likely Apaches, which proves to be the case. In THE DESERTER (Spanish-Italian, 1970) directed by Burt Kennedy, Bekim Fehmiu is out leading a Cavalry detail when he discovers the local mission has been attacked by Apaches. Fehmiu's wife is strung up and has been skinned alive. He shoots her and then goes berserk, carrying on a one-man war against the Apaches until John Huston, as General Miles, enlists him to train Cavalry volunteers in Apache war arts and he leads this highly efficient force to an Apache camp where they kill 325 Apache warriors.

In ROCKY MOUNTAIN (Warner's, 1950) directed by William Keighley, Errol Flynn has organized a group of renegade Confederates to snatch California from the Union. They encounter a band of Shoshonis attacking a stagecoach and by the end of the picture unite with Union soldiers to kill Indians, Flynn taking the Shoshoni chief with him when he dies. THE LAST OUTPOST (Paramount, 1951) directed by Lewis R. Foster is another variation on this theme, of subsequent interest perhaps because of its star, Ronald Reagan. Reagan was cast as a Confederate officer who risks capture in his effort to save a Union post from marauding Apaches. When a Washington bureaucrat proposes to Reagan that maybe the Indians should be enlisted as Union allies to fight Confederates, Reagan makes an eloquent speech about how the Indians hate the entire white race and do not distinguish on the basis of uniforms. Not only does this speech ignore the historical fact that a number of Indian nations, the Five Civilized Tribes among them, joined the Confederate war effort because they were promised freedom and self-government after the war; or that Stand Watie, a Cherokee, distinguished himself sufficiently to become a Confederate general; but it also glides over the post-war revenge exerted by the Union on "disloyal" Indian nations, involving the confiscation of their tribal lands as punishment.

John H. Lenihan in SHOWDOWN: CONFRONTING MODERN AMERICA IN THE WESTERN FILM (1980), armed with no discernible knowledge of Indians not learned from movies but with the Henry Nash Smith thesis, declared that this theme prominent in THE LAST OUTPOST and "prominent in Westerns of the early 'Fifties, of former opponents who become fast friends against a common enemy, was obviously relevant to a country that was seeking national unanimity against communism and defensive alliances among World War II antagonists."[16] As comforting as such a political and military projection might be, it does not answer to the facts. As early as D.W. Griffith's AMERICA (United Artists, 1924), viewers learned that the British were not the real enemies during the Revolutionary War, but rather Lionel Barrymore and his band of Indian renegades. Zoltan Korda's SAHARA (Columbia, 1943) was remade as LAST OF THE COMANCHES (Columbia, 1953) directed by Andre de Toth; dialogue given to Humphrey Bogart in the former was given to Broderick Crawford in the latter; the roles played by the Nazis in the former were given to the Comanches in the latter; and in both the Perception of the film is that freedom-fighters have to pull together to defeat the enemy. It is but the John Ford/James Warner Bellah racial nightmare reversed, with white men uniting to kill men with darker colored skin or other white men—whomever the enemy happens to be at the moment.

In a footnote, Lenihan recalled a visit with Delmer Daves in June, 1973, and dutifully repeated the fallacy that in DRUM BEAT Daves "intended an accurate account of the Modoc incident, based upon his research of military records. Having presented the Indian's (sic) point of view in BROKEN ARROW, Daves wanted to offer the settler's side of the story, which his researched account of Captain Jack allowed him to do. Like most other writers and directors I have interviewed in Southern California, Daves had no recollection of intending any analogy with contemporary problems."[17] However, Lenihan did add that Daves, upon reflection, had been willing to concede that perhaps the Cold War had influenced him unconsciously. This was not the impression I got from Daves when talking with him, but it is really a moot point. A book such as Lenihan's, which was deemed sufficiently well researched for him to earn a Ph.D. on the basis of it, actually does little more than extend the propaganda contained in the films themselves.

"The whites are sincere," Vine Deloria, Jr., wrote in his Foreword to THE PRETEND INDIANS: IMAGES OF NATIVE AMERICANS IN THE MOVIES (1980), "but they are only sincere about what they are interested in, not about Indians about whom they know very little. They get exceedingly angry if you try to tell them the truth and will only reject you and keep searching until they find the Indian of their fantasies. So if you have to deal with them to get the job done, that comes with the job. The first ones, if you remember, were convinced that Seven Cities of Gold existed somewhere in Northern Arizona and even when the Indians told them that no such cities existed they refused to believe them. Instead they tortured countless Indians in an attempt to find the Seven Cities. The next expedition we saw was convinced that a 'Fountain of Youth' existed somewhere in the Florida-Louisiana-Mississippi area. They also tortured Indians in the mistaken belief that we were trying to keep them from learning the secret . . . . The obvious solution to the whole thing would be for the whites to achieve some kind of psychological and/or religious maturity. But the whole psychological posture of American society is toward perpetual youth. Everyone believes that he or she must be eternally young. No one wants to believe that he or she is getting old or will ever get old. Somehow only Indians get old because the coffee table books are filled with pictures of old Indians but hardly a book exists that has pictures of old whites. A strange thing, perhaps, for a vanishing race—having one's pictures on display everywhere—but therein lies the meaning of the white man's fantasy about Indians—the problem of the Indian image. Underneath all the conflicting images of the Indian one fundamental truth emerges—the white man *knows* that he is an alien and he *knows* that North America is Indian—and he will never let go of the Indian image because he thinks that by some clever manipulation he can achieve an authenticity that cannot ever be his."[18]

If there is any political reflection to be drawn from the dialogue given to Ronald Reagan in THE LAST OUTPOST, it is not what was happening in international affairs when the film was made. It is rather that the image of the American Indian embodied in the Declaration of Independence—"merciless Indian Savages, whose known rule of warfare, is an undistinguished destruction of all ages, sexes, and conditions"—had survived unchanged into Twentieth-century entertainments. Indeed, is there an attitude toward Indians more typical of Anglo-Americans over the last two hundred years than that in THE LAST OUTPOST?

However, the Indians against whom Reagan was sounding an alarm are definitely more fearsome opponents than they have been in other films. In DANIEL BOONE (RKO, 1936) directed by David Howard, Boone is able to scare off an attacking horde simply by pretending to swallow a knife. The Indians are plainly too stupid to do their own thinking—another of the Founding Fathers' assumptions embodied in the Declaration of Independence—and so they require leadership from the likes of John Carradine, a scheming white man in DANIEL BOONE as he is later in John Ford's DRUMS ALONG THE MO-

HAWK (20th-Fox, 1939). In chapter plays such as THE PAINTED STAL-LION (Republic, 1937) and THE SCARLET HORSEMAN (Universal, 1946), the Indian hordes are led by women. In the sexist context of these films, this is a significant circumstance.

When one occasionally meets an Indian educated in the white man's ways, as Levi Talking Bear in THE WAR WAGON (Universal, 1967) directed by Burt Kennedy who claims he is no "dumb Indian," his philosophy usually reduces, as it does in this film, to a policy of "grab all you can any time you can." Conversely, white men educated by Indians—such as the character played by John Wayne in HONDO (Warner's, 1953) or that played by Rory Calhoun in APACHE TERRITORY (Columbia, 1958), both films based on novels by Louis L'Amour—are always shown to excel their teachers, *ergo*: an Indian is never a match for a well-trained white man. Nor is a white man ever as morally reprehensible. In AMBUSH AT TOMAHAWK GAP (Columbia, 1953) directed by Fred F. Sears, no matter how badly David Brian, John Derek, and John Hodiak behave, they redeem themselves in the eyes of the viewer when they die in a battle with the Apaches in which they take a lot of Apaches with them—primarily because in this film the Apache military strategy is to ride back and forth in front of a fortified saloon so they can be shot down.

In terms of political organization, Indian tribes and nations were never organized along the autocratic lines of the whites. Europeans never grasped this in their colonial dealings with Native Americans any more than Anglo-Americans did in their dealings with Indians in the Nineteenth century. In depicting Indian government, filmmakers only perpetuated the error. Quite the most effective way to stop an Indian attack is to kill the Indian chief. Victor Mature does this in ESCORT WEST (United Artists, 1959) when he throws a rattlesnake at the renegade mixed-blood leading the Modocs. The renegade chief behaves as if the rattler were a python and thus Mature can get a clear shot at him, after which his followers disperse. At other times it is the medicine man who must be removed, as in THE GUNS OF FORT PETTICOAT (Columbia, 1957). In this film, Audie Murphy and a detachment of stereotypical women, trained as infantry while their husbands are away during the Civil War, kill a great number of Comanches as the Indians circle a besieged mission where they have forted up; but the battle comes to an abrupt end when Murphy slips behind the Indians' lines, finishes off their medicine man, and hangs his corpse up in front of the mission doors. In THE STAND AT APACHE RIVER (Universal, 1953), Stephen McNally ends an Indian siege by showing the chief, Charra Blanca, who is his prisoner, that almost all of his people have been killed. Wounded and himself dying, the chief calls off the hostilities, speaking to his people in Spanish.

Infectious diseases have often been made allies of the white man in Western films. In THE COMMAND (Warner's, 1953), based on an original story by James Warner Bellah, the John Ford/James Warner Bellah racial nightmare of many tribes uniting in a genocidal war against all white men following Custer's defeat is prevented by an orgy of Indian-killing. But this is only the tip of the iceberg. In the course of their promiscuous raiding, the Indians contract chicken pox—not smallpox!—and the resulting epidemic wipes out virtually all the Indians who are left, thus finally foiling any hope for racial alliance.

Oddly enough, the only film which shows the Indians completely successful—that is, where every white person is killed and there are no reserves—is AGUIRRE, THE WRATH OF GOD (German, 1973) directed by Werner Herzog. In THE LOST PATROL (RKO, 1934) directed by John Ford, a British detail in the desert is preyed upon and killed off by Arab marauders one by one until only Victor McLaglen is left. The viewer does not see these Arab enemies, only their effects, until the final scenes when McLaglen single-handedly shoots them down in large numbers before he is relieved by reinforcements. In AGUIRRE, no reinforcements arrive and the Indians are never seen except for brief moments. The film is set in South America and the Spaniards are all German actors speaking German, rather an interesting contrast with so many American films in which Spaniards, Mexicans, Indians, and Germans all speak English in highly stereotyped accents. There is an eerieness at the end which not even the ripples of the water caused by the motorboat on which the camera was mounted can wholly dispel and Herzog, in his own way, effectively demonstrated just how much Native Americans were a part of their natural environment.

In Hollywood films, the reverse is the rule. What happened to the Seminoles after all those films showing how they retreated to the Florida everglades rather than be sensible and get on the white man's road (to make their act of removal active rather than passive) and even then still had to be beaten into submission? WAR ARROW (Universal, 1954) directed by George Sherman attempts to supply the answer. Jeff Chandler was cast as a Cavalry major who is sent to the fort commanded by John McIntyre to fight Kiowas. Chandler's idea is to organize the Seminoles to do the fighting—in the dialogue the Kiowas are universally referred to as Kioways. McIntyre is skeptical. After the fight in Florida, he reminds Chandler, the Seminoles scattered, laid down their guns for good, and now are groveling cowards. Chandler meets with the Seminoles and, in exchange for six months of solid fighting against the Kioways, they can have some land of their own. The chief's daughter sets her heart on Chandler and tells her people: "No one will give you anything unless you fight for it." The Seminoles agree and Chandler begins to train them in modern military strategies, e.g., having them dig trenches in which they hide to ambush Kioway war parties as the Kioways unwittingly ride past. "A Kioway a day keeps me in pay," a Cavalry sergeant, played by Noah Beery, Jr., remarks. "Tomorrow I'm going to have a special: two for a quarter." Suzan Ball, cast as the chief's daughter, has not much chance against Maureen O'Hara, the wife of the white deserter acting as an advisor to Jay Silverheels, cast as Satanta, chief of the Kioways. The Kioways decide to attack the fort and Chandler has all the women and children hide in the powder house so they can be blown up if the Kioways overrun the white defenses. But the Kioways prove no match for the Anglo-Americans and their Seminole allies.

Jeff Chandler's objective in THE GREAT SIOUX UPRISING (Universal, 1953) directed by Lloyd Bacon is to prevent the John Ford/James Warner Bellah racial nightmare from happening during the Civil War. When Anthony Quinn as Crazy Horse in THEY DIED WITH THEIR BOOTS ON (Warner's, 1941) begins to enumerate the many allied Indian tribes, he treats the Oglalas and Sans Arcs (Itazipchos) as if they were somehow separate nations from the Sioux rather than branches of the Sioux nation. The same split is true in this picture and Stand Watie is trying to recruit both the Sioux and the Oglalas as well as the Cheyennes and Nez Perce to join the Confederacy. While holding the Cavalry at bay, Chandler exposes Lyle Bettger as the trouble-making villain. The Cavalry promises peace and justice after the war and Stand Watie is sent packing back to Indian Territory. In a variation of the John Ford/James Warner Bellah racial nightmare, Dana Andrews in SMOKE SIGNAL (Universal, 1955) directed by Jerry Hopper tells Cavalry captain William Talman that the Ute chief, War Cloud, has become war-crazed and is forming an alliance with the Sioux and the Navajos. After a number of harrowing adventures, Talman decides to let Andrews go talk personally to Apache chief Guranío, who supposedly will foil War Cloud's *entente*.

Just as all the trouble can often be laid at the door of some renegade white villain who has organized the Indians to fight in his own personal cause or who can trick them into doing so, sometimes the major source of dissension is caused by a megalomaniacal white Cavalry leader. It might be a case such as that of Everett Sloan cast as Colonel Templeton in MASSACRE AT SAND CREEK (Screen Gems, 1956) directed by Arthur Hiller. "Redskins hunt, murder, and steal," Templeton observes to Indian agent Roy Roberts. "Whites work." To which Roberts responds: "Work and vote." The narration tells the viewer that in 1864 the Cheyennes were drained of spirit by too many battles and too many defeats. Because the Arapahos are at war, the Cheyennes are moved to Sand Creek where Templeton surrounds their village and destroys it. The Cheyenne chief murmurs, "From where the sun now stands, I will fight no more"; but his braves rush off to join the Arapahos. Unlike John Ford's FORT APACHE, the U.S. Cavalry's honor is not maintained by making a hero and a legend out of Templeton: instead he is discharged from the service! Another ridiculous, if well-intentioned, effort to treat the Sand Creek massacre was SOLDIER BLUE (Avco-Embassy, 1970) directed by Ralph Nelson, in which Nelson hoped to put the event on the screen more or less as it happened. As THE WILD BUNCH, much of the notoriety attached to this picture came from the sensational amount of killing, rivaling in this regard the European Westerns then in vogue. Unfortunately the participants as depicted in the film are *not* those involved in the historic battle itself and the military conflict is framed by the routine formulary plot ingredients derived from the literary source, T.V. Olsen's ARROW IN THE SUN (1969).

The plot of William S. Hart's WAGON TRACKS (Famous Players-Lasky, 1919) directed by Lambert Hillyer incorporates that incident whereby an Indian is inopportunely killed by a member of a wagon train and the Indians demand a white life for his life with Hart, although innocent, volunteering. There is a similar episode in THE WAY WEST (United Artists, 1967) directed by Andrew McLaglen—albeit not in the original A.B. Guthrie, Jr., novel on which the film was based. An Indian follows after a wagon train for several days with his dead son mounted grotesquely on a horse. When I was working as a consultant on IMAGES OF INDIANS (PBS, 1980), the words which this Indian speaks were a kind of Lakotah. They were translated via subtitles in a clip of this sequence, coming out nearly total gibberish, in contrast to what Robert Mitchum on screen translates the Indian as saying. But then, why should a producer have been concerned about lingual accuracy when the intention of the majority of these films is to reinforce the comment made in THE BLACK DAKOTAS (Columbia, 1954) directed by Ray Nazarro: "You can never tell when those savages will break loose and turn against us"? In this particular film, incidentally, the whites are able to establish peace with War Cloud and induce him to kill renegade leader Black Buffalo and his followers in exchange for $100,000 in gold. Of course, sometimes the white villains do not like the price offered. In LAND RAIDERS (Columbia, 1969) directed by Nathan H. Juran, villain Telly Savalas objects to the Indian commissioner offering the Apaches two million acres of land if they will make peace. "Remember Sand's [sic] Creek?" he asks as he leads a gang to raid an Indian village, killing and burning. The Apaches retaliate by attacking the town and, despite all the fighting, still find time to rape white women.

In YELLOWSTONE KELLY (Warner's, 1959) directed by Gordon Douglas an Arapaho maiden played by Andra Martin is named "Eyes Like A Summer Sky" to go with her blue eyes. She is only one in a long line of blue-eyed Indians and the only quality they all have in common is that they do not portray Mandans where having blue eyes might be believable. Chuck Connors, cast as the lead in GERONIMO (United Artists, 1962) directed by Arnold Laven, explained after the film was released that he had done a screen test with his eyes covered by black contact lenses, but that he did not look as menacing with the contact lenses as with his natural blue eyes. Nor had this situation changed by the time Trevor Howard came to play an aged, blue-eyed Cheyenne in WIND-WALKER (Pacific International, 1980) directed by Kieth Merrill. I happened to attend the world première of this film where the author of the novel on which it was based, Blaine Yorgason, asserted that, while he knew nothing about the Cheyenne Indians, the story had come to him in a dream, directly from the Holy Ghost! I definitely would not want to blame the Holy Ghost for WIND-WALKER, since it is basically a Cavalry versus Indians Western with the Crows every bit as nasty as the Cavalry at its worst. In order to identify with the sympathetic Cheyennes, we must hate the Crows.

"From 1913 to the present," Phil Lucas wrote in "Images of Indians" in

FOUR WINDS (Autumn, 1980), "Hollywood has produced literally thousands of feature films on cowboys and Indians . . . . These films, coupled with a preponderance of supportive literature (dime novels, poems, books, essays, journals, and plays), art, and, more recently, television and advertising erase the varied cultural and ethnic identities of over 400 distinct tribes and nations of the original inhabitants of the Americas, and have successfully replaced them with a permanent fictional identity . . . the Hollywood Indian."[19] Accepting Lucas' point, that there is no cultural or historical validity in the portrayals of Indians in most Western films, there are nonetheless discernible patterns into which these variations of the Indian Story plot setting fall in the mode of the formulary Western or of the romantic historical reconstruction. Depending on the specific ideology in each of these films, they can be isolated into a variety of pure types.

In an essay on ULZANA'S RAID (Universal, 1972) directed by Robert Aldrich contained in WESTERN MOVIES, Jack Nachbar subscribed to that erroneous dichotomy between savagery and civilization which one-sided critics like to project into Western films. He also felt that while "anti-Indian racism does indeed exist in Western movies . . . the problem is not one of vicious stereotyping but one of the romantic distortions of history for purposes of creating mythic narrative."[20] I have given so many examples in this chapter because, if I demonstrate nothing else in it, I would hope the reader can agree with me that most Westerns dealing with Native Americans are in fact guilty of vicious stereotyping. However, I did not bring up Nachbar to harangue him for what he wrote, but rather to make mention of a distinction which he made in this essay, that is, that there are pro-progress and anti-progress Westerns. In the pro-progress Western Indians are stereotyped "as treacherous, cunning, and sadistically violent . . . to make their defeat . . . all the more symbolically satisfying."[21] In the anti-progress Western, "tribal life becomes stereotyped as nobly virtuous, a proper alternative to the vulgarities of white society."[22] As examples of anti-progress Westerns, Nachbar selected BROKEN ARROW and Arthur Penn's LITTLE BIG MAN (National General, 1970). The basis, of course, for the latter film was Thomas Berger's novel and, as mentioned above, the novel was intended as parody. But it is flawed in that Berger had little understanding of the Plains Indians and less knowledge of Western history, and so Arthur Penn could scarcely be expected to adapt historical and cultural perspectives not to be found in the original. The most comic situation in the film is how the protagonist, Jack Crabbe, played by Dustin Hoffman, becomes dissolute among white men and sober and upstanding among the Indians, as the story follows him back and forth.

In a sense, Nachbar's distinction between pro-progress and anti-progress Westerns is an extension into plot structure of the division between noble and demonic savages which began with James Fenimore Cooper. Provided we are agreed on what is meant by the idea of progress, it is possible to classify Western films featuring Native Americans both according to the presence or absence of noble and demonic savages and according to whether or not the ideology of the plot supports the advance of Anglo-American society at the expense of indigenous cultures. When it comes to ULZANA'S RAID, Nachbar felt it is a dialectical Western, incorporating both pro-progress and anti-progress elements. The plot intercuts Ulzana's party of renegade Apaches in its reign of terror against whites with their pursuit by the Cavalry. Among the atrocities committed by Ulzana's party are the hacking out of a heart of a trooper and playing catch with it, burning a victim alive, and raping a woman into insanity. "Aldrich," Nachbar observed in a footnote, "[was] so intent on dramatizing Ulzana's rampage as stereotyped that he apparently ignored cultural accuracy. According to one study [AN APACHE LIFE-WAY: THE ECONOMIC, SOCIAL, AND RELIGIOUS INSTITUTIONS OF THE CHIRICAHUA INDIANS (University of Chicago Press, 1941) by Morris Edward Opler], Chiricahua Apache[s] were traditionally reticent in sexual matters. The raping of women when on raids was looked upon by the Chiricahua[s] with extreme disfavor and it rarely took place."[23] The dialectic enters Aldrich's film through the behavior of the white troopers as, for example, when they mutilate the body of Ulzana's slain son. The scout, played by Burt Lancaster, who is named McIntosh points this out to the officer of the pursuit detail when he remarks: "What bothers you, Lieutenant, is you don't like to think of white men behaving like Indians. Kind of confuses the issue, don't it?" According to Nachbar, by rejecting the thesis and antithesis of pro-progress and anti-progress Westerns, a synthesis "in which 'ain't none of us right' " might emerge "and the treatment of the Indians on screen will cease to be exploitive."[24] I find this rather too facile. I do not think any new synthesis will become possible until screenwriters and filmmakers generally are willing to present audiences with historical reconstructions, until there is a legitimate concept of historical reality informing both the structure and the characters in a Western film. Just as in Westerns dealing with historical personalities, when a Western deals with diverse cultures it must strive to represent them accurately, as they existed at the time during which the film is set. While I accept Nachbar's distinction as valid, I also reject it as an adequate critical framework for evaluating Western films featuring Native Americans and Native American cultures, since progress as it must be defined is essentially an Anglo-American interpretation of an historical process of excluding the right of other cultures to exist. It should rather be required of filmmakers, if they expect their films to be taken seriously and not classed as a form of racist propaganda, to be truthful not only to the period and the place but to the people as well.

When it comes to relations between Anglo-Americans and Native Americans, a basic concept of historical reality would also permit us to make a wide variety of distinctions between the various kinds of films which have been made or which may be made in the future, as opposed to only two. THE DEVIL'S DOORWAY (M-G-M, 1950) directed by Anthony Mann, for example, could readily be evaluated on where it fits into the canon of Mann's films; it could be identified as a romantic historical reconstruction with a doomed hero; and, as a narrative structure, it is an instance of the Indian Story in which the hero is portrayed as a virtuous man forced by social circumstances into becoming an outlaw: thus a combination Indian Story/Outlaw Story. In REPRISAL! (Columbia, 1958), the hero played by Guy Madison appears in a romantic historical reconstruction which combines the Indian Story with the Justice/Revenge Theme plot setting insofar as social pressures force him to become violent. In the Indian Story featuring a mixed-blood in Anglo-American society, we have romantic historical reconstructions in which the ideology reveals a mixed-blood who remains noble throughout the story despite white machinations, as in BROKEN LANCE (20th-Fox, 1954); or a mixed-blood who succumbs to evil ways because of white machinations, as in THE HALF-BREED (RKO, 1952); a mixed-blood who by virtue of his mixed blood combines the worst qualities of both races, as in HAWK OF THE HILLS (Pathé, 1927); or a mixed-blood who embodies the noblest qualities of both races, as in FLAMING STAR (20th-Fox, 1960). We can distinguish that ideology in Western films which shows the effects of Indian cultures on white men raised in them: be it (1) Richard Widmark in THE LAST WAGON (20th-Fox, 1956) whose knowledge of Apache ways helps him to protect a wagon train and kill marauding Apaches effectively; or (2) Charlton Heston in THE SAVAGE (Paramount, 1952) whose Sioux training has taught him to become violent only as a last resort, but who, once he becomes violent, is more terrifyingly capable because of that training; or (3) Paul Newman in HOMBRE (20th-Fox, 1967) whose Apache upbringing has doomed him and caused him to vanish, that is, to die for the benefit of the surviving white race. According to the ideology, Indian biography films can present Native American historical personalities such as Geronimo as a demonic savage, as in GERONIMO (Paramount, 1939); as a noble savage forced into violence by white machinations, as in GERONIMO (United Artists, 1962); or as a candidate for religious conversion, as in WALK THE PROUD LAND (Universal, 1956). Lastly, a basic concept of historical reality will permit the informed viewer to realize that in RUN OF THE ARROW (RKO, 1957) when Jay C. Flippen, cast as a Sioux, claims that the Sioux got their name from the French and that it means "cut-throat," no one working on the picture even bothered so much as to look up Sioux in a standard dictionary to learn its origin.

"Our nation was born in genocide when it embraced the doctrine that the original American, the Indian, was an inferior race," Malcolm X is quoted in THE AUTOBIOGRAPHY OF MALCOLM X (1966). "Even before there were large numbers of Negroes on our shores, the scar of racial hatred had already disfigured Colonial society. From the Sixteenth century forward, blood flowed in battles over racial supremacy. We are perhaps the only nation which tried as a matter of policy to wipe out its indigenous population. Moreover, we elevated that tragic experience into a noble crusade. Indeed, even today we have not permitted ourselves to reject or to feel remorse for this shameful episode. Our literature, our films, our drama, our folklore all exalt it. Our children are still taught to respect the violence which reduced a red-skinned people of an earlier culture into a few fragmented groups herded into impoverished reservations.''[25]

Are there no Western films which represent Native Americans accurately? What of BUCK AND THE PREACHER (Columbia, 1972) directed by Sidney Poitier or ONE FLEW OVER THE CUCKOO'S NEST (United Artists, 1975) directed by Milos Forman? In connection with BUCK AND THE PREACHER, there is no question that its portrait of Native Americans is sympathetic, probably motivated by the fact that white prejudice is its basic theme. In the picture the Indians even rescue a caravan of black homesteaders being pursued by a posse of white bigots. But, as in the case of LITTLE BIG MAN, a film that distorts history in an atypical way does not, for that reason, escape being a distortion. A formulary Western with black protagonists does not cease being a formulary Western.

There are those who would say that ONE FLEW OVER THE CUCKOO'S NEST is definitely not a Western. It was based on Ken Kesey's novel, a book cited by Leslie A. Fiedler in THE RETURN OF THE NATIVE AMERICAN (1962) as supporting his thesis that any story featuring a Native American is *a priori* a Western. For me, ONE FLEW OVER THE CUCKOO'S NEST is that most elusive of all types of fictional narrative, the kind I questioned in the first chapter of this book, an allegory. In it the whites have imprisoned themselves in an insane asylum from which there is no escape and from which a Native American, named Chief Bromden, breaks out and seemingly alone can gain freedom. When working on IMAGES OF INDIANS, I asked Will Sampson, who was the host/narrator and who had played Chief Bromden in the film, if he felt this ending to be tragic. Not at all, he assured me. He interpreted the picture to mean that the white man is destined to live in a world of his own creation which must ultimately deny him his liberty, whereas the Native American lives in the world of Nature and can only be destroyed if he remains in the white man's world.

I must say that I do not find this kind of mutually exclusive ideology any more palatable than the old Anglo-American idea that color lines are inviolable. I have learned much in my life from my association with Native Americans and I would hope that in the future, with a more accurate understanding of their various cultures, a truly meaningful dialogue would develop. Until that happens, however, I would hope that we may once and for all put to rest that killing ''mythical'' Indians is only so much ''newspeak'' for enjoying genocide and that the Western film as it has been made deserves the strongest censure which can be brought to bear for the lies it has told.

Epilogue

Before I come to a summing up of what I have tried to do in this book, I should like to mention, albeit only briefly, the ritual aspect of motion pictures. Television has long replaced the movies as the primary medium of mass entertainment for the majority of Americans. Television productions have their own peculiar formulae: there is a violent episode, usually resulting in death, on the average of every seven minutes; but, on the average of every four minutes, there is what might be called a heart-warming moment. This combination of aggression and sentimentality would seem to meet the psychological needs of most viewers.

What has happened to motion pictures in the meantime is that they have become directed to more specific audiences than was formerly the case. On New Year's Day, 1984, I attended a showing of SCARFACE (Universal, 1983) directed by Brian DePalma. The audience for most movies is made up of persons between the ages of seventeen and twenty. There were about four hundred people who came to see SCARFACE when I did. This audience consisted largely of black and Hispanic males in this age group; there were very few women of any age. In addition to experiencing the customary ritual elements of viewing a film in the dark on a gigantic screen, this particular audience in many cases had brought whiskey or marijuana in which it indulged as the screen violence—which originally earned the film an "X" rating before the decision was appealed and amended—increased as the film ran its course.

In the beginning of this book, I rejected the "decades" approach of viewing motion picture productions. My reasons for this, I trust, have become evident. I shall not concern myself here with why young people would need depressants to view a depressing motion picture. What must be stressed, however, is that the violence is well choreographed and that the presentation of screen violence over the years, in the Western as in the gangster picture, has become standardized. SCARFACE concludes with a blood bath, vividly realized through sophisticated special effects. Motion pictures have managed to make violence palatable for a very wide audience. Of course, there is a segment of the population, admittedly a very small one, for which this kind of choreographed violence is insufficient. For them there are the so-called "snuff" films which can be attended, sometimes for as much as a hundred dollars a person, in which it is possible to see real people, at times children, at others adults, being actually put to death in front of a camera. For most who attend films, however, the preference obviously still is for pretended violence, not the real thing.

Americans live in an electronic culture in which, in 1983, at the same time as a former motion picture actor was in the White House and another motion picture actor was made the ambassador to Mexico, a former Secretary of State, Henry Kissinger, agreed to make a guest appearance on the popular evening soap opera, DYNASTY. Americans are accustomed to having the news dramatized and the same techniques used for so many centuries to tell fictional stories have now been cleverly adapted to treat reports of actual occurrences. It is an immersion into the conventions, techniques, structures, stereotypes, and formulae of fantasy unparalleled in the history of civilization.

I have sought in this book to apply techniques for "defantasization" which I adopted in developing my course, "Images of the American West." I must confess, however, that these techniques, as indeed my classes, were found most useful by women and other minorities and, accordingly, such were generally my best students. A male white Caucasian who views himself as part of the successful Establishment and identifies with the existing power structure tends, much of the time, to resent this kind of analysis. One time when I taught a special course for teachers on just motion picture images of Indians, the female teachers, who included a black and a Nez Perce, began to study enthusiastically various Native American cultures in order to contrast how the historical reality was distorted and to speculate as to what the purpose had been in distorting it in various motion picture treatments; whereas the male teachers, midway through the course, initiated what they called a "revolt," by which they meant that Western films, and in particular John Wayne, embodied what they considered the finest moral values any society could have and what did I mean by daring to question those values. On the other hand, undergraduates, both male and female, perhaps because at their age they feel a degree of alienation from the dominant culture, always find "defantasization" an exhilarating experience. If I screen for such a class a print of John Ford's STAGECOACH (United Artists, 1939) and ask them to submit it to a careful structural and stereotypical analysis, I can follow it with TWO RODE TOGETHER (Columbia, 1961) and these young people are able, if I turn off the projector before the final reel, to predict which of the two heroines will go to the character played by Richard Widmark and which to the character played by James Stewart. They are able to perceive the ideological manipulations in a motion picture and to separate themselves from those manipulations sufficiently to understand how they are intended to work.

Most that has been written about the Western film has been written, at least in English, by men who cherish the fantasies embodied in these films and who, therefore, resent any effort at dispelling those fantasies. I cannot imagine that what I have had to say in this book will have any effect on them, one way or the other. But for those who are not enamored of the Western film as a form of special pleading, for them I feel I have devised a series of methodologies whereby the fantasies can be dissected and analyzed. In order to do this, one must begin by breaking down the structure of the Western film, as was done in the first part of this book, in terms of its relationship to historical reality. It is possible today in some states to graduate from high school having taken little or no history whatsoever, so one positive advantage of this approach is that it does require one to study history to learn how it has been distorted to suit the needs of a particular entertainment. Once a film has been shown to be a romantic historical reconstruction, then it becomes a matter of determining just what the ideology is in the film and how that ideology functions in order to bring about the situation at the end of it in contrast to the situation at the beginning. This can best be achieved by studying the works of a particular director, such as those who were studied in this fashion in the second part of this book. Or it might be achieved by contrasting the historical reality of an individual with the perpetuation of the legend which has grown up around that individual, primarily for the purpose of prescribing what is or is not acceptable behavior as far as the individual filmmaker was concerned. Or, finally, it might be achieved by contrasting the historical reality of a particular cultural or social group, such as Native Americans or women, with the carefully constructed cinematic distortions of that group. Whatever the approach, the result will invariably be the same; having undergone a "defantasization" experience, a viewer will have some of the tools necessary to remain more in possession of his or her own faculties in a society devoted to fantasy, indeed immersed in it.

And what of the Western film itself? Very few of them are made any more. One advantage of this is that the Western film can thus be studied more easily, due to this degree of cultural estrangement, than most of the other genres still very popular at the box office. Moreover, I believe one of the reasons the Western film has found itself to be in this state of disuse is that, throughout its history, it remained for the most part a sentimental entertainment and it found it difficult, if not impossible, to survive in a commercial and psychological climate in which sentimentality and the American agrarian dream had increasingly less emotional currency in the lives of viewers. While I myself would like to see Western films that, although embodying well-made stories with beginnings, middles, and ends, depict events and people with historical accuracy and truthfulness simply because I am convinced that there is more to be learned from the history of the American West as it happened than can ever be learned from illusions and comforting fantasies about an American West that never was and never could have been, the fact is the Western film has been preoccupied with the latter for so long and so many such Western films have been made, their imagery, plots, and stereotypical characters all being so familiar, to make this transition might amount to making a film that most would not even consider a Western. Moreover, to object to the kinds of Western films which have been made is to overlook the reasons for which they were made; the purpose was never to depict the history of the American West, but rather to prescribe to viewers what they ought to believe, think, and how they ought to behave. In this context, to tell of the actual history of the American West as it happened might be considered by some people to be both depressing and subversive: in a word, unAmerican. Therefore Robert Altman may have been correct: the best we could ever have hoped for was for the Greatest Show on Earth to go on and on and on.

A Western film that is not a mandate to go forward proudly, a Western film that reveals the crimes and follies of the past rather than pretending only to find triumphs and righteousness rewarded in that past, a Western film with still enough sentimentality to show people pulling in a common cause, be it only a drunken foray to exterminate Indians, a Western film in which everyone is consumed by some form of materialism and calling this the American dream?—I doubt if such a Western film would be commercially feasible. The few attempts that have been made in this direction have not been especially successful and many of them have been dismal failures. Yet, unless some new alteration is made along these lines, if there are any Western films at all in the future, I imagine they will be only more of the same. It is indeed ironic that in telling about some of the most *unconventional* generations of human beings the world has ever known, we should have become so hopelessly mired in these rigid, formulary conventions . . . ironic, but I do not think it has been accidental. Freud perhaps stated it best when he observed that "ein Nichtverstehen ist oft ein Nicht-verstehenwollen" [not understanding is often willing not to understand].[26]

If there is any hope for the truth about the American West becoming as well known as the fantasies about it, it resides in the fact that its history is being better written, and more accurately researched, now than at any time in the past; and, above all, in the fact that Western American literature has undergone an artistic and spiritual renaissance since World War II, that many of the finest authors of Western fiction are living and writing now. It may be that a combination of these two new forces will produce a new kind of Western film and one that will find a new, enlightened audience to view it. When it comes to the Western films that have been made, all I can do is express my regret that an ostensible entertainment medium should have so consistently reinforced the notion that murder is frequently the only solution to social problems and a prerequisite for entering upon a better life; that an entire race of people can be virtually wiped out only to be regarded as "mythological" by filmmakers and film critics alike; and, most of all, to know even as I write these words, there will be persons who will read this book who are more in sympathy, or at least complacent about, such ethical aberrations than are inclined to object to them.

Notes

INTRODUCTION

1. Sallust, BELLUM CATILINAE [CATILINE'S WAR] III.2.
2. Cohen, Morris R., THE MEANING OF HUMAN HISTORY (Open Court, 1947), p.33.
3. Ibid., p.34.
4. Quoted in Lucas, F.L., TRAGEDY (Collier Books, 1962), p.81.
5. Excerpted in Danto, Arthur, and Sidney Morgenbesser, editors, PHILOSOPHY OF SCIENCE (Meridian Books, 1960), p.236.
6. Ibid., p.236.
7. Also excerpted in Danto, Arthur, and Sidney Morgenbesser, editors, loc. cit., pp.246–247.
8. Cohen, Morris, op.cit., p.277.
9. Wasserman, Harvey, HARVEY WASSERMAN'S HISTORY OF THE UNITED STATES (Harper's, 1972), p.35 and p.38.
10. Neihardt, John G., BLACK ELK SPEAKS (1932; Pocket Books, 1972), p.181 and p. 184.
11. Wasserman, Harvey, op.cit., p.35.
12. Quoted in Otto, Max C., SCIENCE AND THE MORAL LIFE (New American Library, 1962), p.127.
13. Boatright, Mody, "On the Nature of Myth," in MODY BOATRIGHT, FOLK-LORIST: A COLLECTION OF ESSAYS (University of Texas Press, 1973) edited by Ernest B. Speck, p.114.
14. Pilkington, William T., and Don Graham, editors, WESTERN MOVIES (University of New Mexico Press, 1979), p.3.
15. Ibid., p.48.

PART I: VARIETIES OF MONTAGE

1. Eisenstein, Sergei, FILM ESSAYS AND A LECTURE (Praeger, 1970) translated by Jay Leyda, p.158.

2. Pilkington, William T., and Don Graham, op.cit., p.8.

3. Ibid., p.8.

4. Lovell, Alan, "Robin Wood—A Dissenting View," SCREEN (2 October 1969), pp.47–48.

5. Tudor, Andrew, THEORIES OF FILM (Viking, 1973), p.130.

6. Ibid., p.131.

7. Pilkington, William T., and Don Graham, op.cit., p.9. Italics theirs.

8. Orwell, George, NINETEEN EIGHTY-FOUR (1949: Signet Classics, 1961), p.36.

9. Pilkington, William T., and Don Graham, op.cit., p.9.

10. Bluestone, George, NOVELS INTO FILM: THE METAMORPHOSIS OF FICTION INTO CINEMA (1957; University of California Press, 1973), p.62.

11. Pilkington, William T., and Don Graham, op.cit., p.10.

12. Sandoz, Mari, CHEYENNE AUTUMN (1953; Avon Books, 1964), p.vi.

13. Pilkington, William T., and Don Graham, op.cit., p.10.

14. Piekarski, Vicki, "Sydney Pollack," in CLOSE-UP: THE CONTEMPORARY DIRECTOR (Scarecrow Press, 1981) edited by Jon Tuska and Vicki Piekarski, p.34.

15. Frye, Northrop, THE CRITICAL PATH: AN ESSAY ON THE SOCIAL CONTEXT OF LITERARY CRITICISM (Indiana University Press, 1971), p.19.

16. Pilkington, William T., and Don Graham, op.cit., p.10. Italics theirs.

17. Ibid., p.11.

18. Woods, Michael, AMERICA IN THE MOVIES, OR "SANTA MARIA, IT HAD SLIPPED MY MIND!" (1975; Delta Books, 1976), p.19.

19. Ibid., p.23.

20. Smith, Henry Nash, VIRGIN LAND: THE AMERICAN WEST AS SYMBOL AND MYTH (1950; Harvard University Press, 1970), pp.vii–viii.

21. Ibid., p.91.

22. Cohen, Morris R., A PREFACE TO LOGIC (1944; Meridian Books, 1956), p.87.

23. Tudor, Andrew, op.cit., p.159.

24. Cohen, Morris R., A PREFACE TO LOGIC, op.cit., p.88.

25. Wollen, Peter, SIGNS AND MEANING IN THE CINEMA (Indiana University Press, 1969), p.101.

26. Pilkington, William T., and Don Graham, op.cit., p.11.

27. Eliot, T.S., THE COMPLETE POEMS AND PLAYS: 1909–1950 (Harcourt, Brace, 1958), p.7.

28. Fergusson, Francis, "Introduction," to Aristotle's POETICS (Hill and Wang, 1961) translated by S.H. Butcher, p.9.

29. Fergusson, Francis, THE HUMAN IMAGE IN DRAMATIC LITERATURE (Anchor Books, 1957), p.202.

30. Pilkington, William T., and Don Graham, op.cit., p.30.

31. French, Philip, WESTERNS (Viking, 1974), p.29.

32. Ibid., p.29.

33. Ibid., p.31.

34. Wright, Will, SIXGUNS & SOCIETY: A STRUCTURAL STUDY OF THE WESTERN (University of California Press, 1975), p.32.

35. Ibid., p.48.

36. Ibid., p.41.

37. Ibid., p.42.

38. Ibid., p.45.

39. Quoted from Charlie Ohnhaus' transcript of the conversation, reproduced in Cunningham, Eugene, TRIGGERNOMETRY: A GALLERY OF GUNFIGHTERS (Caxton Printers, 1941), p.372. Horn's own account of his life, including his letter to Ohnhaus questioning why Ohnhaus deleted certain of his statements can be found in the facsimile version of Horn, Tom, LIFE OF TOM HORN (1904; Crown Publishers, 1977).

40. Horn, Tom, op.cit., p.284.

41. Ibid., pp.308–309.

42. Tolstoy, Leo, WAR AND PEACE (1862–1869; New American Library, 1968) translated by Ann Dunnigan, p.907.

43. Calvin, John, INSTITUTES OF THE CHRISTIAN RELIGION in two volumes (1536–1559; Westminster Press, 1960) translated by Ford Lewis Battles, Vol.2, p.964.

44. Balzac, Honoré de, THE COUNTRY DOCTOR (1833) in Volume X of THE WORKS OF HONORÉ DE BALZAC IN EIGHTEEN VOLUMES (Harper's, no date), no translator, p.89.

45. Albert, Marvin H., APACHE RISING (Fawcett, 1957), p.32.

46. Leutrat, Jean-Louis, LE WESTERN (Librairie Armand Colin, 1973), p.137.

47. Cohen, Morris R., THE MEANING OF HUMAN HISTORY, op.cit., p.5.

48. Bell, Daniel, THE CULTURAL CONTRADICTIONS OF CAPITALISM (1976; Harper's, 1978), p.69.

49. Ibid., p.117.

PART II: SIX STUDIES IN AUTHORSHIP (AUTEURISME)

1. Quoted in Lucas, F.L., op.cit., p.13.

2. Place, J.A., THE NON-WESTERN FILMS OF JOHN FORD (Citadel Press, 1979), p.44.

3. Sinclair, Andrew, JOHN FORD (Dial Press/James Wade, 1979), p.38.

4. Ford, Dan, PAPPY: THE LIFE OF JOHN FORD (Prentice-Hall, 1979), p.290.

5. Ibid., p.310.

6. Duckett, Margaret, MARK TWAIN AND BRET HARTE (University of Oklahoma Press, 1964), p.237.

7. Blair, Walter, MARK TWAIN & HUCK FINN (University of California Press, 1960), p.113.

8. Harte, Bret, "The Outcasts of Poker Flat," Volume I of THE WRITINGS OF BRET HARTE IN NINETEEN VOLUMES (Houghton Mifflin, 1897–1904), p.14.

9. Ibid., p.16.

10. Ibid., p.19.

11. Ibid., p.22.

12. Ibid., p.26.

13. Ibid., p.26.

14. Quoted in Drinnon, Richard, FACING WEST: THE METAPHYSICS OF INDIAN-HATING AND EMPIRE-BUILDING, A MAJOR INVESTIGATION OF THE HISTORICAL LINK BETWEEN AMERICAN RACISM AND EXPANSIONISM (Meridian Books, 1980), p.96.

15. Ibid., p.99.

16. Bogdanovich, Peter, JOHN FORD (University of California Press, 1978), p.22.

17. Rieupeyrout, Jean-Louis, LA GRANDE AVENTURE DU WESTERN (Éditions du cerf, 1964), p.395.

18. Ibid., p.241.

19. McBride, Joseph, and Michael Wilmington, JOHN FORD (De Capo Press, 1975), p.55.

20. Tuska, Jon, "Yakima Canutt," in CLOSE-UP: THE CONTRACT DIRECTOR (Scarecrow Press, 1976) edited by Jon Tuska and Vicki Piekarski, p.284. Canutt did do some second unit work on a later Ford picture, MOGAMBO (M-G-M, 1953), but it was not under Ford's supervision nor did he so much as talk to Ford.

21. Sinclair, Andrew, op.cit., p.84.

22. Ford, Dan, op.cit., p.214.

23. Ibid., p.214.

24. Bellah, James Warner, THE APACHE (Fawcett, 1951), p.4.

25. Bellah, James Warner, "Massacre," in REVEILLE (Fawcett, 1962), p.82. I have reprinted this story in my anthology, THE AMERICAN WEST IN FICTION (Mentor Books, 1982), pp.246–259.

26. Bogdanovich, Peter, op.cit., p.86.

27. Bellah, James Warner, "The Devil at Crazy Man," in REVEILLE, op.cit., p.59.

28. Wallace, Ernest, and E. Adamson Hoebel, THE COMANCHES: LORDS OF THE SOUTH PLAINS (University of Oklahoma Press, 1952), p.264.

29. LeMay, Alan, THE SEARCHERS (1954: Gregg Press, 1978), p.263.

30. Place, J.A., THE WESTERN FILMS OF JOHN FORD (Citadel Press, 1974), p.162.

31. McBride, Joseph, and Michael Wilmington, op.cit., p.162.

32. Cook, Will, COMANCHE CAPTIVES (Bantam Books, 1960), p.94.

33. Bellah, James Warner, SERGEANT RUTLEDGE (Bantam Books, 1960), p.vii.

34. Ibid., p.viii.

35. Ibid., p.1.

36. Ibid., p.2.

37. Ibid., p.11.

38. Ibid., p.77.

39. James Warner Bellah novelized his screenplay in collaboration with Willis Goldbeck based on Dorothy M. Johnson's short story. Although difficult to obtain, it makes for an instructive contrast with the perspective in Johnson's story and the film which Ford made. Bellah, James Warner, THE MAN WHO SHOT LIBERTY VALANCE (Permabooks, 1964).

40. McBride, Joseph, and Michael Wilmington, op.cit., p.178.

41. Drinnon, Richard, op.cit., p.465.

42. Sandoz, Mari, op.cit., p.262.

43. Bogdanovich, Peter, op.cit., p.104.

44. Letter from John Wayne to the author dated 24 September 1973.

45. McBride, Joseph, and Gerald Peary, "Hawks Talks," FILM COMMENT (May–June, 1974), p.46.

46. This article is reproduced in Bogdanovich's JOHN FORD, op.cit., pp.109–112.

47. Belton, John, THE HOLLYWOOD PROFESSIONALS: Volume Three (Barnes/Tantivy, 1974), p.43.

48. Aurelius, Marcus, [TO HIMSELF], III:5.

49. Rivette, Jacques, "Genie de Howard Hawks," CAHIERS DU CINÉMA (May, 1953), p.17.

50. Quoted in Rieupeyrout, Jean-Louis, op.cit., p.318.

51. Chase, Borden, RED RIVER [BLAZING GUNS ON THE CHISHOLM TRAIL] (Bantam Books, 1948), p.147.

52. Willis, Donald C., THE FILMS OF HOWARD HAWKS (Scarecrow Press, 1975), p.49.

53. Tuska, Jon, "Howard Hawks," in CLOSE-UP: THE CONTRACT DIREC-TOR, op.cit., p.419.

54. Ibid., p.421.

55. Ibid., pp.422–423.

56. Rieupeyrout, Jean-Louis, op.cit., p.319.

57. Eliot, T.S., op.cit., p.6.

58. Guthrie, A.B., Jr., "The Historical Novel," in WESTERN WRITING (University of New Mexico Press, 1974) edited by Gerald R. Haslam, p.51.

59. Wollen, Peter, op.cit., p.88.

60. Ibid., p.90.

61. Bacall, Lauren, BY MYSELF (Knopf, 1978), p.83.

62. Ibid., p.114.

63. Brackett, Leigh, "Working with Hawks," in WOMEN AND THE CINEMA: A CRITICAL ANTHOLOGY (Dutton, 1977) edited by Karyn Kay and Gerald Peary, p.196.

64. Tuska, Jon, "The American Western Cinema: 1903–Present," in FOCUS ON THE WESTERN (Prentice-Hall, 1974) edited by Jack Nachbar, p.38.

65. Ibid., p.38.

66. Willis, Donald C., op.cit., p.57.

67. Quoted in Wood, Robin, "Rio Bravo," in FOCUS ON HOWARD HAWKS (Prentice-Hall, 1972) edited by Joseph McBride, p.129.

68. Ibid., pp. 123–124.

69. Bogdanovich, Peter, "El Dorado," in FOCUS ON HOWARD HAWKS, op.cit., p.147.

70. Ford, Gregg, "Mostly on RIO LOBO," in FOCUS ON HOWARD HAWKS, op.cit., p.153.

71. Ibid., p.160.

72. Rieupeyrout, Jean-Louis, op.cit., p.410.

73. Nogueira, Rui, "Henry Hathaway Interview," FOCUS ON FILM (Summer, 1971), p.12.

74. Leutrat, Jean-Louis, op.cit., p.42.

75. Gruber, Frank, ZANE GREY: A BIOGRAPHY (World, 1970), p.210.

76. Nogueira, Rui, "Writing for the Movies: Wendell Mayes Interview," FOCUS ON FILM, loc. cit., p.39.

77. Canham, Kingsley, THE HOLLYWOOD PROFESSIONALS: Volume One (Barnes/Tantivy, 1973), p.158.

78. Gruber, Frank, op.cit., p.206.

79. Canham, Kingsley, op.cit., p.151.

80. Drinnon, Richard, op.cit., p.149.

81. Ibid., p.149.

82. Nogueira, Rui, "Henry Hathaway Interview," op.cit., pp.16–17.

83. However, in history, such things were occasionally done *to* the Apaches by the Maricopas. "Looming up on the side of the hill, in bold outline against the sky, stood a rude cross upon which hung the dried body of an Apache, crucified about two years

ago by the Maricopas," J. Ross Browne recorded in ADVENTURES IN THE APACHE COUNTRY: A TOUR THROUGH ARIZONA AND SONORA, 1864 (1869: University of Arizona Press, 1974). " . . . It was a strange and ghastly sight. The Maricopas do not profess the Christian faith, but this much they had learned from the missionaries who had attempted their conversion, that crucifixion was a species of torture practiced by the whites." [p.104.]

84. Twain, Mark, ROUGHING IT (1872; Signet Classics, 1962), p.97.

85. Bazin, André, "The Evolution of the Western," in WHAT IS CINEMA?: Volume Two (University of California Press, 1971) translated by Hugh Gray, p.156.

86. Ibid., p.156.

87. Ibid., p.156.

88. Bazin, André, "The Western: or the American Film *par excellence*," loc. cit., p.145.

89. Kitses, Jim, HORIZONS WEST (Indiana University Press, 1970), p.69.

90. "Entretien avec Anthony Mann" ["Interview with Anthony Mann], POSITIF (September, 1968), p.26.

91. Rieupeyrout, Jean-Louis, op.cit., p.388.

92. Kitses, Jim, op.cit., p.68.

93. Ibid., p.44.

94. Quoted in Drinnon, Richard, op.cit., p.466.

95. Silver, Charles, THE WESTERN FILM (Pyramid Books, 1976), p.87.

96. "Entretien avec Anthony Mann," op.cit., p.25.

97. Quoted in Kitses, Jim, op.cit., pp.72–73.

98. Quoted in Leutrat, Jean-Louis, op.cit., p.92.

99. Meyer, William R., THE MAKING OF THE GREAT WESTERNS (Arlington House, 1979), p.260.

100. Flynn, T.T., THE MAN FROM LARAMIE (Dell Books, 1954), p.6.

101. Ibid., pp.22–23.

102. Ibid., p.33.

103. Ibid., p.41.

104. Ibid., p.56.

105. Ibid., p.71.

106. Ibid., p.134.

107. Ibid., p.144.

108. Ibid., p.221.

109. Kitses, Jim, op.cit., p.62.

110. Ibid., p.63.

111. Ibid., p.43.

112. "Entretien avec Anthony Mann," CAHIERS DU CINÉMA (June, 1966), p.48.

113. Kitses, Jim, op.cit., pp.39–42.

114. Caesar, Julius, DE BELLO GALLICO [THE GALLIC WAR] I.1.

115. Quoted in Rieupeyrout, Jean-Louis, op.cit., p.389.

116. "Entretien avec Budd Boetticher," CAHIERS DU CINÉMA (September, 1963), p.7.

117. Quoted in Drinnon, Richard, op.cit., p.96.

118. "Entretien avec Budd Boetticher," op.cit., p.11.

119. Kitses, Jim, op.cit., p.109.

120. Ibid., p.108.

121. Silver, Charles, op.cit., p.121.

122. Rieupeyrout, Jean-Louis, op.cit., p.341.

123. Arrian, THE MANUAL, XVII.

124. Sherman, Eric, and Martin Rubin, THE DIRECTOR'S EVENT (Atheneum, 1970), p.40.

125. Ibid., p.51.

126. Ibid., p.49.

127. Kitses, Jim, op.cit., p.93.

128. Sherman, Eric, and Martin Rubin, op.cit., p.47.

129. Ibid., p.52.

130. Maltin, Leonard, BEHIND THE CAMERA (Signet Books, 1971), pp.174–175.

131. Ward, Jonas (pseud. William Ard), THE NAME'S BUCHANAN (Fawcett, 1956), p.9.

132. Ibid., p.21.

133. Ibid., p.34.

134. Ibid., p.50.

135. Ibid., p.101.

136. "Entretien avec Budd Boetticher," POSITIF (January, 1970), p.16.

137. Kitses, Jim, op.cit., p.97.

138. Silver, Charles, op.cit., p.119.

139. Quoted in Parkinson, Michael, and Clyde Jeavons, A PICTORIAL HISTORY OF WESTERNS (Hamlyn Publishing Group, 1972), p.168.

140. For a more detailed portrait of this director, vide Tuska, Jon, "Sam Peckinpah," in CLOSE-UP: THE CONTEMPORARY DIRECTOR, op.cit., pp.99–132.

141. Rieupeyrout, Jean-Louis, op.cit., p.358.

142. Seydor, Paul, PECKINPAH: THE WESTERN FILMS (University of Illinois Press, 1980), p.56.

143. Heston, Charlton, THE ACTOR'S LIFE (Dutton, 1978), p.190.

144. Seydor, Paul, op.cit., p.69.

145. Kitses, Jim, op.cit., p.146.

146. Quoted in Seydor, Paul, op.cit., p.54.

147. Ibid., p.54.

148. Kitses, Jim, op.cit., p.151.

149. "Interview with Sam Peckinpah," PLAYBOY (August, 1972), p.74.

150. Kitses, Jim, op.cit., p.161.

151. Pettit, Arthur G., "The Polluted Garden: Sam Peckinpah's Double Vision of Mexico," in WESTERN MOVIES, op.cit., p.101.

152. Kitses, Jim, op.cit., p.169.

153. Seydor, Paul, op.cit., p.79.

154. White, Stewart Edward, ARIZONA NIGHTS (McClure, 1907), pp.27–28.

155. Ibid., p.39.

156. Seydor, Paul, op.cit., p.154.

157. Silver, Charles, op.cit., p.133.

158. Nogueira, Rui, "Henry Hathaway Interview," op.cit., p.19.

PART III: FRONTIER LEGENDS

1. Fisher, Vardis, and Opal Laurel Holmes, GOLD RUSHES AND MINING CAMPS OF THE EARLY AMERICAN WEST (Caxton Printers, 1979), p.1.

2. Quoted in Settle, William A., Jr., JESSE JAMES WAS HIS NAME (1966; University of Nebraska Press, 1977), p.27.

3. Ibid., p.33.

4. Ibid., p.46.

5. Ibid., p.81.

6. Ibid., p.112.

7. Ibid., p.125.

8. Ibid., p.131.

9. VARIETY (19 October 1927), p.16.

10. Sherman, Eric, and Martin Rubin, op.cit., p.126.

11. Ibid., p.127.

12. HARRISON'S REPORTS (11 November 1950), p.178.

13. HARRISON'S REPORTS (2 December 1950), p.191.

14. Graham, Don, "THE GREAT NORTHFIELD MINNESOTA RAID and the Cinematic Legend of Jesse James," in WESTERN MOVIES, op.cit., p.132.

15. Ibid., p.136. Italics Graham's.

16. My book, BILLY THE KID: A BIO/BIBLIOGRAPHY (Greenwood Press, 1983), provides a lengthy historical construction of the Kid's life and the Lincoln County War in which he participated, followed by chapters on the growth of his legend in popular histories, Western fiction, and Western films, and concludes with an analysis similar to that which ends this part of THE AMERICAN WEST IN FILM, save that the focus is strictly on the Kid. In the present book I have been able to extend my methodology to apply to a number of other frontier legends.

17. Metz, Leon C., PAT GARRETT: THE STORY OF A WESTERN LAWMAN (University of Oklahoma Press, 1974), p.37.

18. Quoted in Adams, Ramon F., A FITTING DEATH FOR BILLY THE KID (University of Oklahoma Press, 1960), p.26.

19. Case No. 532, TERRITORY v. WILLIAM BONNY (sic), District Court, 3rd Judicial District, Doña Ana County, quoted in Metz, Leon C., op.cit., p.73.

20. Ibid., p.73.

21. Ibid., p.76.

22. Sonnichsen, C.L., FROM HOPALONG TO HUD: THOUGHTS ON WESTERN FICTION (Texas A&M Press, 1978), pp.18–19. While this makes an engaging anecdote about the capricious attitude of filmmakers, I seriously doubt if Sophie Poe did know the Kid. She first came to New Mexico in 1882, almost a year after the Kid's death!

23. Sherman, Eric, and Martin Rubin, op.cit., p.105.

24. Quoted in Parish, James Robert, and Michael R. Pitts, THE GREAT WESTERN PICTURES (Scarecrow Press, 1976), p.192.

25. Williams, Wirt, Introduction to THE AUTHENTIC DEATH OF HENDRY JONES (1956; Harrow Books, 1972), p.vii and p.x.

26. Ibid., p.225.

27. INDEPENDENT FILM JOURNAL (13 November 1972) Entry #1995.

28. Seydor, Paul, op.cit., p.188.

29. Ibid., p.202.

30. Cunningham, Eugene, op.cit., p.249.

31. Rosa, Joseph G., THEY CALLED HIM WILD BILL: THE LIFE AND ADVENTURES OF JAMES BUTLER HICKOK (University of Oklahoma Press, 1964), p.268.

32. Quoted in ibid., loc. cit., p.268.

33. Schoenberger, Dale T., THE GUNFIGHTERS (Caxton Printers, 1976), p.79.

34. Quoted in ibid., loc. cit., p.79.

35. Sandoz, Mari, THE BUFFALO HUNTERS: THE STORY OF THE HIDE MEN (Hastings House, 1954), p.139.

36. Fenin, George N., and William K. Everson, THE WESTERN: FROM SILENTS TO THE SEVENTIES (Grossman, 1973), pp.105–106.

37. Hart, William S., MY LIFE EAST AND WEST (1929; Benjamin Blom, 1968), pp.339–340.

38. Adams, Ramon F., BURS UNDER THE SADDLE: A SECOND LOOK AT BOOKS AND HISTORIES OF THE WEST (University of Oklahoma Press, 1964), pp.240–241. Italics Adams'.

39. Fenin, George N., and William K. Everson, op.cit., p.107.

40. Quoted in Parish, James Robert, and Michael R. Pitts, op.cit., p.268.

41. Quoted in ibid., loc. cit., p.269.

42. Quoted in Steckmesser, Kent Ladd, THE WESTERN HERO IN HISTORY AND LEGEND (University of Oklahoma Press, 1965), p.158.

43. Quoted in Schoenberger, Dale T., op.cit., p.33.

44. Rosa, Joseph G., THE GUNFIGHTER: MAN OR MYTH? (University of Oklahoma Press, 1969), p.199.

45. Quoted in Waters, Frank, THE EARP BROTHERS OF TOMBSTONE: THE STORY OF MRS. VIRGIL EARP (1960; University of Nebraska Press, 1976), p.173.

46. Earp, Josephine, I MARRIED WYATT EARP: THE RECOLLECTIONS OF JOSEPHINE SARAH MARCUS EARP (University of Arizona Press, 1976) collected and edited by Glenn G. Boyer, p.248. When this book was adapted for a television movie, I MARRIED WYATT EARP (NBC, 1983), starring Marie Osmond as Josephine, I was telephoned by a radio station in Tucson to ask my opinion, on the air, if I felt that this film, then currently in production on location, was going to usher in a new age of realistic movies about the American West. My answer was I would have to wait until I saw it. Since in this version Josephine is shown as a participant in the gunfight and kills two men, my answer would have to be a definite: No.

47. Brownlow, Kevin, THE WAR, THE WEST, AND THE WILDERNESS (Knopf, 1979), p.280.

48. Lake, Stuart N., WYATT EARP: FRONTIER MARSHAL (1931; Bantam Books, 1959), dedication.

49. Ibid.

50. In Earp, Josephine, op.cit., p.249.

51. Ibid., p.251.

52. Ibid., p.258.

53. Adams, Ramon F., BURS UNDER THE SADDLE, op.cit., p.317.

54. Everson, William K., A PICTORIAL HISTORY OF THE WESTERN FILM (Citadel Press, 1969), p.118.

55. Place, J.A., THE WESTERN FILMS OF JOHN FORD, op.cit., p.60.

56. Quoted in Haggard, Mark, "Ford in Person," FOCUS ON FILM (Spring, 1971), p.35.

57. Hutchinson, W.H., CALIFORNIA: TWO CENTURIES OF MAN, LAND, AND GROWTH IN THE GOLDEN STATE (American West Publishing, 1967), pp.106–107.

58. Quoted in Frederick W. Turner III's Introduction to GERONIMO: HIS OWN STORY (1906; Ballantine Books, 1970) edited by S.M. Barrett, p.12.

59. Ridge, John Rollin (Yellow Bird), THE LIFE AND ADVENTURES OF JOA-QUÍN MURIETA, THE CELEBRATED CALIFORNIA BANDIT (1854; University of Oklahoma Press, 1955), p.158. Italics Ridge's.

60. Quoted in Wilson, David, "William Wellman," in CLOSE-UP: THE HOL-LYWOOD DIRECTOR (Scarecrow Press, 1978) edited by Jon Tuska and Vicki Piekar-ski, p.230.

61. Steckmesser, Kent Ladd, op.cit., p.175.

62. Custer, General George A., MY LIFE ON THE PLAINS (1872–1874; Univer-sity of Nebraska Press, 1966) edited by Milo Milton Quaife, pp.21–22. Italics Custer's.

63. Excerpted in Turner, Frederick W., III, editor, THE PORTABLE NORTH AMERICAN INDIAN READER (Viking, 1974), p.225.

64. Neihardt, John G., op.cit., p.105.

65. Correspondence of Ernest Haycox on deposit at the archives of the University of Oregon, Eugene, Oregon.

66. Jung, C.G., THE ARCHETYPES AND THE COLLECTIVE UNCONSCIOUS (Princeton University Press, 1969), p.270.

67. Reik, Theodor, THE SECRET SELF: PSYCHOANALYTIC EXPERIENCES IN LIFE AND LITERATURE (Farrar, Straus, 1952), p.47.

68. HARRISON'S REPORTS (2 June 1951), p.88.

69. Sandoz, Mari, THE BATTLE OF THE LITTLE BIGHORN (1966; Curtis Books, n.d.), p.215. Sandoz included a list of the names of all the enlisted men known to have been killed in the battle, pp.232–233.

70. Quoted in Parish, James Robert, and Michael R. Pitts, op.cit., p.73.

71. Fenin, George N., and William K. Everson, op.cit., p.156.

72. Dippie, Brian W., CUSTER'S LAST STAND: THE ANATOMY OF AN AMERICAN MYTH (University of Montana Press, 1976), p.102.

73. Ibid., p.102.

74. Dippie, Brian W., op.cit., p.109.

75. Turner, Frederick Jackson, "The Significance of the Frontier in American His-tory," in FRONTIER AND SECTION: SELECTED ESSAYS OF FREDERICK JACK-SON TURNER (Prentice-Hall, 1961) with an Introduction and Notes by Ray Allen Bil-lington, p.38.

76. Drinnon, Richard, op.cit., p.463.

77. Cawelti, John G., THE SIX-GUN MYSTIQUE (Bowling Green University Popular Press, 1975), p.38.

78. Moore, Robin, GREEN BERETS (Crown, 1965), p.122.

79. Leutrat, Jean-Louis, op.cit., p.155.

80. Cawelti, John G., ADVENTURE, MYSTERY, AND ROMANCE: FORMULA STORIES AS ART AND POPULAR CULTURE (University of Chicago Press, 1976), pp.232–233.

81. Tatum, Stephen, INVENTING BILLY THE KID: VISIONS OF THE OUT-LAW IN AMERICA, 1881–1981 (University of New Mexico Press, 1981), p.x.

82. Ibid., p.153.

83. Ibid., pp.41–42.

84. Ibid., p.95.

85. Ibid., p.175.

86. Ibid., p.174.

87. Ibid., p.176.

88. Steckmesser, Kent Ladd, op.cit., p.250.

89. Ibid., p.32.

90. Lerner, Gerda, THE MAJORITY FINDS ITS PAST: PLACING WOMEN IN HISTORY (Oxford University Press, 1979), p.148.

91. Steckmesser, Kent Ladd, op.cit., pp.76–77.

92. Ibid., p.77.

93. Ibid., p.85.

94. Ibid., p.100.

95. Ibid., p.100.

96. Boatright, Mody, "The Western Bad Man as Hero," in MESQUITE AND WILLOW (Southern Methodist University Press, 1957), p.97.

97. Ibid., p.97.

98. Ibid., p.98.

99. Ibid., p.98.

100. Ibid., p.99.

101. Ibid., p.100.

102. Ibid., p.102.

103. Twain, Mark, op.cit., p.111.

PART IV: TYPES AND STEREOTYPES

1. Lucas, F.L., op.cit., p.43.

2. Lerner, Gerda, op.cit., p.174.

3. Myres, Sandra L., WESTERING WOMEN AND THE FRONTIER EXPERIENCE: 1800–1915 (University of New Mexico Press, 1982), p.98.

4. Ibid., p.76.

5. Cook, Will, THE PEACEMAKERS (Bantam Books, 1961), p.140.

6. Tudor, Andrew, IMAGE AND INFLUENCE: STUDIES IN THE SOCIOLOGY OF FILM (St. Martin's Press, 1975), p.150.

7. Sandoz, Mari, THE CATTLEMEN: FROM THE RIO GRANDE ACROSS THE FAR MARIAS (Hastings House, 1958), p.341.

8. Myres, Sandra L., op.cit., p.125.

9. Ibid.,p.66.

10. Quoted in McBride, Joseph, and Michael Wilmington, op.cit., p.93.

11. Georgakas, Dan, "They Have Not Spoken: American Indians in Film," in THE PRETEND INDIANS: IMAGES OF NATIVE AMERICANS IN THE MOVIES (Iowa State University Press, 1980) edited by Gretchen M. Bataille and Charles L.P. Silet, p.136.

12. Hassrick, Royal B., THE SIOUX (University of Oklahoma Press, 1964), pp.112–113.

13. Excerpted in Bataille, Gretchen M., and Charles L.P. Silet, editors, op.cit., p.61.

14. Geronimo, op.cit., p.184.

15. Quoted in Brownlow, Kevin, THE PARADE'S GONE BY . . . (Knopf, 1968), p.142.

16. Lenihan, John H., SHOWDOWN: CONFRONTING MODERN AMERICA IN THE WESTERN FILM (University of Illinois Press, 1980), p.32.

17. Ibid., p.43.

18. Deloria, Vine, Jr., Foreword to THE PRETEND INDIANS, op.cit., p.xv.

19. Lucas, Phil, "Images of Indians," FOUR WINDS (Autumn, 1980), p.69.

20. Nachbar, Jack, "ULZANA'S RAID," in Pilkington, William T., and Don Graham, op.cit., p.140.

21. Ibid., p.141.

22. Ibid., p.141.

23. Ibid., p.147n.

24. Ibid., p.146.

25. X, Malcolm, THE AUTOBIOGRAPHY OF MALCOLM X (Grove Press, 1966) with Alex Haley, p.368.

26. Quoted in Jones, Ernest, PAPERS ON PSYCHO-ANALYSIS (Beacon Press, 1961), p.i.

Bibliography

BOOKS

Adams, Ramon F., A FITTING DEATH FOR BILLY THE KID (University of Oklahoma Press, 1960).

———, BURS UNDER THE SADDLE: A SECOND LOOK AT BOOKS AND HISTORIES OF THE WEST (University of Oklahoma Press, 1964).

Albert, Marvin H., APACHE UPRISING (Fawcett, 1957).

Arrian, THE MANUAL.

Aurelius, Marcus [TO HIMSELF].

Bacall, Lauren, BY MYSELF (Knopf, 1978).

Balzac, Honoré de, THE COUNTRY DOCTOR (1833).

Bataille, Gretchen M., and Charles L.P. Silet, editors, THE PRETEND INDIANS: IMAGES OF NATIVE AMERICANS IN THE MOVIES (Iowa State University Press, 1980).

Bazin, André, WHAT IS CINEMA?: Volume Two (University of California Press, 1971) translated by Hugh Gray.

Bell, Daniel, THE CULTURAL CONTRADICTIONS OF CAPITALISM (1976; Harper's, 1978).

Bellah, James Warner, THE APACHE (Fawcett, 1951).

———, SERGEANT RUTLEDGE (Bantam Books, 1960).

———, REVEILLE (Fawcett, 1962).

———, THE MAN WHO SHOT LIBERTY VALANCE (Permabooks, 1964).

Belton, John, THE HOLLYWOOD PROFESSIONALS: Volume Three (Barnes/Tantivy, 1974).

Blair, Walter, MARK TWAIN & HUCK FINN (University of California Press, 1964).

Bluestone, George, NOVELS INTO FILM: THE METAMORPHOSIS OF FICTION INTO CINEMA (1957; University of California Press, 1973).

Boatright, Mody, editor, MESQUITE AND WILLOW (Southern Methodist University Press, 1957).

———, MODY BOATRIGHT, FOLKLORIST: A COLLECTION OF ESSAYS (University of Texas Press, 1973) edited by Ernest B. Speck.

Bogdanovich, Peter, JOHN FORD (University of California Press, 1978).

Browne, J. Ross, ADVENTURES IN THE APACHE COUNTRY: A TOUR THROUGH ARIZONA AND SONORA, 1864 (1869; University of Arizona Press, 1974).

Brownlow, Kevin, THE PARADE'S GONE BY . . . (Knopf, 1968).

———, THE WAR, THE WEST, AND THE WILDERNESS (Knopf, 1979).

Caesar, Julius, DE BELLO GALLICO [THE GALLIC WAR].

Calvin, John, INSTITUTES OF THE CHRISTIAN RELIGION in two volumes (1536–1559; Westminster Press, 1960) translated by Ford Lewis Battles.

Canham, Kingsley, THE HOLLYWOOD PROFESSIONALS: Volume One (Barnes/Tantivy, 1973).

Cawelti, John G., THE SIX-GUN MYSTIQUE (Bowling Green University Popular Press, 1975).

———, ADVENTURE, MYSTERY, AND ROMANCE: FORMULA STORIES AS ART AND POPULAR CULTURE (University of Chicago Press, 1976).

Chase, Borden, RED RIVER [BLAZING GUNS ON THE CHISHOLM TRAIL] (Bantam Books, 1948).

Cohen, Morris R., THE MEANING OF HUMAN HISTORY (Open Court, 1947).

———, A PREFACE TO LOGIC (1944; Meridian Books, 1956).

Cook, Will, COMANCHE CAPTIVES (Bantam Books, 1960).

———, THE PEACEMAKERS (Bantam Books, 1961).

Cunningham, Eugene, TRIGGERNOMETRY (Caxton Printers, 1941).

Custer, General George A., MY LIFE ON THE PLAINS (1872–1874; University of Nebraska Press, 1966) edited by Milo Milton Quaife.

Danto, Arthur, and Sidney Morgenbesser, editors, PHILOSOPHY OF SCIENCE (Meridian Books, 1960).

Dippie, Brian W., CUSTER'S LAST STAND: THE ANATOMY OF AN AMERICAN MYTH (University of Montana Press, 1976).

Drinnon, Richard, FACING WEST: THE METAPHYSICS OF INDIAN-HATING AND EMPIRE-BUILDING, A MAJOR INVESTIGATION OF THE HISTORICAL LINK BETWEEN AMERICAN RACISM AND EXPANSIONISM (Meridian Books, 1980).

Duckett, Margaret, MARK TWAIN AND BRET HARTE (University of Oklahoma Press, 1964).

Earp, Josephine, I MARRIED WYATT EARP: THE RECOLLECTIONS OF JOSEPHINE SARAH MARCUS EARP (University of Arizona Press, 1976) edited by Glenn G. Boyer.

Eisenstein, Sergei, FILM ESSAYS AND A LECTURE (Praeger, 1970) translated by Jay Leyda.

Eliot, T.S., THE COMPLETE POEMS AND PLAYS: 1909–1950 (Harcourt,Brace, 1958).

Everson, William K., A PICTORIAL HISTORY OF THE WESTERN FILM (Citadel Press, 1969).

Fenin, George N., and William K. Everson, THE WESTERN: FROM SILENTS TO THE SEVENTIES (Grossman, 1973).

Fergusson, Francis, THE HUMAN IMAGE IN DRAMATIC LITERATURE (Anchor Books, 1957).

———, "Introduction" to Aristotle's POETICS (Hill and Wang, 1961) translated by S.H. Butcher.

Fisher, Vardis, and Opal Laurel Holmes, GOLD RUSHES AND MINING CAMPS OF THE EARLY AMERICAN WEST (Caxton Printers, 1979).

Flynn, T.T., THE MAN FROM LARAMIE (Dell Books, 1954).

Ford, Dan, PAPPY: THE LIFE OF JOHN FORD (Prentice-Hall, 1979).

French, Philip, WESTERNS (Viking Press, 1974).

Frye, Northrop, THE CRITICAL PATH: AN ESSAY ON THE SOCIAL CONTEXT OF LITERARY CRITICISM (Indiana University Press, 1971).

Geronimo, HIS OWN STORY (1906; Ballantine Books, 1970) edited by S.M. Barrett.

Gruber, Frank, ZANE GREY: A BIOGRAPHY (World, 1970).

Hart, William S., MY LIFE EAST AND WEST (1929; Benjamin Blom, 1968).

Harte, Bret, THE WRITINGS OF BRET HARTE in nineteen volumes (Houghton Mifflin, 1897–1904).

Haslam, Gerald R., editor, WESTERN WRITING (University of New Mexico Press, 1974).

Hassrick, Royal B., THE SIOUX (University of Oklahoma Press, 1964).

Heston, Charlton, THE ACTOR'S LIFE (Dutton, 1978).

Horn, Tom, LIFE OF TOM HORN (1904; Crown Publishers, 1977).

Hutchinson, W.H., CALIFORNIA: TWO CENTURIES OF MAN, LAND, AND GROWTH IN THE GOLDEN STATE (American West Publishing, 1967).

Jones, Ernest, PAPERS ON PSYCHO-ANALYSIS (Beacon Press, 1961).

Jung, C.G., THE ARCHETYPES AND THE COLLECTIVE UNCONSCIOUS (Princeton University Press, 1969).

Kay, Karyn, and Gerald Peary, editors, WOMEN AND THE CINEMA: A CRITICAL ANTHOLOGY (Dutton, 1977).

Kitses, Jim, HORIZONS WEST (Indiana University Press, 1970).

Lake, Stuart N., WYATT EARP: FRONTIER MARSHAL (1931; Bantam Books, 1959).

LeMay, Alan, THE SEARCHERS (1954; Gregg Press, 1978).

Lenihan, John H., SHOWDOWN: CONFRONTING MODERN AMERICA IN THE WESTERN FILM (University of Illinois Press, 1980).

Lerner, Gerda, THE MAJORITY FINDS ITS PAST: PLACING WOMEN IN HISTORY (Oxford University Press, 1979).

Leutrat, Jean-Louis, LE WESTERN (Librairie Armand Colin, 1973).

Lucas, F.L., TRAGEDY (Collier Books, 1962).

McBride, Joseph, editor, FOCUS ON HOWARD HAWKS (Prentice-Hall, 1972).

————, and Michael Wilmington, JOHN FORD (DeCapo Press, 1975).

Maltin, Leonard, BEHIND THE CAMERA (Signet Books, 1971).

Metz, Leon C., PAT GARRETT: THE HISTORY OF A WESTERN LAWMAN (University of Oklahoma Press, 1974).

Meyer, William R., THE MAKING OF THE GREAT WESTERNS (Arlington House, 1979).

Moore, Robin, GREEN BERETS (Crown Publishers, 1968).

Myres, Sandra L., WESTERING WOMEN AND THE FRONTIER EXPERIENCE: 1800–1915 (University of New Mexico Press, 1982).

Nachbar, Jack, editor, FOCUS ON THE WESTERN (Prentice-Hall, 1974).

Neider, Charles B., THE AUTHENTIC DEATH OF HENDRY JONES (1956; Harrow Books, 1972).

Neihardt, John G., BLACK ELK SPEAKS (1932; Pocket Books, 1972).

Orwell, George, NINETEEN EIGHTY-FOUR (1949; Signet Classics, 1961).

Otto, Max C., SCIENCE AND THE MORAL LIFE (Mentor Books, 1962).

Parish, James Robert, and Michael R. Pitts, THE GREAT WESTERN PICTURES (Scarecrow Press, 1976).

Parkinson, Michael, and Clyde Jeavons, A PICTORIAL HISTORY OF WESTERNS (Hamlyn Publishing Group, 1972).

Pilkington, William T., and Don Graham, editors, WESTERN MOVIES (University of New Mexico Press, 1979).

Place, J.A., THE WESTERN FILMS OF JOHN FORD (Citadel Press, 1974).

——, THE NON-WESTERN FILMS OF JOHN FORD (Citadel Press, 1979).

Reik, Theodor, THE SECRET SELF: PSYCHOANALYTIC EXPERIENCES IN LIFE AND LITERATURE (Farrar, Straus, 1952).

Ridge, John Rollin (Yellow Bird), THE LIFE AND ADVENTURES OF JOAQUÍN MURIETA, THE CELEBRATED CALIFORNIA BANDIT (1854; University of Oklahoma Press, 1955).

Rieupeyrout, Jean-Louis, LA GRANDE AVENTURE DU WESTERN (Éditions du cerf, 1964).

Rosa, Joseph G., THEY CALLED HIM WILD BILL: THE LIFE AND ADVENTURES OF JAMES BUTLER HICKOK (University of Oklahoma Press, 1964).

——, THE GUNFIGHTER: MAN OR MYTH? (University of Oklahoma Press, 1969).

Sallust, BELLUM CATILINAE [CATILINE'S WAR].

Sandoz, Mari, THE BUFFALO HUNTERS: THE STORY OF THE HIDE MEN (Hastings House, 1954).

——, THE CATTLEMEN: FROM THE RIO GRANDE ACROSS THE FAR MARIAS (Hastings House, 1958).

——, CHEYENNE AUTUMN (1953; Avon Books, 1964).

——, THE BATTLE OF THE LITTLE BIGHORN (1966; Curtis Books, n.d.).

Schoenberger, Dale T., THE GUNFIGHTERS (Caxton Printers, 1976).

Settle, William A., JESSE JAMES WAS HIS NAME (1966; University of Nebraska Press, 1977).

Seydor, Paul, PECKINPAH: THE WESTERN FILMS (University of Illinois Press, 1980).

Sherman, Eric, and Martin Rubin, THE DIRECTOR'S EVENT (Atheneum, 1970).

Silver, Charles, THE WESTERN FILM (Pyramid Books, 1976).

Sinclair, Andrew, JOHN FORD (Dial Press/James Wade, 1979).

Smith, Henry Nash, VIRGIN LAND: THE AMERICAN WEST AS SYMBOL AND MYTH (1950; Harvard University Press, 1970).

Sonnichsen, C.L., FROM HOPALONG TO HUD: THOUGHTS ON WESTERN FICTION (Texas A & M Press, 1978).

Steckmesser, Kent Ladd, THE WESTERN HERO IN HISTORY AND LEGEND (University of Oklahoma Press, 1965).

Tatum, Stephen, INVENTING BILLY THE KID: VISIONS OF THE OUTLAW IN AMERICA, 1881–1981 (University of New Mexico Press, 1981).

Tolstoy, Leo, WAR AND PEACE (1862–1869; Signet Classics, 1968) translated by Ann Dunnigan.

Tudor, Andrew, THEORIES OF FILM (Viking Press, 1973).

——, IMAGE AND INFLUENCE: STUDIES IN THE SOCIOLOGY OF FILM (St. Martin's Press, 1975).

Turner, Frederick Jackson, FRONTIER AND SECTION: SELECTED ESSAYS OF

FREDERICK JACKSON TURNER (Prentice-Hall, 1961) edited by Ray Allen Billington.

Turner, Frederick W., III, editor, THE PORTABLE NORTH AMERICAN INDIAN READER (Viking Press, 1974).

Tuska, Jon, THE FILMING OF THE WEST (Doubleday, 1976).

———, and Vicki Piekarski, editors, CLOSE-UP: THE CONTRACT DIRECTOR (Scarecrow Press, 1976).

———, and Vicki Piekarski, editors, CLOSE-UP: THE HOLLYWOOD DIRECTOR (Scarecrow Press, 1978).

———, and Vicki Piekarski, editors, CLOSE-UP: THE CONTEMPORARY DIREC-TOR (Scarecrow Press, 1981).

———, editor, THE AMERICAN WEST IN FICTION (Mentor Books, 1982).

———, BILLY THE KID: A BIO/BIBLIOGRAPHY (Greenwood Press, 1983).

Twain, Mark, ROUGHING IT (1872; Signet Classics, 1962).

Wallace, Ernest, and E. Adamson Hoebel, THE COMANCHES: LORDS OF THE SOUTH PLAINS (University of Oklahoma Press, 1952).

Ward, Jonas, THE NAME'S BUCHANAN (Fawcett, 1956).

Wasserman, Harvey, HARVEY WASSERMAN'S HISTORY OF THE UNITED STATES (Harper's, 1972).

Waters, Frank, THE EARP BROTHERS OF TOMBSTONE: THE STORY OF MRS. VIRGIL EARP (1960; University of Nebraska Press, 1976).

White, Stewart Edward, ARIZONA NIGHTS (McClure, 1907).

Willis, Donald C., THE FILMS OF HOWARD HAWKS (Scarecrow Press, 1975).

Wollen, Peter, SIGNS AND MEANING IN THE CINEMA (Indiana University Press, 1969).

Woods, Michael, AMERICA IN THE MOVIES, OR "SANTA MARIA, IT HAD SLIPPED MY MIND!" (1975; Delta Books, 1976).

Wright, Will, SIXGUNS & SOCIETY: A STRUCTURAL STUDY OF THE WEST-ERN (University of California Press, 1975).

X, Malcolm, THE AUTOBIOGRAPHY OF MALCOLM X (Grove Press, 1966) with Alex Haley.

ARTICLES AND INTERVIEWS

"Entretien avec Anthony Mann," CAHIERS DU CINÉMA (June, 1966).

"Entretien avec Anthony Mann," POSITIF (September, 1968).

"Entretien avec Budd Boetticher," CAHIERS DU CINÉMA (September, 1963).

"Entretien avec Budd Boetticher," POSITIF (January, 1970).

Haggard, Mark, "Ford in Person," FOCUS ON FILM (Spring, 1971).

HARRISON'S REPORTS (11 November 1950).

HARRISON'S REPORTS (2 December 1950).

HARRISON'S REPORTS (2 June 1951).

INDEPENDENT FILM JOURNAL (13 November 1972).

"Interview with Sam Peckinpah," PLAYBOY (August, 1972).

Lovell, Alan, "Robin Wood—A Dissenting View," SCREEN (2 October 1969).

Lucas, Phil, "Images of Indians," FOUR WINDS (Autumn, 1980).

McBride, Joseph, with Gerald Peary, "Hawks Talks," FILM COMMENT (May–June, 1974).

Nogueira, Rui, "Writing for the Movies: Wendell Mayes Interview," FOCUS ON FILM (Summer, 1971).

Nogueira, Rui, "Henry Hathaway Interview," FOCUS ON FILM (Summer, 1971).

Rivette, Jacques, "Genie de Howard Hawks," CAHIERS DU CINÉMA (May, 1953).

VARIETY (19 October 1927).

Index

About the Author

JON TUSKA is a writer whose interest has long centered on the film industry. He has published several books, including *Billy the Kid: a Handbook* (1983; reprint, University of Nebraska Press, 1986) and *Dark Cinema: American Film Noir in Cultural Perspective* (Greenwood Press, 1984). His book, *In Manors and Alleys: A Case-Book on the American Detective Film,* will be appearing early in 1988.